**BRUCE NEUBURGER** is the author of *Lettuce Wars: Ten Years of Work and Struggle in the Fields of California*. He has worked on farms and in factories, as a cab driver, an ESL teacher, and a video arts instructor. His writing is shaped by the great social justice movements of the 1960s and by his experiences as a child of German Holocaust survivors.

# POSTCARDS TO HITLER
## A German Jew's Defiance in a Time of Terror

BRUCE NEUBURGER

MONTHLY REVIEW PRESS
*New York*

Copyright © 2024 by Bruce Neuburger
All Rights Reserved

Library of Congress Cataloging-in-Publication xata
available from the publisher

ISBN: 978-1-68590-054-0 paper
ISBN: 978-1-68590-055-7 cloth

Typeset in Minion Pro

MONTHLY REVIEW PRESS, NEW YORK
monthlyreview.org

5 4 3 2 1

# Contents

Prologue | 9
Introduction: September 20, 1941 | 11

**PART 1 THE FAMILY | 21**
1. Anna and Benno, 1907 | 23
2. Prosperity, 1907–1914 | 53
3. War, 1914–1918 | 95
4. Revolution, 1918 | 127
5. The 1920s | 152
6. Shocks | 173
7. 1933 | 184

**PART II "THE JEWS ARE OUR MISFORTUNE" | 199**
8. Race Riots and Racial Laws, 1935 | 201
9. Trogerstrasse | 206
10. Hani's Escape, 1937 | 216
11. Max Holzer, 1937 | 225
12. The Fight, 1938 | 231
13. Fritz | 237
14. June to November, 1938 | 246
15. Klara | 257
16. Shattered Glass | 263
17. After Dachau | 274
18. Slave Labor | 296

**PART III: DESPAIR BECOMES DEFIANCE | 303**
  19. Trapped in Munich | 305
  20. Berg am Laim | 317
  21. Resettlement | 336
  22. The Letters of November 18 and 20 | 357
  23. Late November 1941 to Mid-March 1942 | 360
  24. September 18 and 19, 1942 | 375

Epilogue: Red Posters and the White Rose | 428
Benno's Role in History | 433
Those Who Perished in the Holocaust | 433
The Memorial in Munich | 435
Family Tree | 436
Persons in *Postcards to Hitler* | 437
Characters in *Postcards to Hitler* | 442
Acknowledgments | 444
Key Sources and Bibliography | 449
Notes | 455

*for*
Madeline Moeller
Eleanor Moeller
Batsheva Labowe-Stoll
Katya Labowe-Stoll
Elijah Labowe-Stoll
Jaden Labowe-Stoll
Jacob Stoll
Emily Stoll
Maya Ferchaw
Lincoln Ferchaw
Rachael Villaran
Joshua Villaran
Julia Villaran
Rebecca Villaran
Romeo Risdon
Jacob Dolinka
Samantha Dolinka

*The great-great-grandchildren of
Anna and Benno Neuburger.*

*To them and all those who inherit this beautiful and
abused world of ours, we must insist:*
NEVER AGAIN TO ANYONE!

# Prologue

WHILE I WAS ON A visit to my parents' home in Long Beach, California, in the early 1980s, my father handed me a thick folder of letters he and his sister had received from their parents, Benno and Anna Neuburger, between 1938 and 1941.

This much I knew at the time: During those years, my grandparents, Benno and Anna, tried to leave Germany to join their children, who had emigrated to the United States. They were unsuccessful. Both died in 1942, a day or two apart, in very different places. My father had told me that his mother was murdered in a camp somewhere east of Germany, and his father was executed in Berlin after having been convicted in the Nazis' so-called People's Court for having written a letter of outrage to Hitler.

In the early 1990s, my Aunt Johanna (Hani) gave me a copy of a transcript of Benno's trial. I didn't know it at the time, but the discovery of that document was made possible by the reunification of Germany, when court archives stored in the former East Berlin became accessible to a wider body of researchers. The transcript revealed that Benno was arrested, tried, found guilty of treason, and executed—not for writing a letter to Hitler, but for having written a series of postcards denouncing Hitler and the unfolding genocide and placing them anonymously in the mail. That is a part of the story my father, who died in 1987, never knew. That act of resistance ultimately inspired my determination to investigate the lives of Benno, Anna, and other relatives in order to write their stories.

In the 1980s, I interviewed surviving members of my family. Years later, I was able to retrieve hundreds of documents from the German Bundesarchiv and the Munich and Bavarian Archives. These shed light on the lives of my grandparents and the events that led to Benno's execution and enabled me to reconstruct those events in this book.

In the years since the release of the court records, Benno's story has drawn the attention of historians, especially German historians, seeking to unearth and make known acts of Jewish resistance to German fascism. Their writings have provided important information and inspiration that have greatly assisted my efforts.

Furthermore, historians have published new details of what befell Jews in places such as Munich, Laupheim, Traunstein, and Wolfratshausen, German cities where Benno's and Anna's family members lived. Some of those historical writings dealt directly with members of those interrelated families, the Neuburgers, Einsteins, Holzers, and Spatzes. Those historical works have also been invaluable to me in the writing of this book.

In my effort to bring to life the people whose stories are told here and the social environment in which they lived, I have necessarily imagined situations and relationships beyond the facts that I acquired directly through these sources. This includes several of the many letters that are part of this text. I have sought to use the knowledge I gained through extensive historical research and travel to reconstruct the drama of those times. I can promise you, the reader, that I have taken care to reflect the historical moments recounted here as accurately and truthfully as I can.

# Introduction: September 20, 1941

BENNO NEUBURGER WAS SITTING IN the office that was once his son's bedroom. He had been there for some time, contemplating a blank postcard on the large wooden desk in front of him. He ran his open hand over his hairless head as he thought about what to write. His mind also wandered to the dreadful reality of his diminished life—his diminished person. Not so long ago, his broad face, wide gray mustache, and firm jaw gave him what he regarded as a look of calm strength. Now, when he dared look in a mirror, what he saw staring back was a gaunt and aged man, whose dulled eyes seemed to have receded into his head. Benno was seventy. But it wasn't age that had so quickly changed him. It was the unending wretchedness of life that he, his family, and his community now endured. And now too, the terrifying rumors one heard about Nazi violence in the east . . .

He sat back in his chair and glanced over at his old suit coat, which was draped over the back of an armchair. The coat had a yellow cloth badge that his wife, Anna, had sewn on that morning. The rage he felt looking at that demeaning star, with the word *Jude* in thick black letters at its center, pushed aside for a moment the fear and paralysis that often gripped him.

Benno turned away from the coat and looked over the photos displayed on the bookshelves next to his desk. Here were the images that spanned much of his life: those of his children, Fritz and Hani, at different ages; he and Anna on their wedding day in 1907; several photos of the two of them with friends at Munich beer halls. There were vacation photos of himself and Anna standing near their Opel sedan by the Rhine River in Cologne, on a forest road near Salzburg, Austria, and still others in the Alps including Berchtesgaden—long before it became Hitler's Austrian hideaway. One of his favorite photos was of Fritz, Hani, and their "country" cousins from Traunstein, all in their late teens or early twenties, posing playfully, one behind the other. It was taken around 1927.

How shockingly different, those times were, he thought.

There were other photos, too—recent ones of Fritz with his new wife, Kate, and Hani with her husband, Ludwig, all taken in New York.

He reached for the photo of Hani standing in front of a brick apartment building. In it, her left hand was on her forehead, shading her eyes from the sun, while in her other arm she held her infant daughter, Karoline. Benno picked up that picture of his granddaughter wearing only a diaper and, as he had done before, looked closely at her face, searching for a family resemblance. He found what he thought were his own mother's eyes.

He set that photo down and looked at one of his own parents, surrounded by their five children. He, Benno, stood out, not only as the youngest among the four boys, but as the only one wearing lederhosen. He reached for another photo of himself with Anna and Fritz on his son's Bar Mitzvah Day in front of the old Munich Haupt Synagogue—that grand temple that Hitler ordered torn down in June 1938. Benno's hand trembled as he set the photo back on the shelf.

The photos on the bookcase had multiplied in recent years. Benno had taken them from boxes and albums, set them in frames or pasted them on a stiff backing, and put them on display. In this way he tried to fill a deepening void as his and Anna's personal and community lives were reduced bit by bit and detached from anything one could call a tolerable existence.

On the same chair where his coat lay, there was a letter, on thin onionskin paper, that Benno had written that morning to his son and daughter. He reached over and picked it up. It was short and contained the usual assurances, now so dramatically out of sync with reality. For years he and Anna had been writing carefully worded letters, assuring their children that they were fine, but also expressing an ever more fervent wish to be with them. This letter read:

September 20, 1941

Dear children,

Even though I'm expecting mail from you here, I'm writing you again. I got word that through a certificate of employment in connection with a sponsor, it might be possible to emigrate to the USA sooner. So, I included a copy with this letter. Please send it with the other documents right away to Washington. Who knows, it might work.

We are doing fine, and we hope the same is true for you. . . . We are so ready to leave. Let's just hope it will happen soon . . .

For now, I'm sending you greetings, and I'll be writing again soon.

Loving greetings from your father.[1]

Benno reread the letter several times and then put it in an envelope and placed it in the desk drawer.

He turned his attention to the blank postcard and thought again about what to write. He was a well-read man. Even the commanding officer from his World War I unit had noted on his military discharge papers that he was an "educated man." But this card was not going to require literary skills. In the desperate effort he was about to undertake, he would have to make his message as simple and direct as possible.

When not weighed down by the thought that what he was about

to do was likely to be completely useless or worse, he buoyed himself with the idea that whoever saw this card might be moved by the fact that someone—by courage or despair—risked breaking the silence.

As he carefully wrote a few words in large letters on the card he clung to the thought that one could not fully predict what one's actions might produce. Maybe the postal worker, after turning the card over to the authorities, which, of course, he would have to do, would mention it to a friend or a trusted fellow worker. Maybe it would spark a conversation about the wretched state of affairs in this country. Maybe it would encourage someone already fed up with things to speak up!?

He thought about an incident a few weeks ago on the Luitpold Bridge. He was out for a walk and, as he crossed the bridge, he stopped to look down at the Isar River. He looked down at the water for a moment, transfixed by shapes that were formed as it swerved around rocks and other obstacles before meandering under the bridge and out of sight. He had been absorbed by these images for a few precious moments, until someone suddenly stopped next to him—close enough for Benno to feel a coat brush up against his shoulder. He could tell that this person was taller and probably heavier than himself. Fear had just begun to take hold of him when he heard the man's voice "Don't let those Nazi *bastards* get you down!"

A hand briefly touched Benno on the shoulder. A moment later, the man was gone.

Benno thought he recognized the voice and that stocky figure that walked away with a slight limp. But he wasn't sure.

Was he another Jew?

Benno wished to believe he wasn't. He wanted to think that the man was one of those non-Jewish Germans who hated what he hated—though likely not as bitterly, nor as fearfully. Regardless, this man clearly wanted Benno to know that there were people like him.

*How did he know it was safe to speak to me? Was that not an act of defiance? Was that not also meant to have an effect?*

Then there was the well-dressed, middle-aged couple whom Benno saw passing in front of a newsstand where the Nazi paper *Völkischer Beobachter* was prominently displayed with a screaming headline from the Eastern Front. They spoke just barely within earshot. "Oh, yes," Benno heard the man say to his partner with unmistakable sarcasm. "Yet another world historic victory in the east!"

These little things gave him hope. Or, if not exactly hope—that word no longer seemed relevant to this moment—a recognition that there were little cracks in the walls. Cracks.

This made him think again about this enigma called Germany—and how this whole nightmare began—how a country that was his country, which he felt such a part of, for which he had sacrificed so much and which he had taken such pride in, was now his deadly sworn enemy.

His mind drifted back to a day more than sixty years earlier. His family was having a little party at their old home on Liebherrstrasse to celebrate his birthday. His older brothers—Markus, Heinrich, and Hugo—were there, and so were his sisters—Berta, then three, and his infant sister, Lina, who died of scarlet fever a few years later. Benno's mother, Judith, whom everyone called Jette, had made a batch of cheese blintzes and Benno's favorite desert, apple kugel.

His father, Max, normally stern and unexpressive with his children, especially with the boys, was in a playful mood that day. He spoke in a loud voice, drawing everyone's attention, "My boy, you are now growing up. Tell us how old you are."

Benno answered quietly, "I'm six, Papa."

"Benno, when people ask you how old you are, you must say to them, 'I'm as old as Germany!'" His father laughed. Everyone around the table smiled, Benno recalled, but it was his Papa's laugh, loud and a little wobbly from the beer he'd had with his dinner, that Benno remembered most vividly.

It was only later, in school, that Benno would come to understand his father's meaning. As with every young German, he would come to know 1871, the year he was born, as the year that twenty-seven German states were unified under the Prussian chancellor, Otto von Bismarck, giving birth to Germany's Second Reich.

*As old as Germany*. He considered how that coincidence of dates had affected his life.

For a long time, 1871 felt like a good year to be born. Nationhood emerged with Prussia's triumph in a war with France, elevating Germany into the ranks of the great powers of Europe. Those first forty years of Benno's life were peaceful ones, prosperous times for the most part, or so it now seemed in light of the cataclysm of four years of war that followed.

He thought about the events after Germany's defeat in November 1918, and how anger, disillusionment, and division had spread through the population. It was then that the horror now engulfing the Jewish community was set in motion. When the war ended, he was released from active military duty at the Dachau weapons depot and arrived home to a Munich in turmoil. That was more than twenty years earlier, but he recalled it clearly. A revolution with stunning swiftness had driven out the old Bavarian monarchy. Within days, the old Reich was gone. Then, just a few months later, came the assassination of the revolution's leader, Bavaria's prime minister, Eisner—a shock—and the beginning of a new kind of fear, like a wave that crested and ebbed, but never completely disappeared.

The anger and the passions at that time were to some degree understandable. So many had suffered, and so much had been lost in that deadly four years of war. But the hatred persisted. Even when life seemed to return to some normalcy after times of inflation and hunger, that hatred hung in the background, like some brooding demon biding its time, only to reemerge in a fury—not directed at the war with all its suffering and death, but at people like himself: Jews!

It was from this hatred that the beast was nourished and grew.

*Yes, we saw it. But one would have had to have been a fortune-teller to really foresee all its implications. It took a while for it to grow. But it did so right before our eyes, right in our midst, here in Munich, right on these streets!*

Benno thought about one of the guiding hands that set the hellishness in motion—a former general, and a man well known to every German of that era, who, in the waning days of the war, lied to the people, claiming "imminent victory" even as *he knew* the war was lost! And when in that November 1918 the Baltic sailors finally had had enough and marched off their ships with red flags and set the spark of rebellion for what threatened to become an uncontrollable blaze across the country then he—that general—that oh so "honorable" *Ludendorff*—pointed his finger, yes, blamed it ALL on the leftists . . . and on the JEWS—on US! He among a growing chorus claimed we had stabbed Germany in the back! He knew the sacrifices that Jews had made for the war effort, every bit in lockstep with the rest of the nation. Yet he stoked the flames of persecution. That bastard! I saw him walking arm in arm here in Munich with that scum, Hitler, in 1923 . . .

There was a knock at the door.

Benno heard his niece Hedi's voice: "Onkel Benno, there's dinner. Tante Anna says to come before it gets cold."

"Okay, I'll be there."

Benno took a breath. He looked again at the postcard and added a few words in the space between the original words.

His hands were shaking when he picked up his old coat from the stuffed chair. As he put it on, he noticed how worn it was around the wrists and along the other hemlines. He took the postcard from the desk and slipped it into an outer coat pocket. "On the left," he reminded himself, not wanting to fumble for it later.

Benno looked down at that yellow star on the left front of his coat and felt that sting again. They'd taken everything—everything but his anger. And that anger had worn through his caution, burned through his lifelong acquiescence.

*Whenever I leave this apartment I'll have this mark on me. There will be no place I can go without being identified, despised, pitied, or shamed.*

With that thought, he opened the door onto the hallway and passed by the kitchen. Anna and Hedi had just served themselves some potato pancakes and soup and were sitting down to eat. "Where are you going?" asked Anna. "We're having dinner now."

Benno couldn't help noticing how weary his wife looked. He imagined how anxiety and grief had aged her and dimmed her once luminous green eyes. "I know, I know. I won't be long. That letter to the children . . . I want to get it in the mail by this evening."

"You could send it tomorrow." Then, looking at the yellow star, she added, "I don't think you should go out."

"I'm just going to mail a letter. I'll be okay."

"But why?"

"I'm going out, Anna, with this brand of the slave on my chest. I'm not going to let *this* keep me from mailing a letter to my children." And then, in response to the worry on his wife's face he said, "I'll be back soon. Before the food gets cold."

He opened the door quietly, slipped out, and closed the door softly behind him. He did that so a certain neighbor wouldn't hear him, wouldn't open his door to the building's hallway, wouldn't stare and grin at the yellow brand on Benno's coat . . .

*Herr Kandl! That hateful turd of a man!*

Benno slipped quietly down the hall, down the stairs, and out to the street. It was still light, but the day was fading. He had only a block and a half to go. The dimming light made him feel less exposed, his branding less noticeable should someone pass him on the street. Still, he put his left hand up to his forehead, as if he were scratching something as he walked.

At the corner, a young woman appeared. Benno looked down. He had an urge to turn away but thought that would look suspicious. The woman looked at him as she passed the corner.

*Did she see the star?* He wasn't sure. All he was sure of was that the mark was doing what it was meant to do—rob him, rob Jews, of their last remnant of dignity.

As he approached the mailbox, he reached into his coat pocket and felt the sudden heat of panic. The card was gone! *Did it fall out on the street?* He turned to look in the direction he'd come. There was nothing on the ground that he could see. He would have to retrace his steps. But someone was coming toward him from that direction. He felt dizzy. *What if I dropped it in front of my apartment, and someone finds it?*

He searched again. He reached into his left coat pocket this time, felt the card, and cursed himself for having forgotten what he had so carefully told himself *not* to forget. He stuck his hand down into the tattered lining and pulled it out from between the silk and the wool. He looked down at the words he'd written in large letters where an address would normally be: "THE ETERNAL MASS MURDERER, HITLER, I SPIT ON YOU!"[2]

He put the card in the mailbox, turned, and walked back to his apartment.

# PART I
# THE FAMILY

---— 1 ——

# Anna and Benno, 1907

ONE FRIDAY EVENING IN EARLY March 1907, Benno Neuburger's friend Berthold invited him out for a drink to celebrate Benno's thirty-sixth birthday. They went to the Hofbräuhaus, a popular beer hall up the street from Benno's apartment on Liebherrstrasse.

It was one of the first warm spring afternoons of the year, so the crowd at the Hofbräuhaus was large and lively. Groups gathered around tables, singing boisterously to the traditional Bavarian tunes played by a live quintet. The two men had just sat down when Berthold leaned across the table and said loudly, "I think we need to find a spot where we can hear ourselves think." Benno glanced up to see Berthold push a lock of dark hair out of his face, his eyes alive with earnest intensity. Benno lifted his shoulders in resignation. They left for another restaurant up the street.

"You must have something really urgent to tell me," Benno commented as they settled into their seats and surveyed the menu. He ordered Bismarck herring with fried potatoes and a dark malt beer, while Berthold asked for duck, a baked potato, and a pale wheat beer. When the beers arrived Berthold held up his glass and proposed a birthday toast, then watched his friend take a long drink from his stein. Benno still looked youthful, but Berthold saw signs of greater maturity lurking. Berthold had often noted how Benno's heftier build contrasted with his own slender frame and narrow face, and now his naturally stocky build was thickening further. Benno's once thick dark hair had thinned and a few white hairs peeked out from the dark mustache that accented his broad face. Berthold had also noticed a change in his friend's demeanor after Benno joined his father's real estate business, five years earlier in 1902. He was now more subdued and his manner more conservative. He wore suits of a darker color. And he carried a watch and chain in his vest pocket that lent him an air of respectable maturity, as did the ascot ties he now almost always wore in public.

While they waited for their food, Berthold reminded Benno that Passover was coming.

"Seriously, *that* is what you're so anxious to tell me about?"

"Benno, I wanted to know if you had plans."

"I haven't talked it over with my father yet, so I can't say."

"Well, I intend to invite you to a seder at my uncle's house, in my old hometown, Laupheim." Berthold reached for the glass of beer in front of him.

"You know my mother died a month ago. This will be the first Passover without her." Benno shook his head. "I don't think I could leave my father alone."

Berthold looked intently at his friend. "My uncle has a good friend who comes every year with his family."

"Why are you telling me this?" Benno was annoyed that his concern was being ignored.

"Well, this friend has daughters, Benno."

"Daughters?"

"Two unmarried daughters. And they'll be at the seder. Look, Benno, call this matchmaking if you like, but what have you got to lose?"

"Laupheim, if I recall, is quite a distance from here."

"Not so far." Berthold sniffed the aroma of the food on his plate. "You know this place serves some of the best duck in Munich."

"Good. But let's stick to one subject at a time, Bert."

"They put a rail link from Ulm to Laupheim a few years ago." Berthold looked intently at Benno. "That cut transport time. In fact, the line takes you practically to my uncle's doorstep. I think you'll like these young women. The youngest is in her twenties."

Benno swirled the beer in his glass mug, took a drink, and looked on as a waiter set a dish of rolled-up pickled herring and onions noisily in front of him. Benno cut a slice of herring.

As Berthold watched his friend, he recalled their days together at Königsberger's fabric store. By the time Berthold started working there both he and Benno were in their mid-twenties, but Benno was an old hand, having started as an apprentice when he was just fourteen. They soon became good friends, sharing humorous rumors about the store owner and his family and exchanging jokes about eccentric customers. They found a mutual interest in hiking and travel in the mountainous areas of southern Bavaria, Austria, and Switzerland, not unusual among young Bavarians.

Berthold cut into his baked potato. "Come, and meet my Laupheim family. I'm sure you'll enjoy the place. Even if things don't work out—I mean, with my friend's daughters—I can guarantee you a good meal!"

Benno shrugged as he cut off another piece of herring.

"It's said," Berthold continued, "that my uncle's seders serve the best brisket and sauerbraten in Wurttemberg."

"Said by *whom*?" Benno slipped a piece of fried potato into his mouth.

"I suppose by his family!" Berthold noted with a grin. "It's rumored that the food is so good, the Kaiser once asked for an invitation."

"I don't think that recommends it at all. The Kaiser's hardly known for his good taste."

"Okay, Benno. I think I heard you say, not long ago, we're not getting any younger."

Benno pursed his lips. "My father's been dropping hints on that subject. And about the 'old days,' when parents arranged these family matters for their children."

"He has a point." Berthold shrugged. "We're on our own, are we not? And look, to be honest, we're lucky. So many Jewish guys have emigrated from small towns like Laupheim that there are more women than men. I'm offering you a chance to meet a few of them. I don't think you'll be disappointed."

"Quite a sales pitch, Berthold." Benno raised his glass as if offering a toast.

"A salesman's only as good as the product he's selling," Berthold said, returning the gesture with his beer. "But let's call this *community service*."

"Okay, Bert. But I need to talk to my father. How could I leave him alone so soon after my mother died?"

"Bring your father." Berthold waved his fork that held a piece of duck. "He'd be welcome."

"I'll talk to him, and I'll let you know. By the way . . . these young women, what are their names?"

"Anna and Mina. Their father is Moses . . . Moses Einstein. Anna's the younger one. They're both friends of my fiancée, Hilde."

Benno raised the issue to his father, Max, the next day. Max was enthusiastic about Berthold's invitation. "Benno, I think your friend has an excellent idea. You should go to Laupheim. I'll be fine. I'll spend Passover with some of Jette's family. Don't worry about me."

## LAUPHEIM

On Friday, March 29, 1907, the first day of Passover, Benno and Berthold met at Munich's Hauptbahnhof, the downtown train station. They boarded the noon train with a route through Augsburg to Ulm.

On the way, Berthold told Benno about his life in Laupheim before his family's migration to Munich. Moving to the big city was not what Berthold had had in mind. Instead, after graduating from the *realschule* and working briefly with a local hops dealer, Berthold flirted with the thought of going to America. As in many places around Germany, the uncertainties of economic life and bouts of discrimination in the 1880s and 1890s had encouraged young Jewish men to emigrate abroad.

"We'd heard that America welcomed Germans and being Jewish was of little or no concern," Berthold said, describing his thinking. "America was interested in enlarging what they called their European population. And here we were Jewish, but as European as they come! However, my father got a good offer for a job in Munich, so I dropped the idea and went along with the family. But I had a few friends who left the country. Probably attracted as much by romantic visions of 'pioneer life' in America as they were disgusted by the problems here."

"Like my brothers," Benno mused. "I think they thought they might become cowboys. Heinrich went to Colorado, and Markus and Hugo to Chicago, where it's my understanding that few cowboys are to be found!"

"We had some Laupheim boys go to Chicago. I don't know what they expected to find there." Berthold shrugged. "One of them, one of the Laemmles, got his father to finance his trip. And now he's gotten himself into the theater business of some sort. He's becoming a bit of a *macher*, I'm told."

"Well, I'm happy I stayed." Benno looked out at rolling hills that stretched to the horizon. "Bad times come, and bad times also go. We have the world's best beer, we have schnapps, we have the Alps. And this is not bad." He gestured to the Danube, which had just come into view outside their window.

At that moment, the train was on a rise, with a view of flatlands, rolling hills, patches of forest, and the outline of a distant village beyond the slow-moving river. A spring sky was studded with lumbering clouds that cast their shadows on the fields of various shades of brown and green. This was Benno's homeland. Unlike Berthold and other friends, he'd never even considered leaving it.

## The Seder

The Laupheim train station was just a few blocks from Berthold's uncle's large house on Kappelenstrasse. After a ten-minute walk from the tiny station to Laupheim's Judenberg district, its "Jewish Hill," the two men reached the house just as people began arriving from the Sabbath evening service at the synagogue.

Benno greeted each of Berthold's relatives and friends with a slight bow and forgot their names as soon as he moved from one to the other. Yet there was warmth in this Laupheim crowd that he felt immediately.

Benno and Berthold made their way around a large room, its walls covered in dark wood wainscotting and wallpaper with a floral pattern. Wooden beams crossed the ceiling. Benno felt the charm of the room and thought of rural comfort. Young women were moving around the space filling glasses with wine.

Noticing that all the men wore head coverings, Benno pulled out a yarmulke he'd brought from home.

When an older man with a full white beard and mustache entered the room, Berthold took Benno's arm and moved him in the man's direction. "Here's a friend of the family I want you to meet," Berthold said. Benno suspected that the man, with his dark suit and colorful yarmulke, was a rural rabbi. "Moses, this is my friend Benno."

Benno took hold of an outstretched hand and was surprised by its firm grip and its rough calluses—decidedly not what one would expect of a rabbi.

"This is Moses Einstein." Berthold gestured toward the man respectfully.

"The young man from Munich." Moses smiled. Benno realized that Berthold must have been talking about him. "Your first visit to Laupheim, is it?"

"Yes. And I'm pleased to be here." To justify such a statement about a place he'd arrived at only an hour before, Benno added, "My friend Berthold has had a lot of good things to say about this community."

Moses held Benno's hand in his rough grasp "We're a small community, in a small town. But there is a long history to us here. Thank you for coming." Moses put a hand on Benno's shoulder. "Don't let me keep you. I think Berthold has plans to introduce you to others here in Laupheim." At that, Moses smiled and turned to head toward a group of people who had just entered the room.

Benno walked with Berthold along the long tables formally set with dinnerware and wine glasses. There were extra plates on table corners topped with blue linen napkins that covered stacks of matzoh. Each place setting had a colorful Haggadah with large Hebrew lettering and pictures depicting the scenes from the Passover story: slaves pulling massive stone blocks, and Egyptians in their chariots being swept away by the raging waters of the Red Sea.

Benno noticed a familiar smell coming from the kitchen. "Berthold, my guess is that there's a sauerbraten in the oven somewhere."

"Don't say I didn't warn you," Berthold said jovially. The two men watched the room fill with people who were chatting as they approached seats at the tables. Talk trailed off as two women lit candles, one at each of the two long tables, and a tall man wearing a white yarmulke intoned a prayer: "*Baruch atah Adonai. . . .*"

"My Uncle Nate," Berthold whispered.

The prayer continued, joined by other voices: "*l'hadlik ner shel yom tov. . . .*"

When the words *Shabbat Shalom!* echoed around the room, smiles, greetings, and laughter erupted. Men, women, and children in their Sabbath clothes settled into the seats around the tables. Berthold brought Benno to a place near the middle of one of these tables before moving to join his fiancée, Hilde, and her family. Benno found himself opposite a young woman with medium-length light brown hair and luminous green eyes. "My name is Benno, I'm from Munich," Benno volunteered. "I came here with my friend Berthold."

"I'm Anna. Glad to meet you." The young woman spoke quietly with a slight nod of her head. "I'm glad you could come."

A short time later, a slightly older woman with a thinner build and shorter hair sat down next to Anna. Benno noted a resemblance. "This is my sister, Mina," Anna said, gesturing to the woman. "And this is Benno, Berthold's friend from Munich."

Mina smiled. "Nice to have you, Benno. All the way from far-off Munich!"

"Not so far as I'd thought—just two and a half hours from Munich to Ulm. And the train from Ulm took us almost to the doorstep of this house."

Anna looked at her sister and then back to Benno. "We still think of Munich as being far away. But you're right. It's really not so far with the new train lines."

It wasn't long after their introduction that Anna and Mina left the table and disappeared behind what Benno assumed was the door to the kitchen. Benno took the moment to look around at two long tables running parallel across the room, and another, smaller table, where children were seated. There were fifty or sixty people in the combined living room and dining room now being used for the seder. To Benno the place had the feel of a dining hall in an inn more than a house.

When Anna and Mina returned to their seats, Benno asked if the seder preparations had kept them busy. "Very," Mina sighed. "We've been preparing for a week. We had to clear the house of every crumb of *chametz*! Now we have to watch over the sauerbraten."

"One of my favorites!" Benno was about to mention Berthold's joke about the Kaiser, but then thought the better of it.

"We've spent the better part of the last several days on that dish," Mina continued. "Our father Moses," Mina nodded to the rabbinical looking man Berthold had introduced to Benno, "is very particular about his sauerbraten. So we try hard to get it right."

"What's the secret to that?"

"Spices, marinade, cooking time. . . ."

"And self-sacrifice," Anna joked.

Mina looked at her sister. "You must give yourself to the food.

You have to watch the temperature, and the time, and the order you do things. If you don't do it right, the meat will come out tough and dry."

"And then our sweet father will come out a little bitter!" Anna laughed.

Mina nodded. "Our mother taught us how to cook it. She also warned us about our father's judgments on cooking."

"Your mother?"

"Our mother, Hannchen."

"She passed away four years ago," said Anna.

"I see. I'm sorry." Benno paused. "My mother passed away in February." And as he spoke those words, it struck him that this was the first seder in his life without his mother present. "She was a good cook. Some of my earliest memories were of her kugel."

Mina gave Benno a sympathetic look. "I'm sorry about your mother. But you're in luck. We're having apple kugel tonight, along with other desserts. But I suppose we should keep some surprises."

"My mother would be happy—I mean, that I'll be eating so well." As Benno spoke, a baritone voice rang out with another prayer, this time for wine, joined by voices from around the room: "*Baruch atah Adonai eloheinu melekh ha'olam borei peri haggafen, ah, ah, amen.*" Berthold's uncle and Moses were standing at the ends of the long tables with their wine glasses raised, along with everyone else's.

Anna, Mina, and Benno lifted their glasses to their lips. With the reading of the order of the seder and the first blessing of the wine, the seder began. Benno had been to seders all his life. He understood the service very well, the order of the prayers, the storytelling, the wine drinking, the eating of the bitter herbs and other ritual foods. But seders with his family and friends in Munich had been conducted in Hebrew and German. He relied on the German to understand all the nuances. This Laupheim seder, conducted in Hebrew alone, had him struggling. He read the Hebrew parts assigned to the "congregation" quietly, under his breath, and somewhat self-consciously. He had taken classes in Hebrew as preparation for his bar mitzvah, but he'd forgotten most of it and had little opportunity—or motivation—to practice it.

I'm going to have to brush up on my Hebrew, Benno thought. If I ever have to lead a family seder, I don't want to be caught short.

At each table, there were several beautiful metal platters, specially designed for Passover, with matzoh, bitter herbs, a cup of salt water, and a boiled egg. These were passed around at the appropriate times during the service. Moses Einstein and Berthold's Uncle Nate took turns instructing the congregants when to eat the symbolic foods, when to drink the sweet wine, when to speak and when to sing.

This seder in Laupheim was more formal, more ornate, and, Benno felt, more spirited than those in his family circle. He was struck by the care with which the children read the four questions, the way an older child diligently guided a younger one through newly learned Hebrew words, and the seriousness with which these children performed the rituals.

Benno glanced at Anna during the service. She was wearing a white, long-sleeved blouse with large black buttons and vertical ruffles that extended to just below her high-neck collar. She had a roundish face and features that were not fine or delicate, but soft and robust in a way that struck him as friendly. Her light brown hair was nearly shoulder-length, in contrast to Mina's, which was darker and shorter. If looks are an accurate measure of personality, he thought Mina must be more reserved and strait-laced and Anna more open, in a sweet kind of way. Benno realized that this was just superficial guesswork and tried to dismiss it. Still, there was attraction, and with that came incentive.

After the first part of the seder service came dinner and conversation. An older woman sitting next to Benno introduced herself as an aunt of Berthold. She asked Benno what he thought of the seder. "I think this is the most beautiful seder I've ever attended," he replied earnestly.

Pleased, the aunt leaned over and as she grasped Benno's upper arm she said, "This first night of Passover is special. It brings a lot of us together from around Laupheim and Ulm."

As Berthold had promised, the food was remarkable. To begin with, there was matzoh ball soup. Then plates of meat—outstanding sauerbraten and beef tongue with wine sauce. There was matzoh knodel (dumplings), spätzle, and beets and parsnips in a mushroom sauce. Benno was impressed with it all. The sweet wine served at the seder service gave way to other wines, most of them local varieties from a region near the Rhine River in Württemberg. As Benno ate, he chatted with people around him. Meanwhile, Anna and Mina were busy serving: first the meal, then wine, and then dessert.

When the sisters finally had time to enjoy their own meal, Anna asked Benno about Passover in Munich. "Smaller and less formal," he replied. "And the Haggadah text is also in German. After my brothers left Germany for the United States, it was just myself, my sister, and our parents, so we started rotating between the homes of different relatives and friends. Sometimes, my mother's relatives would come to our apartment, or we'd go to their home. One year, we went to Nördlingen, near my father's hometown of Mönchsdeggingen. Do you know those places? Little villages east of Ulm, really quite small—smaller than Laupheim."

Anna shook her head, indicating she did not. Then she added casually, "We pass through Munich every now and then on the way to see our sisters."

"They live in Traunstein." Mina looked at Benno. "Are you familiar with Traunstein?"

"I know where it is. I've passed it on the way to Salzburg a few times."

"We've talked about stopping in Munich, but never gotten around to it." Anna stood up to go again to the kitchen and came back with kugel, as Mina had promised. Then, with some fanfare, came the king of the desserts, so to speak, the Kaisertorte, or Emperor's cake—a dish that Benno knew of but had never eaten. The Laupheim version was multilayered with chocolate and slices of apple.

After the meal, the seder resumed for a short time. When it

concluded, someone tapped a wineglass and called for a toast to a relative who was celebrating a birthday. Then another man rose, announced the birth of a new child, and insisted on yet another toast. After several more toasts Benno heard a familiar voice in a slightly higher pitch than normal. Berthold held his wine glass high and looked around the room. "I have two toasts. One to Hilde and our engagement." This was followed by applause. Berthold's aunt leaned over to Benno and whispered, "You see, these young Laupheim men run away from here to America or to some big city, and then they come back to take away our girls!" Benno didn't know if she was kidding or serious, but he heard the Passover wine in her voice. He nodded at her remark just as he heard Berthold say, "And another toast to my friend, Benno, who came all the way from Munich to enjoy our Laupheim seder."

Shouts of "*Prost!*" and "*L'chaim!*" could be heard from people around the tables. Some of them looked at Benno as they raised their glasses. When Benno nodded in reply, he saw Anna and Mina raising their glasses, and he raised his glass, too.

It was past midnight when the seder dinner came to an end with the eating of the *afikoman*, the hidden matzoh, which some of the older children brought around as people sang hymns as part of the Nirtzah. "May the Lord God of Israel shine His face upon you," Moses sang out from the end of the table. The words *Next year in Jerusalem! Next year in Jerusalem!* rang out, as those who still had wine in their glasses took a final drink.

Finishing his wine, Benno looked across the table. Anna and Mina were gone. Berthold appeared with his fiancée Hilde. After introductions and a goodbye to Hilde, Berthold took Benno's arm. Together, they walked a little unsteadily out the door and headed toward the house of another of Berthold's relatives, where Berthold had arranged for them to stay for the night.

The next morning, they attended Sabbath service at the small synagogue. The women were seated in the mezzanine and were not visible to the men, sitting in the pews on the ground floor. Benno commented quietly to Berthold during the service, "I'm not used to this rather drastic separation of men and women in the synagogue."

To avoid offending any of Berthold's relatives by taking a train on the Sabbath, they stayed in Laupheim that night also. On Sunday, one of Berthold's cousins gave them a ride to Ulm, for the train to Munich. On their trip back, Berthold asked Benno about his impression of Laupheim. "It's a pretty town. It feels very friendly. And if you mean Anna and Mina, I enjoyed their company. But they disappeared not long after desserts were served, so I had no way to say goodbye to them. They were certainly busy the whole evening."

"Well, as Hilde likes to say, 'Jewish holidays are for women to prepare and for men to enjoy.'" Berthold shrugged. "Will you be seeing Anna again?"

"I intend to try," Benno replied as he watched the German countryside glide by the train window and wondered how he could make that happen.

## Munich

When Benno returned to Munich, he wrote to Anna and Mina, asking them to thank everyone for their hospitality and especially the cooks for their excellent work. He put in a special word for the sauerbraten, the beef tongue, the kugel, and the Emperor's cake.

He then added a P.S.:

If you plan to pass through Munich, let me know. I think you'll find Munich's a good place to visit. I can show you some places of interest here.

With warm regards, Benno.

A week later, he received a reply in the form of a brief note:

Thank you for your letter and your kind words. Mina and I are planning to visit Traunstein in two weeks. We'd like to stop by Munich on the way. Let me know if that's convenient. It was very nice meeting you. I look forward to seeing you again.

I am yours truly,
Anna

It was an early May morning when Anna and Mina stopped in Munich on their way to Traunstein. Benno was at the train station to meet them. He watched nervously as the train from Ulm pulled up to the platform. Added to his nervous anticipation was a worry that he would have trouble finding his Laupheim guests on the crowded platform. But the two Laupheimers came off the train near to where Benno was standing. They recognized each other instantly.

Anna was wearing a white blouse with a high collar and a dark skirt. She had her light brown hair in a pompadour style with a blue silk scarf around her neck. Mina was wearing a yellow print dress with long sleeves and a dark hat with a thin brim, out of which came a large silver goose feather. To Benno they looked every bit the middle-class German women—nothing "country" about them.

After they greeted each other warmly, Benno offered to buy them breakfast.

"We're fine," said Mina. "We ate before we left."

"Okay. We'll have lunch later after I've worn you out walking this town." Benno smiled as he looked down at his guests' shoes. "I hope those are comfortable for walking." Benno led them out of the station through the crowded street toward Munich's central plaza. Cars, horses pulling wagons, bicycles, and pedestrians all competed for road space.

"So busy." Anna spoke with a bit of wonder in her voice as she dodged traffic and then stared up at large Baroque and Gothic buildings on the street outside the Hauptbahnhof.

At Marienplatz, Munich's central square, they stopped in front of an immense neo-Gothic building, its façade an elaborate pattern of arches, spires, and statuary. "This is the New Town Hall," Benno said as his guests looked on, stunned by the tall central tower and massive ornate structure. "It houses the Bavarian state and Munich government offices. There are four hundred rooms in there."

"And the statuary?" asked Mina.

"Most of the figures you see are representative of the Wittelsbach line, Munich's royalty. Their reign goes back quite a few centuries." Benno pointed to the central tower. "Behind the construction covering on that tower is what will soon be a very large mechanical clock—an elaborate mechanism with music, Medieval figures, dancers, and performers. This is Munich showing off its mechanical prowess. We've been promised quite a show. It's the re-creation of a famously obscene, opulent wedding feast, so we're told."

"This building reminds me of the Ulm-Minster church," Mina commented.

Anna nodded. "The style is similar to this. It's also quite impressive in size."

"The tallest church in the world." Mina looked at her sister. "Isn't that right, Anna?"

Anna nodded. "That's what I've heard people say."

"I should see that sometime." Benno motioned for them to continue.

When they came to another plaza, a few blocks from Marienplatz, Benno paused and had his guests turn around. They saw a stage with a portico held up by pillars. In the center, there was a stairway flanked by two stone lions. "This is Feldherrnhalle," Benno explained. "And this plaza where we're standing is the Odeonplatz. All this was commissioned by King Ludwig I of the Wittelsbach family. It's modeled on an Italian museum, whose name I don't recall." Benno pointed in the direction opposite the Feldherrnhalle. "At the other end of this street there's a Roman triumphal arch called the Siegestor. You can just barely see it from here. These structures, this plaza, and the wide street in front of us are all part of Ludwig's grandiose vision for Munich. Thanks to his building mania, Munich got the nickname 'Athens on the Isar.' But I've never been to Athens to see if there's any resemblance!"

"Ludwig was that crazy prince who built that castle," Mina paused to remember, "Neu—"

"Neuschwanstein," Anna reminded her sister.

"Well, that was a different Ludwig . . . Ludwig II." Benno said, gesturing for them to follow him. "Opinions differ as to whether he was actually crazy. There are those who say he just had a passion for building crazy palaces."

"And his death was rather strange. Am I right?" asked Anna.

"Murdered. And at a rather young age." Benno, a history buff, was impressed with how much Anna knew. "Some say he was murdered because he was crazy, others because he was homosexual and an embarrassment to the monarchy. What we know is that no one was ever charged for his death! Now, how could that be?" As Benno completed the question he stood at an ornate stone gateway at the far edge of the Odeonplatz. Through the archway he pointed to a building that extended a great distance from where they stood with a seemingly endless series of rectangular and curved windows, and doorways framed by carved figures. Benno pointed toward the long building. "The modest Residenz Palace of our humble monarchs, the Wittelsbachs. Don't ask me how many rooms—I've lost count!" Benno laughed.

"Enough to keep them comfortable?" Mina teased.

Benno smiled. "Let's hope so!"

Benno and his guests walked along Ludwigstrasse, the wide street that flowed north from Odeonplatz, rimmed by impressive stone buildings. Benno paused in front of one long yellow-and-red brick building that stretched at least half a block. He told Anna and Mina to look up at a building with four large stone figures in front of its arched doorways. "The Bavarian State Library. Its collection goes back to the 1500s—the biggest collection of books and documents in Germany. Here you'll find a copy of every written work in Bavaria . . . with the exception of our two letters."

"Of course our letters wouldn't be here," Anna responded matter-of-factly. "Since my letter was from Wurttemberg."

"So true," Benno laughed.

It was a short exchange that communicated a lot. They could joke with each other!

The tour along Ludwigstrasse took the three of them past the Catholic University and then the Siegestor monument. Benno pointed out the trolleys powered by overhead electric wires, recalling how only a few years before they had been pulled by horses. He then took them through part of Munich's largest park, the English Garden. He mentioned its amenities including the Chinese pagoda and its huge central beer garden.

They walked through the park to the Isar River, passing several bridges. Benno gave a short description of each bridge. At the largest one, Benno said, "This is the Ludwigsbrücke. I suppose I don't need to tell you who this bridge is named after!" About halfway across the Ludwigsbrücke, Benno led his guests up a narrow path and pointed to a construction site. "We're on an island in the river. This is—or will be—the Deutsche Museum of Sciences and Technology. There's a temporary building here, as you can see. It opened last year. The main building has yet to be constructed. But once it's completed, it will be the world's largest science museum."

"The soon-to-be Ludwig Science Museum?" asked Anna playfully.

"I don't think any Ludwigs, at least the royal ones, have had much to do with it. The city donated this island to the project. It's called Coal Island."

"Coal Island?" Mina said. "Is there coal in the ground here?"

"No," Benno replied. "But it was from here that coal was brought into the city."

Anna and Mina laughed quietly at Benno's passion for Munich's history. And, in truth, he impressed himself with all the information he'd gathered over the years and the way it now flowed from him.

## Max

From the museum, Benno took Anna and Mina to his family's

apartment a block from the river. As they approached a building on Liebherrstrasse they saw an older man standing in a doorway, his thin face rimmed by neatly trimmed gray sideburns and a beard. His dark frock coat was buttoned up to just below the top of his gray tie. He wore a brown homburg and carried a cane.

The man came out of the shadows, grinned broadly, and bowed slightly. "These must be the girls from Laupheim. So glad to meet you! Certainly am! I've heard nothing but good things about you Laupheimers. I'm Benno's father, Max, in case you hadn't guessed."

Benno blushed at this unusually effusive introduction. "Papa, this is Anna and Mina."

"So happy you could come to Munich. Should we go to lunch? I know some good places not far from here. You must be hungry after your walk around the city, no?"

"Yes," Anna and Mina answered at the same time.

"I feel like we've seen a lot in a short time," Anna commented.

"I hope Benno didn't wear you out with all that touring."

Anna laughed. "We'll recover."

"Well, Benno was born here, as you must already know, and he . . . and we . . . have seen the town grow up right in front of us."

They made their way to a street that intersected Liebherrstrasse—Zweibrückstrasse. After being seated at a restaurant on that street, Max asked his guests if they would like "a real Munich lunch." When they nodded favorably, he ordered several large servings of beef knuckles, sauerkraut, and a platter of bratwurst and cheese. Max smiled as he looked across the table at the young women. "You come from a large family, am I right?"

"Five of us—four sisters and a brother," Mina said, glancing at Anna. "I'm the oldest. We have two more sisters, Fanny, and Bertha, who live in Traunstein. Which is where we're going today—"

"And a younger brother who still lives in Laupheim with us," Anna said.

"I have four boys and a girl who grew up here in Munich." Max looked at the two women guests and then at his son. "Benno was the only one of the boys who was *born* here. And the only boy who stayed. My daughter, Bertha, lives here in Munich. We saw some rough times. One by one, Benno's brothers left for America. In the Nineties it seemed that every young German, or at least every young German Jewish man, wanted to go to America! You could just go there and get free land, get rich, and so on. So they say. I never understood where all that land came from."

"From people who were there before the English came," Benno commented.

"I wish they hadn't gone. If they'd stayed I think they'd have done fine here . . . they might even have been better off." Max picked up a glass of beer that had just been set in front of him. "America is not the paradise some would believe. It's rich because they have people over there working for nothing."

"*Had*, Papa," Benno interjected. "Slavery ended."

"Well, not everyone is treated so well over there. That's what I hear. There are opportunities here now—more than there were."

"There was a time," said Mina, "when our father was ready to sail off to America." Anna looked at her sister with surprise. "The way he told me the story, he wasn't interested in being drafted for one of those Prussian wars."

Max nodded. "Could have been the war with Denmark or Austria. I remember them. But I was too old for either. And I was married. Militaries want their soldiers young and reckless. What year was your father born, Mina?"

Mina looked at her sister. "1841 or '42, I think."

"Well, you see, I was born in 1836. Jette and I got married in April 1862. Just a week after we met."

"Just a week?" Benno sounded surprised. "I hadn't heard that before."

"Your grandfather Mathias brought Judith—everyone called her Jette—over from Huerben to meet my family. They were nice enough to invite me to the gathering." Max laughed. "I was okay with that. We got married in Krumbach, a larger community with its own synagogue. It turns out we got along okay. We lived together in Mönchsdeggingen for seven years." Max looked at Anna and Mina. "You probably have never heard of that place. A tiny village in Bavaria. Then we came here. But to go back a bit . . ."

Benno took a breath and was about to interrupt the story he'd heard several times before, but then thought the better of it. Max continued, "When I was eighteen, my uncle gave me a small wagon and a horse and taught me the selling trade. I went from farm to farm with materials for clothing. I was at the mercy of the farmers. If they had a good year, things went okay. But when they were doing poorly, I suffered with them. The farmers hired young girls as maids and field workers. The farmers paid them with the products, the fabrics they bought from people like me. I think you know what I'm talking about."

Mina and Anna nodded that they did.

"Well, you know that the girls made clothes for their own use and for their dowries. The farmers had a hold on those girls so long as they didn't slip out of their hands through marriage, which was great incentive for these girls to *get* married! For me it was a hard way to make a few marks. I spent a lot of hours on the road in that wagon!"

"What made you decide to move to Munich?" Mina asked.

"A few things. When factories started making clothing, the girls didn't need my fabrics. They could buy ready-made clothes more cheaply. So that was a big loss for me. Then it was decided *not* to put a rail line to our little town. What chance would there be for commerce in our poor little village?" Max shrugged. "Jette brought up the idea of moving. She had family here in Munich, and they encouraged us. It wasn't so hard to let go of life in Mönchsdeggingen. We had nothing to hold on to."

Anna took a sip of beer. "And starting out here in Munich with a family, how was that?"

Max looked over at his son. "If we hadn't had Jette's relatives here, it would have been difficult. But our timing was good. Benno was born two years after we got here. At the time the economy was doing well. So, we got a good start here in Munich, selling textiles. Of course, things also went down for a time after that"—Max paused for a moment—the changes I've seen in my time here are quite amazing. I'd say we were lucky. Not everyone has done so well in these times. I think my generation is a little more sensitive to that fact. Whereas the younger generation tends to take things for granted."

"For example?" Mina asked.

"Well, take my old business in Mönchsdeggingen. When the factories came along, they destroyed a lot of trades, including mine! Not everyone's been able to find new ways to make a living. That's caused resentment. As I've said to Benno, modernization has been good in many ways. But let's not forget the negative side."

Benno looked at his father impatiently. "Papa, maybe Anna or Mina would like to say something about Laupheim?"

Mina looked at her sister. "There's not much to say. Things don't change that quickly in Laupheim. Our grandfather was a leader in the community. Papa's proud of that. He has a cattle business and makes a decent living. Anna and I help with bookkeeping and such."

"Laupheim has some very prosperous businesses," Anna added. "Papa supplies the farmers in the area with oxen for their field work. What he makes has usually been enough. I'd say it's not been too hard a life. We hear stories of hard times, but we've never gone hungry that I can remember. Papa is devoted to the synagogue, to religion. We have a community that's very—"

"Close-knit," Mina said, taking a bite of beef. "Mmm. This is quite good!"

"But the opportunities for women are limited," Anna added.

"Benno told me about your seder. He can hardly stop talking about the food! Especially that ah—"

"Sauerbraten, Father."

"Yes. Jette, Benno's mother, used to make quite a good sauerbraten, but Benno says yours was better."

Anna laughed. "When you have a father who trades in cattle..."

"Are you still selling textiles?" Mina wanted to know.

"No. I'm retired. Benno runs everything now. We got out of the textile business years ago." Max looked over at his son. "Benno can tell you the story of our land business."

"But you know it from top to bottom." Benno took a piece of bratwurst and cheese off the large platter in the center of the table.

Max nodded. "One day, Karl, a cousin of Jette's, asked me to take a ride with him. We went to an area not more than a few miles from here. It was still farmland then. We stopped at the side of a field and Karl said, 'Max, look at this land. You know, you can buy land like this.' Well, we'd come from a place where Jews were not allowed to own land. I knew things were different here in Munich. But still, I said, 'Fine, but what would I do with land?' I had a little money, but not enough to build a house, and I'm not a farmer. Karl said, 'You don't have to do a thing. Just pay the taxes on it.' And I couldn't see any point in that! Then he said, 'That's because you're from a place where land prices don't change. Here in Munich, land prices are going up, and they'll continue to go up because the city's growing.' And, of course, he was right. So, we—Jette's family and I—started to buy little plots of land together with other families. We pooled our money, got a few loans, and so on. And we bought little parcels of land. Some we rented, and some we sold. That's how we've made a living."

"Now you know everything about us!" Benno laughed.

"This is a really remarkable place," Anna said. "I mean, so different from Laupheim. And what about life for Jews here?"

"Being Jewish here is not the same as it was in Mönchsdeggingen or Krumbach," Max began. "There, no matter what, you were a Jew. Here, no one really knows or really cares much. Right, Benno? That's not to say there's no prejudice here. Of course, there is. If you look at the statues on the New Town Hall at Marienplatz, you'll see a few of them have anti-Jewish themes."

"I didn't mention that during our tour. But it's true," Benno concurred.

"Do Jews go out on the streets here on Sundays?"

Benno looked at Mina. "Of course. Why wouldn't we?"

"We go out, but we stay in our neighborhood," Anna explained.

"The gentiles sometimes take offense seeing Jews in their part of town on their holy day."

Benno winced. "First of all, here in Munich no one knows who is and who isn't Jewish. I'm speaking about us native German Jews, not the Jews from the east, of course."

Max added, "We go out no matter what day of the week it is. I don't think the *goyim* in Munich give a hoot about that."

"Papa!" said Benno.

"Benno doesn't like me using words like '*goyim*.' But I grew up with expressions like that."

"Most of the non-Jews here in Munich are about as religious as we reform Jews." Realizing what he had said, Benno stopped to see the reaction from Anna and Mina. But his casual attitude toward religion didn't seem to bother them. "We respect the holidays, but we don't take religion that . . . solemnly."

"Things are different in Laupheim. On any given day, a man in our community might be asked to be part of a *minyan* so there are enough congregants to have a service. I think I could live without that." Anna blushed when she realized the implication of her remark.

Mina looked at her sister. "Anna, we have a train to catch this afternoon." After thanking Max for his stories and for the lunch, the young women said goodbye to him. Benno accompanied them to a tram stop, and the three rode together to the main train station. As they neared it, Mina turned to Benno. "You didn't take us to the Jewish quarter."

"Munich doesn't have a Jewish quarter. Or I should say, we don't have a *German* Jewish quarter. There's an area where you'll find a lot of Jewish immigrants from Russia, Galicia, Poland, and so on. It's near the Gärtnerplatz, which is not that far from where we met my father."

"In Laupheim we have our own district, Judenberg. Until a few years ago, we weren't allowed to live anywhere else," Anna explained.

The three of them got off the tram across from the Hauptbahnhof.

As they walked into the train station, Anna turned to Benno and said, "We'd like to invite you to Laupheim. It would only be fair to give you a tour. Then we can show you our own 'new town hall.'"

"Yes, such a grand place!" Mina gave an exaggerated flutter of her hand which Benno found amusing. "How many rooms, Anna?"

"Six, at least—maybe eight." Anna paused as Benno laughed. "We'll show you around our Jewish hill and the rest of the town. And, of course, the synagogue. . . . Oh, I forgot! You were at our synagogue during Passover! But we haven't seen your synagogue here."

Benno realized that he hadn't even thought to bring his guests to one of Munich's synagogues. "We have two large temples here in Munich. The next time you come, I'll show them to you."

A conductor was waving to people on the platform. Anna turned and took a step up to an open door, and Mina stepped up behind her. "Let us know when you can come to Laupheim," they called.

"Of course!" Benno waved back, smiling.

DURING THE MONTHS THAT FOLLOWED, Benno and Anna exchanged postcards and letters as they grew closer together. Since both were looking for a permanent relationship, it wasn't long before the question of marriage came up. After a few trips to Laupheim, several walks around the town, a Sabbath evening service at the Laupheim synagogue, and several meals at the Einstein home, Benno asked Anna if she wanted to come join him in Munich. "This time, as my wife."

And she happily agreed.

## Moses

Munich attracted Anna. There was something about the anonymity of the large city that gave her a sense of freedom. In Munich, she could imagine herself living, not as someone's Jewish daughter or wife, but as a woman in her own right. There, she saw doors being opened to a life broader than could be found in Laupheim. And someone had come to Laupheim to find her and walk her through that door!

Not that she would go without some regrets. With her mother gone, she worried about leaving her father. She knew how much Moses wanted her to stay and raise a family in Laupheim, a town where their family went back at least four generations and where Moses's father had been the *Judenvorsteher*, the community leader. Moses regarded the bonds of tradition and community as the bedrock of social existence. Anna, however, felt these bonds from a different angle. She felt them limiting her options and perspectives as a woman. Anna worried about her father's well-being, but took comfort in the fact that her older sister Mina intended to stay and look after their father, as would the community. Her younger brother, Ludwig, was still living in Laupheim too, and, up to that point, he had made no move to leave.

After Benno and Anna agreed to marry, Benno promised to meet Moses in Laupheim to discuss the marriage decision. They met in late July in the small garden behind the Einsteins' whitewashed home at 49 Kappelenstrasse. Moses gestured for Benno to sit at a small table under a beech tree. As Benno contemplated his opening remarks, Moses went right to the point without hesitation: "You and Anna are going to get married. I'm not unhappy about that. I think you know that. You make a good living. But I will tell you what I told the Holzer boys when they stated their intention to marry Anna's older sisters Bertha and Fanny. This Laupheim Jewish community has been around for a few centuries, and it's been through its ups and downs. But it has survived, and I think survived well, because we've held on to our religious traditions. I know that sounds quaint to your modern ears, but you'll find that the strength of a community comes from its determination to defend its traditions. Judaism could not have survived in the Diaspora without that commitment. I know you have a penchant for history, and so you know what I'm talking about."

Benno nodded but said nothing. He recalled Anna's story of the scandal that erupted in the Einstein household when her sisters Bertha and Fanny told their parents of plans to marry two brothers, Louis and Willi Holzer—thus breaking with the long-standing tradition of arranged marriage, which had brought Moses and Hannchen, and so many others of their generation, together. When the sisters informed their parents they were moving to Traunstein, a small Bavarian town with no organized Jewish community, Moses was beside himself. "How will you even remain Jewish there!?" In the end he insisted that Bertha, Fanny, and their husbands-to-be agree to maintain a kosher household in exchange for his blessing to the marriage.[3]

"Without tradition," Moses insisted as he sat at the garden table across from Benno, "people will be blown here, there, and everywhere. I see it happening. I see a danger in it. And just because one has ridden out a storm, and you've probably seen a squall or two already in your days . . . I certainly have . . . and just because the calm has returned, it doesn't mean that another wind won't come along." Moses paused. Benno just nodded again.

"You were too young to have really experienced what happened in the 1870s," Moses said gravely. "Things were going well after unification . . . and our 'emancipation.'" Benno noted a bit of sarcasm in Moses's voice. "My business was very robust. Then the bad times set in. We all suffered. I had to sell off cattle below the price I'd paid for them, and we almost lost our house. The suffering was spread all around. But the blame all went in one direction. If a Jew was doing poorly, no one noticed. If a Jew was doing well, it had to be because he was manipulating the economy to benefit himself." He paused and pointed a finger toward the village. "Here in Laupheim, we have a family, the Steiners, who've done quite well in hops and other things. They were insulated to some degree from the worst effects of the economic problems because of their foreign trade connections. But they became a target, not as a prosperous family, but as *Jews*. Some extreme measures were being floated about, and the community began to wonder what our fate would be."

"My father's business also had a few rough years," Benno noted.

"But Munich kept growing, and new possibilities came along. I personally haven't had any really bad experiences. But I remember, when I was a teenager, my brother Hugo swore he'd never return to school. That was after a teacher humiliated him as a Jew in class one day. The insult stayed with him. I suppose some wounds never fully heal."

"I've seen how discrimination affected my children. My older daughters wanted to get away from Judaism altogether." Moses looked intently at Benno. "If they'd met some gentile boys, they might have gone that way. There are plenty of others who did, and still are. Anna was rebellious in a different way. When she and her friends were called names, she didn't sulk or go into hiding." Moses paused and smiled. "One day, after school, she was walking home with Jewish friends from the neighborhood when some children yelled at them, 'Jews, go away,' or some such thing, and threw rocks at them. Well, my Anna picked up one of those rocks and threw it right back! Where she got that kind of spunk, I don't know." Moses had a twinkle in his eye. "She can be shy, but don't let that fool you. As the saying goes, she's someone who won't allow ignorance to degrade her dignity."

"Good for her," Benno said quietly.

"We Jews are riding high right now." Moses leaned forward in his chair. "I don't mean that in a bad way. Everywhere you look, there are Jews in the spotlight. It hasn't happened quite like this before. I see the younger people like you anxious to break with the old ways and become a part of this new society and all. But not everyone is happy to see that happening. That I also know." Moses tapped the table. "So, I'm cautious. Maybe too cautious. Maybe too worried. But I also know we're vulnerable. Maybe living in a small town like this makes us that way. Anna tells me that in Munich you can go out anywhere, on any day, as a Jew, without worries. But here we tread more lightly. Until recently we weren't allowed to live outside our own neighborhood. Even now, we have to pay attention because some people take offense when they see a Jew in certain neighborhoods. Do you get what I'm saying?"

Benno nodded again. He understood Moses's concerns. But he was moving along a different path, one that was not bound or defined by religion. And he wanted to continue to follow that, even if he had no intention of breaking with his Jewish identity or the religion itself. He struggled to find the words to express this; "I think Laupheim represents what Germany has been. Munich is what Germany is becoming."

"A very clever turn of phrase, Benno. I mean that in a good way. But I don't have your confidence." Moses paused. "It's said that it only takes one good fall to make you fearful of climbing. If we lose the sense of who we are, we'll be defenseless, rootless." Moses looked at his future son-in-law sternly. "Keep the traditions. If you have children—you plan to have children?" Benno nodded. "They have to have their roots, so that when the next wind comes, it doesn't blow them down. How can we survive if we're not rooted in our religious traditions?"

Moses's tree metaphor was one that Benno had heard before. He'd even made reference to it in a statement he wrote for his Bar Mitzvah service. But he also included another idea that he considered important. He recalled the words he had written: "Judaism is a living tree. But like all living things, it must bend and adapt to its environment. A tree that can't bend will break in a stiff wind." He was about to repeat those words to Moses, then he thought better of it. Instead, he assured his future father-in-law that he intended to raise his family as Jews.

Benno exaggerated a bit about his religious practices. In keeping with the practices of many urban Jews, these consisted of attending synagogue for the high holidays and going to an occasional Bar Mitzvah. But he was sincere when he promised to raise his family in the Jewish tradition. Having been cued on this by Anna, Benno promised that they would keep a kosher household. Knowing little about how to actually do that, Benno knew he would have to rely on his wife for direction. Hoping to move beyond this topic, Benno quickly added, "You have quite a wonderful community here. I intend to keep a connection with it." In this he was sincere, and thanked Moses for his hospitality and guidance.

Moses looked at Benno. "Well, let me say that, with four daughters and not much to go round—"

"I'm fine, Herr Einstein. I don't expect or need a dowry. My father and I are doing well now. Business has been good."

Moses nodded. "We can talk about that on another occasion. For now, I wish the best to you both. Maybe my words will have more resonance in times to come." Then, smiling at Benno, he said, "You know, I've passed by Munich on my way to see my girls in Traunstein, but I never stopped to see it. I still wonder what this big city excitement is about!"

Benno laughed. "Of course. You will be coming to our wedding?"

"If I'm invited!" Moses put his hand on Benno's shoulder. "I want you to know how glad I am you accepted Berthold's invitation to seder."

"So am I."

After that conversation, Benno realized that his soon-to-be father-in-law was more than just the stern religious man he'd seen at the seder and a few other occasions when Moses was in his role as family patriarch. Now he got a glimpse of the jokester beneath the piety and of a more active and thoughtful intellect than he'd given Moses credit for.

Even so, he thought of the old man as something of an anachronism—a man from another era with a worldview that was out of step in this new Germany. Benno listened to Moses's advice about religious tradition in a world of adversity, but he didn't really feel like it pertained to him. For Benno, a new world beckoned. Germany, despite its prejudices, was moving away from old restrictions and antiquated bigotry. Jews were moving toward a place of greater acceptance and influence in society. And their increasing involvement was also changing the country. Jews and Germany were being mutually transformed. Munich, Berlin, and other large cities encapsulated that new reality. And his own future wife, Anna, like so many other Jews, was drawn by the city's gravitational pull.

### The Marriage

Benno and Anna were married on October 12, 1907, at Munich's Haupt Synagogue. After the wedding, they spent several weeks traveling through the Austrian Alps. When they returned, they settled into the apartment at 19 Liebherrstrasse with Max.

The apartment was within easy walking distance of the Isar River, the English Garden, Munich's beer halls, the Marienplatz, and other centers of the city's commercial, political, and cultural life—all places that would soon become familiar to Anna.

Benno and his bride were about to begin the hectic years of starting a new family. These were years of relative social calm and middle-class prosperity.

They both took them for granted, believing that they would last indefinitely.

## 2

# Prosperity, 1907–1914

THERE WERE REASONS WHY BENNO and Anna felt optimistic about their future together. Germany was prospering. Munich was coming of age as the nation's second major city as its economy, population, and cultural importance grew. Its museums and plazas were gaining a reputation beyond Germany's borders. Because they lived near the Alps, Munich's residents had ready access to beautiful areas of rest and recreation.

Benno's real estate business, which he had managed alone since Max retired, was doing well. Many of Germany's Jews were breaking through long-existing social barriers to achieve advances in economic, social, and cultural life. Jews were benefiting from political rights, acceptance, and recognition in German society as never before and were becoming prominent in many fields of endeavor. An optimism for the future was shared widely in the Jewish community.

### GERMANY AND EUROPE IN THE WORLD

Benno and Anna's upbeat mood reflected the relative good fortune of all middle-class Germans, and indeed Europeans in general, during this time. By the turn of the century, the major Northern European nations had achieved political, economic, and military dominance in the world. England, France, Germany, and lesser powers, such as Belgium and Holland, were amassing immense wealth from industrial development, burgeoning trade, and colonization. European success in its colonial pursuits contributed enormously to the rising prosperity.

By some estimates, more than 80 percent of the world's finance capital was shared by just a few industrialized countries. Among all of them, Germany was growing the fastest economically. It had started late in the race toward industrialization, but it was catching up to its European rivals in key areas, and by the early 1900s Germany surpassed France and England in all the major indices of industrial growth. For example, by 1913, the German economy generated and consumed 20 percent more electricity than Britain and Italy combined.

By the beginning of the second decade of the twentieth century, Germany's economy had grown larger than that of any other country except the United States. In Britain, the words *Made in Germany* carried a threatening connotation as they challenged England's economic dominance.

Germany's population growth also outstripped that of its major rivals. By 1914, Germany had 68 million people—a third more than either England or France.

These changes had a profound impact within Germany. The traditional middle class of craftsmen, shopkeepers, medium-sized farmers, bureaucratic officials, and other persons of authority declined, and a new middle class of lawyers, doctors, merchants, stock exchange investors, cultural workers, and owners of large retail businesses rose to prominence.

### German Jews

Industrialization, modernization, and the growth of the cities brought significant changes to the status of German Jews. Many of them had risen from poverty in the period of social liberalization during the decades preceding German unification in 1871. By then, as many as 60 percent of Germany's Jews could be counted as members of the country's middle class. As the pace of modernization and urbanization accelerated in the latter 1800s, the pathway widened for Jews to achieve greater integration into the larger society.

This integration took a further leap politically in 1871 with the implementation of the constitution of the newly united Germany. It contained language abolishing restrictions on civil and political rights due to "religious differences." German Jews thus achieved *on paper* the political emancipation that had long been denied them.

While 80 percent of Germany's Jews lived in small towns or villages prior to 1871, 60 percent lived in cities of 100,000 or more by 1910. By that year, a quarter of all Germany's Jews lived in Berlin, where they made up 4 percent of the city's population. As a measure of their rising affluence, Jewish Berliners accounted for almost 15 percent of the city's tax revenue.

In 1871, Germany's 512,000 Jews represented 1.25 percent of the population. Over the next forty years, as Germany's population exploded by nearly 60 percent, the Jewish population increased by only 20 percent due to emigration and a birthrate among Jews that declined as they rose economically to middle-class status. By the first decades of the twentieth century, Jews made up less than 1 percent of the German population.

German intellectual accomplishments surged in the years after unification. Jews played a significant role in this, in such arenas as literature, science, music, medicine, and psychology. Among the fifteen German Nobel Prize winners in science and literature in the first decade of the new century, four—Otto Wallach, Paul Heyse, Paul Erlich, and Adolf von Baeyer—were Jews. Many factors contributed to Jews' success. But certainly one of them was their determination to prove themselves worthy while proving their detractors wrong.

Urban Jews integrated most readily into the broader society. As they became more intertwined with the economic, cultural, social, and political life of Germany, they began to identify more closely with the nation. Younger Jews, whose parents and grandparents regarded themselves as Jews living in Germany, now saw themselves as Germans with Jewish roots.

With modernization and urbanization, traditional Jewish religious practices were gradually pushed aside, and new forms of religious observance, known as Reform Judaism, emerged. Reform synagogues conducted their services in German rather than Hebrew. They revised religious services to reflect their participants' growing sense of assimilation into German society. They integrated music into the services and brought men and women together in the congregation, thereby modifying or abandoning the old practice of strict gender segregation..

### Benno, Anna, and Family

Benno's father, Max, was seventy-one when Benno and Anna married. Thanks mainly to their land holdings, Benno and his father had combined assets of 160,000 marks. This was roughly equivalent to $40,000 at that time—not a great fortune, but enough to provide relative security.[4]

The Neuburgers' first child, Fritz, was born on October 2, 1908. A second child, Johanna, or Hani, came the following October. Anna embraced her role as a stay-at-home mother.

### Integration: A Businessman's Social Life

Before marriage, Benno had been part of a circle of friends drawn mainly from his business acquaintances, both Jewish and Christian. That continued as he and his friends moved from bachelorhood to married life.

Benno's old friend Berthold, whom Benno jokingly referred to as his "godfather," was part of that group, as was Otto Götz, whose family were partners with Benno in some landholdings. The circle included Julius, a clothing store owner who attended the same synagogue as Benno; Rolf, a non-Jewish clothing shop owner whose business was near Berthold's store; Gustav, a land investor and friend of Rolf's; and Werner, a civil attorney who knew members of this group through legal work.

Another, less consistent, non-Jewish member of the group was Arnulf, a part-owner of a ski shop, who spent a lot of time on the road selling ski equipment. A bit of an odd man out, Arnulf was younger than the others and still single. And whereas the other members of the group leaned toward one of Germany's liberal or centrist parties, Arnulf, whose father and several uncles were active in Munich trade unions, was a member of the Social Democratic Party, the party that had emerged from Germany's socialist-minded workers' movement. As a member of a more politically involved family Arnulf took a greater interest in political issues and from a different angle than others in the group.

The group's get-togethers were irregular and, by necessity, almost always in the early evenings, after work. Yet, for a few years, the group became tight enough, and their gatherings frequent enough, that they had their own table at one or another of Munich's beer halls.

For both the Jews and gentiles in this group, religious differences were both important and irrelevant. All of the men had their roots in rural German towns, where separation of religious communities had largely been the rule. But in Munich's cosmopolitan environment, intermingling was both more possible and more appealing.

Jews welcomed the city's lowered social barriers that offered hope for an end to exclusion and suspicion. For the non-Jews in the group, association with Jews carried an element of cultural subversion and the appeal of breaking with old social prejudices. As the men got to know each other, they developed a camaraderie based on common interests in business, family, sports, and, at times, local and national affairs—in addition to their true mutual love, Bavarian beer! They shared a sense of unity as Germans, which was a sentiment that was gaining momentum as the new century proceeded and as rivalries between European nations grew more contentious. They shared a common dialect and culture as Bavarians.

As married men with children, their get-togethers held an element of illicit pleasure. A furtive glance at a watch or clock in the middle of a boisterous conversation reflected an awareness of moments stolen from homelife. During their meetings they could forget for a moment the pressures of sales to be made, bills to be paid, investments to ponder, debts to fret over, children's illnesses to worry about, or domestic disputes to confront. Their mutual ties were thickened through banter—their camaraderie measured by the laughter they provoked while poking pointed remarks into the soft flesh of personal idiosyncrasies.

The group's most ardent practitioner of jokes and the razzing arts was Gustav. He was a man of medium height, with a wide face, close-cropped hair, and an unusually thickset body. His slightly bent nose positioned on a thick, broad face gave him the appearance of a street brawler, and provided the perfect foil for the would-be comic. One of his favorite jokes, which typified his brand of humor, was about two Bavarian acquaintances he called Wilfred and Hugo. In Gustav's telling:

"Hugo is out on the street one day when he runs into his friend Wilfred.

'Wilfred,' says Hugo, noticing his friend's dour expression, 'you don't look so happy! What's going on with you?'

'Well, I was at the doctor yesterday.'

'And?'

'He said I have just two weeks to live!'

'Two weeks? My God! Just two weeks? Do you drink?'

'No! No, I don't drink.'

'Do you smoke then?'

'No, I don't smoke!'

'Ach. You must play around with the girls, eh, eh?'

'No, not at all. I never play around with the girls.'

'Well, then,' says Hugo, placing his hand on Wilfred's shoulder, and looking at his friend with a dour expression, 'why live?!'"

More humorous than the joke itself, especially for those who'd heard it before, was Gustav's hefty frame shaking with laughter from his own punchline, which somehow didn't diminish even with repeated tellings. It was the irony that got to Gustav. It left the others somewhat less amused—even while they found ways to appropriate the punchline for various occasions.

### Common Dreams and Nightmarish Memories

Economic growth stimulated optimism and ambition. Occasionally, this ambition gave rise to talk of grandiose schemes as these middle-class businessmen cast an envious eye at the upper strata of wealth and considered strategies that might propel them to greater economic heights. Speculative land deals and investments that promised outsized rewards became fodder for conversations. This was most often just talk, bravado, like the fantasies of armchair athletes.

Rolf and Julius, both small shop owners, whose eyes were always on the margins where success and failure were decided, were the most frequent purveyors of schemes for acquiring a cushion of wealth to forever banish their insecurities. Most of their proposals fell apart as impractical when subjected to the scrutiny of the group. But they added an element of lively conversation to the gatherings and so they were appreciated on that level, even when not taken very seriously.

The civil lawyer Werner placed one such idea on the beer table from one of his clients, a man with his own robust ambitions. The man was seeking backing for an invention that would allow reproduceable sound to be added to a film strip so that movies, thus far silent, could "talk." Movies had become explosively popular in Germany, making the man's idea intriguing. But it also provoked objections from some in the group. Julius maintained that talking movies would never catch on because, as he argued, "People are too fond of the silent films and their live musical accompaniment."

Arnulf claimed that adding sound to films would have the negative consequences of putting musicians, who made their living playing music in the theaters to accompany movies, out of work.

After reflection and discussion, during which it was often difficult to tell whether an assertion was being argued seriously or tongue-in-cheek, a consensus emerged. The means to permit films to "talk" was technically unfeasible and therefore something for the far distant future. And, in any case, this was a project that was out of their league.

Benno enjoyed these conversations—the speculations and the get-rich-quickly schemes—even if *he* was very unlikely to ever be part of them. In his own business, he was a far cry from the gambler. He only put money in properties he was certain would retain their value. He was satisfied with, and even preferred, modest growth. As a result, he occasionally missed out on a deal that could have, in hindsight, brought substantial gains. But his regrets were always short-lived.

Benno's aversion to risk came directly from Max's stories about the economic crisis of 1873. Many businesses that began or expanded in the years of economic fervor following German unification in 1871 collapsed in a heap when the stock market crashed. Tens of thousands of middle-class and aristocratic German families were riding high one day, then woke up broke and broken the next. What emerged from the wreckage were stories of excessive borrowing, wild speculation in risky stocks, and blind faith in an ever-expanding economy. The catastrophe struck just as Max was getting his bearings in Munich. The lessons he summed up from this debacle led him to approach his own business decisions with caution.

Germany's Depression, which began in 1873 and lasted well into the 1880s, was part of a worldwide downturn and was the most serious global crisis up to that time. Right-wing forces in Germany were quick to turn public anger and frustration at the economic hardships against the tried-and-true target of bad news—the Jews. Books appeared that portrayed Jews as stock market swindlers and accused them of being "immoral." Rightists made angry speeches in the Reichstag denouncing Jews and submitted measures to strike the 1871 constitution's emancipatory language. They even proposed to strip Jews of their German citizenship.

None of these measures passed. And as the economy improved, the clamor died down. By the middle of the 1890s, strident anti-Jewish rhetoric had subsided, and the threats had disappeared. But it took years for the scars to fade, and its influence lingered.

Out of this experience Max clung to a belief in restraint as a guardrail against economic turmoil, and he preached restraint to anyone who would listen. He avoided debt as a hiker would avoid a dangerous cliff's edge. In Benno he found a willing disciple who was, if anything, even more cautious than his father. Years later, Benno would pass this same business ethic to his son, Fritz.

### A Holiday's Dispute

When this group of friends met at the Hofbräuhaus on a cool, cloudy day in January, Julius noted that it was the 17th of the month. The following day there were events planned to celebrate the fortieth anniversary of the founding of the German Second Reich. He proposed that they toast the successful unification of the country and its architect, Otto von Bismarck.

Arnulf slammed his beer stein noisily on the table. "A toast to German unity, but never to that wretched autocrat!"

What started out as a lighthearted and relaxed conversation suddenly turned serious. "Bismarck may not be the perfect democrat," Benno asserted, "but I'll give him credit for bringing Germany along the path to unity. Not an easy project."

Like most Germans of their generation, this group of Bavarian friends were well acquainted with Otto von Bismarck as the architect of German unity, but they were mostly fuzzy on the details of how that unity was achieved. Benno was known among these friends as someone who took an interest in and read a good deal about history. And this was the reason why Rolf stood up and declared in a rather theatrical way, "Well, I'm interested in what our good friend and visiting lecturer Benno has to say about this episode in our national history."

"Yes, of course. So sit down, Arnulf!" Gustav scolded jokingly. "No one called on you. Where are your classroom manners?" Arnulf nodded his amused approval and then Gustav turned to Benno. "Excuse the interruption. You may proceed with your remarks. We all agree, don't we?"

With a half-finished stein of dark beer in front of him and a newly lit cigar in his hand, Benno was in a good mood and, moreover, in a talkative frame of mind. "Let's remember," he began, "that the French in 1870 considered themselves the premier power on the European continent."

"Arrogant SOBs that they are," said Götz to approving laughs.

"And," Benno continued, "they were determined to keep it that way. Germany—or, I should say, Prussia—was coming off several successful wars; the most recent, against the Austrians. This worried the French. They clearly saw a rising and potentially united Germany as a challenge to them."

"Keep Germany weak and divided . . ." Gustav said, nodding in assent.

"And Bismarck, looking for a way to rally the discordant German states into a unified country saw France's antagonism as a possible pathway to that German unity."

"Discordant. Benno, that sounds like Bavaria," joked Götz.

"Yes, Bavaria, but also the other twenty-six states," added Benno, taking a drink from his stein, and looking to see if others at the table were in the mood to hear more.

"Go on Benno," Rolf encouraged. "I don't hear any snoring yet. We could all use a little refresher on our history."

Benno let out a stream of cigar smoke. "And as we know, we Germans are notorious for our regional idiosyncrasies. Bismarck could see no way to bring all these German states together except through some common threat. And there was France on its border, hostile and, apparently, ready to fight."

"Spoiling for a fight," Rolf growled.

"As was Bismarck. But how to get into a fight with France on terms favorable to Prussia?" Benno paused and looked around the table. "Then, conveniently, came the crisis of the Spanish queen."

There was a brief silence. Then Werner spoke. "If we were in class I'd be raising my hand now."

"Go ahead, Werner." Benno chuckled.

"Let's see—the Spanish queen, Isabella, if memory serves me, was facing some kind of internal rebellion and decided it would be wise to leave the country. She renounced her throne, got on a train, and off to Paris! And there she stayed. And as a replacement it was suggested that a relative of Prussia's King William take the throne."

"Which would have put Hohenzollerns on *two* borders with France," Berthold added emphatically.

"France, already looking ahead to a war with Germany, was, understandably, unhappy with the idea of having a German ally on their southern border," Benno said.

"That relative of King William was a cousin. Am I right?" asked Berthold.

"I don't recall. But a relative," Benno answered. "And Napoleon III, or Louie Napoleon as some prefered to call him, demanded that William withdraw his candidacy."

Julius tapped his index finger on the table. "And he did withdraw. But this was not enough for Napoleon, who decided to go to war with Germany."

"Yes, but here's an important detail that needs to be added." Some at the table leaned in as Benno spoke. "Bismarck secretly encouraged this young relative of King William to persist in efforts to gain the Spanish throne. And Napoleon, pushed by his advisors, or his wife, Eugénie, depending on whose account you read, demanded that William promise not only to oppose this selection but *any future* candidacy of this kind as well."

"Sounds like an effort to humiliate," Rolf groused.

Benno nodded, then continued. "Then the French foreign secretary sent his ambassador to the resort, Bad Ems, where the King was vacationing demanding a promise *in writing* that William would never again promote a member of his family to the Spanish crown. And here is where another detail is relevant. It's said that William wrote his reply to the French in an effort to be diplomatic. *But* he asked Bismarck to look over the note before sending it to Napoleon. Bismarck did some *amending*"—the word provoked laughter at the table—"that removed some of its diplomatic language so that it came off as, well, a little rude. And this proved to be a shrewd step. Because to a neutral observer it seemed like a fairly harmless reply. But it angered Napoleon, his advisors, and that energetic empress. All were eager to find an excuse to go to war and they found it in this Ems telegram."

"So Napoleon played into Bismarck's hand," Werner commented.

"Exactly."

"Bismarck was looking for a way to provoke a fight without appearing to do so." Werner turned to Arnulf. "If you'll forgive me, Arnulf, that was the art of Bismarck's diplomacy. He played on Napoleon's arrogance."

Berthold laughed. "And we're talking about a man who was in no short supply of that! This is the Napoleon who, when his term as president expired, just named himself Emperor!"

"Arrogance is a pretty common quality among our European leaders," commented Arnulf.

"And here Bismarck was poking old Napoleon to provoke him." Gustav made a jabbing gesture with his index finger.

Benno took another sip of beer. "When Bismarck made *public* his version of William's message to Napoleon, well, Napoleon's people believed they had a pretext to attack Germany."

"In other words, Napoleon and his crowd took the bait!" Gustav grinned.

"Bismarck reasoned that if France attacked Germany for a mildly insulting telegram, Germany would have the moral advantage in world opinion." Benno flicked the ashes from his cigar. "Including, most importantly, among the German states whose people were now ready to join Prussia against what they saw as unjustified French aggression!"

"A clever strategy," Julian observed, "but only in hindsight. If Germany had lost the war, we would not have thought him so shrewd."

"True," Benno said. "But I think Bismarck realized Germany was better prepared for war than France was. And he had a psychological advantage."

"He was more calculating," Werner commented.

Benno turned to Werner. "Yah. Bismarck was acting out of a plan, a strategy. Whereas, I'd argue, Napoleon was acting more on impulse."

"I'd give the French a bit more credit," argued Werner. "They had that Chassepot rifle which had better range than our German needle gun. And they also had a machine gun—unwieldy in some ways, but deadly. They had reason to believe that they had a good shot at rolling Germany back to the Rhine."

"True," Benno countered, "but, on balance, the Germans had the advantage. We had better railroads, a better system of calling up troops and, of course, Krupp's cannons."

"Krupp's guns," Julius put in. "We've all heard stories about the effects they had. They tore the French lines to pieces."

Benno stabbed the air with his cigar. "The French made that most fatal of mistakes in war. They underestimated their enemy. French soldiers went into battle thinking their opponents were pushovers and when they found out that was not the case, they quickly lost heart."

"Looking back, I think that's a reasonable conclusion," Werner agreed.

Götz added, "The French army crumbled, and Napoleon surrendered within weeks as I recall."

"Napoleon was captured and held as a prisoner," Werner responded.

"Then there was that long siege of Paris," said Berthold.

"The French have not forgotten that!" Rolf sounded gleeful.

Werner looked over at Rolf. "Nor that Bismarck held Germany's unification ceremony in the Hall of Mirrors in Versailles of all places!"

"The French lost the war, and we Bavarians lost our independence," Werner said provokingly. When no one spoke he said, "Of course, I'm kidding about that, we're all proud Germans now, aren't we?"

"Not so fast," Gustav said as he scanned the table crowd. "I may not agree with all of Arnulf's objections, but I think we Bavarians would do fine on our own without that arrogant buffoon of a Kaiser! What do you say, Benno?"

Benno shrugged and looked at Arnulf. "The Kaiser aside, I think the 1871 constitution, even with its shortcomings, did us good."

"That constitution had some positive provisions," Arnulf replied. "Of course I favor the rights Jews won in that document. But we still live under something that's more like autocracy. The Prussian landlords still hold most of the power even though they're a small minority."

"But we have elections," objected Götz.

"Rigged ones! I mean, it's set up so that no matter how many votes a popular party might get, the Prussian oligarchs will still call the shots!" Arnulf insisted.

"Is that Bismarck's fault?" asked Götz. "We can't praise Bismarck for bringing Germany together and then criticize him for using the tactics to make it possible."

"Bismarck wanted a united Germany because he knew that a fractured Germany would be weak in the face of other powers." Arnulf looked intently at his drinking partners. "But he wanted it under the thumb of the Prussian Junkers. Look how he outlawed the Social Democrats when he saw the workers gaining strength and threatening the power of the aristocracy."

Rolf set his beer down on the table with a thud. "We Bavarians are, in a sense, just pawns of the Prussians then, eh?"

Götz shook his head. "I don't feel that way."

"Nor do I," Julius added. "Arnulf has his points. And I feel resentment or just disgust sometimes with the Prussians, but I agree with Benno. I feel like this unity with all its problems is more advantageous than negative."

"Those of us in Munich, and in the cities, with the way the

voting system is set up, our vote counts for very little." Werner shrugged. "But we're in a better position as a country. And all in all . . . maybe I'll contradict myself here . . . I think Bismarck, and those who have followed him, have been acceptably fair."

"Bismarck was a bloodhound in defending this undemocratic system!" Arnulf said, and then, when no one else spoke up, added, "He supported the French bourgeoisie when they slaughtered the workers in Paris after the war!"

"The Commune," said Benno.

"Yes." Arnulf held his index finger upward. "The workers of Paris drove the French government out of the city! And they organized a more egalitarian society and put a scare into the pampered French bureaucrats. And not just the French—"

"Well, my friend," Gustav put a hand on Arnulf's shoulder, "I don't think a lot of Germans really care about that. And anyway, it was the French that did that slaughtering in Paris, no? Can't blame that on the Prussians!"

"Interesting history, but ancient history," Götz mused.

"Well, the French have not forgotten the reparations, nor their loss of the Alsace province," Benno observed.

"Simply a just punishment for starting the war!" Rolf said loudly.

Berthold stretched. "We live in an imperfect world, but I'm glad that Germany came together as one country. I think we've all benefited from that."

Arnulf shook his head. "Not equally."

"I'll grant you that," Gustav agreed.

"You'd better," Götz joked. "Some of us have gotten *fat* in this German empire, as we can clearly see." Götz pointed to Gustav's ample frame. "While others have a little extra to count on." He stood up and turned around indicating his own thin build.

"Absolutely right!" Gustav roared. "Bring Götz a beer! No, make that two! We'll equalize you yet!"

Arnulf laughed and rolled his eyes along with the rest.

"If you're buying, I'm taking," Götz was still standing. "But not now. I've got to go while I still can on my own steam."

Rolf rose. "And before Benno decides to assign homework!"

With that, they wished each other a pleasant night and headed off to their respective homes.

### Refugees from the East

In her first years in Munich, Anna's life was largely restricted to the home and family as a mother of young children. But she gradually began to find her way into the social life of the city and its Jewish community by attending Sabbath services at the reform Haupt Synagogue.

During the winter of 1910, as she entered the synagogue, a young woman handed her a flyer announcing a meeting of the Jewish Women's Association. She saw in bold letters the words "The Struggles of Our Brethren from the East." She put the flyer away without much thought. But during the service the rabbi spoke of the hardships faced by immigrants arriving from Galicia, Russia, and East Poland. When he reminded the congregation that in Jewish tradition one must welcome the stranger, she pulled the flyer from her purse. The meeting was to convene immediately after the service. Since Benno was home with the children and she didn't need to rush home, Anna decided to attend the meeting.

There were about a dozen women sitting in classroom chairs when Anna arrived. She didn't recognize any of them. Two women sat at a table at the front of the room in animated conversation. One looked to be in her fifties, the other in her twenties. Anna had seen the older woman at the synagogue but didn't know her name.

Anna had just sat down when a thin woman with short silver hair handed her a paper. At the very top it read, *You too must love the stranger, for you were strangers in the land of Egypt.* There was a brief description of several families who'd left their towns and villages in Russia and Galicia and come to Germany seeking shelter. Anna knew of the growing community of eastern Jews in Munich. She saw them on the streets of the city or occasionally in a store where she would overhear them speaking in Yiddish, or, she assumed, Russian, but she otherwise had little contact with them.

Anna began reading a section of the paper titled "Conditions since 1905," when she heard a voice from the front of the room. The older woman at the table had risen to speak. "My name is Ilse. Our Munich Jewish Women's Association welcomes you to this very special meeting to discuss the situation of refugees from our eastern communities." As she spoke several more women entered the room and Ilse nodded to them. Anna looked around. There were now several dozen women in the room and most seats were taken.

"How many of you are here for the first time?" Ilse asked the crowd.

Anna raised her hand timidly. This was all new to her. She couldn't recall having attended any kind of public meeting like this before. She felt relieved to see others also raising their hands.

"Thank you for coming. A special welcome to our new attendees." Ilse looked directly at Anna, who nodded. "The purpose of our meeting is to continue our discussion of the problems facing members of our community—those from Poland and Russia especially. We are blessed to have two of our immigrant sisters here today." She gestured to two women sitting off to the side of the room by a row of windows. "I'm going to turn the meeting over to Henny, who will talk to you..."

"Do they have names?" someone asked loudly.

"I'm sorry." Ilse motioned toward the two refugee women again. "Our guests are Riva and Sonia. Forgive me for not introducing them. Henny Kosman," Ilse turned to the young woman next to her, "will talk to us more about our guests, and we'll hear from one or perhaps both of them."

Henny stood up from her seat at the table. She was short and wore a light jacket over a white blouse open at the neck. Her auburn hair was pulled into braids at either side of her head. Anna wondered about how someone so young had the courage to stand in front of a group like this and speak. "I hope everyone can hear me well," Henny began. People nodded affirmatively. "My family is originally from Kyiv, but I was born in Munich. What is happening to immigrants from our eastern communities is very near and dear to me. How many people here know that over the last few years Jews in the East, especially in Russia, have experienced violent attacks on their communities?"

Everyone raised their hands.

"And how many of you know that many of them have been forced to leave their homes to seek safety?" Again, everyone raised their hands. "Does anyone here have an idea of how many of these refugees are now in Munich?"

"It says 'nearly 15 percent of the Jewish population' in the flyer," came a reply.

"Yes. In Germany as a whole. And here in Munich it's even higher—more than 20 percent. One in every five members of our Jewish community in this city are immigrants from countries to the east. That may seem like a lot, but it is a tiny fraction of the people who've been forced to leave their homes and towns. We think that up to two million Jews have fled Bialystok, Kyiv, Kishenev, Odessa, and other places."

"Where are most of them going?" asked a woman sitting behind Anna.

"Most are passing through on their way elsewhere—like America, for those who have the means or the assistance to do that. And that is one of the things our community can and has been doing—helping them with their passages, usually to America."

As she spoke, she moved from behind the table in the direction of the two women sitting off to the side. "Some of the refugees don't want to move on from Germany—or they can't. For one thing, they don't necessarily want to leave their homelands forever. If they stay here, then of course they have a better chance to return home."

A woman down the row from Anna raised her hand. "How are these refugees treated here?" she asked.

"It's a mixed situation," said Henny. "Those that are clearly moving through Germany on their way somewhere else are usually left alone. You know most of those moving on will be taking German ships wherever they're going—business, money . . ." Henny shrugged. "But for those who choose to stay, they are vulnerable to deportation. Just how vulnerable, that depends. If there is help—including legal help, if there is a place to stay, if they find work, if there's a school to learn the language, a way to blend in— it's more likely they won't be sent back." Henny paused and looked around the room. When she saw no hands raised, she went on. "So that is why we're here. We assist people who need refuge and help. And we're fortunate to live in a country where we can offer that help."

Ilse spoke up. "Our association has decided that this is our main work at present. And we will get into what that means. But first I'd like to ask one of our sisters to come and tell us about why she's here. I want to warn you, what you will hear is not pleasant. And I think these women are extraordinarily courageous to even come here and be willing to tell their stories. Henny will translate for us."

Henny said something to Riva in Yiddish and Riva got up and passed the child on her lap to Sonia. "This is Riva Mishnik," Henny stated. "She's from Siedlce, east of Warsaw, and she's been in Germany for two years." Riva was a short woman. She was wearing a long dress that hung below her ankles. Her dark bangs were just visible under a light blue scarf. Henny offered her a seat by the table. She sat stiffly, with her hands on her lap and did not look at the other women in the room.

Henny nodded to Riva who began to speak in a voice barely audible to the audience. Her hands moved nervously as she described her small town. Through Henny's translation, she told the group that she and her husband had run a business there, one he had taken over from his father. Their town had been usually quiet and peaceful and had had no great troubles until after the turmoil in the winter of 1905.

Henny interrupted her translation to say, "You might remember the events in Russia five years ago. The massacre in Petrograd in

January of 1905." Most of the women nodded. "I just wanted to be sure that you understood that, while the violence against Jews did not begin in 1905, it worsened after the Revolution of that year. Thousands of people who were peacefully protesting, petitioning the Czar, were shot down by the Czar's soldiers. Strikes spread to industries and fighting spread in cities throughout Russia. This is when the Czar and his followers made concerted efforts to turn the explosive anger of the people away from the Russian monarchy—the source of their lack of rights, the source of their hunger and terrible conditions—by directing violence at the Jews of Russia. These attacks on Russia's Jewish communities are not the result of some age-old animosity coming to the surface, some spontaneous hatred among people of different religions."

She turned to Riva and spoke to her again in Yiddish.

Riva continued by describing how the Jews in her town had lived many years side-by-side with non-Jewish people. Then the troubles started. Sometimes groups of young men would come to the district where Jews lived or where Jewish shops were located and yell, "Jews out!" They'd even throw rocks. She went on to describe how, one evening, they were still in their shop when they heard glass breaking. "Hang the Kikes!" and "Death to the dirty Kikes!" they shouted. She and her husband locked the door of the business but a group of young men, some of whom had been drinking, broke into the shop. They smashed merchandise and began pushing her husband, eventually hitting him, and knocking him down." Riva paused. She was trying to control her voice. "They picked things off the shelves and started throwing them at him. He was bleeding, but they kept hitting him." With these words Riva stopped. Her eyes were red, and her body began shaking.

"We should stop," a woman sitting in the front pleaded. "This is really hard on her."

Henny spoke to her in Yiddish. "Riva wants to tell her story. She wants people to know."

The room was quiet. The women could see Riva taking deep breaths. When she continued, Riva described how she was pushed to the floor and how one of the men got on top of her as she lay only feet away from her husband. The man had a chain with a cross dangling from his neck. "He pushed the cross into my mouth as he abused me," Riva said. Then she stopped and began sobbing.

Henny, fighting back tears, put her arm around Riva. The room went quiet, soundless except for Riva's sobs. Anna closed her eyes and felt tears running down her cheeks. Henny said, "I asked these sisters to tell us about the things that they've gone through, what compelled them to leave their former lives behind, take a chance—risk crossing a border, with its dangers. Things the newspapers very rarely mention. We need to know that people aren't just coming here for vacation or to take advantage of German society."

A tall woman with red hair sitting next to Anna raised her hand and Henny called on her. "I would like to say, without taking anything away from the terrible, terrible things that are happening in Russia to the Jewish communities, I think we also should consider"—she hesitated a moment—"that the actions of the Jewish communities in Russia also play a role here." When Henny didn't respond, the woman went on. "I mean, don't you think these assaults on Jewish neighborhoods are partly a result of some actions of Russia's Jews themselves?"

Henny stood up. "The Czar and his people claim Jews are a subversive force in Russia. This claim has provoked a lot of violence. They also spread terrible lies among the people. In one town, the people who act for the government, the ones they call the Black Hundreds, went through the street with a piece of meat they stole from a Jewish butcher shop claiming that it was the butchered carcass of a Christian child! These are the kinds of slanders they use to provoke these murderous rampages. There have been protests by Jews, by individual Jews and by groups of Jews—the Jewish Bund for example. All this has happened because Jews, like every group so horribly slandered and mistreated must speak out, has a right to speak out. You can't call the protest of injustice subversion! People should not be beaten into silence for demanding to be treated fairly!" At that the room erupted in loud applause.

Ilse rose from her seat. "Time is going by," she said, "and we need to move to another part of our meeting. My heart is heavy for our dear sisters, and I want to thank Riva and Sonia for coming. We have much to learn from their strength and courage." She placed her hand on her heart. "If anyone has time and wants to talk to our sisters more, Henny and I will stay a while after this meeting, to translate." The older woman who passed out the information sheet now began to walk around with a sign-up sheet. "We have employment counselors, a German language school on weeknights for immigrants at the synagogue, and an emergency food system. And we're organizing childcare for parents who are working. You should know that these sisters and brothers want to work, and many are working. We have newly arrived immigrants who come to our synagogue looking for help and we try to put them in contact with a resident who can counsel and assist them. If that idea interests you, let us know. All our services require help and, of course, money. Please volunteer if you can and if you don't have time to volunteer you can help in that way."

When a box came to her, Anna put what money she had into it. When a list went around for those interested in helping in other ways, Anna signed her name, her hand shaking with emotion from the story she'd heard.

As the women left the room, Anna found herself near the tall woman who'd sat next to her. The woman had shoulder-length red hair and looked like she was several decades older than Anna. She turned to Anna and asked, "What do you think?"

"I didn't know how awful things were for these immigrants. I knew some things, but I can see I didn't know very much about their situation."

The woman sighed. "I sympathize with them—how could we not? What they have gone through—are going through—is terrible. But I also think that sometimes these Jewish people from Russia make things worse for themselves. What I mean is that the government is going to attack you if you criticize the government.

There are Jews involved in the revolution there. Do you see what I'm saying?"

"I honestly don't know enough about it," Anna said as she reached the bottom of the synagogue steps. "What I heard tonight, I see no justification for that—for that cruelty."

The woman shrugged. "We don't always hear the whole story." Then she added, "We Jews are under scrutiny already. It's just common sense that we need to be cautious. That's all I'm saying." At that she turned to go down the synagogue steps into the street.

"Goodbye," Anna called after her. And the woman waved a hand as she walked away.

## An Uncomfortable Conversation

It was a warm evening in May at the Burgerbraukeller on Rosenheimerstrasse and the group of friends was busy exchanging stories about business. The prospect of a locomotive factory locating in an area where Benno and Götz had a piece of property was grist for conversation, as was Julius's worries over a department store opening near his clothing store.

While the conversation was in progress Horst, an acquaintance of Gustav's, wandered over to their table. He was clearly tipsy as he greeted Gustav, who introduced him to the group and, as was his custom, asked Horst if he had any jokes to tell his friends. When Horst came up empty, Gustav volunteered, "I have one."

"A new one, I hope." Julius's wary look spoke for others at the table.

"A new one, yes!" Gustav grinned. "I sort of came up with this one myself."

"Brace yourselves," said Rolf.

"Grab a seat," Gustav pushed his friend Horst gently into a chair next to Werner before turning to the others. "What's the difference between beer drinkers in Berlin and Munich?" Gustav asked, as he gazed around the table.

When silence ensued, Gustav bellowed with bravado, "In Berlin they watch people drink and listen to them speak." He paused for effect. "In Munich, we listen to people drink and watch them speak."

Julius, caught sipping his drink when Gustav delivered his punchline, coughed up a spray of foaming beer onto the table in front of him.

"What did I tell you?" yelled Gustav. hitting the table with his fist. "That's one real Munich man among us!"

Meanwhile, Rolf and Werner made loud slurping sounds as they sucked beer from their steins.

"All right. Enough of that," Gustav bellowed with his infectious laugh.

"Well, you guys are in a damn good mood tonight," Horst said.

"And why not. Otherwise, why live?" Berthold said and cast a mischievous glance at Gustav.

Gustav turned to his friend. "You look like you have something on your mind, Horst."

"Faammily." Horst had the voice of one moving his tongue through a thickening haze of intoxication. "My uncle just had a heaart, heaaart attaaack."

Gustav touched his friend's arm. "Sorry to hear that."

"Pressures. Pressures, you know?" Horst looked down at the table.

"What pressures?" asked Gustav.

Horst took time to answer. "Helluva carpenter—ruined. Ruined by competition. It ruined him."

"Rough," Julius said, thinking about his own situation.

"Yah, and it's all 'bout what we gotta put up . . . nowadays . . .from the Jeeewws." There was silence. "The Jew fact'ries puttin' craftsmen out of *business*." Horst was almost swaying in his seat.

"Why *Jewish* factories?" Götz asked.

"Don't know why. But seems like Jeewws pretty much taakking things over."

Gustav broke in. "Horst, I think you might want to change the subject, friend."

"No. No. We've gotta face up to what's happ'ning to us, Gustav. Jewish business—have you been down to Kauf . . ., Kauf'ner Strasse—Kaufiner Strasse—nothing but Jew shops!"

"Jewish shops," Gustav corrected. "Horst, you might be offending some people here."

"Do I care? Jew lawyers. Jew doctors. Jew merchants. Jew bankers. Hell, I've got a Jew-ishsh landlord!"

"We have some Jewish friends at this table," Werner said sharply. "And I'm a lawyer, and I'm not Jewish."

"An excepppshun." Horst laughed. "Let me guess, your law professor was a Jew, and you're married to a Jew . . .ess."

"Not true," Berthold rolled his eyes.

Horst shrugged. "I guess I stumbled on a nest of . . ."

Gustav put his arm around Horst and asked to speak to him, in private. Horst got up and staggered with Gustav to another area of the hall. When Gustav returned, he apologized for his friend. "Too much drink can make a man stupid."

"Or honest," Rolf replied.

"What does that mean?" asked Berthold.

"I mean, he's just saying what a lot of people—unfortunately, okay—are thinking, Bert. I have relatives who have been hurt with all the changes going on. And they—"

"Blame Jews for it," Benno put in.

"Yah. It's not right. But it happens. It seems every time you turn around there's another example."

"Of what?" asked Götz.

"Of some person in the news who's a Jew. Some department store owner, or a theater owner or . . ."

"Factory owner?" Berthold was struggling to remain calm. "But that's only because when someone is a factory owner and happens to be Jewish it becomes an issue."

"There's a diner down the street from my shop"—Rolf's voice rose—"that's been losing business ever since a Jewish delicatessen opened up next door to it. The Jewish business expanded its menu to draw customers away from that small restaurant."

"And your point, Rolf?" Benno's voice conveyed his incredulity.

"My point is that when people get hurt, they grow resentful. I'm just relating what I hear people say. Jewish businesses are aggressive."

"It's in the nature of business to be aggressive," Werner commented dryly.

"Fine. But I think we can all agree that Jewish businesses are often . . . pushier," Gustav said in defense of Rolf.

"I don't go along with that," said Julius.

"None of us is ever just a shopkeeper or an investor, or lawyer; we're a Jewish shopkeeper, a Jewish investor, a Jewish lawyer." Benno turned to Rolf. "When I come from a bakery, I don't say, 'I just bought this loaf of rye from a Catholic baker.'"

"It's not the same thing," Rolf insisted.

"Why not?" asked Berthold.

"Because Christian bakers are not—"

"Not what?" asked Julius.

"Not . . ." Rolf hesitated.

Gustav looked at Benno. "How many doctors are Jewish?"

"I don't know. What difference does it make?"

"It seems like so many of the professionals . . ."

Benno cut Gustav off. "You know, Jews are less than one percent of the population!"

"Well, that's the point!" Rolf waved his hands as he spoke. "Jews play an outsized role in this country. Why deny that? How many journalists and theater producers are Jewish?"

"How many mine owners and generals are Christians?" countered Benno.

"Mine owners and generals don't shape the culture," Rolf fumed.

"Well, there's some truth in that," Werner remarked.

"I think," Rolf began, "what we're trying to get at here is people's—"

"Prejudice," Berthold finished. "I'm trying to make a go with my small business. You and I, Rolf, have small shops. What makes us any different?" Berthold threw his cigar into an ashtray. It missed and rolled off the table and onto the floor.

"You should know we're not talking about you, Berthold—or Benno, Julius, Götz—you're our friends." Rolf now sounded defensive. "But look. A younger cousin of mine just started college. He says half his class are Jews. Half the class! And a lot of them are Eastern Jews, immigrants."

"You see them all over Munich now. Most are not citizens," Gustav added.

"It makes it harder for those of us Germans . . ." Rolf grumbled.

"We're Germans!" Julius shouted.

"You know what I mean," Rolf shouted back.

"You mean the 'Volk.'" Julius scowled.

"Yah!" Gustav raised his voice. "There is such a thing."

Arnulf, who had watched the conversation unfold, suddenly broke his silence. "We're all Germans. We all try to do what's best for this country. Am I right? I see differences of opinion here. I see differences. But this is nothing. You should hear the arguments at the Social Democratic meetings. Those are arguments! This is just a little squabble among friends." Arnulf looked around the table and paused. "Maybe that's a good excuse for a . . ."

"For a toast!" Gustav raised his beer stein, happy to see a way out of an uncomfortable conversation.

Arnulf smiled appreciatively and also raised his stein. "Let's have a toast to differences among friends. *Prost!*"

"Differences among friends," repeated Benno with little conviction in his voice. "But agreement on the most important of all questions . . ."

"Which is?" Götz asked.

"Bavarian beer. What else?" Benno spoke to a mechanical clinking of steins.

### Healing Wounds

For Benno, Berthold, Julius, and Götz, the Jewish participants in the evening's conversation, the following days felt like a long-lasting hangover. They were not so naïve as to believe that anti-Semitism had disappeared from German society. There were self-proclaimed anti-Semitic political parties that won representation in the Reichstag, though they typically polled less than one percent of the vote. Still, many of Benno's generation believed anti-Semitism to be on the wane. Because Benno and his friends rarely encountered it personally, having it set out so starkly in a gathering of people they considered their friends was a shock.

After that gathering, Benno spent more evenings at home reading and taking walks with Anna and the children. Anna noticed the change and brought it up at dinner one evening.

"Everyone's been too busy to meet after work," Benno commented. "And I think we're all feeling the need to spend more time with family."

As if to emphasize the point, one late afternoon in September 1910 Benno surprised Anna with tickets to a concert at the Munich Musik-Festhalle to hear a presentation of a Gustav Mahler composition, his Symphony No. 8. It was to be their first night out together since the birth of their children. Benno and Anna were so taken by the power of the Mahler piece, with its long choral segments from Goethe's *Faust*, that the performance became a topic of conversation with friends for weeks thereafter. For Benno this helped to ease the sense of loss he felt when the get-togethers with his friends were put on pause.

## Crisis

Over time the beer group returned to their gatherings. Initially they all took care to avoid certain subjects. Their banter returned but was noticeably subdued. Time healed wounds and new issues crowded into their lives and conversations. The memory of the unpleasant conversation gradually lost its sting.

One evening they arranged to meet at one of their typical haunts, only to find it closed. Outside the beer hall, there were people protesting over the rising price of beer. It was one of many such protests taking place across Munich.

The beer rebellion of 1910, however serious for some, was quickly overshadowed by international tensions. In the spring of 1911, a colonial dispute between Germany, France, and England threatened to erupt into war. Germany made no secret of its ambitions in Africa. While Germany had several colonies in Africa most of the continent was controlled by other European nations, and Germany's efforts to expand its interests had been repeatedly rebuffed.

Germany had managed to get iron mining rights in Morocco, a country where France was seeking to expand its influence. When a conflict erupted in that North African nation in April, France sent 17,000 troops to the country's interior. Germany sent a Panther warship to the Moroccan coastal port of Agadir to show the national flag and to convey Germany's determination to defend its national interests. The British stood with the French against the Germans. In the face of such united opposition, Germany backed off.

Public opinion was brought to a boil in all three countries, but the outcry was especially pronounced in Germany. The Morocco dispute was the continuation of tensions that had increased ever since France signed its Entente pact—a "war pact" in the words of the pro-German press—with Russia in 1904. The agreement's aim was to contain Germany's growing power. English hostility toward Germany had been on the rise ever since Kaiser Wilhelm made clear his country's interest in building a naval force to match that of England.

Many Germans—and Benno's group of friends was among them—considered the Kaiser a headstrong buffoon. But they also considered England, by far the dominant colonial power on the globe, thanks to its overwhelming naval power, as arrogant and belligerent. They supported the buildup of the German navy and the military generally as necessary measures to defend the nation's interests.

On a warm summer afternoon in late July, the beer group met at an outdoor restaurant near the Marienplatz. Julius had just come back from the Tyrol, and he and Werner were arguing over whether Salzburg or Berchtesgaden made the better vacation. Götz, meanwhile, pulled out a newspaper and laid its front page on the table in front of him, nearly tipping over his stein of bock beer. "Look at this crap!" Götz pointed to a headline. "You should read this speech by the goddamn British Chancellor. It may affect all of our vacation plans." Julius and Rolf paused their conversation to listen. Götz looked up from the paper. "He's saying very clearly that if Germany wants war, he'll give us war."

"He's talking about Morocco, isn't he?" asked Julius.

"Morocco's the pretext. They want to scare us into backing down on plans to build a stronger navy," said Berthold.

"Listen to what Lloyd George says." Götz began reading: "'If Britain were to be forced to choose between peace on the one hand and surrender of her international preeminence . . .peace at that price would be a humiliation intolerable for a great nation like ours to endure.'"

"It's like France and England own the friggin' world and we better watch where we step or they'll arrest us for trespassing." Gustav raised his large arm in a threatening gesture.

Benno lifted a cigar to his mouth and let out a plume of smoke. "As long as England rules the waves—isn't that what they say? They'll never give that up. Here there's a chance that Germany might get a port in Morocco, on the Atlantic—one port—and Britain declares itself ready for war!"

"The British are always talking about what a peace-loving power they are, but they're the most aggressive saber-rattlers of all," Rolf added.

"*Blutsauger der welt*—bloodsuckers of the world. Isn't that what some people call them?" Julius put in.

Werner gestured with his hands, "France on one side, Russia on the other, with England backing things up with their navy. Germany is being surrounded. It's about humiliating us."

"An alliance of thieves and tyrants," Gustav said as he took a piece of sausage from the plate in front of him.

"To say nothing of hypocrites," Julius added.

"What are we going to do?" asked Götz.

"Well, friends, invest in weapons," bellowed Rolf, only half facetiously.

"I have a brother-in-law in Traunstein who breeds special horses for the Prussian cavalry," Benno mentioned.

"There we go, we could all become cavalry soldiers," Gustav mumbled as he bit into the sausage.

Berthold bent forward, his arms dangling toward the ground. "I'd feel sorry for any horse that would have to carry you around, Gustav."

"First off," said Rolf, "they'd have to have a crane to put our cavalryman up on the goddamn horse."

"You guys have no idea. In my younger days I was quite the horseman."

"Your younger days, Gustav?" Berthold questioned.

"When he rode with that guy from Spain," Benno explained.

"Here we have Sancho Panza." Götz stretched his arms toward Gustav. "Come to think of it . . ."

They were all laughing, Gustav as much as the rest.

When the laughter died down Julius said, "If war does come, I'm afraid we're already too old for the fight."

"Well, the French certainly have lucked out there." Rolf raised his stein and the others joined in.

Benno was relieved—and commented as much to Götz a few days after this conversation—that the rancor that had erupted among their beer crowd months before now seemed to have subsided, replaced by a common feeling of national concern.

## 1912

In early February 1912, Benno was with the usual group at a restaurant called the Kunstlerhaus when Arnulf joined them. He was, on this evening, unusually gregarious, having just returned from skiing in the Bavarian Alps with stories to share of his exploits. Everyone took them as exaggerations, which they were, but they were amusing ones. It included the unlikely tale that he'd lost one of his skis on the mountain but made it to the bottom, in a blinding snowstorm no less, on the one remaining ski. After some good-natured interrogation, his tale began to unravel. But no one cared. It was an amusing story.

However, it was not skiing that most occupied the minds of the seven compatriots who met over beer and bratwurst. It was election politics. The Reichstag national election had been held the previous month and to the surprise of many, and to Arnulf's satisfaction, the Social Democrats (SDP) won a plurality with more than four million votes, nearly 35 percent of the votes cast and by far the largest share of any party in the election.

Arnulf, as a supporter of the SDP, was happy, but the others were to one degree or another unsettled by the election. They related to the liberal parties: the National Liberal Party, the Progressive Party, and the Liberal Party. All those parties supported German armament as a necessary measure to defend German national interests, with which they identified. They therefore were wary of the Social Democrats whom they considered to be radical socialists.

The SDP began as the Socialist Workers' Party in 1875 with a base of support among Germany's growing working class. Rising industrialization in the early 1800s brought a rapid growth of an industrial workforce that labored under miserable and dangerous conditions. Workers who saw their conditions deteriorate even as the wealth brought about by mass production mounted, flocked to the party that advocated a radical change in social organization to address these injustices.

By the second decade of the 1900s the SDP had lost much of its revolutionary energy as the radical spirit among the workers had been cooled by government reforms. The SDP was becoming ensconced as a loyal opposition party anchored by the trade unions whose demands were limited to economic reforms. Even so there were groups within the SDP that remained hostile to the growth of the military and colonial expansion and denounced what it described as militarism in Germany and Europe generally. Because there were different voices within the SDP, there was confusion about what the party's stand really was. And Arnulf, as its lone supporter at the table, came under some intense questioning about the SDP's stand on German arms buildup.

"The growth of these absurdly large militaries is dangerous," Arnulf replied when asked about the SDP's stand on German arms buildup. "And it is also very costly. Most of the cost is borne on the backs of people like those in my family, workers, union people. Look how much beer prices have gone up because of the taxes we pay for the armies and the rest."

"We're all paying for that," Gustav insisted. "My beer is taxed just as much as your uncle's, or whoever's."

"But when you live on a low wage, that tax takes more out of your hide."

"So, what's the alternative?" asked Julius.

"Tax incomes and property," Arnulf asserted. "Why shouldn't people with more, pay more?"

"Are you ready to pay more?" several asked.

"I think it's a question of fairness. That's what the SDP campaigned on, and I think the voters agreed."

"Maybe you have a point," Benno said. "But the Social Democrats also call for cutting back or even ending military spending. I believe that's dangerous. Sometimes to avoid a fight you have to be ready for one. We're more likely to be attacked if we appear weak."

Rolf nodded. "I agree with Benno. And, in this case, though I hate to admit it, I also agree with the Kaiser!" There were assents around the table.

"All the countries say they're building up armies to guarantee peace." Arnulf ran his hand through his thinning but still ample blond hair and spoke with a tone meant to mock certain conservative political speech: "With all these huge armies built to 'defend the peace' war will soon be impossible!"

"Clever, my friend," said Benno, "but let's be practical. How can Germany defend itself without a big military? The French are arming, as are the Russians, the British, even the Italians. It would be suicide for Germany to not keep pace."

Gustav pounded the table lightly with his fist. "Will the SDP defend Germany if we're attacked? I think that's what people want to know."

"There are those who say that they would oppose war under *any* conditions. That was in the statement set out by the socialist groups in Basel." Arnulf looked at the others around the table. "And there are those who favor military spending as a defensive measure. Which, I should say, is also the point of view of the unions." Arnulf paused. "Of course, I stand with that faction. We'll defend our country if it's attacked. But I can't support this aggressive approach to becoming a colonial power. Look at what's been happening in South West Africa. Terrible things going on there."

Berthold nodded. "Okay, Arnulf, I'll concede that to you. This country has stepped out of line in its treatment of Africans—"

"I'm not so sure," Rolf cut in.

"Let me finish my point." Berthold held up an open hand. "What I see is Britain and France, the Americans, and the others, too—Belgium, for example, and the Russians—planting their flags around the world and not being so nice about it. And when Germany does something along those lines on a much smaller scale, we get criticized and threatened. I don't see anyone else disarming or giving up colonies."

"I think that's quite obvious," added Götz. "Britain had half the world under its thumb before we Germans began to think about colonies."

"Let's not forget," Werner put in, "the advantages the so-called colonized people derive from European technology, European farming practices and science, industry, and so on."

"Whether that's true or not the people in those countries haven't a word to say about it," said Arnulf. "And, it should be obvious that the German people, including us here, have not a word to say about any of it, either!"

"The SDP now has a big voice in the Reichstag," Götz noted.

"SDP representation is small compared to our actual vote," Arnulf argued. "We need a more equal voting system."

"Well, I agree with that!" Berthold said, nodding. "The Prussians stack the deck for themselves. Those of us in the cities count for less than the Prussian Junkers and the rural yahoos they keep ignorant by design. All of us should have an equal voice."

"That's what the SDP is trying to achieve. But it needs a majority in the Reichstag. Which means unity with other parties in coalition." As there were shrugs around the table but no immediate reply, Arnulf continued, "So, I propose a toast!"

Benno laughed. "We should have seen that coming."

Gustav grinned. "A well-played shot. *Prost!*"

"Well, why not." Berthold raised his stein. "A toast to—"

"A toast to some great bullshit ski stories!" Gustav stood with his imposing bulk behind his chair.

"And may Arnulf find his other ski come spring," added Rolf.

"*Prost!*" they all repeated.

"Time to go home before my wife locks me out of the house and I miss dinner!" Rolf slammed his stein on the table and rose from his chair.

## A Seder in Traunstein

Passover came in late April 1913. At the urging of Anna's sisters, Anna and Benno accepted an invitation to have seder in Traunstein. Max was at first reluctant to travel. But after some coaxing, he agreed to join them. As the elder in the family, he presided over the service.

The three Einstein sisters, Bertha, Fanny, and Anna, prepared an elaborate meal of brisket, roasted chicken, hot potato salad, and a string bean casserole. Once dinner was over and the children had drifted off to bed, the adults took the time to drink wine, relax, and catch up on their lives.

The discussion wandered over various terrains, settling for a time on the ups and downs of cattle and horse raising in Traunstein. The

Holzer brothers, Louie and Willi, had begun their livestock business in Traunstein after their marriages to Bertha and Fanny in 1902. As time went on Louie took charge of the buying and selling of horses while Willi concentrated on the cattle and oxen trade. Louie's business was booming because of the rapid expansion of the Prussian cavalry. "I can't get ahold of these Trakehner horses, the special breed for heavy work, fast enough!" Louie exclaimed as he sipped from a tall wineglass. "I've been telling Willi we should drop the cattle business for now and use the space and resources we have for the horses. There's a huge market right now!"

This clearly irritated Willi. "That's short-sighted. What will we do if the horse trade goes slack? It's good now, but who knows what's ahead. Cattle, on the other hand, will always be in demand. People are not likely to give up eating meat!"

"I don't see people giving up horses anytime soon either," countered Louie.

"Well, you might have heard of these 'horseless carriages'? Even on farms there's talk of horses being replaced by machines."

"A long way off," Louie scoffed. "And right now, I've got these Prussian buyers picking up every animal I can supply them!"

Willi shook his head. "The local farmers complain that we send all our stock up north. They're saying that we're just out to get rich by selling to Prussians and ignoring their needs."

Louie threw his arms in the air. "And there are those who complain we're *not* patriotic when we hold back stock for the local farmers!"

"Take it from me," Max jumped in, "no matter what you do, they'll say, you're doing this or that because you're a Jew!"

"We don't hear that kind of talk here, thank God," Louie sighed.

Fanny came into the room. "I have coffee here, for anyone who wants to sober up. And I'd like to hear something from Munich. I'd like to hear about Anna's volunteer work with the refugees."

Anna sat quietly for a moment as eyes turned toward her. "I've learned a lot from the immigrant women who've come to Women's Committee events at the synagogue."

Louie poured himself a cup of coffee and asked, "Which women are these?"

"Refugees from Russia, Galicia, Poland . . . Women . . . and children, forced to leave their homes to seek refuge in Germany, or England or the United States." She described some of the circumstances as told to her by the immigrants.

"What do you do for them?" asked Fanny.

"We try to assure them that they're safe here in Germany. We help find them jobs. Some of the congregation hire them for domestic work or put them up in their homes temporarily. We've had several work for us as child-sitters." Anna looked over at Benno and then Max who had fallen asleep on a chair in the corner of the room. "We have clothing drives. The community has a German language school for the adults. We get tutors for the kids, who are still learning German. We help with school supplies. That sort of thing."

"How many of these Eastern Jews are in Munich?" Louie asked.

As Anna thought about it, Benno blurted, "Too many."

Anna looked at her husband. "What do you mean 'too many'?"

"I mean, there are quite a lot. You see them all over the city. They're very noticeable on the streets. Some come to the synagogue—which is fine. But you can also see some begging."

"Most are hardworking people." Anna's voice wavered with emotion. "I don't hear people complain about them when they're washing windows or working in the laundries or helping out around our homes."

Benno shrugged. "Well, you'll find those who say that they are taking jobs from Germans. The problem is not the people. They come here running from dire situations. The problem is that a lot of Germans look at these Russian Jews, these Eastern Jews, with their clothing and habits and judge us—all of us—by what they see in them."

Anna looked at her husband. "How's that their fault? That they're poorer than us or that their situations are so desperate?"

"It's not their fault," Benno replied. "It's Russia, it's the Czar, and these ugly pogroms . . . but it's also true that people have to confront problems and not run from them."

"So easy for us to say."

"I didn't say it was easy."

Louie leaned forward in his chair. "Well, someone has to stand up to that bastard, the Czar and his goons. Can't let them drive every Jew out of their country."

Bertha got up from her chair. "I almost forgot. I have some good dessert. Benno, I think it's something you had in Laupheim a few years ago, if I'm not mistaken." At that Bertha went into the kitchen.

Fanny looked at Anna. "I think it's great, what you're doing for our people from Russia. Something has to be done. With all these stories about shtetls being raided by these Black Hundreds, or whatever they call them, and Jewish parents being butchered in front of their children . . ."

As Fanny spoke Bertha came into the room carrying a platter. "Empire cake!" She set the platter down in the center of the table and handed Franny a knife. The two began cutting pieces from the large round cake covered in chocolate frosting and placing them on dessert plates.

Louie looked at his wife. "I was wondering what you had cooking in there. But I think it's called *Emperor's* cake."

"I call it Empire cake because it takes as long to make as it takes some empires to form!" Bertha laughed. Everyone's attention now turned toward the plates in front of them with their generous helpings of multilayered chocolate cake.

"Very rich, Bertha." Benno had a twinkle in his eye as he looked over Bertha, then Anna. "I can taste the Laupheim influence here."

"Let's not forget to thank those who also worked hard for this dish." Fanny spoke as her mouth filled with the chocolate covered dessert. "The hens and cows! Eggs and milk, the secret of it all!"

On the return from Traunstein, Benno and Anna both thought about their argument over the immigrants, but neither raised the subject.

## Storm Clouds on a Clear July Day

In mid-July 1914, Benno and Anna were out with their children at Munich's English Garden. At one of the meadows Benno stopped for a moment to tell his children how he'd come to carnivals at that very spot when he was young. He had just begun to tell them about the rides and booths when Fritz and Hani began bouncing up and down impatiently. "We wanna go to the river, Papa." They ran down to a spot where the meadow sloped gently into a narrow stream. Anna unfolded blankets on the grassy area near the water's edge and Benno sat down heavily with a book, but he read little as he kept falling asleep. Anna kept a wary eye on the children but resisted their pleas to join them in the water.

"Tell Papa to come in the water with us," urged Hani.

But Benno was now snoring, his head resting on the pages of the open book. "Papa's asleep. Let him rest," Anna called.

In the afternoon they met their friends Rudy and Greta at the huge beer garden by the Chinese Pavilion, a large structure built in the 1800s. Benno and Rudy had known each other since they attended religious school classes together as children. Now they both had children attending the same school. Rudy and his wife, Greta, ran a small bakery near the Marienplatz. The two couples sat together over beer and food while their children played.

It was a stunningly beautiful day, and the beer garden was alive with music, loud talk, laughter, and occasional outbursts of singing. But amid the revelry, beer, healthy portions of chicken and corned beef, sausages, pickles, sauerkraut, and salad, on many of the tables where families and friends gathered, the conversation drifted from personal news and small talk to the topic occupying all of Europe at that moment. Three weeks earlier, on June 28, 1914, in the city of Sarajevo, Austria's Archduke Franz Ferdinand and his wife, Sophie, were shot dead by a young Serbian. Details coming out in the papers told of a group of Serbian youths who'd traveled to the Bosnian capital with the intention to murder the heir to the Habsburg throne.

Most Germans—most Europeans, in fact—would have been hard-pressed to explain the anger that motivated this act of political terror. The complex politics of the Balkans were not easy to follow from afar. As shocking as the murder of these ruling figures was, it was widely believed at first that no great consequence would come of it.

But, by that late July day, the Austro-Hungarian government had delivered a threatening and humiliating ultimatum to the government in Serbia, while Russia was declaring it would come to the aid of its Slavic brothers in Serbia. Suddenly, things began to look more serious.

Benno set down several steins of beer, surveyed the crowded garden and took off his coat and draped it over a chair. "Seems like all of Munich is out here today."

Greta looked up from her seat at the table and joked, "My! Who would have thought it could get warm enough in Munich to get Benno out of his coat. And in public!"

"Well, I hope I'm not revealing too much," said Benno wryly as he sat down.

"Yep, a gorgeous day," commented Rudy. "But now they say that storm clouds from Serbia are on their way. So maybe we should eat quickly and go home before they arrive."

"If you're talking about the Archduke's killing, it was a terrible thing" commented Greta. "But let's hope nothing more terrible comes of it."

Anna, seated next to her, nodded. "They caught the young man who did the shooting and he'll be put on trial. That should end it."

"But it won't," Rudy cut a piece of sausage. "The Habsburgs want revenge. It looks like they might even bomb Belgrade. It'll be a very uneven affair."

"And it probably won't stop there," said Benno.

"Where do you see this going?" asked Greta.

Benno sipped his beer. "If Russia gets involved, it's hard to say. They say they'll back up the Serbs. And Germany is committed to the Austrians. One thing can lead to another."

"Let's hope it doesn't go beyond Austria and Serbia," Anna asserted.

"I don't think Russia or Germany would risk war over this Archduke, do you?" Greta asked Benno. "He wasn't a very popular character to begin with."

"I'm not so sure," Benno replied. "Russia has ambitions. Germany has necessities that might make it worth the risk."

"Really, Benno?" Greta asked dubiously. "Risk a war, for what?"

"We know that France and Russia—and England too—would like to strangle Germany. They see us as a threat. France has never gotten over its defeat in the Franco-Prussian War. It wants to get back at Germany and recover Alsace-Lorraine." Benno brushed the ashes off the tip of his cigar. "Countries need to defend themselves."

Anna looked over at her husband. "So, you want to see a war?"

"No, I don't but . . ."

"But, it may be necessary," Rudy put in. "I agree with Benno, a country has a right to defend itself. If Russia were to attack Austria, Germany would have to respond because of our agreements with the Habsburgs."

"Maybe such agreements are a mistake," Greta suggested.

"Without Austria, Germany would be at the mercy of Russia and France." Rudy reached for a beer. "And probably England, too."

"Germany's the strongest country in Europe right now," Benno asserted. "That might not always be the case. Russia is gaining strength. And it is a hellish place, especially for Jews. Let's not forget that."

"So, you are for a war, Benno!" Greta exclaimed.

"War can be terrible and it's a big gamble. But war sometimes becomes necessary, or at least unavoidable if you want to defend the things you care about."

"I think that Germany is strong enough to be able to win a war, and fairly quickly," added Rudy.

"Like in 1870?" asked Benno.

Rudy shrugged. "Maybe."

"The armies are much bigger now. More countries will be drawn into it. The armaments are more deadly." Benno spoke as though he was thinking to himself.

"Long or short, I don't want to see any war at all," Anna insisted. "The only thing that is certain in war is death."

"So, you're a pacifist, Anna?" chided Rudy.

"I don't see what can be gained from this. Wasn't there a war in the Balkans a few years ago? What did it resolve? Seems like every country wants this piece of land or that. Whatever happens, someone ends up unhappy. War just raises the level of anger and desire for revenge. One war just creates conditions for the next one."

"Benno," Rudy looked across the table at his friend, "your wife has been studying some history I see."

Greta looked at her husband. "You find it surprising that women can learn from history?"

"Of course not," said Rudy defensively.

"Austria got control of Bosnia Herzegovina to ensure peace after the war with the Ottomans," Anna said, looking at the two men. "But that only angered the Serbs who thought they had a right to a piece of the Bosnian coast. And now here we are."

Benno nodded and took a puff from his cigar. "Yah, she's right. Of course it's a bit more complicated . . ."

"Isn't that always the case? But I agree with Anna," Greta chimed in. "And this is a beautiful summer and things are not going so badly. So, let's not spoil it. Besides, we've got to get ready for Walter's Bar Mitzvah in September." Greta looked over at her friend. "And let's not forget, Anna has a new baby to bring into this world soon!" Anna smiled and touched her swollen belly. "We don't have time for a war right now!" Greta lifted her stein . "Cheers!"

# 3

# War, 1914–1918

ON JULY 23, 1914, THE Austro-Hungarian government, encouraged by the Germans and assured of German support in the case their action against Serbia put them in conflict with Russia, issued an ultimatum to the Serbs. Their demands were so strident that the Austro-Hungarians were confident they could not be met. When the Serbian government failed to capitulate on all of the demands, Austria-Hungary declared war on Serbia on July 28 and brought heavy guns to shell the Serbian capital of Belgrade.

Russia, which had pledged to support Serbia in case of a conflict with Austria-Hungary, announced the mobilization of its army on July 30. On August 1 Germany, declaring it was coming to the aid of Austria-Hungary per its treaty commitment, declared war on Russia. On August 2, France, in line with prior commitments, ordered military mobilization in support of Russia. On August 3, Germany declared war on France.

### War Fever

On August 4 thousands of people gathered in Munich's Odeonplatz. Word had spread that advance troops of the German army had crossed into Belgium on their way to France. England denounced the invasion as a violation of Belgium's neutrality and declared war on Germany. Many found in these events cause for celebration. Benno was among the revelers. He was caught up in the excitement, as he held the hand of his six-year-old son, Fritz, at the edge of the crowded Odeonplatz. For the moment a broad public sense of common purpose seemed to promise a stronger, more prosperous, and more inclusive Germany.

As hundreds of thousands of young German soldiers moved west and east toward a war on two fronts, as many other young Germans lined up at recruiting stations to join up, Kaiser Wilhelm spoke to the German public from his palace in Berlin, declaring, "I no longer recognize any parties or any confessions . . . Today we are all German brothers and only German brothers." He asserted that German soldiers marching off to war would be "back home by the time the leaves begin to fall"—in other words, within months.

The Social Democrats in Germany and similar parties in other belligerent nations, all of which had denounced the coming war and vowed to build mass opposition to it, now backed away from their commitments. Pointing out that Russia was first to mobilize its military the leaders of the German Social Democratic Party, with few exceptions, declared that Germany was being forced to fight a defensive war and pledged their support to the war effort. They seemed to take little note of Germany's support for Austria-Hungary's artillery attack on Belgrade.

Each of these parties did exactly what they had insisted they would never do: They accepted the words of their own governments, all of which insisted that their rivals were the real instigators and aggressors.

### Late August 1914

Benno was at the Viktualienmarkt, the outdoor market area near Marienplatz, when he heard someone call his name. Behind a row of crowded tables Benno saw Werner, one of his old beer-drinking partners, approaching him. "Congratulations," Werner bellowed as he set a hand on Benno's shoulder. "I've heard a new child's on the way. Coming soon, is that right?"

"So it seems." Benno looked down at a bag he'd set on the ground. "I've been out shopping for things to prepare for the new arrival."

As they spoke Julius and Götz appeared with steins of beer. Götz handed one to Benno and shook hands with Werner, as did Julius.

"We should find a table," said Julius. "I just saw Berthold and Rolf. Anyone know about Gustav?"

"He won't be joining us," said Werner as he grasped a chair at a table being vacated by a large group. "Gustav's brother-in-law was injured at the front. There's a lot of turmoil at his home and he can't be out right now."

Benno shook his head as he sat down. "Sorry to hear that, Werner."

Rolf arrived and set a large plate of potatoes and onions in the center of the table. The old friends sat and exchanged stories about their personal and business lives in a country now at war. All of them had stories of young men they knew who had volunteered or been drafted and sent into the fight. But aside from a rise in food prices caused by a British naval blockade, they noted that their lives, thus far, had not been affected much by the war.

At a pause in the conversation Benno asked about their old drinking partner Arnulf.

"I saw Arnulf a few hours ago," Berthold replied, "with a woman friend. He says he's busy this evening and can't join us. I gathered that he's not so happy about the war. Nor, it seemed, was the woman he was with."

"Why shouldn't they be happy?" Werner responded. "This'll be a short war. It could well be over in a few months."

Julius nodded. "And Germany'll have righted some wrongs." As he spoke the sounds of celebration came from several nearby tables. At one, a group of men, quite far along in their drinking, had begun singing lines from a poem, "A Song of Hate for England," written by a German-Jewish poet, Ernst Lissauer.

*We love as one, we hate as one,*
*We have one foe and one alone—England!*

"Catchy words, that poem," Rolf said as he nodded acknowledgment to the singers.

"Maybe a bit over the top," Berthold replied.

"It's motivation for the troops, Bert," Werner said. "Every soldier in Prince Ruprecht's Bavarian corps carries Lissauer's poem to the front!"

"And look here," Götz said, tapping the table with his index finger, "we're doing pretty well on both fronts. You've all heard about the battle at Tannenberg, right? What a blow to the Russians! Their entire Second Army's practically wiped out. Hindenburg and his aide-de-camp . . . uh—"

"You mean Ludendorff!" Julius asserted.

"Yes. I'd never heard of him before, but he's turning out to be quite the commander." Götz paused as he slid a slice of potato in his mouth. "He and Hindenburg sent Russia's First Army running back to Nicholas in a panic!"

Rolf smiled broadly. "Who'd have thought that Russia could be routed by just a small part of the German force? And so quickly!"

"Not quite routed yet," Benno sat back in his chair and then paused at a round of loud singing and shouting at a nearby table. "The Russians have a huge army and it's only been partially mobilized. It's also unclear just how effective our Habsburg allies will be in this fight."

"Benno," Julius said as he rested his arm on Benno's shoulder. "This is August. Winter is months away and you're already raining on our parade!"

"A few sprinkles—just to keep you awake," Benno said with a laugh.

"The place to watch is the western front. If Paris falls, it's over." Rolf pounded the table so hard one of the dishes started bouncing, but Berthold caught it before it fell.

"Hah, good work, Bert," Rolf roared, to a round of laughter. "The invasion through Belgium was a masterstroke!"

"And so much for those 'impregnable' Belgian fortresses!" Werner added. "We're seeing what Krupp's guns and aggressive tactics can do!"

"And now our fellows are sweeping across Flanders and northern France in a big arching movement." Rolf held his arms curved in front of him. "Moltke's set out a huge net to trap the French and Brits. Once they snap the trap shut," Rolf slapped his hands together, "then it's on to Paris!"

"The Schlieffen Plan!" said Benno.

Berthold emptied his stein and set it down hard. "What do you make of the noise about Germany violating Belgium's neutrality? We're accused of brutality against the Belgians."

Götz turned to Berthold. "That noise is coming from the British! And I say to hell with them! In war you do what you have to do, right?"

Werner nodded. "The Belgians should just stay out of it. It's not their fight!"

"You get in the way of Germany, you get hurt. That's just the way it is." Benno shrugged.

"And what's this concern about neutrality?" Werner added. "Where was 'neutrality' when the British went after the Boers in Africa, huh? The British want the world to believe they're so *cultured* but really they're a bunch of self-righteous, tea-drinking brutes!"

"Exactly," came the response from several in the group.

"I find myself in agreement with that Jewish poet," Rolf added. And he began reciting Lissauer's poem:

> *Throughout the Fatherland, make it heard.*
> *We will never forgo our hate,*
> *We have all but a single hate,*
> *We love as one, we hate as one,*
> *We have one foe and one alone—England!*

"I think Germany is showing the world that it deserves the respect it's not always been granted," Julius added to nods of assent.

"The German military needs to make a quick end to this war before the British can mobilize the resources of their empire," Benno observed. "But a victory for us this time will be more significant than 1871. Then it was just us and the French. Now the British and Russians are also in it."

"Germany'll teach them all a little humility. It's our moment!" Rolf beamed.

"Another beer, Benno?" Götz asked. "It's on me. You know, a little present for the new one coming."

Benno laughed. "No, thank you. I hate to be a spoiler. As much as I've enjoyed this gathering, I've got to get along." Benno held up a shopping bag.

At that Julius stood up. "My wife has drafted me for domestic service. I've been ordered to find a good cut of meat for a family gathering. So I'll be getting along, too."

"Luck to you. Good-quality meat is becoming harder to find," Berthold commented.

"And more expensive!" Julius exclaimed. "But, a small price to pay—to my mind."

"Whadaya say we meet again when Paris falls?" Werner suggested as the gathering was breaking up.

"And we'll get Gustav and Arnulf to join us," Götz threw in.

"And then we'll celebrate the end of war!" Berthold exclaimed.

"Victory to Germany," Rolf roared. And they all shouted, "*Prost!*"

### Birth and Death at Home

On September 6, 1914, Benno's sister Berta and a midwife rushed to 19 Liebherrstrasse after receiving urgent phone calls. The midwife, Frau Schröder, a tall woman with a straightforward but friendly manner, supervised the birth of Ernst, the third child of thirty-six-year-old Anna. While he was taking his first breaths, the midwife took note of a troubling sound from the infant's lungs. She mentioned this to Benno and Berta, taking pains not to worry the mother. A doctor came the following day and left hopeful, with instructions to watch the infant carefully. But, during his sixth day out in the world, Ernst died in his sleep.

The death threw Anna into a state of depression. It was psychological more than physical pain that kept her bedridden for several weeks. Benno suspended other activities to be at home, and Berta became a regular house companion. She came to the house nearly every morning to cook, help with chores, and look after Fritz and Hani.

As the family was recovering from its pain, Europe was passing through an immense shock of its own.

## The Marne

By late August six German armies had come within a hundred miles of the English Channel and had turned south toward Paris. The Germans were moving rapidly all along the line. Confident of victory, the German high command sent two army corps from the western front to East Prussia to shore up the fighting with the Russians, who were sending more divisions to the front. This left the western front weakened. On September 6, near the Marne River, the British cavalry attacked at a gap between Germany's 1st and 2nd Army; the gap had opened when German troops were sent to counter the French 6th Army attacking them from the north. At this crucial juncture six thousand French soldiers, newly arrived from Tunis, and ferried from Paris by two thousand Parisian taxis, attacked the Germans in the same vulnerable area.

The French and British moves broke the German advance. German troops began to pull back beyond the Marne River. German failure to destroy key bridges allowed the British to advance rapidly. To halt their retreat, the German command ordered its troops to dig trenches and set up defensive positions near the Aisne River. The German army's defensive positions on the Aisne were the first of what would become a maze of trenches running for hundreds of miles on either side of the war front.

It soon became clear that the nature of war itself had changed from previous wars. The use of more advanced weapons—especially powerful long-range artillery, machine guns, flame throwers, grenades, and later, poison gases—made offensive ground operations very costly while greatly increasing the importance of defense. By late fall 1914 it was apparent that this was not going to be another 1870, another quick victory by Germany. The conflict settled into what would become a long, bloody war of attrition and a virtual stalemate punctuated by episodes of colossal slaughter in such places as Verdun, the Somme, and Ypres.

## Max's Long Walks, Spring 1915

Benno's father, Max, continued to be physically active well into his seventies. He occupied himself with frequent long walks around Munich. Sometimes he would go to his daughter Berta's apartment on Damenstiftstrasse, and they'd walk to nearby Marienplatz and the surrounding area. They had a route that took them through Alter Botanischer Garten, the botanical garden and the nearby Konigsplatz. But Max, even at his age, or maybe because of it, was restless for challenges and wanted to take longer strolls. Berta, who complained of sore feet, knee pain, or discomfort in a hip, cut their walks short. So when Max wanted longer walks he would take them on his own.

One day, shortly before the spring equinox, Max left for a walk early in the morning before others in the house were up. He didn't return until late that night, which had Benno concerned. When Max finally returned, he was casual about his extended time away. But he complained that his hips and feet were sore and went to bed.

Over dinner the next evening he explained in detail his route west to Untermenzing, then a rural area outside the city. He described a walk along country roads that skirted hay and flax fields that brought back memories of his old days traveling country roads as a rural peddler.

He looked in on Herr Friederichs, the farmer who rented land Max and Benno jointly owned with the Götz family.

"Did Herr Friederichs have much to say?" asked Benno.

"He's very upset about the war. He was grousing and at times practically yelling. 'What with the British blockade and all we have a country suffering from a lack of food, and I can barely get a crop in the ground because the young men needed on the land are being taken off to be killed in the war'—that's just the way he put it! 'They're fighting over pieces of land somewhere, and there's no one to work the land here!' He went on quite a long while about that."

After leaving Friederichs's farm Max expected to catch a ride with a bus back to the center of town but got confused and missed the connection. He ended up walking the entire way back—a distance of almost 26 kilometers. Max drank several tall beers to celebrate his achievement and spent the next several days recuperating.

In the first week of April 1915, after weeks of steady rain, Max left home intending, as he told Anna, to make a tour of Munich's spring wildflowers. He described the route he would take along the Isar, to the English Garden and then across town to Nymphenburg, to visit the new botanical garden that had opened the year before. He even brought a pad of writing paper to make notes of the flowers and plants he encountered there and along the way.

When he returned that evening and Anna asked him about his floral tour, he seemed confused and disoriented. He couldn't recall the names of the plants he'd seen nor the route he had taken. He said he felt dizzy and wanted to take a nap before dinner. When he didn't wake up for dinner Anna let him sleep. Benno found him later that evening passed out on a chair in the living room. They were able to rouse him, but he could barely speak, or walk. They took him to a hospital, but it was too late. He'd suffered a massive stroke at home and died shortly after arriving at the hospital. He was several months short of his eightieth birthday.

### The Shivah

Max's death hit Benno hard. He had always been very close to his father. With his physical vitality, Max didn't seem like someone ready to die.

It was Anna who insisted they sit shivah for her father-in-law. Benno resisted at first, saying he preferred to be alone for a time. But he relented and later thanked his wife for insisting they mourn the traditional way.

For five days Benno and Anna remained at home while friends and relatives came by. Anna's father, Moses, came from Laupheim with Anna's sister Mina and their younger brother Ludwig. Anna was distressed by how weak and pale Ludwig looked. But he evaded her questions about his health.

Several relatives of Jette, Benno's mother, stopped in to give their condolences. Some of Benno's beer-drinking friends were there: Otto Götz came with his wife, Thekla; Berthold came with Hilde; and Julius with his wife, Margaret. Anna's sister Bertha came from Traunstein with her daughter Hansi.

As is the custom, everyone brought food. Benno and Anna's friends Greta and Rudy came with generous offerings of apple cake, pear tarts, strudels, and pumpernickel bread from their small bakery. Other visitors brought potato salad, nuts, fruits, cheeses, latkes, kugel, blintzes, sweet and sour cabbage, pickles, and sauerkraut. Mina cooked a brisket at the apartment from meat she brought from Laupheim. Bertha brought chicken from Traunstein. Berthold and Hilde brought several large salamis and some smoked fish from a friend's deli. For five days the house overflowed with food. At one point, the dining room table was so full of food offerings that there was no place left to sit. Visitors ate on chairs and sofas with plates on their laps.

Yet the talk of food, when it did come up, was not about its abundance, but its scarcity. Food was becoming difficult to find in Germany and prices were rising sharply. The rationing of flour had begun the previous December. Certain that more rationing would come, everyone cherished this moment of abundance, even as it came on a sad occasion.

A big surprise for Benno was to see Gustav at his door on the third day of Shivah. Benno and Gustav had not seen each other since before the war began. When Gustav entered, he embraced Benno with his bear-like arms and gave his condolences. He then added, like a man who couldn't get far away from humor even in the darkest circumstances, "I've never been to a shivah before. It's said you *sit* Shivah. Yet here you are standing in front of me. I'm disappointed."

"Well, Gustav," Benno answered, "here you are witness to my fall from grace." They both laughed, as they had in the days of their beer get-togethers.

When Benno asked Gustav about his family, Gustav lamented that he had a nephew and an in-law who had been injured in the war, one on each of the two main fronts. But then Gustav added with some relief, "It's our good fate or fortune that we are fathers too old to serve, with children too young to fight." When Benno suggested that as the war was going, Germany might have to extend the age of those eligible for the military, Gustav scowled, "When they start taking old sots like us, we'll know just how desperate they are!"

After a short visit, Gustav excused himself and Benno accompanied his friend to the door.

As they parted, Benno grasped Gustav's hand and thanked him for the visit.

Anna, Benno, and his quiet sister Berta were together for five days accepting condolences, thanking their visitors, and talking about Max. It was this time of tragedy in the family that brought the very introverted Berta closer to her brother and his family than she had ever been as an adult or would be again.

In the days of shivah visitors took care to avoid talk of war casualties. Yet this reality hung in the air. The newspapers carried lists of Munich soldiers who died or were badly injured. Nearly everyone knew of someone whose name appeared on that list. Few could avoid the thought that while friends and family came to console the passing of a nearly eighty-year-old father, every day in France, East Prussia, the Balkans, and elsewhere, eighteen-year-old boys were being blown into bloody fragments.

On the last day of shivah, Herr Katz, a longtime friend of Max's, and someone who knew him as a boy more than seventy years before, came by the apartment. Katz was a short man with a large, exposed scalp rimmed with wild wiry silver hair. He walked with some difficulty with the help of a cane and with his body bent forward. Benno and Berta introduced themselves to this man they could not remember having met before. He gave each an energetic embrace. With a voice that seemed outsized for his frame, Katz recalled that the last time he'd seen them they were young children, though he couldn't recall the year. "My Max's children," he called them.

Katz shuffled into the living room, accepted a cup of coffee from Anna and sat down on a sofa, insisting that Benno and Berta sit nearby. He began to recount stories from his and Max's youth. "We were among the last Jews to live in that town," said Herr Katz referring to the village of Mönchsdeggingen. "There are no Jews there at all now." One hand rested on the round top end of his wooden cane, while his other hand moved restlessly over the side of his scraggly goatee as he talked. He was alone with Benno and Berta at first, but others came into the room as he was talking. "Max and I were in the same school. I should say, the same room, since there was only one schoolroom for all of us! Just one teacher. That was such a small town, Mönchsdeggingen!"

Herr Katz wore glasses perched high up on his prominent nose. His bushy eyebrows moved as he spoke giving his face an animated, comical quality. "I left that town soon after your father, you see. I saw no point. There was no point. No way to make a living. Your father saw that. It took me longer. He had that wife to help him ..."

"Judith," Benno volunteered.

"Yes, I knew her by another name."

"Jette," Berta interjected.

"Yes. She helped him, the family, get out—with the boys—you were one of the boys, right?" Herr Katz looked over at Benno with watery eyes as he leaned on his cane.

"No, I was born here in Munich."

Herr Katz gave Benno a sidelong look and nodded. "When we were boys your father and I used to walk to Nördlingen. That was a town, not far, but in those days, it seemed far. Nördlingen to us was a big town. But it was this tiny, tiny place. But it was bigger than Mönchsdeggingen, so it seemed big to us young boys! When you're young everything is big! When you're big, everything is small. The law of proportions," Herr Katz pointed out as though he was lecturing in physics. "What is it that fellow from Ulm says?"

Benno and Berta shook their heads, not quite sure where this was going.

"Relativeness. An important concept." Benno thought Herr Katz probably meant to say "relativity," but he didn't comment.

"They say no one understands it," Katz continued, "and so I don't think I do either. But I do understand things are relative. The older you get the more relative everything becomes. You know, sharp lines disappear, and you see this in that and that in this. Do you see what I'm saying?" He looked over at Max's children, who were nodding more from politeness than anything else.

"And we would go to this store, Max and I, and buy candy and little cakes, wrapped with scenes from German history, you know. That was a great store to us. It seemed big but it was just the bottom floor of a house. But it had more variety than any place in our town. They had these young girls working there, daughters of the owner or some such. I mean they were older than us. We were maybe twelve—before Bar Mitzvah. The people in that store must have thought we had the sweetest tooths in Bavaria. We came so often to get cakes and cookies and candies . . . But it wasn't that kind of sweets we were most interested in. And the owner would say, 'Oh here are those Jewish boys again.' And it wasn't said in a bad way at all. Just like a matter of fact. And how did she know we were Jewish boys? We didn't wear yarmulkes, that I can recall."

By the time Herr Katz reached this point in the story, his audience had grown and it appeared that he was playing to it.

"How would that store woman know we were Jewish?" He

paused and looked around, "A mystery to this day. Look at me. Would you think I was Jewish?" He said this with a strong upward sweep of his voice. By this time Berta, Anna, Anna's sister Bertha and her niece Hansi, Götz and others were all laughing to themselves—less at the story than at the way Herr Katz told it, and to the way his eyebrows moved when he asked the question. He was amusing. And they were in the mood to be amused.

Caught up in the moment Götz burst out, "Not at all, Herr Katz, I would have thought you were the Pope."

At that, the entire room convulsed. Maybe it was the tension of the war, the days of solemnity surrounding Max's death, their unease over what the future would bring such that they needed something they could laugh at or with, and the laughter gushed like water from behind a broken dam. Berta, Benno's normally quiet sister, laughed so hard tears came to her eyes, and she had trouble catching her breath. Anna was on the couch covering her face as her body vibrated. Herr Katz joined in the laughter and pointed an appreciative finger at Götz, like a comedian acknowledging a good punchline.

Benno too, uncharacteristically, laughed convulsively. His face was red and tears that began as tears of laughter soon became tears of sorrow, tears of loss. Benno, normally so controlled, lost himself in emotion, in the realization that he was laughing about these stories of his father—this father he would *never* see again. Benno embraced his father's old friend, even as he was embarrassed because such a show of emotion was not becoming for a German man.

Everyone in the room shook the old man's hand and thanked him for coming and for enriching them with his stories.

And it was fitting that with Herr Katz's stories and then with the Kaddish prayer for the dead, led by the rabbi who arrived about this time—*Yis'ga'dal v'yis'kadash sh'may ra'bbo* . . . the shivah came to an end.

## War Bonds

During 1915 the German government began running short on funds to finance the war. Lacking outside sources of finance, and reluctant to raise taxes for fear of the effect on public morale, the government issued war bonds and appealed to the patriotism of its citizens to invest in them. Benno responded to the call, joining wealthy, middle-class, and even some working-class Germans roused by patriotic fervor and incentivized by the promise of 5 percent interest on the bonds over a ten-year period.

The initial campaign proved successful. During the first round of bond sales the government raked in 24 billion marks ($160 billion in today's money). Each subsequent campaign recorded an increase over the previous one thanks to middle-class Germans who sought to prove their patriotism by buying larger quantities of bonds. Investing in war bonds meant buying a direct stake in the war's outcome.

Anna, who was far less supportive of the war from the outset, was not happy that Benno risked a large part of their savings on its outcome. Benno held to his belief that Germany was the victim in this war and that it could triumph if the people stood fast in their support.

When Germany launched a huge offensive at Verdun in February 1916, Benno followed the news stories of the battle closely. Germany threw two million soldiers into this monstrous campaign. They shelled French fortresses with millions of artillery rounds in the belief that they could smash through Verdun's strategic position, or at least bleed the French dry as they threw in reserves to defend it. The German press predicted the battle would be a turning point in the war. Germany made early gains, but the French were able to blunt the offensive and the battle settled into a mutual slaughter as armies fought over yards of terrain on either side of the trenches. The battle came to an end in December 1916. In those 10 months 800,000 soldiers died or were wounded; 143,000 of the dead were Germans.

The warring nations unleashed numerous offensives on the western front. New, more powerful, and deadly weapons were introduced to the conflict with the expectation of a decisive breakthrough in the fighting. In late April 1915, at Ypres in the northern section of the front, the Germans unleashed clouds of yellow chlorine gas that killed and maimed British and French soldiers as it drifted over their trenches. The deployment of chemical weaponry, however much it contributed to the deadliness of the war, was not decisive.

## Fractures on the Home Front

The growing numbers of women, parents, and children devastated by the loss of husbands, sons, or fathers in the war became an ever more prominent factor in daily life. So were the growing numbers of wounded veterans on German streets. The German press nevertheless persisted that Germany would win the war.

The extent of the bloodshed, and Germany's barbaric role in it, couldn't be completely hidden from the public. By February 1916, pacifist flyers and posters started showing up in Munich and other cities. They declared the war a huge "swindle." An antiwar faction within the SPD, calling itself the Independent Social Democratic Party, or USDP, denounced the war and called for an end to it. By March the split over the war in the SDP became public.

While the gatherings of Benno's old beer hall crowd had come to an end several years earlier, mainly due to personal issues, Benno, Berthold, and Götz still got together on occasion. They talked of war strategy and prospects. As businessmen drawn to practical matters, philosophical discussions were not the norm. But these were not normal times, and the war was challenging their previously held views of their country, the world, even humanity itself.

They asked themselves if this war with all its terror and barbarism was revealing something basic to human nature. Or was it, as the pacifists wrote in their antiwar flyers, a scam concocted by the military in league with big arms producers for the purpose of amassing great fortunes? Or was it, as the socialists claimed, not a result of human nature per se, but of the nature of capitalism-imperialism, this system that humans had constructed to organize their affairs? Was this war revealing some essential flaw of capitalism that could only be rectified by a revolutionary change? This argument was now capturing broader attention.

In one of their conversations, Götz pointed out something that Benno and Berthold had been hesitant to say: the war pitted Jews in Germany against Jews in the "enemy" nations. "Aren't German Jewish soldiers shooting at, and likely killing, Jews from France, England, and Russia?" Götz asked his friends. "Can this be justified? And isn't this similar to Arnulf's argument, back when he explained to us why many in the SDP opposed the war—that it would have German workers murdering French workers, or Russian workers, and so on? Arnulf had asked us why workers, who had nothing to gain from the bloodbath, should support it, and I wonder about that now."

"But we do have a stake in this fight," Benno argued. "We're part of this nation and how it fares directly affects us."

In any case Benno held, and Berthold and Götz generally agreed, the idea that humanity, or the workers, as the socialists put it, could unite as one across national boundaries for their mutual benefit was unrealistic. Benno was explicit about it: He chose to identify with the nation of his birth and push these other suppositions aside.

Berthold asked, for the sake of argument, what distinguished them as a German nation from any other nation? Customs and language? Doesn't every nation have customs and language? Isn't this just happenstance? Accidents of birth? And weren't they all, regardless of which side of some imaginary line they were born, striving for the same thing?

These were troubling concepts. Benno, and most others like him, chose to dismiss these thoughts, even if he, and they, could not totally ignore them. As a practical matter, Benno concluded that he had no choice but to do so.

And here was another disturbing aspect of the situation that was not so easy for German Jews to shove into a quiet corner of the mind. Even while large numbers of Jews were in uniform at every level of the military, even as they were among the best fighters, and among the wounded and killed in similar proportion to the broader German population, even so, prejudice against Jews did not seem to be diminishing. Even while prominent Jewish public figures like Walter Rathenau—a friend of the Kaiser no less—and the Jewish shipping magnate Albert Ballin were making significant contributions to the economic aspects of the war, there were indications that anti-Jewish sentiments were persisting—even increasing.

Nothing seemed to change the fact that an influential and vocal minority of Germans spoke of Jews, not as patriots and "brothers," as had the Kaiser at the beginning of the war, but as slackers and worse—war profiteers. When someone spoke of "black marketeers," the word "Jew" would somehow hang in the air, but when the word "soldier" was mentioned, the word "Jew" seemed, to the popular mind, inappropriate.

This, too, seemed to be a problem without a solution.

### "Total War"

War difficulties brought a major shift in governance. At the end of August 1916, German Generals Paul von Hindenburg and Erich Ludendorff, heroes of one of the early battles on the eastern front at Tannenberg, were, with great fanfare, put in command of the military. They were also put in charge of policies on the home front, giving them near total power as a de facto military dictatorship. They used this power to mobilize the population for "total war."

In December 1916, the military announced a new measure, the Auxiliary Service Law, that raised the age of compulsory military service to sixty. This brought an extra 300,000 men into the army.

Louis, Willi, and Benno, all of whom were in their early forties, went to register for service at the beginning of December and were told to go home and await orders. On June 1, 1917, Willi and Louis were called up, underwent some weeks of training, and were sent to the western front to join an artillery unit. Benno entered later in June and in early September was sent to Dachau as a guard for a munitions factory.

With their husbands on active duty, Anna and her sisters Fanny and Bertha struggled to provide for themselves and their eleven children. Fanny and Bertha faced the challenge of maintaining the families' businesses of raising and selling livestock and maintaining their farm. For Anna, as for people in cities throughout the country, securing adequate food was becoming more difficult. By fall 1916, there was widespread rationing of meat, eggs, potatoes, and other food. Long lines at food stores and short supplies sparked protests in some places.

But winter 1916–1917 brought something far worse. Bad weather and disease decimated the country's main staple, the potato crop. In its place authorities called on the populace to use turnips, heretofore mainly used as livestock feed, as a replacement for the potato. During this "turnip winter" newspapers featured articles with cheery suggestions on how to make up for food shortages by the creative use of this tough and tasteless vegetable. Meanwhile, the average caloric intake among some people dropped to as low as 900 calories a day and ultimately led to hundreds of thousands of deaths, either directly through hunger or as disease got the better of a population weakened by malnutrition.

City dwellers like Anna, with connections to people on farms, fared better than most. When Fanny or Bertha came to Munich, they brought food from their farm, where they still had adequate supplies of potatoes, meat, eggs, and milk.

## The Holzers of Traunstein

The Holzers lived in a large house on the western edge of Traunstein. Bertha with her three daughters lived in the upstairs rooms. Fanny with her four boys and two girls lived on the next floor down. The ground floor held the offices of the Holzer cattle and horse businesses. A big yard outside the office was rimmed with stables. Here horses and cattle were brought in for trade, were cared for and sold as work animals or breeders, and occasionally, for slaughter. Behind the stable were chicken coops and a plot of land for growing vegetables.

In the prewar years the Holzers brought their horses and cattle to a central market area where buyers came to inspect the animals and make deals. From the time the Holzers set up shop in Traunstein at the turn of the century they earned a reputation for being fair and maintaining a high-quality stock. Their business flourished and they were well received in the town. In their husbands' absence, Bertha and Fanny, with help from their children, worked to keep the business alive.

Anna, Fritz, and Hani made regular trips to Traunstein which helped Anna secure needed food. The city cousins looked forward to these visits, especially in summer months when they could take advantage of the area's abundance of outdoor sports and recreation opportunities.

One such visit occurred in early September 1917. The two older Holzer boys—Leopold, fourteen, and Benno, thirteen—came to the train station to help their Aunt Anna and their younger cousins get to the farm. It had not been so very long since Anna had seen the boys, but she was startled at how much they'd grown and how much older they'd begun to act.

Fritz and Hani, impatient to take advantage of the sunny day, ran on ahead to the Holzer house where Bertha's daughters, Tilli and Hansi, now young teenagers, offered to take the Munich cousins with their younger siblings, Klara and Max, to the Traun River for a swim. It was one of those fall days that felt more aggressively summer than summer itself. It was downright hot.

With the children exploring the bliss of a warm country day, the sisters chatted at a table near the company office, across from the horse and cow stables. They sipped coffee and ate boiled potatoes and chicken—virtual delicacies for the city dweller Anna after nearly two years of war-imposed scarcity.

"I expected to see Papa here," Anna said as she tried to cool herself with a newspaper fashioned into a fan.

Fanny handed her sister a plate of sliced tomatoes from the Holzers' garden. "Papa left two days ago. He wasn't feeling well, and Mina thought he'd be better off at home."

"He wasn't looking that good when he got here," Bertha said as she pulled her chair back into the shade. "But Mina told us he insisted on seeing his grandkids. He complains that we don't go to Laupheim. But how are we supposed to do that? With Louie and Willi gone we've got our hands full."

"Papa's not having a great time of it," Anna remarked. "I've noticed how he's aged since Ludwig passed away."

"Losing his only son . . . And the way our poor brother died." Fanny's voice wavered with emotion. "No death's pretty, but he was down to like a hundred pounds at the end. And the pain!"

"When we saw him at the shivah for Max he wasn't doing well," Anna sighed. "But he didn't want to talk about it. I wonder if he knew then he had stomach cancer."

Fanny shook her head. "No. Mina said they only found out about the cancer around this time last year."

As was often the case when the Einstein sisters were together, their talk turned to the children. Bertha's three daughters, Tilli, 15, Hansi, 14, and Ilse, 13, were no longer able to attend public schools because of rules that barred girls from continuing school after their primary years. Fanny's daughters, Hedi, 11, and Klara, 9, were still in public school but would soon be facing the same situation. Bertha, adamant that her daughters would continue their schooling, had arranged to meet with the sisters who ran the Traunstein Catholic parochial school. Much to her relief, the school accepted her daughters.

"What does Papa think of that?" asked Anna.

Bertha looked intensely at Anna. "That was one topic we kept *off* the table. Papa was in a bad mood as it was. He complained about not having a synagogue in town. 'What's wrong with this place? No synagogue, not even a room to meet for Sabbath?' Since we've been here for some fifteen years, I suppose he thinks we should've built a synagogue by now. 'Papa,' I said, 'we now have more Jews in *this house* than in the entire rest of the town put together.' 'Well,' he said, 'you'—he meant Louie or Willi—'could invite the others, whoever they are, have a little service, read from the prayer book.' I had to explain to him we don't have a lot of contact with the other Jews in town. Then he asked, 'How are your children learning about Judaism?' I wasn't going to tell him, 'Well, you see, Papa, the girls are going to Catholic school—maybe they'll pick it up from the nuns!'"

The three of them laughed at that. Fanny laughed so hard she had to run to the kitchen for a drink of water.

Bertha went on: "Papa's not concerned that the girls are not allowed to go to high school, but I am. And I'm happy the girls have a school to go to. And I'm grateful to the Catholic sisters. They take great care of our kids. If the school serves some non-kosher food like ham, the sisters go out of their way to get the girls special food. They're always very respectful of the holidays. I'm so happy I made that arrangement. My girls are going to get an education!"

"It's hard with Papa here, Anna," Bertha went on. "Not only do we have to run the business and take care of the house, the kids, and everything, he's very watchful of how we keep the traditions."

"He's always been that way," Anna insisted. "Isn't that why we wanted to get away from Laupheim? I love Laupheim, but now thankfully, from a distance. You know the men can talk all they want about following traditions, but the burden falls on the women."

"Oh, Papa got so upset one day!" Fanny's expressive face was somewhere between a grimace and a laugh. "Klara had a friend over, a gentile girl from her school. It was Friday and Klara asked if she could stay over. So I told Klara, 'Your grandfather is here, be sure to respect the Sabbath. Explain to Greta, that's her friend, we have to observe the Sabbath.' Well, if that Klara doesn't bring Greta into the kitchen on Saturday morning to show her how to cook spätzle! I said, 'Klara what are you doing cooking, it's the Sabbath!' Papa was there, but she said, 'Well so what!' And Papa just looked at me, very disapproving."

Anna laughed. "What did you say?"

"I said something like, 'You know with her dad gone off to war Klara's upset and forgets things.' What I *wanted* to say was, 'Don't worry, Papa, Klara's not really mine, someone left her here by mistake.' I thought of maybe throwing her down the well. Only, I know it wouldn't bother her at all. She'd just stay down there swimming like the fish that she is." They all laughed. Klara was known in the family for her passion for swimming.

"Oh, my..." Anna rolled her eyes. "Did she say that on purpose?"

"Of course!" Fanny shook her head. "She's such a rebel. She and little Max, both of them are such goofs. I have to hold my breath when they're around, especially when Papa's here. People around our neighborhood say, 'Oh little Klara and Max, such playful children, always laughing and joking.' And I say to them, 'I'd be the first to laugh about them—if they weren't mine!'"

"What about Fritz and Hani?" Bertha asked.

"Well, we talk to them about traditions—I do that more than Benno. And they pick some up in religious school. But I'm not strict about the food. I try to keep ham out of our kitchen. But if Fritz or Hani want some milk and they eat a piece of meat, I'm not going to have a heart attack."

Fanny nodded exuberantly. "I know! I said, Papa, it's wartime, there's enough to worry about without getting so twisted about upholding the old ways. Take Willi and Louie—do you think they're going to worry about keeping kosher while the shells are falling on them? Anyway, I think we Jews have to be careful about drawing attention to ourselves. There'll always be someone around to say, 'Look how those Jews are always seeking special favors with their kosher stuff and everything.' Sometimes for us the less talk about religion the better."

"What's going on with Benno?" asked Bertha.

"I think he's bored at Dachau. He's not one to care about keeping kosher but being away seems to have made him homesick for the traditional food. I visited him with the kids last week. He asked me if I could bring him some latkes, but there are almost no potatoes in the stores, just turnips."

"Turnip latkes!" Fanny shook her head. "I can't think of a better argument for ending this shitty war."

Bertha nodded. "I tried to cook up some turnips, mash them like potatoes, but the kids wouldn't eat them. We had to feed them to the horses. Thank God we still can get potatoes from our own garden. That's our luck. We have chicken, eggs, and milk, or we can trade for them with other farmers. We can even help the neighbors, which is a blessing. It's the bright side of all this war misery."

Anna's face darkened. "Speaking of the war, Benno's very worried about how the war is going. If Germany loses, a lot of bad things are going to happen. Benno's put almost all our savings into war bonds."

"And we'll all have to learn French!" Fanny observed.

"Or Russian," added Anna.

"I'll take the French, *s'il vous plait*." Fanny picked up her dish from the table.

"At least the Czar is gone. Good riddance!" Anna said emphatically.

"The Czar is gone but the war rages on," Fanny replied.

Bertha pushed her chair back, away from the encroaching sun. "They say that one of the reasons the Russians have done so poorly in the war is that Jews there would just as soon see Germany win. At least Germany treats Jews with some humanity."

"I am thankful to be German," Fanny said. "But let's not get too carried away. There's that Jewish census business in the military—and these rumors you hear that Jews are not doing our part in the war and all that. Or that we're making out big time in the war. I've heard of people saying that."

"I've heard that talk," Anna remarked.

"If they think we're making out so well they should come look at us." Bertha exclaimed "We're barely getting by."

Anna looked at Fanny. "By the way, what do you mean by the census?"

Bertha turned to her sister. "Louie wrote me about that. Let me see if I can find the letter." Bertha went into the office and returned with a paper in her hand. "Here Louie says, 'Last year the military conducted a census of Jewish soldiers. We are singled out. We Jewish soldiers had to fill out a form describing what we do. We had to prove we're part of the fight and not just hanging out in some safe job.'"

"Oh, you mean like sitting around all day counting our money?" Anna joked.

"While eating plates of matzoh brie and liverwurst. Isn't that just so typical of those Jews!" Fanny added.

"Matzoh brie and liverwurst?" laughed Anna. "Where did that come from?"

"It's humiliating!" Fanny exclaimed. "We have to prove our loyalty."

"We thought we were over that. Didn't the Kaiser say, 'We're all in this together?'" Bertha put in.

"Yes, when the war started, and things seemed to be going well," Anna observed.

"We all thought this would be a short war and that things would be better in the end. Except you, Anna." Bertha looked at her younger sister. "I remember you said, early on, that this war would be no good for anyone. You were right. You see these poor boys back from the front, missing a leg, face all burned. It's horrible."

"And the children playing war games," added Fanny. "Little Max and his friends run around pretending to shoot, yelling, 'We are Stormtroopers, no froggies, no dirty tommies—they have their names for the French and British—'can match us!'"

"Hani thinks it's so funny to see her dad in a uniform, with his rifle. Actually, he did look funny when I first saw him in that uniform," Anna laughed. "The first time we visited him, he showed us around—this pretty garden by the munitions factory. Not something you'd expect to find at such a place. Hani was giggling the whole time. Benno was asking me, 'What's gotten into that girl?' I didn't want to say..."

"Doesn't sound like such bad duty," Bertha commented.

"It's given him time to read. He asked me to get him some books."

"Romantic novels?" Bertha asked.

"You know better than that! A book about the history of nations. You know how he loves history books."

Fanny shrugged. "I say good for Benno that he has time to think about such things and not have to worry about shells falling on him. I'm glad they didn't send him to an artillery unit like Willi and Louis... It's so hot out here, maybe we should go inside."

As they were cleaning up, Leopold, Fanny's oldest son, appeared leading a horse. "Hi Tante," he said to Anna. "Meet Rickenbacker. He's young and smart and he'll make a good war horse." As he spoke, Leopold patted the neck of a sleek, chestnut horse with rippling neck muscles and a long dark mane.

"Isn't Rickenbacker a pilot?" asked Anna, struck by the majesty of this animal.

"Yes. And this guy can fly too in his own way."

"You ride him?" Anna asked. Leopold nodded. "It's not dangerous?"

"Can be. You have to know how to handle a horse."

"He's nice-looking, Leopold. And you seem to know what you're doing."

"I'm learning, Tante." Leopold turned and led Rickenbacker back to the stable.

"That's the special breed we've raised for the Prussian cavalry," Fanny pointed out. "I can't help but wonder how these animals are faring in this war. Not much is said about it, but they must be having a terrible time of it."

As they walked into the office a framed pencil drawing of a horse on the wall caught Anna's eye. "That looks just like the horse Leopold brought over to me."

"That's one of Benno's drawings," Fanny explained. "He's the artist in our family. I'm not sure where he got his talent from. Certainly not from me or Willi."

"Very lifelike," Anna offered. "Looks like the boys are doing a good job here."

"Thank God," said Fanny. "They all learned from their father, and uncle. And they want to prove themselves. They've grown up a lot this year."

"Bertha's girls too," Anna remarked. "I must say. I can see the change in them."

Bertha came into the dining room holding another letter. "I want to show you this." She sat down at the dining room table. "This is what Louie just wrote me. 'The talk here is that Russia's going to give up and Germany will only have to fight on one front.' Here he says, 'If this is true Germany can move to a one-front war and we can end this thing, win this, and go back to living again.'"

"I want this to be over with, too. But who cares about winning?!" Fanny exclaimed.

"It's about *not losing*. That's really what it's about for most of us," Bertha responded. "The way the boys write about it, everyone's tired of it all. It's not easy being a soldier. And when you're forty-three years old? There are a lot of older soldiers now. So many of the younger ones have been killed, or maimed, for what?"

"I just want our husbands back," Fanny asserted.

### Russian Revolutions

After two and a half years of war, five million Russian soldiers had been killed, wounded, or captured. Conditions among soldiers and civilians alike were awful. Hunger and misery were widespread but were most severe in the industrial centers of Petrograd and Moscow, where workers in Russia's factories labored under terrible conditions and suffered deadly shortages of food. They also lacked coal or other means for heating their homes in the bitterly cold winters. Hunger and death, especially for the children, brought mothers into the streets in angry waves.

Under the corrupt and incompetent regime of Czar Nicholas II the population lost any hope for a successful outcome to the war. The Czar had taken over command of the military, which only added to general resentment from all sides. Scandals in the increasingly dysfunctional ruling family ripped holes in the unity of the aristocracy and set in motion plans to depose and replace Nicholas with his brother.

Signs of disintegration and possible revolution in Russia were seized upon by the German military. There was a growing consensus in the German command that the war in the west was unwinnable so long as Germany was fighting on two fronts, and efforts to negotiate a way out did not look feasible. But disaffection among Russians, especially Russian soldiers, opened possibilities. The Germans intensified their efforts to undermine the morale of the Russian soldiers by encouraging contact between German and Russian troops.

In January and February 1917, the Czarist government began to unravel. Huge strikes swept Petrograd and Moscow. The Cossack cavalries, long reliable pillars of Czarist rule, refused to repress the movement. Then the soldiers began to side with the protesting workers. By February, Czar Nicholas was forced out of power and none of his Romanov relatives dared step in. This was the February Revolution, and it brought a liberal bourgeois government to power led by Alexander Kerensky, the new government's minister of war.

While these changes were going on among the ruling sectors of society, from below workers and soldiers had begun to form committees, or councils, to exert their own influence on governing power. They forced the Kerensky government to accept democratic reforms. But the new government was unable to satisfy the most widespread and deeply felt demands of the people for land, food, and an end to the war.

Kerensky's government was allied to and dependent on its Entente allies, France and England, and to Russia's landowning elite and capitalists. They could not and would not end the war.

Kerensky was a talented orator and he stumped up and down the front addressing crowds of troops, arguing that fighting the war was necessary to "save the gains of the revolution." But growing numbers of Russians, including millions of Russian soldiers, wanted nothing more to do with the war and believed that the February Revolution was worthless if it couldn't put an end to the bloody and useless slaughter.

The Bolshevik leader Vladimir Ilyich Lenin was living in exile in Switzerland as this upheaval shook his homeland. The Bolsheviks had long held that the war was a conflict among "imperialist" or "colonialist" powers to redivide the world and inimical to the interests of the Russian workers and peasants. Thus they made ending the war a central goal of their political program. Lenin and other Bolsheviks had fled the country to avoid imprisonment or death. Now, with the abdication of the Czar, they sought to return to Russia. The German military command, recognizing that Bolshevik influence could help end the war on the eastern front, arranged travel for Lenin from Zurich on a sealed train through Germany. Lenin arrived by train in Petrograd in mid-April 1917.

By that summer Kerensky's war offensive was failing, and his government teetering. An attempted right-wing coup against Kerensky failed, in large part because of help from the left-wing parties, most of all the Bolsheviks, whose following among the people, especially among workers and soldiers, was growing rapidly. As the Kerensky government continued to flounder, the Bolsheviks gained support in the workers' and soldiers' councils (soviets).

In addition to promising an end to the war, the Bolsheviks promised to carry out changes that would free the people from the binds of a corrupt system. They had a core of supporters who believed in a longer vision of social transformation and a larger mass of people who were just fed up with the old order and wanted peace. This combination, along with fractious infighting among the ruling powers, paved the way for another, more radical revolution.

In late October 1917 the Bolsheviks seized the levers of power.

## The End of the War on the Eastern Front and the Offensive in the West

Negotiations for a peace treaty between Germany and the now Bolshevik-ruled Russia took place in the town of Brest-Litovsk from late December 1917 to early March 1918. The German military command used the threat of a continued war against Russia to extract huge concessions. The Bolsheviks thus ceded to Germany land that held more than 30 percent of Russia's population, nearly 90 percent of the country's coal resources and 26 percent of its railroads in exchange for an end to the war.

The German high command used the collapse of the Russian war effort to boost morale among its troops and at home. In late May 1918 the German military launched an offensive on the western front that military leaders promised would bring a final victory over the French, the British, their respective colonial reinforcements, and the newly arriving soldiers of the U.S. Army.

The offensive began with an artillery bombardment of the French and German lines unlike anything the war had produced to that point. It allowed the German armies in the West to make initial advances, but they failed to make a decisive breakthrough. In the counterattacks by the French at the Marne in July and by the British in early August, the Germans were forced to retreat with huge losses. Shortages of manpower and resources reached critical levels as demoralization, exhaustion, and the rapid spread of the Spanish flu among the soldiers all took their toll.

The Russian Revolution, and the end of the war in the east, breathed new life into the German military. But it also put into the wind radical ideas that found their way among German troops, who, much like their Russian counterparts, were fed up with the war.

Despite declining morale among Germany's troops, the German military command continued to boast of imminent victory to the public. As late as September 1918, placards appeared around Munich and in other German cities proclaiming, "We have won the war in the East, and we shall win it in the West."

But privately, military commanders saw the collapse of the German war effort approaching. As Germany's military commander Eric Ludendorff said in late September, "The condition of the army demands an immediate armistice in order to avoid catastrophe." He and General Hindenburg delivered this message to a shocked Kaiser on September 29, 1918. Ludendorff himself was very near a nervous breakdown. But he recovered his calm when he came up with a plan to end the war, while saving his own hide, and protecting the military command. With the Kaiser's assent, Ludendorff arranged to turn over governing power to the Social Democratic Party (SPD). The party that had pledged in 1912 to oppose the war and then threw its weight behind the war effort was now being "rewarded" with the reins of power.

In mid-October word began to circulate that this new Social Democratic-led government was going to sue for peace. On October 24 German papers reported that the Kaiser had lost confidence in his military chief and Ludendorff was removed from his post. A week later Ludendorff, wearing civilian clothes and a fake beard, got passage on a train to Sweden.

### Mutiny

Even as Germany's new Social Democratic government was given the burden, and, just as importantly, the onus, of seeking terms of surrender, the German naval command announced a major offensive to break the British blockade and reverse the course of the war.

Except for its submarine fleet, the German navy had been bottled up in North Sea ports for the better part of the war and the offensive they promised had *no chance* of succeeding. One German admiral admitted as much when he described the offensive as a way of achieving "an honorable downfall."

German sailors, no less fed up with the war than the troops on land and aware that the German government was moving toward surrender, were in no mood to be a blood sacrifice for the honor of the admirals. When the order was given to prepare the battleships *Helgoland* and *Thüringen* to sail from the German North Sea port city of Kiel to engage the British, the sailors refused to weigh anchor. The naval command retaliated with mass arrests of rebellious sailors and with threats of execution. These attempts at retribution triggered an even broader rebellion. Sailors, with the political support of workers in nearby factories, organized mass demonstrations. They also seized their ships and arrested their commanding officers. With red flags flying, they marched from the North Sea ports to Germany's populated cities. As German historian Sebastian Haffner wrote years later: "Wherever the sailors went the soldiers from the garrisons and workers from the factories joined them as if they had been waiting for them; there was no serious resistance anywhere; everywhere the existing order cracked like rotten wood."

This was the first week in November 1918. A war was about to end and a revolution about to begin.

―――― 4 ――――

# Revolution, 1918

WHEN THE TRAIN FROM DACHAU pulled into the Munich main station in mid-November 1918 only a few weeks had passed since the war had come to an end with Germany's surrender. Benno, discharged from the military, saw the crowds in the station and felt an excitement that had not been there when he'd left for duty fourteen months before. There were young guards in uniform among the crowds. They bore guns. Their upper arms sported red armbands. They were stern but polite and called people "comrades." For Benno this was very disorienting.

Anna, Fritz, and Hani were at the station awaiting Benno's arrival. Benno came off the train wearing a long green-gray trench coat and a wide-brimmed hat and happily greeted his family. "Fritz and Hani, you look so much more grown up! I can't believe it's been only a few months since I last saw you." After giving them big hugs, he asked if they could all walk the two and a half kilometers to their apartment. In his last days at Dachau, he'd heard what sounded like wild rumors of a city in turmoil, and he wanted to see it for himself. As they walked together past the towers of the Frauenkirche and the New Town hall at Marienplatz, Anna reminded Benno that they were retracing the steps of her first tour of Munich eleven years earlier.

Benno was struck by the scars of war evident on the streets. There were now more wounded veterans in the crowds—men missing limbs, men with grievous facial wounds evident even behind high collars and hats pulled down low. There were people who seemed weakened by the deprivations of the war, and there were more people asking for help than he had ever seen.

But there was new energy as well. Benno gazed with amazement at walls and posts plastered with a variety of flyers and posters—calls for meetings, notices of new policies, bulletins with appeals to the public to conserve fuel in the face of shortages. There were colorful flags everywhere: the blue and white flag of Bavaria; the black and yellow Munich city flag; the black, red, and gold of the new German Federal Republic. Most conspicuous for their uniqueness and significance were the red flags flying from government buildings and tied to light posts—the emblem of the new socialist Munich that had been proclaimed eleven days earlier. Conspicuously absent were the black, white, and red flags of the Kaiser and the Second Reich—the ones that were flying when Benno left for Dachau.

The revolution that began among sailors in Germany's northern seacoast cities set off waves of protests for peace and democratic reforms throughout the country. On November 2, 1918, Bavaria's king, Ludwig III, hastily approved democratic reforms meant to pacify a war-weary but energized population. The Bavarian government would now rule by parliamentary majority rather than royal consent. But this change in governance failed to calm the revolutionary passions.

Anna described to Benno a flyer she'd seen for a rally on November 7 at Munich's Theresienwiese parade grounds. It was that rally that would mark the beginning of the Munich revolution.

"I saw such a flyer myself," Benno remarked. "I don't know how it got out to us in Dachau."

The November 7 demonstration was organized by different factions of the Social Democratic Party. The more conservative mainstream SDP allied with the new political authorities in Berlin wanted to rally and then march to "boil off" some of the rebellious steam building up among the people. The more radical Independent Social Democrats, or USPD, wanted a rally that would arouse and direct this rebellious energy against the ruling authorities, in order to bring about a change in power.

At the end of the rally at the Theresienwiese the demonstration broke into two distinct marches. One procession was led by Erhard Auer, leader of the more conservative SDP. It moved south from the rally site, intersected the broad Prinzregentenstrasse, and headed toward the Isar River. Anna was out on Prinzregentenstrasse with her children just as the huge, noisy, but good-natured crowd moved past.

"You should have seen all the people marching!" Hani enthused to her father. "We waved to the crowd. And they waved back!"

"It was the biggest march I've ever seen," Anna commented.

"Where did it end?" Benno asked his family.

"At the Friedensengel?" Fritz answered, not certain that was correct.

"You're right," said Anna.

Benno looked at his son and daughter, "The 'Angel of Peace' Monument. Do you know why that monument was built?"

"No," they both answered.

"To honor the years of peace following the Franco-Prussian War." Benno turned to his wife. "It seems every monument to peace has its built-in irony."

### Kurt Eisner

While Anna, Fritz, and Hani waited on Prinzregentenstrasse for the procession under the leadership of the mainstream SDP, a second march, led by Kurt Eisner, a Jewish-born writer and a leader of the more radical antiwar USDP, left the Theresienwiese parade grounds heading in a different direction. Eisner's march headed north toward a public school that was being used as a military barracks. The aim of the protesters was to challenge the soldiers to join them. As they approached the school, the soldiers inside hung red flags out of their windows as a sign of rebellion against the government. This brought loud cheers from the crowd. The soldiers answered the chants and calls from the marchers with their own chants of "Down with the war!" "Long live peace!" and "Long live the Republic!"

At eight o'clock that evening of November 7 the Bavarian Minister of War sent word to Bavaria's King Ludwig III and the Wittelsbach royal family of what had suddenly become apparent—he had lost control of the military. The royal family realized that they had best leave Munich. They decided to go to Switzerland. But in order to do so they had to hire a car and driver because the family's regular chauffeur had joined the revolution! The Wittelsbachs planned to return to Munich as soon as tempers calmed. But this return never happened. The royals eventually made their way to Hungary, and thus the 738-year rule of the Wittelsbach dynasty in Bavaria came to an end.

By ten o'clock the night of November 7, the rebels under Kurt Eisner's leadership formed a political structure of the kind that was beginning to appear all over Germany: a Workers' and Soldiers' Council. The new Council elected Eisner as its chairman, while his supporters fanned out to occupy key buildings in central Munich. Eisner led a group of rebels to the nearby Parliament building where he proclaimed the founding of a new government. It had been barely a month since Eisner had been released from Munich's Stadelheim Prison for leading a strike of Krupp munitions workers in protest of the war. Now he was the president of the newly formed "Free State of Bavaria."

The new government came to power without a shot being fired. The rapid collapse of the old order shook society to its core. The revolution stirred hope in some and despair in others but society at large was awakened. The city was awash with announcements that the "Workers' and Soldiers' Council" had taken over the city government and that the military and civil authorities had submitted. Across Germany, kings, princes, and dukes were being deposed, but *nowhere* had the more radical wing of that anti-militarist movement taken hold of power as it did in Munich.

### AT THE SYNAGOGUE

On November 9, two days after the revolution brought the new government to power in Munich, Anna went with her children to the Haupt Synagogue. The sanctuary was packed with congregants too excited to stay home. They were anxious to hear what the rabbi had to say and to discuss the stunning events with fellow congregants. At that point Germany was still officially at war and little was known about the terms Germany would have to accept as a consequence of its defeat.

On their way back from the synagogue Anna paused at a newspaper stand where a crowd had gathered. Someone was excitedly discussing the news that Kaiser Wilhelm had abdicated.

"He's on a train to Holland," a tall woman in a long blue work coat yelled.

"And I hope they seal the border!" one man shouted.

"They should send him back here, let him explain to the people what all those years of sacrifice were about!" yelled another.

"I say we put him on a diet of turnips for a few years." The remark, by an older woman in a nurse's hat and a shawl, drew laughter.

"Scheidemann declared a parliamentary republic in Berlin," someone called out.

"Who's Scheidemann?" someone else asked.

"A Social Democrat, with Ebert, one of the leaders of the new government." An elderly man explained. Friedrich Ebert, the leader of the Social Democratic Party, would soon be named president of the new republic.

"But," the woman in the work coat spoke excitedly, "Liebknecht has declared a socialist republic . . ."

"How many governments can we have at one time?" Someone called out, either in anger or astonishment, it was hard to tell.

Amid debates over what kind of government Munich should

have Anna heard someone say, "We certainly don't want the Jews running things!" eliciting murmurs of agreement. Then someone else responded, "We don't need that kind of divisiveness. It's the militarists, not Jews, who've brought us to this sorry state." Anna was relieved to hear that sentiment. She thought of the words she would use if she found the nerve to speak. She felt contempt for the military leaders and cheered at the passionate denunciations of the war.

The future was unsettled and uncertain. Anna's family's economic standing was in doubt. But the depressed anxiety that had gripped Munich in the last year of the war was giving way to this explosion of political awakening and initiative. Anna found the situation stimulating, even exhilarating. But what to make of it all? She headed home, hoping to see a neighbor or two just so she could compare notes and continue the conversation. She thought of her sisters in Traunstein and wished she could talk things over with them now. And her father? What would Moses say in a moment like this? She thought of his old metaphor, "You need to cultivate the roots of Jewish tradition so we can withstand the storm." "Well, Papa," she thought, "the storm's arrived."

### Postwar Munich

Benno also found the atmosphere of the city exciting, and he took a great interest in Anna's descriptions of events she'd witnessed. But he was alarmed at the radical, egalitarian talk he heard coming from the partisans of the new governing order. He had heard rumors about the Workers' and Soldiers' Councils but knew little about them. He did not support a radical overthrow of the old order. He was mainly concerned about restoring economic stability. He had little faith that the Eisner government could do that.

Benno hoped to see things settle down and return to a more accustomed "normalcy." With their savings depleted and the government edging toward defaulting on war bonds, Benno realized that a great deal of his modest fortune was now either gone or withering. His only hope was that land prices would begin to rise so he could sell some properties for much needed cash. For that to happen there would have to be economic stability.

If he'd had his way Benno would have gladly returned to the Germany that existed before the war. This was a point on which he and Anna disagreed. Yes, it was a time of relative prosperity and social peace, Anna conceded, "But if that world before 1914 gave us this horrifying war, why would we want to go back to it? Don't we need to address the conditions that produced such a disaster?"

"You're listening to the radicals, Anna," was Benno's reply. "And their program will not be good for Germany or for us."

Such discussions were taking place throughout the country in gatherings with friends, at beer halls, in restaurants and cafés, in churches and synagogues, and on the streets.

Most of those in Benno and Anna's circle of family and friends shared feelings of deep disgust toward the war, its horrific cost in lives—two million German soldiers killed, seven million wounded, tens of millions more across Europe and Russia—and the lies promoted to sustain it. But there were others in Munich, a minority at first, who did not regard the war itself as the disaster. They held that the real disaster wasn't the *war*, but the *defeat* Germany suffered in the war.

What began as opposed opinions, soon became opposed orientations. And those who held different views gradually began to isolate from each other. A polarization of opinions was rapidly setting in.

## Radicalization and Repression

The old parliamentary-monarchial system, the Second Reich, was over, carried off on the train that took Kaiser Wilhelm to a comfortable, if restless, retirement in Holland. But the new government that came to power, led by the mainstream Social Democratic Party, and generally referred to as the German Republic (and later, the Weimar Republic) left intact nearly all other institutional powers, including, very importantly, the old military.

There were sharp divisions within the governing structure from the very beginning of the new republic. Nowhere were these divisions more evident than in Munich. Eisner was successful for a time in reconciling opposing sides—those who wanted to continue with something like the old parliamentary system, essentially the old order without the royal Wittelsbachs—and others who wanted to replace the power of the ruling elites with Workers' and Soldiers' Councils at the center of political power, as a step toward a radical reorganization of society from the bottom up. Eisner was able to maintain a certain stability amid these wrenching divisions because he had the support and trust of many Bavarian farmers and workers. Meanwhile many middle- and upper-class Bavarians were skeptical of Eisner, if not openly hostile.

### An Assassination

In January 1919, treaty negotiations between Germany and the victorious Allied Powers (France, Great Britain, the United States) began in Versailles, France.

Meanwhile, Bavarian parliamentary elections were held in Munich. The Bavarian People's Party, a conservative Catholic group that promoted openly anti-Jewish views, won the majority. The SDP, which was the party that held power in Berlin, came in a close second. Eisner's party, the USDP, garnered little more than 2 percent of the vote. This was a devastating defeat for them.

February 21, 1919, was a cold, rainy Friday morning, and Kurt Eisner, accompanied by his wife, a political associate, and several bodyguards, set off on foot to an assembly of the Munich Parliament and the Councils. Eisner carried with him a resignation speech he intended to read to the assembly. He never arrived. En route to the meeting a young man who had been waiting for Eisner in a doorway shot the Bavarian prime minister twice, hitting him in the head and lungs. One of Eisner's bodyguards fired at and wounded the shooter, but Eisner died on the spot.

The murderer, who called himself Count Arco auf Valley, was

a right-wing nationalist and an admirer of a Munich group called the Thule Society, one of a number of groups in Munich that were coalescing around extreme nationalist views. Count Arco had been rejected from membership in that group because his mother was Jewish. To prove himself worthy Valley took it upon himself to murder Eisner—the radical Jewish politician, an avowed opponent of the war, and the embodiment of the social reforms hated by the extreme nationalists.

Rage and revulsion occupied Munich in the days following the murder. Marches, gatherings, and flyers called for a "second revolution." In a spasm of violence Erhard Auer—the leader of the conservative SPD majority, a Minister of the Interior in Eisner's government and a political rival of Eisner's—was shot and wounded by an Eisner follower.

Like so many others in Munich and in the surrounding region, Benno and Anna were shaken by Eisner's murder and the events that accompanied it. They made a point of going to the synagogue the day after the assassination, feeling a need to be with their community. Benno and Anna greeted friends and joined one of the clusters of people engaged in discussion.

"I was not a supporter of Eisner," said Herr Klein, a young lawyer and a relatively new member of the congregation, "but I give him credit for trying to bring people with different views and programs together."

"It's the crowd he surrounded himself with that's the problem," offered a cantor, who pulled a prayer shawl around him to fight the morning chill. "There are people among them who would have us go the direction of Russia."

Herr Klein replied, "We don't even know what is going on there! People are just using Russia and what they claim is happening there as a scare tactic!"

"What was he to do?" asked Herr Neuman, an active member of the congregation and a business acquaintance of Benno's. "Eisner took a stand against the war and went to jail for it. It took courage to do that. Now he's been murdered for it."

"He was moving toward a Council government with the revolutionaries. It's too extreme," the cantor replied. "The people rejected that road in the election. The people want a normal republic."

"Let me tell you something." An older man in a dark suit coat pulled a paper out of an inside pocket. "The people who went after Eisner are not our friends, regardless of what we think about him or whether he'd have been successful or not. I got this flyer on the street yesterday." He unfolded the paper slowly, his hands shaking as he began to read. "'Eisner, the Bolshevik Jew, got what he deserved. He and the cowardly Jewish filth he is part of had better beware. We know how they betrayed us in the war and sold us out to our enemies, and we will never forget that. We will never let the Jews rule us!'"

It was as if an icy wind had passed over them. Then came an angry voice: "Betrayed, in the war? What a filthy lie! Who signed that?"

"Some group calling itself the 'Union of Patriots.'"

A tall man wearing a dark gray cap shouted out in a raspy voice: "Damnable lies! The Kaiser and the military dragged us through this bloody war for four years—left us wounded and starved—but now we Jews are to blame for it all! Seriously?"

A woman in a long dark woolen coat standing next to him was also very agitated. "We lived through this. We know who kept telling us the war was won— kept people going, believing, stringing us along!"

"I think you're talking about Ludendorff," Herr Klein put in.

"Our hero!" came the loud reply from the raspy voice. "Don't talk bad of him. The war's been hard on him."

"Ludendorff and Hindenburg now accuse the new government of negotiating surrender behind their backs," said Herr Neuman.

The older man who'd read the flyer spoke: "Some say Germany could not have lost the war—there had to have been betrayal."

The woman in the dark coat was indignant. "Betrayal? Our soldiers were starving while the British were getting fat! My nephew was at the Marne when our army overran the British trenches. He said, 'Mama, you should see the food they had. We were living on worms, and they were dining on corned beef! Seeing that, you knew the war was lost.' That's what he wrote me!"

"It's just a fringe group promoting those extreme views. I wouldn't worry too much about that," counseled the cantor.

Anna, feeling nervous but angry spoke up at that point. "My brother-in-law, Louie, wrote from the front that soldiers he was with were fed up with the terrible food and conditions, and were talking about how they wanted to go home. Louie overheard one of the officers say to a group of the soldiers in his unit, 'Don't give up, this is what the Jews want you to do!' The officer didn't have the nerve to say that in front of my brother-in-law."

"It should not be a surprise that the military's spreading this stuff too," Herr Klein added.

Benno listened intently, but quietly. He was happy that Anna had spoken up. He felt shy about speaking in this situation. He felt he could give a cogent argument for why Germany could not have won the war. But he would wait for a time when he felt more comfortable to make that case.

Benno was critical of the people who were either naïve or stupid enough to go along with the lies that Germany was somehow betrayed. But Anna disagreed. She said she could understand why some people were shocked and were questioning how the defeat could have come so abruptly. "All along, the military leaders and the newspapers told us the war was going well—especially after the Russians pulled out of the war. This was disorienting," she argued. The German collapse seemed especially sudden for those who had no contact with demoralized soldiers.

Now the war was over and a war within Germany was raging. Benno feared that the radical people in Eisner's government would seek revenge for his murder and would push for a more extreme revolution, even a Council Republic along the lines of the Bolshevik government in Russia. At the same time, he was shaken by the hateful talk about Eisner and the vicious accusations against Jews. All this made him feel a fear he had never experienced before.

Benno and Anna had always related to the Liberal Party, a

moderate party that supported a parliamentary democratic order. It rejected the extreme nationalist and racialist groups like the Thule society and opposed those on the left advocating for socialism as well. But the Liberals were losing their support. From where Benno stood, it felt like the middle ground was disappearing.

### "Fluttering Birds"

The following day Anna took ten-year-old Fritz along to a market a few blocks from their apartment. They were on their way back when they heard the sound of a motor reverberating among the buildings. Anna saw several airplanes swoop down low just above apartment rooftops. They made several passes and during the third pass a cloud of objects that looked like birds flew out of them. Fritz ran down the block to where the objects were fluttering to the ground. Anna panicked. "Stop!" she screamed.

But he continued to where the "birds" had landed. He picked one up and ran back to her.

"It's just a paper, Mama," he shouted.

Anna's heart was pounding wildly, and her face flushed with heat. "You listen, and don't you run from me like that!" She grabbed the paper from Fritz's hand and put it in her purse.

Later, in a calmer moment, Anna fished the flyer out of her purse. It was a notice to the Munich population that martial law was being declared and a curfew would go into effect at 7 p.m. beginning that evening and for the foreseeable future. It was signed, "By order of the Council Republic." This government was led by the more radical left members of Eisner's former administration.

"What does 'martial law' mean? And 'curfew'?" asked Fritz.

"It means we have to get home early and not leave until morning, because the Bavarian president was killed."

### The Funeral March

Five days after Eisner's assassination, tens of thousands of people gathered in downtown Munich for a funeral march. Benno joined them, in part out of curiosity, and in part from sympathy. In the crowd there were farmers from rural villages around Bavaria and members of workers' groups who saw Eisner's program as something partisan to them. Some people came out of respect for his courage in speaking against the war when it was dangerous to do so. There were middle-class Germans like Benno who came to show a solidarity with Eisner in death that they would have never demonstrated for him in life.

Anna stood among the crowd that packed the sidewalks to view the funeral procession. She was dressed in a warm sweater and a long wool coat but still felt cold. She was happy to blend into the crowd that sheltered her from the chill breeze, though it also blocked her view of the procession.

Fritz, trapped by a wall of people in front of him, scampered through the crowd and found a streetlight platform where some other boys were standing. He scrambled up to get a better view. Anna tried lifting Hani so she could catch a glance of the march, but she was too heavy and gave up.

"Why are all these people marching?" Hani wanted to know.

"Because Herr Eisner, the prime minister, was killed," said Anna.

"Why was he killed?"

"Because he wanted to have a different kind of government, and some people didn't like that."

"What kind of government?"

"One where there is no war," Anna said.

Fritz was able to see the funeral march from his vantage point and later described to his mother and sister the casket surrounded by flowers and the groups of mourners in work clothes and soldiers in uniform. He also remembered the words on one of the banners that called for revenge for the death of the murdered prime minister.

Anna felt grief for Eisner who, for all his weaknesses, had the courage to stand up for a more humane Germany, a Germany without its militarism. The things that Benno disliked in

Eisner—his poetic bent, for example, which he thought would not make for a good political leader—Anna saw as an asset. She also felt intuitively, though she had no concrete proof, that an Eisner government would be better for women's concerns.

Despite the assassination, Anna also felt more hopeful than Benno that the November 7 revolution could open the way for something better. The size of the funeral strengthened her conviction that this was possible.

### New Governments

The Bavarian Parliament, brought to power in the January 1919 election, disbanded under the pressure of the revolutionary upsurge following Eisner's death. In April a group of pacifist intellectuals proclaimed a "Räte," or Council Republic ruled by Workers' and Soldiers' Councils. But this government was quickly replaced by one with a more radical approach inspired by the Russian Bolsheviks. That effort was bolstered by news that a revolutionary government had come to power in Hungary under the leadership of Bela Kun, a Lenin supporter. For a moment the socialists in Munich were buoyed by what seemed like a revolutionary wave about to sweep Europe. There was even talk of a second revolution in Munich.

But the effort to carry out a radical transformation in Bavaria lacked both a clear plan and the popular support needed to face a powerful enemy that was mobilizing against it. The German revolution that began among the North Sea sailors and spread across the country had been met by a counterrevolution spearheaded by well-armed militias called Freikorps. These military units, made up mainly of war veterans, were inspired politically and ideologically by the German military command, by monarchists, and by right-wing nationalists. But they were supported by the Social Democrats and were led by Gustav Noske, the Social Democrat Minister of Defense.

Freikorps troops violently suppressed the revolution in Berlin, in the Ruhr Valley, and in other places where it had risen most strongly. By the spring of 1919, Freikorps units were heading toward Munich.

## The Counterrevolution

By April 1919 Freikorps troops, destined for Munich, clashed with members of Munich's revolutionary government near Dachau. The radical leaders of Munich's government formed a militia they called the "Red Army." As the Freikorps headed to Munich members of this militarized force arrested a number of local aristocrats and adherents of the Thule Society, and held them hostage in the Luitpold Gymnasium (a high school). On April 30, as the Freikorps neared the city, enraged members of the Red Army killed the hostages.

On May 1, thirty thousand Freikorps troops entered Munich. A few hundred committed revolutionaries fought them, but their resistance was quickly overcome. Other supporters of Munich's revolutionary government, seeing the momentum turn against the revolution, quietly put away their red flags and arm bands and tried to blend into the population. In the days that followed, roving groups of heavily armed rightists wearing white arm bands rooted out and murdered hundreds of members and supporters of Munich's revolutionary government and others who were considered "subversives." Thousands were jailed. In justifying the widespread murder and terror, the Freikorps cited the killings of the hostages at the Luitpold Gymnasium.

The Freikorps promoted themselves as a fortress of order and masculinity in what they considered a hostile world of democratic egalitarianism, communist internationalism, feminism, and gay rights. While carrying out repression against the leftists, Freikorps units made no secret of their contempt for Jews. They were influenced by propaganda from the military command that Jews were complicit in Germany's defeat in the war. They further demonized Jews by claiming that Munich's revolution was a Jewish affair. As conservative forces gained the upper hand these views attracted a widespread following.

The fighting between the Red Army and the Freikorps continued throughout the week of May 1 to May 6, 1919. In their home on Liebherrstrasse, Benno and Anna could occasionally hear the sounds of mortar, artillery, and machine-gun fire on Ludwigstrasse and the buzz and whine of attacking aircraft sent to crush the Munich revolution.

### A Chilling Reunion

Berthold and Rolf were already nursing beers on the awning-covered patio of the Kunstlerhaus when Benno and Götz arrived. While both men had had recent contact with their friend Berthold, neither had seen Rolf since shortly after the war began. He looked older, as they all did, but he seemed healthy.

They all shook hands and slapped each other's backs on this late summer afternoon, and then Berthold roared, "Seems we've all survived war, bad governments, and even blood in the streets. How many more plagues to go for us?"

Benno laughed. "I think we just passed eleven. That should put us in the clear."

"But who got free after all this suffering?" asked Rolf.

"The Kaiser, I suppose!" said Benno as he pulled up a chair next to Berthold.

"And he didn't have to cross the Red Sea to get there—only the Dutch border!" Götz noted with a smile.

At that moment Gustav and Werner appeared. Gustav still had his rotund stocky figure, but its dimensions had changed. The war's deprivations had trimmed him down some, as it had all of them. Still, the men all bellowed to each other how they looked exactly as they had before. Gustav snorted. "We've all become such talented liars. And they say no blessings come with age!"

Like Benno, most of the group had served during the war as older soldiers assigned to guard or logistics duties. Only Berthold had been outside German borders—in Belgium, where he had been attached to the supply detail of an artillery unit. "I must have loaded enough artillery and mortar shells to blow up half the continent," he joked.

Just as Benno asked if anyone had heard from Julius, he appeared like an apparition from behind a waitress delivering their beers and pretzels. Of them all, Julius had aged the most. There was something more in his face than the passage of time—a weary look in his eyes as he greeted his old friends. Götz reached a hand to his friend. "Julius, we've just begun discussing our exploits in the war. Seems to me the war might have had a different outcome if the heroes at this table had been given the chance at the front."

"Well, I was with all of you then—nowhere near the front. I was sent to Alsace. And because I speak some French, I was asked to question French prisoners to get to their state of mind."

Götz's face lit up. "What did you find out?"

"By the time I got there they were tired of the war. But they wanted Alsace back and deeply resented our control of it."

"You all got to play soldier but me," Gustav lamented. "They sent me home when I reported, claimed they couldn't find a uniform to fit me."

Werner regarded Gustav with a wry smile. "Just as well. Why use up an entire platoon's supply of cloth for one recruit?"

The men drank a toast to their wartime survival. Then Julius spoke up. The emotional break in his voice brought the table to silence. "My son was part of the spring offensive. He turned eighteen toward the end of 1917 and was sent to the Marne with a lot of other young boys. He was a fast runner, so they trained him to be a stormtrooper." He took a deep breath. "The plan was to overrun the British lines and bring the war to an end before the Americans could arrive. But his first week in battle, he was hit with flying metal from a shell." He put his hands over his eyes and rubbed them. "The shrapnel tore into his shoulder and face."

Gustav put a bear-like arm around him. "You don't have to say any more. We're sorry."

After a few moments, Julius lifted his head. "We've all suffered losses. But it's hard to see a young man, such a young man . . . so horribly wounded."

There was a pause. Then Rolf said, "Every day I hear stories of the terrible sacrifices of our soldiers at the front." There was a silent shaking of heads. "And I've heard informed comments on how we had the war won—could have won—but the troops were betrayed."

"Betrayed?" Werner looked at Rolf with a puzzled expression. "I don't believe that. You know how many thousands of American troops were on their way to join the British last summer? We didn't have a chance."

Rolf's expression was stone-like. "Take a closer look. We had the British on the run. We might've ended it before the Americans arrived if morale hadn't collapsed—if the support of our troops at home hadn't been undermined."

Berthold shook his head. "I think the German soldier was tired, fed up with it all. Yah, a lot of the young ones were enthusiastic—and brave—but not determined. There's a difference. Young guys get excited. But the excitement disappears quickly when you're outgunned, out-resourced, out-manned. And let's not forget how the Spanish flu spread through the ranks. It almost did me in!"

"I wonder what Arnulf would say about all this," Gustav said.

Götz jumped in. "I saw him! He's not doing well. He got hurt—not at the front, but in some accident on duty behind the lines. Now he's torn up by what's happened here in Munich."

"Meaning what?" Benno inquired.

"Meaning, he has friends who've been killed or arrested since . . ." Götz lowered his voice "Since the Freikorps arrived. Friends who were part of the Councils. He's bitter because the SPD and Noske sent these assassins—that's how he describes the Freikorps—to Munich."

"Well, someone had to stop our Bolsheviks." Werner folded his arms over his chest. "They got a bit out of hand."

Rolf leaned forward and pressed his hands into the table. "They did what they needed to do."

Götz looked nervously around the table. "Please, let's keep this conversation to ourselves. There are people still being picked up on rumors that they supported the socialists. Arnulf told me he has friends who were killed or jailed, simply for their ideas."

Without lowering his voice, Rolf continued. "Some of the people he seems to call friends did some killing too—those hostages at the Luitpold Gymnasium, for example."

"In any case, the Freikorps' violence has been much worse," Julius insisted.

"But necessary!" Rolf slammed his fist down.

Götz stood up. "So, instead of uniting us, the war is dividing us."

"You don't speak out against a war when your country is at risk!"

"We've heard the talk, Rolf." Benno spoke slowly, in a low voice. "They're looking for someone to blame."

"We know who's to blame!!" Rolf popped up out of his chair. "There's Eisner. And then the other socialist bandits—those Munich Council leaders, you know—Landauer, Toller, that guy Levien, Mühsam . . . I forget all their names." He paused. "It's not a secret, they're all Jews!"

"Levien's a Christian!" Berthold responded. "And what is this? Why is it that whenever something goes wrong in this country, people turn on Jews?"

Rolf shrugged. "There are reasons . . ."

Benno tried to remain calm. "We need to talk more about this." Benno motioned to Götz to sit, which he did, reluctantly. Benno continued. "What about all the supporters of the Council Republic who were not Jews?"

"It appears to me, and others, that Jews led the whole show." Rolf's face reddened.

Götz looked like he was ready to jump up again. "The ones you mentioned were Jews by birth only. They wouldn't know a Torah if they ran into one!"

"Who do you think undermined the war effort? If it wasn't the Jews . . ."

"You can't be serious, Rolf!" shouted Götz.

"And do you count Julius's son among those who undermined the war effort?" asked Berthold.

"Of course not." Rolf took a big swig of his beer. "These are matters of life and death for the *country*. And there are things that have been kept from us—all of us, you as well. Someone has to speak the truth."

Gustav shook his head. "Benno, you usually have something to say along these lines, I mean as a student of history and such, no?"

Benno looked up from the beer in front of him. "We fought a two-front war for three years. France and England had only one front to contend with. England never lost control of the seas and choked off our imports. Germany had the advantage in a short war, but the disadvantage in a long one." He paused and stroked his chin. "I don't believe in simplistic answers or finding someone to blame. We have to look at the bigger picture."

Berthold turned to Rolf. "You've known us for years, Rolf. Are you saying we betrayed the country?"

Rolf, breathing heavily, looked away from the table. "Not you personally. But I don't know if you're just naïve or trying to...hide something."

"Hide something?" Benno's eyebrows arched.

Gustav raised his hand. "I think, my friends, we're all tired."

"We've all been through a lot," Werner added. "We should just calm down, drink our beers, go home, and get some sleep." He offered a round of goodbyes, then stood up and left.

Benno and Berthold were the last to leave the Kunstlerhaus. After the others had gone, they spoke about how this reunion had felt both bewildering and disheartening. They had all anticipated a different outcome to the war. Now an undercurrent of hatefulness was surfacing—even among those they'd considered friends.

Nevertheless, they would go on believing that the inevitable challenges and events of everyday life would cover the wounds. Over time, the sting of the war and its loss would fade, and, with it, so too the irrational finger pointing. Perhaps a deeper understanding of what happened would emerge.

As they left the restaurant, they saw a small group of young Freikorps soldiers across the street from the café. They were standing on the sidewalk near a truck. They were wearing their long gray coats and leggings, and high leather boots. They had the relaxed demeanor of young fellows on an outing and did not appear to be armed. Several of them had white markings on their helmets that caught Benno and Berthold's attention—a crooked cross that they'd heard was called a "swastika." They'd seen the design in pictures, but this was the first time they'd seen one in public.

## A Dark Undergrowth

In the early winter of 1920, Anna went with a group from the Jewish Women's Association to a prayer room in a small building on Reichenbachstrasse. During the war members of the committee had been meeting there with Ostjuden women—Eastern European Jews from Russia, Austria-Hungary, and Poland who lived in Munich's Isarvorstadt district. Together they were working on problems such as food shortages, schooling, and health matters. After the war, these meetings became even more important, especially after March 1920, when the right-wing politician Gustav von Kahr became Bavaria's prime minister. Kahr, pandering to the anti-immigrant and anti-Semitic sections of the Bavarian population, soon began making loud public threats to deport these Jewish immigrants.

Anna's Jewish women's group was meeting to discuss how they might marshal their leverage as German-born Jews to defend their immigrant sisters and their families. As they arrived at the Isarvorstadt district prayer room they were met by a group cleaning up paint that had been thrown on the building the night before. The group dropped their cleaning rags and tools and greeted the visitors. Raissa, a tall woman with hair covered by a brown scarf, greeted Anna with an enthusiastic hug.

Anna had become friendly with this animated woman, who had gray-green eyes and prominent eyebrows. Raissa was always quick to joke. Her willingness to express whatever thought came to her in a newly acquired, if sometimes crudely used, German made her both an object of some amusement but also admiration.

When Anna asked Raissa how she was doing, she answered, "A little afraid now, we all a little afraid now. Munich not so friendly for us. I not go out much as before."

After exchanging information on the state of their children, Raissa fished a paper out of a pocket of her long, black skirt and unfolded it. On it she had written the name of a book she'd seen in a Munich bookstore, *Die Geheimnisse der Weisen von Zion*. The words "*der Weisen von Zion*," which she understood to mean "the wise men of Zion," had caught her eye. She suspected this book was like one that had appeared in Russia years before. But she wanted to be sure. "*Die Geheimnisse*," explained Anna, "means 'the rules, the guide' for something."

Raissa nodded. "Yes, must be that I think. This is book of Jewish, how to say, not talk about things. But no real, pretend . . . um, not true things."

Anna paused trying to piece together Raissa's broken German. "Not true things? You mean lies?"

Raissa nodded. "Very no good for us, for Jews. The hate people use book, very much hate. The killers, you know? Where I from."

"Okay, you mean the anti-Semites in Russia use this book?"

"Ahh, yes!" Raissa nodded vigorously.

Anna mentioned the book to others in the women's group and later to Benno. None had heard of it. But in months to come word about it began to seep out, and it appeared on the shelves of several Munich bookstores in the early winter of 1920. Benno first saw a copy at a gathering called by a Zionist group. Benno almost never went to meetings of any kind, including ones called by Zionists, who, for the most part, he did not like. He thought they purposefully exaggerated anti-Semitism in Germany to attract adherents, and he strongly disagreed with their message that Jews could not live in a country with non-Jews. But he went to this meeting because the poster advertising it promised to present new information on how anti-Semites were operating in Munich.

The presenter was a young man who introduced himself as Robert. His round glasses and receding hairline gave him an intense and scholarly look. He wrote for a Zionist paper called *Judische Rundschau*. After greeting the small audience, Robert began his presentation. He described how Munich's anti-Semites were becoming more aggressive in their campaign to blame Jews for the loss of the war. A rash of small groups were gaining adherents among bitter and disoriented demobilized soldiers and middle-class Germans eager to find a culprit both for Germany's postwar troubles and their own personal economic distress. He described these groups' compositions and showed copies of the flyers and posters they used to popularize their views and seek new members. "Furthermore," he explained, as he paced the front of the room, "they're all filled with vitriol for the now defeated revolution. They all describe the Council Republic as a Jewish blemish on German society—even a diabolical Jewish plot to dominate the German nation."

At this point the presenter held up a copy of *Protocols of the Elders of Zion*—the book Anna had mentioned to Benno some months before. "This," Robert paused to find the right words, "elaborate lie first appeared in Russia around 1903. This volume is the first version of this slanderous rubbish I've seen published in German." Robert handed the book to a person in the front row and asked them to pass it around. "It was and continues to be hailed as the revelation of a great secret—a Jewish conspiracy dedicated to taking over the world!" He turned to someone who'd let out a laugh. "We may find it ludicrous. But in Russia and Poland it deepened the hatred of Jews and amplified the violence of the pogroms. We've traced this work to a pro-Czarist journalist. It was widely distributed in Russian after 1905. It's said that the original version of this document was an accusation directed against the Bonapartists and Freemasons in France—accusing them of plotting to take over the world. The anti-Semites just substituted the word 'Jew' in place of 'Bonapartists.' Now this *shanda*, this sham, has surfaced in Germany. The anti-Semites find it useful." He rested his hands now on the table in front of him and leaned forward. "And that's because it 'explains' the obvious contradiction that Jews are, at once, denounced as the great exploiters under capitalism, the bankers, and so on, and the 'dark forces' behind the Communist revolution against capitalism. *Protocols* has an explanation!" Here he paused and looked around the room at the fifteen or so attendees. "Jews promote two opposing political and economic systems, as tools in an elaborate conspiracy *to enslave* the non-Jewish world!"

Robert described *Protocols* as tediously boring and repetitive, but he said that its simplicity serves its purpose. "Its message is easy to grasp. And as an 'underground' movement, belief in the *Protocols* lives outside the realm of open public discourse. Shielded from rational scrutiny, its poison can seep into the veins of those who want simple explanations for the complex and painful realities of our world. It has a fantastical quality that makes the reader feel like they have come upon some dark and powerful secret. It validates and magnifies whatever misconceptions and prejudices of Jews they may have. Here, the anti-Semite says to himself—as I've heard people say in so many words—'I *knew* there was something sinister about those people, and now the truth has been revealed!'"

Questions followed about how to counter the lies Robert spoke to and what Jewish organizations were doing to expose them. "We have our 'solutions,'" said Robert, "and we write about them in our paper, so I hope you'll subscribe. The problem, of course, is that if *Judische Rundschau* publishes an article—with evidence—exposing this fraud and what it represents, the anti-Semites will say, 'Well of course the Jews will deny it, that's part of how they operate!' And if a non-Jewish source does likewise, the anti-Semites will say, 'See how many useful idiots are in pay to the Jews!' But we can't give up, and we won't! Even as we realize that for every lie we swat away," here he waved his hand as if batting away a mosquito, "a new one comes to take its place."

After some discussion among the attendees that included some heated disagreements about the Munich revolution and about its Jewish leaders, Benno got up to leave. As he reached the door an older woman pressed a copy of *Judische Rundschau* into his hand and urged him to subscribe. He took the paper home and left it on the dining table with the intention of reading it and showing it to Anna. But he felt conflicted about whether to bring this up with her and soon, in the shuffle of other events, he forgot about it.

# 5

## The 1920s

ONE MORNING, ELEVEN-YEAR-OLD Hani was walking to school with her brother Fritz, then twelve. They were on Thierschstrasse, several blocks from their family's Liebherrstrasse apartment, when a dog walker wearing a trench coat passed them. Fritz turned to his sister. "You know who that is?"⁵

Hani looked back as the man moved away from them. "No. I've seen him before. But I don't know him." Hani looked at Fritz with an indifferent expression. "Why should I?"

"His name is Hitler and there are posters of him around announcing his speeches at the beer halls. People come and hear his speeches. And he has a newspaper, the *Völkischer Beobachter*."

"So?"

"Well, he's a Jew hater."

"How do you know that Fritz?"

"They talk about him at school."

"What do they say about him?"

"Some of the older students like him. Some teachers, too. Well, they liked the Kaiser, and they want to go back to the old German Reich, before this government now. They hate this German Republic. They say it's selling out Germany. That's what I hear a lot of them say." He stopped to kick a stone. "Anyway they like this

Hitler guy because he's saying those same things. Some of them wear his group's emblem."

Hani remained silent.

"You know what I mean, right?" Fritz looked over at his sister.

Hani shook her head. "No."

"It's a kind of cross." Fritz stopped walking and took a piece of paper and a pencil from the shoulder bag he was carrying and sketched out a swastika.

"Okay, I've seen that. What is it?"

"It's called a swastika. People at my school who wear it hate Jews."

Hani's eyes widened. "Do they hate you?"

"No!" Fritz answered emphatically. "I'm a student at the school. I get along with everyone."

"But you're a Jew!"

"Okay, but they don't hate me, they hate the *Jews*."

"I don't get that."

Fritz shrugged. "I don't either, exactly."

"Does it bother you?"

"Of course it bothers me!" Fritz replied sternly. "But I can't do anything. And it's just talk."

## Hani's Distress

Posters and newspapers announcing meetings of the dog walker, Adolf Hitler, the leader of the small but growing National Socialist German Workers' Party, were becoming more visible around Munich in the early 1920s. And the symbol that Fritz had noticed among his classmates was being seen more frequently among groups of men marching in the street. They wore armbands with the black, white, and red colors of the old German Reich with a swastika in the center.

When Hani returned to her school after an absence for the Jewish high holidays in September 1922, she and several other Jewish students were taunted by their classmates. "It was so nice when you Jews weren't here!" they said. Even Leni, one of Hani's closest friends, joined in this chorus.[6] Later, Leni apologized. "I'm sorry I hurt your feelings Hani. But our country has suffered a lot."

"I know that. I've lived here all my life, just like you."

"Okay, but the Jews have been a part of that."

"Really? How is that?" Hani looked intently at her friend.

Leni turned her face away from Hani. "Well, the Jews did a lot to undermine our country during the war."

Hani felt distressed and angry at those words. "My father was in that war. He was a guard for the army."

"Maybe your family was supportive. But there were others who were not."

"That's no different than in any group of people."

"There are people who know more about these things than you or I." Leni played with the straps of her bookbag. "They lived through those times, and they saw what was happening. For example, some of the teachers in this school."

"Which teachers?"

Leni now crossed her arms in front of her. "I'm not going to say. But it was a history teacher who explained this to us. Don't you think a history teacher would know? There are other people who don't think Jews are so great for our country."

Hani's heart was racing. She had a tightness in her chest and felt a sense of panic. The words of the conversation stayed with her in the months to come as the number of swastikas, anti-Jewish posters, and other signs of anti-Semitic sentiments on walls multiplied. But she kept the school incident to herself.

## A Putschist's March, November 9, 1923

Anna was at home in her apartment just after noon on November 9 when she heard loud shouts, drum beats, and other commotion outside her apartment. Seeing nothing from the window, she went out into the street where she saw a crowd of people moving down Zweibrückstrasse, the wide street that intersected Liebherrstrasse a few yards from her apartment entrance. The marchers wore street clothes and uniforms of various colors. Most wore steel helmets or ski caps. Anna was alarmed by the many red arm bands and red flags bearing swastikas, and by the rifles many of the men were carrying.

Anna headed cautiously toward the procession. As she approached the corner she heard shouts from marchers to the spectators, who, like her, had been drawn by the noise or were watching from passing trolleys. "Join us! March with us! We're going to drive out the Jewish Marxist bastards, and the other Weimar criminals! Munich will be ours!! We'll march on Berlin!!" Some in the crowd were singing "Deutschland Uber Alles."

A group of young men rushed past Anna. One looked back at her and shouted, his face red with excitement—"Ludendorff and Hitler are leading the march! Long live the new Germany!" He and his friends turned up the corner and blended into the moving crowd.

Once the procession cleared the intersection Anna joined a group of people standing around posters pasted next to a corner store window. One of the posters had been almost completely torn down. The remaining words, printed on bright red paper, read, "Fellow patriots, do your duty!" There was a partial signature: ". . . Hitler, Reich Chancellor." Another poster next to the first one was largely intact. It was signed by Bavaria's prime minister, Gustav von Kahr and Bavarian military commander General Hans von Lossow. It denounced "acts of treason" by "criminals falsely claiming to have the backing of the Bavarian government," referring to Hitler's group.

One of the men standing around the posters held up a folded copy of the *Münchner Neueste Nachrichten* (Munich Latest News) from the previous evening. "It says right here," he yelled as he shook the paper, "that the Bavarian government leaders agreed at a meeting at the Burgerbraukeller last night to join with Hitler and Ludendorff to remove the scoundrels in Berlin. It even quotes von Kahr's words!"

A woman in the crowd responded, "Well, I heard on the radio

this morning that reports of the Bavarian government's support for Hitler's people were false."

Anna and several others voiced or nodded their agreement, having also heard that report.

An older woman in a dark duffle coat shook her head. "This is terribly confusing, who are we supposed to believe?"

The man with the newspaper was still waving it in the air. "I hope their revolution succeeds. "What we're going through is intolerable. Those socialist-Jewish bastards in Berlin have got to be taken down!"

"Where are the marchers heading?" asked an older man with a prominent mustache.

"To Marienplatz. To take over the government," the man with the paper answered.

The old man grinned. "Let's hope they succeed. Something has to be done!"

Anna said nothing. She and Benno had heard disturbing news about events the previous evening at the nearby Burgerbraukeller. A friend called late at night to warn them that Jews were being accosted on the streets by Hitler's people and taken to that beer hall.

A woman who stood at the edge of the small crowd turned to the man with the newspaper and shouted at him, "Apparently you haven't heard what Hitler's men did early this morning. They kidnapped Mayor Schmid and some of the city councilmen. That's just criminal!"

"Why should that bother me?" said the man with the newspaper. "I have no love for Schmid or his red friends"—referring, Anna assumed, to the Social Democrats on the city council.

Anna returned to her apartment, wracked with apprehension.

### That Night at Dinner

At dinner Hani described news that was circulating in her school of an army led by "that man named Hitler" which was trying to take over Munich. "I know who he is," Hani asserted. "He lives up the street on Thierschstrasse. Isn't that right, Fritz?"

"Yah," Fritz looked up from his dinner. "We all know who he is, Hani. You see his people everywhere nowadays."

Benno asked Anna to pass him a plate with bread. "But he doesn't have an army. He has a few hundred supporters. And they were stopped by the police this morning at the Odeonplatz. Hitler was shot."

"Did they kill him?" asked Fritz.

"He was injured and got away."

"Too bad," Fritz muttered quietly. "I wish they'd killed him."

"So, Papa, why does he have so many people who like him?" Hani asked.

"There are a lot of people who are desperate right now," Anna answered.

"The inflation," Fritz interjected.

"In times of economic trouble people will listen to those they normally would not listen to and accept things, even if they're not true." Benno paused. "So, you have to be careful who you listen to. Hitler's people have no answers, only hatred."

Anna was hesitant to bring up what she'd seen and heard that day, especially in front of Hani, who was unnerved by events in Munich. Benno too held back. But when he was alone with Anna, he told her that a friend who was at the Marienplatz that morning heard a speaker named Streicher say that once in power they, "the true patriots," intended to hang Jewish leaders from light posts.

Later that night in bed they expressed relief at the news that Hitler's putsch had failed. Nonetheless, Anna found it difficult to sleep.

## Schnapps and Kugel

The next evening, the Neumeiers, longtime friends of the Neuburger family, came for dinner. The economic crisis and the attempted putsch of the previous days had shaken all of them deeply. It also increased their urge to gather for mutual support.

As Benno served schnapps to his guests, he talked about a conversation he'd had that afternoon with business friends at a small Jewish-owned restaurant. The topic there, as most everywhere in Germany, was the colossal inflation that made the German mark all but worthless. Benno explained how the gathering tried to lighten the moment with jokes. "Drink up before the price goes up!" they counseled each other. "If you take too long, you'll have to borrow another billion marks for the next mug!"

Benno recalled one sarcastic wit answering, "You see, there's a bright side to everything. It's now irrefutable that getting quickly soused on beer makes good economic sense!" When one of them tried to light his cigar with a billion-mark note that may well have been worth less than the paper it was printed on, the bill was snatched from him. "Let's pay off the national debt with this, then we'll light up!" Other remarks followed, Benno related, each an effort to outdo the other in absurdity. Still nothing they said could do justice to the outlandish reality of the moment.

The Neumeiers' comments on the situation were more somber. The collapse of the German mark meant that anyone whose wealth was in currency, no matter how large their fortune, was now a pauper. Only goods such as land, buildings, jewelry, and precious metals had any value. Ernst Neumeier was a lawyer and normally made a good living. But his family had little in the way of property other than furniture and a car. Their modest investments in stocks were now, for the moment at least, nearly worthless. The German war bonds he, like Benno, bought as an expression of patriotism were also worthless and would probably remain that way.

Benno confessed that he and Anna's savings were wiped out and that they were now nearly destitute. "I have some plots of land but at the moment that's meaningless, because who has money to buy them?" Still, he said, he counted himself among the lucky. "At least I have land. And its value will return sometime."

"Fortunately, Ernst has a job that pays well," Frau Neumeier said, as they settled at the dining room table. "But if we don't spend his salary on the same day he's paid, by the next day it's practically worthless." She described how they rushed to the store on pay days to get in line with everyone else to get what they could before prices went up. We haven't starved, but who knows if it won't come to that?"

"At least we had some practice at it during the war," Herr Neumeier joked.

"I promise you won't starve tonight." Anna Neuburger went into the kitchen to retrieve a large pan of potato kugel. Anna Neumeier followed with a pitcher of water and platter of bratwurst and cheese. Cabbage followed.

"I don't think this will last long," Frau Neumeier commented once she'd sat down.

"What are you referring to?" asked Anna Neuburger.

"The inflation. You see, I think a lot of this is being manipulated."

"How so, honey?" Herr Neumeier inquired.

"We here are all suffering, this is very true. Ruined. But there are people out there that have something to gain from this."

"Like?" Benno looked at his guest.

"Think about it, Benno. The big industries are in debt from the war. The reparations imposed on Germany by Versailles is a huge burden. Those debts that are payable in German marks have largely been wiped out by the inflation."

"The foreign creditors are not going to accept worthless marks," Benno countered.

"Well, I think they'll bargain."

Benno was quite agitated. "You might be right. But in the meantime the inflation just might bring the whole country down!"

"You're talking about what happened at the Bürgerbraukeller," Frau Neumeier replied.

"Yes. Hitler's people made a pretty good run at bringing down the government yesterday!"

"Do we really know what happened yesterday?" Anna asked.

Frau Neumeier looked at her husband. "Ernst has a client whose uncle was at that meeting in the Burgerbraukeller. It was organized by Prime Minister von Kahr. Rumor had it that von Kahr was going to announce a plan to bring back the Bavarian monarchy. But Hitler has his own ideas about who should rule. Hitler brought his National Socialist thugs into the beer hall and took over the meeting."

"They call them Nazis, by the way," added Herr Neumeier.

"We heard from a friend that Hitler's people were kidnapping Jews off the street and bringing them to the beer hall!" Anna added.

"What a mess," offered Herr Neumeier.

"We should continue this conversation." Frau Neumeier smiled as she took a bite from her plate. "But right now, I want to say a few words about another momentous issue, this potato kugel is . . . the best I've ever had, Anna! And I think you owe it to the world to give us the recipe."

"Well said, dear." Herr Neumeier raised his glass of schnapps and quipped, "After a fascist coup is defeated there's nothing more important than a good kugel!"

Frau Neumeier gave her husband a distraught look. "I wasn't trying to make light of this . . ."

"I'm sorry, honey. I was just joking." Herr Neumeier turned to Anna Neuburger. "Anyway, Anna, I agree with my wife about the food."

"Very good," laughed Anna. "Before I give you the recipe I would like your help in understanding what happened at the Burgerbraukeller. Yesterday morning the *Münchner Neueste Nachrichten* reported that von Kahr and the Bavarian military leader . . ."

"Von Lossow," Benno put in.

"Yes, von Kahr and von Lossow agreed to join Hitler. And that this decision was announced at the meeting," said Anna.

"That's true." Herr Neumeier looked at Anna. "Regarding that meeting on the night of November eighth . . . Hitler, who was armed—that should be understood—interrupted the meeting before von Kahr could finish his remarks . . . and got von Kahr and

Lossow and the police commissioner von Seisser, who was also there with Kahr, to move to a room off the main hall, to negotiate. Meanwhile the crowd waited in the beer hall, for several hours. People were getting very restive. Then General Ludendorff showed up."

"That snake!" Benno scoffed.

"Yah, I agree, a snake. Well, maybe General Ludendorff threatened to bite the Bavarian leaders!" Herr Neumeier laughed. "Because shortly after Ludendorff arrived Kahr and von Lossow, and von Seisser stood with Hitler in front of the crowd and announced they'd agreed to work together to overthrow the Republic."

Benno poured more schnapps. "But later," Benno added, "Kahr and von Lossow changed their minds."

"For whatever reason," Herr Neumeier said, "as soon as the Bavarian leaders left the Bürgerbraukeller, they decided to oppose the coup."

"What do you think changed their minds?" asked Frau Neumeier.

"I think they had just pretended to go along with Hitler," Benno surmised.

Herr Neumeier nodded. "I think that's right. Because as soon as they left the Burgerbraukeller someone ordered posters to be printed and put up around town denouncing Hitler's people and saying it was a lie that von Kahr and the others had agreed to the putsch."

"I saw one of those posters yesterday morning right down the street here," Anna said. "And, by the way, I saw Hitler's people marching right up Zweibrückstrasse."

Herr Neumeier nodded. "Of course, the march from the Burgerbraukeller, the morning after that meeting, came up Zweibrückstrasse toward downtown."

Benno took another sip of schnapps. "My understanding is that the police opposed the coup from the beginning."

"Thank God," said Frau Neumeier.

"I think there were divisions among the police. But the main authorities opposed the coup and organized the roadblocks like the one at the Odeonplatz," Herr Neumeier said.

"When I saw the marchers they seemed pretty confident to me," Anna commented.

"Maybe they didn't know the police were mobilized against them," said Frau Neumeier.

Herr Neumeier sat back in his chair. "Hitler must have known by then that Kahr and the rest had turned on him."

Benno smiled. "He just didn't tell his people. Led them into a trap at the Odeonplatz!"

"Led himself into a trap. That's where Hitler was shot . . . and Ludendorff arrested," Frau Neumeier put in.

"Hitler had Ludendorff marching with him. Maybe he thought police wouldn't fire at them with that pompous general at his side," surmised Benno.

"Where were they headed, exactly?" asked Frau Neumeier.

"To the War Ministry. Some of Hitler's people were under siege by police there," said Herr Neumeier.

"We don't know all that happened. What we know is that Hitler's bodyguard was killed, and Hitler got away." Herr Neumeier reached for the schnapps bottle. "Anyone?" he asked as he poured himself another shot glass. "Have we seen the last of Herr Hitler?"

"We can hope!" Benno exclaimed. "But even if we have, there is still the matter of these right-wing fanatics and this bottomless hatred for the German Republic—which some are now calling the Weimar Republic! These fascists put the blame for the Versailles Treaty on the Republic. Which is absurd since the war was lost before the Republic came into existence!"

"Well, now all the talk is about the French occupation of the Ruhr, and all this economic misery," Herr Neumeier murmured.

"They hated the Republic long before the Ruhr and before this inflation," Anna asserted.

"Of course." Frau Neumeier pushed a strand of her long brown hair out of her face, "The constitution of the Republic gives all women the right to vote. And access to birth control. For Hitler's people what greater crime could be committed?!"

"Munich's become the haven for these haters," Anna added.

Herr Neumeier glanced at Anna. "I'm sorry to have to say this, but we have a Jew to blame for that."

Anna looked incredulous. "Who do you mean?"

"Kurt Eisner, of course. And the other Jewish socialists—Toller, Landauer, and Mühsam—if it hadn't been for that ridiculous revolution the ruffians and misfits would not have descended on Munich like locusts, turning our city into this wasteland of stupidity."

"Eisner was only saying what we all felt about the war and all the terrible things it did to us. He was guilty of having the courage to say and act on these things in public." Anna's comment brought a nod of agreement from Frau Neumeier. "People were justifiably angry at the war. Eisner put their thoughts to words and acted on them."

Herr Neumeier leaned forward. "We Jews had best keep such thoughts to ourselves. As much as we think of ourselves as Germans, there are plenty of those who don't. Nor do they care about what's true or not. If it comes from the mouth of a Jew, it's automatically regarded with suspicion, and convinces no one."

"So, we all just keep quiet?" Anna was thinking of similar sentiments someone expressed about Russian Jews some years before.

Frau Neumeier looked at her husband. "When that group of Hitler idiots tried to shut down Brecht's play at the Residenztheater a few years ago, you were one of the first to stand and tell them to shut up. So, I think maybe you contradict yourself."

"Taking over a government and standing up for the right to hear a play are quite different things, dear."

"I was referring to Anna's point. There are times when we need to speak up for ourselves."

"Okay. But you can't compare those two examples."

"The Jew haters don't make those distinctions," Frau Neumeier insisted.

Anna asked if they were ready for some coffee. When she returned to the table with coffee and a tray of baked goods, she asked the Neumeiers about their children.

"Our children," Anna Neumeier said as she picked up a sweet roll, "are very troubled by all this. Our oldest, Karl, is at the university. He's disturbed by how many of the young people at the school are becoming fanatics. They fall for the idea that Germany has been robbed from achieving its greatness. And to be a true German you have to be against the Jews! You should hear how many of these students believe the country needs someone like Hitler."

Herr Neumeier tapped the table with his palm. "What happened yesterday should put an end to that! If they catch Hitler, if he's still alive, he'll be tried—hopefully outside Munich— and put away for a good long time!"

"Let's hope so," Benno replied. "And the people in Berlin have got to straighten out this mess of an economy before this whole country explodes!"

### Trial

During the shootout at Munich's Odeonplatz in the afternoon of November 9, Hitler fell and dislocated his shoulder. His supporters helped him to a car, and they headed for the Austrian border. Their car broke down before they got to the border, so they sought shelter at the home of a supporter of Hitler's National Socialist Party in the village of Uffing. Hitler was arrested a week later in Uffing by Bavarian authorities.

A wounded Hitler was taken to Landsberg prison in a small medieval town on the Lech River a few dozen miles from Munich. He was placed in what became known as the "celebrity cell," previously occupied by Kurt Eisner's assassin, Count Arco auf Valley. From his arrest through his trial, sentencing, and incarceration after trial, Hitler and his fellow defendants were treated by the Bavarian judicial system more like honored guests of the court than enemies of the Republic.

Hitler and his associates could have been charged with a variety of crimes: theft of government funds, assault, kidnapping, hostage-taking, murder—including the death of police killed at the confrontation at the Odeonplatz—and the seizure and occupation of government buildings, among others. But there was only one charge brought against them: treason. This suited Hitler and his movement. It was the destruction of the German Republic they sought, and their intention to do so garnered them support from the monarchists, militarists, and fascists. Treason is what they wanted to be known for and proudly admitted to at the trial, which began on February 26, 1923. It was held, under tight security, at the Reichswehr Infantry School to the west of Munich's city center. Journalists from across Germany and around the world sat in the audience. Their extensive reports on the proceedings made Hitler a known figure in Germany and internationally.

Hitler, Ludendorff, Hermann Goering, and the other defendants faced a panel of five judges who were themselves right-leaning nationalists, hostile to the central government. The lead judge, George Neithardt, made no attempt to hide his sympathy for the Putschists. He even addressed one of the defendants, General Ludendorff, as "your excellency." Rulings from the bench allowed the Putschist defendants wide freedom to express their views and they took full advantage of it. They delivered long speeches blaming the leaders and supporters of the Weimar Republic for the loss of the war and the painful Versailles Treaty. Hitler declared proudly that once he succeeded in overthrowing Weimar, he would establish a dictatorship.

There were closed proceedings during the trial in which sensitive issues were raised and discussed outside of public view. Evidence presented in these sessions indicated that the Putschists were more intertwined with the Kahr government and the Bavarian military than was publicly acknowledged—a point the defense tried to use to its advantage.

The trial lasted until April 1924.

## Wilheims

During the days of the failed putsch, Fritz was attending Wilheims Gymnasium, one of the most conservative schools in the country. Already, by 1920, the school had defiantly raised the red, black, and white flag of the old Kaiser Reich, and not the red, black, and gold flag of the Weimar Republic.

Many of Wilheim's teachers made no secret of their hostility to Weimar. But many also opposed the attempted coup and viewed the Nazis as ruffians and bullies, demeaning to the cause they espoused: the restoration of the Wittelsbachs and the old Reich.[7]

While much of Munich, Bavaria, and even Germany more broadly was engaged with the spectacle of the attempted coup and its aftermath, Fritz, who was often busy with schoolwork and sports, kept his distance from these political affairs. His friends were other athletic-minded youths. Nearly all were non-Jews. Fritz learned that his opinions would be scrutinized and looked at with suspicion, so he kept them to himself.

## A Sports Field Brawl

One day in the spring of 1924, as the trial was nearing its end, Fritz and his teammates were at track practice taking their turns with timed sprints when a confrontation broke out on the sideline. Fritz turned toward the noise and saw two teammates in a shouting match. Several others soon joined in.

The argument began when one of the track team members mentioned Ludendorff's testimony at the putsch trial. Another boy scoffed, "They oughta put that smug, pompous asshole in front of a firing squad! He's always talking about traitors. He's the biggest traitor himself—and a crappy general too! What kind of pathetic loser blames others for their own defeats!"

For several of his teammates this was a blasphemy too great to ignore. One of the boys exploded in anger—"Shut your stupid mouth about Ludendorff. It's the November criminals who brought

Germany down in the war, and we know who the fuck they are!" By which he meant Social Democrats, liberals, and Jews.

It wasn't clear who threw the first punch but there were bloodied faces on both sides before the coaches intervened to separate the half-dozen boys who entered the fight.

The argument created a pall over the team and the coach issued a ban on any future discussions of politics on the track field under threat of expulsion from the team and possibly the school as well.

The putsch trial ended in early April. Ludendorff was the only defendant to be fully exonerated and given no jail time. Hitler was found guilty of treason but received the shortest sentence legally possible, five years. In the end, he served barely eight months, which he used to write his plans for Germany's future in a book he called *Mein Kampf—My Struggle*. The other convicted putschists served similarly light sentences. More significantly, the trial made Hitler a national figure and gave a huge boost to what was emerging as a robust national Nazi movement.

### Thormann and Dannhäuser

By the beginning of 1925, Fritz, sixteen years old and in his last full year at the gymnasium, decided there was no way, given his family's precarious economic situation, that he could go on to college. He began looking for a job.[8]

A friend of the family mentioned that a Munich sport shoe company was looking for apprentices. This opportunity immediately caught Fritz's attention, especially because the company, Thormann and Dannhäuser, manufactured the running shoes he wore in practice and in competition. He applied to the company for an apprenticeship and was elated when they accepted him. Benno had to sign the necessary papers allowing Fritz to enter the apprenticeship, which began in April 1925.

Impressed with his maturity and initiative, the company sent Fritz on the road as a sales rep in the second year of his apprenticeship in 1926. Fritz traveled by car to the southern regions of

Germany. He spent the better part of the next twelve years as a traveling salesman.

His first sales territory covered a swath of area from the Black Forest in Wurttemburg to the Bodensee, a large lake in southern Bavaria at the conjuncture of Germany, Austria, and Switzerland. Fritz found himself on the road for days and weeks at a time. In between trips he returned to Munich to visit family and friends and engage in training and competition with Munich's 1860 sports club, where he became part of the track and handball teams.

He made his living on sales commissions, which had its downsides. When sales fell, income followed. But, with time, as he became more skilled at his trade, and developed ties with his sport shop customers, his sales increased. In addition, the job afforded Fritz the chance to not only cater to those drawn to alpine sports but to engage in them himself. He hiked in the areas where he visited his customers, such as Pfänder mountain outside Berganz, the Bavarian Alps's deepest gorge at Breitachklamm and the stunning Wutach gorge in Baden-Württemberg. In summer months he walked the valley trails and hill and mountain paths near towns throughout the Bavarian Alps and the Austrian Tyrol. He was guided to these places by reading accounts and hearing about them from people he met in his travels, especially his customers, who sometimes accompanied him on his outings.

Fritz also took to swimming in local waters. He swam in lakes he heard about in conversations and ones he saw from the road, such as the Forggensee near the town of Füssen; the Tegernsee outside the town of Bad Tölz; and the Stanbergersee, which was on a route he took to and from Munich.

His resumé of rivers expanded with his sales territory. He swam in the Rhine, the Lech, the Danube, the Oder, and the Elbe. He was not a particularly accomplished swimmer, but he was drawn to the challenge of testing himself when the occasion offered.

When passing through Traunstein he stopped to visit his Holzer cousins. He took special pleasure reciting his growing list of "conquered" swimming spots to his cousin Klara Holzer, a notoriously adventurous swimmer herself. Klara responded to her cousin's braggadocio with a wave of her hand as though batting a bothersome fly: "Why, sticking your toes in the water, Fritz, hardly counts as swimming." When Fritz protested that Klara was being unfair, she answered with a challenge: "The next time you're in Traunstein we'll go to the Chiemsee together and I'll show you what real swimming is." Fritz acted as though insulted by his cousin's doubts. But he enjoyed this little game of swimming upmanship and verbal sparring.

In winter Fritz skied in the Bavarian and Austrian Alps. As his sales territory expanded, he got to know ski runs in the Thuringian and Harz mountains. He eventually became acquainted with ski runs in the Giant Mountains of Czechoslovakia as well.

These outings had their practical, business value. Fritz included his personal experiences hiking and skiing as testimony to the qualities of the sports shoes he was promoting.

### "Normal" Years

After the debacle of his failed coup of November 1923, Hitler decided to pursue power through electoral means. Not long after he left prison in December 1924, the Nazis attracted growing numbers of votes, especially in Bavaria. Their message combined a "Germany first" attitude with militant condemnation of the Weimar Republic and strident hatred directed toward Jews.

By 1928, German economic and political stability returned thanks to foreign loans, restored farming and industrial production, a new reparations payment structure worked out through an international agreement, and Germany's inclusion in the League of Nations. But this stability was deceptive. The economic damage caused by the war, the inflationary period of the early 1920s, and the ongoing burden of reparations exacted by the Versailles Treaty continued to grind down swaths of the population. Millions of Germans struggled in economic and social distress. Still, the relative normalcy after years of war and economic and political turmoil was a welcome relief for those who could get by.

Bavarian Jews living in the cradle of German fascism were relieved when, in 1928, the share of votes for the Nazi Party in Reichstag elections fell to 2 percent nationally, to 6 percent in Bavaria, and to 17 percent in Munich, where in the early 1920s the Nazis had garnered more than 35 percent of the vote.

As Munich real estate regained its value Benno was able to enjoy some modest economic security and, by the age of fifty-nine, began to contemplate retirement. His thoughts began to stray toward other interests and pursuits.

Every year, he and Anna attended Octoberfest at the Munich fairgrounds at Theresienwiese. They took regular walks around Munich, especially along the Isar and in the English Garden where they met friends for lunches or dinners. They frequented Munich's ever-growing number of movie houses, which showed films produced by Germany's expanding film industry, or imported movies, especially those from Hollywood. They went to theaters and nightclubs. Anna continued with activities at the synagogue, and Benno had his occasional gatherings with old business friends in Munich beer halls.

They also traveled. Better roads and automobiles were opening up a new and appealing form of mobility for those who could take advantage of it. Anna usually chose their destinations. They went to Ulm to see the towering Gothic Münster church and to southern Bavaria, stopping at lakes Fritz had recommended to them. They visited the Austrian Alps region and Salzburg where they stayed with Anna's niece Hansi and her family.

### Weimar Culture

Benno had never been a stranger to books. But the novels of the Weimar period of the late 1920s and early 1930s attracted him in a way that literature had not done before. Among the writers that most drew his and Anna's attention were three prominent Munich authors: Thomas Mann, his brother Heinrich Mann, and Lion Feuchtwanger. Anna was the first in the family to read Thomas Mann's *Buddenbrooks* and she recommended it to Benno. When Thomas Mann won the Nobel Prize for Literature in 1929, Benno was motivated to read it and Mann's popular novel, *The Magic Mountain*. The latter became the subject of conversation among their friends. There was friendly wrangling over the broader meaning of the book, especially when it came to the views expressed in the fierce debates between the characters Settembrini and Naphta. What had Mann intended with this character Naphta—a Jew educated by Jesuits who argued for religious absolutist and anti-democratic views? And what about these debates with his ideological rival, the democratic-minded, "enlightened" Settembrini? The book's bizarre twist—when Naphta challenges Settembrini to a duel and then commits suicide rather than shoot his rival—really stirred the group to argument. What should they make of that?

These discussions over literature had special significance to Benno. He had left public school at fourteen to take an apprenticeship. As a youth he'd been motivated by practical needs. He found his schooling uninspiring, with its Teutonic emphasis on rote learning. With these books Benno found himself, for the first time, seriously discussing philosophical issues and "existential" questions of humanity, like the individual versus the mass, democracy, and autocracy, and the "meaning" of life, and other abstract issues. He developed an interest in the characters and their points of view. And he developed his own interpretations of what Mann was trying to get across. He now found himself arguing over issues he would have once dismissed as irrelevant, if not a total waste of time. And he found himself enjoying it!

In 1929, Alfred Döblin's book *Berlin Alexanderplatz* received a great deal of public attention. Benno read it over time. He was not fond of the book's avant-garde "montage" style, but he eventually got through it. Anna also eventually got caught up in that book. "If nothing else Döblin's book makes Berlin sound like a pretty intriguing place to visit," she argued. And they did become somewhat obsessed with the idea of spending time in the capital city. Benno's interest was further driven by descriptions and commentaries he heard at temple. "The cabarets in Berlin," one congregant told him, "make the ones here in Munich seem like a Bar Mitzvah party."

So, in August 1930 they decided to spend time sightseeing in Berlin. They went to the Neues and Pergamon museums on an island in the Spree River. They saw several theater shows in a city with a bewildering variety of venues. They saw cabaret acts that lived up to their sexually explicit reputations. They found the singing and chorus dancing impressive and the repartee clever and amusing, but Benno concluded that he preferred Munich's "less sophisticated and colorful" and, for him, more humorous comedy shows.

They enjoyed Berlin's hectic bustle. They agreed with the description of one observer who said Berlin was like a machine always at full throttle. But they also realized they preferred living life at a more Munich-like—somewhat slower, more deliberate—pace. Berlin was thrilling, yes. But the visit to Berlin was marred by signs of economic distress and social unrest which had followed not long after the New York stock market crash of October 1929. There were long food lines and angry demonstrations by opposing communist and fascist groups. Clearly the Nazis had become emboldened and their influence, including their strident anti-Jewish fervor, was noticeable. Fear was rising among Berlin's Jews and in Berlin's generally more liberal and progressive community. Anna and Benno brought that disquiet back with them to Munich.

## 6

# Shocks

ANNA AND BENNO RETURNED FROM Berlin in time to vote in the September 1930 election. In the 1928 national election the Nazis had garnered 810,000 votes. This time they received 6.5 million votes, enough to give them a significant presence in the national government and boost their confidence and momentum.

One Sabbath evening after the Neuburgers returned from Berlin, Anna invited to dinner her brother-in-law Louis Holzer and his daughters and their families who lived in the nearby town of Wolfratshausen. Cäcilie, or Tilli as everyone called her, came with her husband, Hermann Spatz, and their son Wilhelm, or Willi. At the last minute, Tilli's sister Ilse called Anna to say she didn't feel well and would not be attending.

With Hani's help, Anna had made a large pot roast, potato dumplings, and pickled beet salad. When they were all seated Anna and Hani brought out the food. Anna placed a large bowl on the table and turned to her niece. "Tilli, your sister called me last night to say she wasn't feeling well. Otherwise we'd have both Hermanns here." Anna was referring to Ilse's husband, Hermann Schuster.

"Ilse didn't tell you?" Tilli looked amused. "Maybe I shouldn't . . . but . . ." She turned to her father, Louie, who made no gesture.

"There's something I should know?" Anna asked.

"More, Tante Anna," Tilli said coyly. "My little sister is . . ."

Hermann laughed. "Little sister? Ilse's twenty-six."

Tilli reached for piece of rye bread from a platter. "I'm two years older, and she'll always be my little sister!"

"Tell us the secret," Anna said, "you're getting me worried."

"Pregnant!"

"Well, that's not so bad!" Anna laughed. "Louie, did you know about this?"

Louie winked at Tilli. "I had an inkling."

"You should be happy. A grandfather . . ." Benno looked over at young Willi who was wiggling in his seat, "again!"

"Better they come now while I'm still young enough to remember their names," Louie sighed.

"Is there a name?" asked Hermann.

"No!" Tilli put her hand on Hermann's shoulder, playfully. "It's too early in the pregnancy for names."

"Well, if it's a boy, tell Ilse or Hermann *not* to name him Hermann. We've enough confusion already in this family!"

"Well, honey," Tilli was suddenly quite cheeky, "if it's a girl could we call her Hermina?"

Hermann suppressed a laugh. "You'll have to get Ilse's permission for that."

Louie looked at Benno and then Anna. "Tell us about your recent trip to Berlin."

Benno began, "One of the best parts of the trip was a long walk we took one day along the Unter den Linden—an imperial boulevard if there ever was one. We started at the Alexanderplatz and walked all the way through the Brandenburg gate to the Tiergarten. Then we went to the Kürfurstendamm district through the Potsdamer Platz. . . . Where else Anna?"

"We stopped at the Reichstag building and visited the Berlin Zoo. There's a lot to see in that city . . ." Anna paused. "It's so fast-paced, and so different from Munich."

"I'd be interested to know what people in Berlin were saying about the September election," Hermann said to Anna.

Anna reached for the bowl of dumplings. "We were there before the election. We came back here to vote. It's very disturbing how many voted for the Nazis!"

"Unemployment is rising out of control," Benno said, cutting a piece of meat. "Hitler's a master at playing on people's misery and finding someone to blame."

"Finding Jews to blame," Louie added.

Hermann nodded in agreement. "And the election has emboldened them."

"Of course." Then Benno quickly added, "I was just reading this morning about a Berlin radio show based on Döblin's novel, *Berlin Alexanderplatz*—cancelled because of intimidation by the Nazis."

"This is a matter I'd like to discuss." Hermann put down his fork and leaned forward. "There's a movie in Berlin that Hitler's people were able to shut down, *All Quiet on the Western Front*. It's the only war movie that has had the balls—excuse me—the nerve, to tell the truth about the war! At least, if it's faithful to the book."

Louie looked at his son-in-law. "That movie was made in the United States."

"Yes. But it's from a book by a German author, Remarque."

Hani looked over at Hermann. "Mama said you were in the war for three years?"

"I was. Much of it at a place called Ypres, in Belgium," said Hermann.

"What was it like there?"

A pained look came over Hermann's face. "Terrible place, Hani. A slaughtering place. Half a million, *half a million* soldiers died there!"

Hani asked hesitantly, "Is that where your brother died?"

"Not at Ypres. He died at a place nearby called Givenchy—in France." Tilli put her arm on her husband's shoulder and leaned her head toward him.

"I'm sorry," Hani began.

"Wilhelm left law school to go in the army. He, like all of us, was taken in by the 'war to defend our nation's glory' talk. It was all a wasteful horror show. The book, at least, brings out the brutal ugliness of it."

Anna looked over at Benno. But his face was still, and he remained silent.

"About Wilhelm"—Tilli wrapped her arm with Hermann's—"he was like one of the characters in the book, right?"

"You mean Paul Baumer . . ." Hermann looked around the table. "Yes, in the book Baumer is this nice schoolboy. He and his school buddies enlist in the army right out of high school. They're sent to the western front. Nearly all of his friends are killed or maimed. Baumer, too, gets injured, and spends time in the hospital but then goes back to the front out of loyalty to his soldier comrades. There's the similarity with Wilhelm! He was at Verdun. When he came down with pneumonia he was sent to the hospital to recuperate. After leaving the hospital he returned to the front, asked to return. And in one of those absurd offensives to 'turn the tide of the war'—but really so the generals could brag about winning a few yards of dirt—Wilhelm was cut down by machine-gun fire. That was in February 1917."

Louie was about to redirect the conversation, but then stopped when he saw Hermann was intent on saying more.

"The book is important to me, because it depicts the war as it really was." Hermann's voice took on a sharper tone. "But in Germany right now it's lies that rule. Everything's become a lie. If you go to a club and say, 'Germany didn't really lose the war!' someone'll pat you on the back and buy you a drink. But if you say, 'Germany lost the war because people at home were starving and the soldiers at the front were fed up with it all'—ahh, you'll be lucky to get out of the place in one piece! No one wants to hear the truth! The idiots have taken over the conversation. Apparently now only idiots have the right to speak. If all of us who know the truth are silenced then pretty soon the idiots will rule the whole roost."

Hermann's intense words had everyone quiet for a moment.

"It's now becoming un-German to tell the truth," Benno conceded.

Hermann hit the table with his palm. "Dangerous. Hitler's flunky Goebbels brought hooligans into a Berlin theater to disrupt the war movie with gas bombs."

"I read that they beat people in the audience," Anna added.

"And now they've shut the movie down . . . !" Hermann struck the table again.

Hani looked at her cousin's husband. "Who shut down the movie?"

"A commission in Berlin," Anna responded. "You didn't hear about that, Hani? A government commission in Berlin said *All Quiet on the Western Front* is too dangerous to show because of violent protests *against* it."

"It's the government's role to stop the violence— to arrest the rioters if necessary." Benno was becoming more agitated.

Louie scowled. "The authorities are playing into Hitler's hands!"

"Exactly my point," Hermann said.

There was a pause and Tilli turned to her husband. "You know it was Carl Laemmle's American company that made the movie. And Laemmle comes from the same town as Tante Anna."

"Laupheim. Yah, I know that. And he's Jewish—another reason the Nazis use to shut the film down," Hermann added.

"But did you know that Anna knew Carl Laemmle when they were kids in Laupheim?"

Anna laughed. "Tilli, I was about six years old, at most, when Laemmle left for America."

"Well, I guess we're lucky you were so young, otherwise he might not have gone off to America to become a filmmaker." Tilli's remark brought laughter from around the table.

Hermann spoke with deliberate calmness: "I'm not a political person. But when it comes to the war, there are things that need to be said—and in public. I want that movie to be seen. I'd take Willi to see it." Hermann looked over at his son who was now asleep on a couch.

Tilli frowned. "He's pretty young for that, honey."

"The young need to know. He wouldn't understand all of it, but he needs to see how it was. It's not a game."

As Hermann spoke, Hani and Anna went into the kitchen. When they returned Hani set a chocolate cake on the table and Anna set down a pot of coffee.

Tilli poured herself some coffee. "People complain that we Germans are always depicted as brutes in foreign films. I've heard this is the one war movie from the United States that shows us Germans as just ordinary people who struggle and suffer."

Louie reached for a plate. "Ahh. We Germans may suffer. But we never lose! That's the sin!"

"Poor Willi. He's going to miss the cake." Anna looked over at the sleeping child on the couch, now covered with a blanket Hani had put over him. "Should we wake him?"

Tilli looked over at her son. "No, Tante, I'll take a piece home and keep it for him, if I can restrain myself."

Hermann took a gulp of coffee and went to the couch and picked up Willi, his son's head on his shoulder. "We should be going, to get this young fella to bed."

"Okay, honey, but I just had a question I wanted to ask before we leave." Tilli turned to Anna. "I haven't seen or heard a thing about Cousin Fritz. What's going on with him?"

"He's on the road most of the time nowadays," Benno answered. "Since the economy's gone down he's taken on a bigger territory, and he's carrying two lines now, Thormann sports shoes and Julius Levy sports clothing..."

Benno opened a drawer in the dining room cabinet. "Here, have a look at this." He held up a thick stack of postcards. "From Fritz—each card's from a different place. Not just Bavaria, he goes to Stuttgart and north of that." Benno picked through the stack of cards. "Here's one from Eisenbach, one from Saalfeld, Gera, Greitz ... He writes about hikes in Thale in the Harz Mountains, in the forest around Thuringia."

"I've never been to those parts," Hermann commented.

"Where does he find the time for all that? And working?" Tilli looked astonished.

"You'll have to ask him!" Benno looked the proud parent. "Here's the latest one. This came yesterday. It's from Ternitz, Austria. He writes 'Best regards from Karwendel, the largest mountain range of the Northern Limestone Alps. I send my greetings. (I got totally soaked today!)'"[9]

"Poor Cousin Fritz!" Tilli laughed. "Please remind your son that the next time he's on his way back to Munich from the south that Wolfratshausen is still there. He should stop by. Tell him if he comes to visit we promise to keep him dry!"

## A Movie in Munich

In 1928 a musical play called *The Threepenny Opera* opened on a Berlin stage to widespread notice and notoriety. Its creators, Elizabeth Hauptmann, Bertolt Brecht, and Kurt Weill, chose an operatic form associated with aristocratic themes, to put working people and society's "down-and-outs" on center stage. This brought the play considerable notoriety in Germany and beyond. The extreme right-wing groups, especially the Nazis, made no secret of their loathing of what they called an example of "degenerate Weimar art."

Fritz, in his travels, had heard a lot of lively talk about the play and made a special trip from the city of Weimar to see it in Berlin. Then, when the movie version opened three years later, Fritz wrote his father asking Benno to get tickets for one of the showings during the time he planned to be home.

At dinner in their home before the movie the four of them talked about the controversy. "I saw the play," Fritz explained. "I won't say too much. I don't want to spoil it. But I will say the story and the way it's put together is something different than I'd ever seen. The lyrics are very . . .bawdy, you might say." He teased his sister. "Hani, you might want to bring some ear muffs if the dialogue gets too rough."

"You don't have to worry, Fritz, I'm not so fragile as you think."

"You could always put your fingers in your ears," Fritz was laughing as he demonstrated this action.

"Enough, Fritz!" his sister scoffed. "I don't remember you being so . . . avant-garde!"

Fritz ignored her remark. "I'll be interested to see how much of the play gets into the movie."

"Did you know that the playwright, Brecht, used to live in Munich?" Anna asked. Fritz shook his head. "He left Munich and went to Berlin in the early 1920s because the Nazis shut down one of his plays with their protests here."

"Why did they protest?" asked Hani.

"Because Brecht is a socialist," Anna answered.

"Hypocrites! They call themselves 'socialists,'" Hani scoffed.

"*National* socialists, Hani," said her father.

"What exactly is the difference?"

Anna grabbed her coat from the closet. "National socialists, like the Nazis, only care about their own little group of people, their race, or whatever you want to call it. Socialists care about everyone."

"How do you know this, Mama?"

"I've known a few socialists." Anna looked over to Benno. "I met them among the refugees from Russia."

"I think it's a little more complicated than that," said Benno.

"Will there be protests tonight?" Hani asked.

Benno looked at Anna and shrugged. "We don't know."

When the family arrived at the theater a long line of people were waiting to get in. There were brown-shirted Nazis out front hawking the party paper, *Völkischer Beobachter*. The Nazis were loud and aggressive. They shouted, "This movie is filth meant for the sewer" and other insults, but people mainly ignored them.

Hani held tight to her brother as they walked toward the theater. "Don't go in there!" a protester in a brown uniform screeched at them. "Don't you know only a Jew could love this trash? Do you want to act like a Jew?" For a second it looked like Fritz was about to say something to the Nazi, but Hani, whose arm was linked with his, pulled her brother through the theater door.

After the theater, as the family walked to a tram stop for the ride home it was Fritz who had the most to say about the evening. "I thought the movie was very innovative—like the play. It's very . . . unconventional, I guess is the word."

"I liked that it was about people you don't see so often in movies," said Anna. "It's sympathetic to people who don't often get treated so well or spoken of well."

Hani turned to Benno. "And Papa, what did you think?"

"I think I'm tired and want to go to bed."

"But what did you think of the movie?" Hani insisted.

"Well, I liked the music. That much I liked a lot."

### The Election of 1932

The economic turmoil of the early 1930s produced mass unemployment, bankruptcies, and a collapse of wages. German factory production fell 50 percent from 1929 to 1932 as loans dried up and capital was hard to come by. Trade slumped, and Germany lacked funds for imports, including for food. Economic suffering drew growing numbers of followers of the Social Democrats to the more radical, anti-capitalist politics of the communists. Meanwhile, the conservative-minded were drawn to the more radical right wing, especially the Nazis. Votes for the liberal parties nearly disappeared and political polarization made it difficult to bring together a parliamentary majority.

German industrialists, bankers, and the wealthy in general, fearful of the country's growing unrest, saw in the conservative parties and Hitler's rising Nazi Party a counterweight to the dangers of rebellion from below—even as they were wary of where Hitler's program would lead.

The more traditional conservative parties of the German bourgeoisie thought they could contain the Nazis by offering to rule in a coalition with them. But Hitler and the Nazi leadership had their eye on winning exclusive power. This set off intense maneuvering within the government and set the stage for the presidential election in March 1932 in which Hitler ran against the Great War's

General Paul von Hindenburg. Hindenburg was elected president in 1925 after the death that year of the first Weimar president, Friedrich Ebert. Other candidates in the 1932 presidential election were Ernst Thälmann of the communist KPD and Theodore Duesterberg, candidate of a right-wing, anti-Semitic militia called the Stahlhelm. The Stahlhelm appealed to the same voting base as the Nazis. The Nazis undermined Duesterberg by making public the fact that he had a Jewish grandfather.

In the weeks before the election Hitler crisscrossed the country by airplane holding rallies in big cities and small towns. Fritz found himself in places where Hitler's election rallies were being held and he attended one of them. He came away impressed, and disturbed, by Hitler's ability to captivate a crowd with his brand of nationalist rhetoric.

Fritz understood the high stakes in this election. When he realized he could not make it back to Munich in time to vote, he wrote a note to his father: "If I do not tell you anything to the contrary by Thursday, I will be in Gera/Thuringia next Sunday. You can send me the ballot paper to the Hotel Sonntag."[10]

Hindenburg won the highest number of votes in that March 1932 election, but he failed to gain a majority. Hindenburg won a subsequent runoff election and a seven-year term by garnering 53 percent of the vote. But support for the Nazi Party was growing, even while it had nowhere near a majority. Ominously, the ranks of the brownshirt militia quadrupled in those months of the elections from 100,000 to 400,000 members.

### The New Chancellor

As president, Hindenburg had the power to appoint a chancellor who had broad executive authority, including over the military. But the chancellor could only rule by forming a majority in the parliament, the Reichstag, which backed his rule. In December 1932 Hindenburg appointed Kurt von Schleicher as German Chancellor. Schleicher was an ambitious man with strong ties to the military. But when he was unable to pull together a stable conservative government Hindenburg dismissed him. At the end of January 1933 Hindenburg appointed Adolf Hitler to the chancellorship.

The traditional conservative parties of the German bourgeoisie accepted Hindenburg's decision because they thought they could contain the more radical Nazis by inviting Hitler into a government whose cabinet members were mostly non-Nazis. It was a fatal miscalculation.

# 7

# 1933

IN A RECURRING DREAM, BENNO'S daughter Hani is walking on a wall. The wall is very high and stretches into the distance. She is nervous, afraid of heights. The wall is thick enough to walk on but there are loose bricks and when she steps, they crumble around her feet. She has a long way to go. But she can't turn back. She's afraid to turn. Suddenly her foot hits one of the loose bricks and she nearly slides over the edge. She catches a glimpse of sharp rocks far below. She's terrified.

A doctor listens as Hani retells her dream and talks of her fears. She tells the doctor how her nervousness and anxiety have been growing, and of her panic attacks.[11] Hani recalls for the doctor the incidents that seemed to have set this sense of terror in motion.

It was an evening in late January. Hani sat in the dining room with her father. He was smoking a cigar and reading the paper. Hani expressed her concern over the news that Hitler had become the new German chancellor. Benno said to her, "Hani, governments come and go in Germany. Besides, the Nazis are a small minority of the cabinet in his new government. Hitler won't be able to do much. It's one thing to be out of office and rile people up with angry ideas to get them to vote for you. It's another thing to run a country. Angry words and marches are not a substitute for dealing with problems in the real world."

Her father's words calmed her. But by the next morning her nerves were acting up again. That's when Anna suggested they take a walk. Perhaps to a café on Hochstrasse and have coffee or breakfast. They crossed the Ludwig bridge to the east side of the Isar and headed up Rossenheimer Street. It was cold. There was frost on the ground, but the sky was clear. She remembered her mother talking and seeing the mist from her mother's mouth as she spoke. Hani thought the words were calming, but in her nervous state there were moments when she only heard the sounds of her mother's words, but not the words themselves.

Several blocks ahead of them they saw a commotion in front of the Bürgerbraukeller. Shouts echoed down the street and Hani told her mother that she'd heard the word "*Juden*."

They turned away from the beer hall toward the paths that parallel the Isar River. They continued to hear loud voices from another direction and the sound of men singing. The words were muffled, but the tune was recognizable as a Nazi anthem called the "Horst Wessel Song," written by a leader of a brownshirt unit— "Millions are already looking at the swastika full of hope. The day for freedom and for bread dawns." The chorus of voices rose and fell, wavering like a drunkard staggering down a street.

Several men came along a path that skirted the river. As they approached Hani and Anna they shouted, "Our time has come. Now the fucking Jews will see the real Germany rise!" One of them made a complete turn of his body with his arms outstretched above his head, "Come out my Jews! Come out my Jews! Your new Germany is here to greet you!"

Hani was terrified, but she tried to walk and act calmly. Anna put her arm around her daughter. They turned up another street to an open area just beyond an apartment complex and turned toward the building as if making their way to it. The men, all wearing some Nazi insignia, and all smiling and jocular, passed them walking in the direction of the beer hall.

What Hani saw in their faces stunned her. They seemed mesmerized by an aggressive joy.

## March 9 and 10

A few months later, Hani was at her cash register in the downtown Munich dress shop where she had worked for several years. It was late morning when a seamstress came in hurriedly from the street. She went straight to the back of the store without greeting Hani.

When Hani took her noon break in the small backroom where store employees went to rest, she saw the worker, Herlinda, in conversation with another seamstress. "It was a lawyer named Siegel," Herlinda said in a strained voice. "Someone on the street identified him. He was barefoot and his pants were torn. You could see his mouth was swollen. It looked like a couple of teeth had been knocked out and there was blood on the front of his shirt." The other girl sat with her hand covering her mouth, as though in shock.

Hani sat down on stool next to a long table with bolts of pink and blue fabric. "What's going on?"

Herlinda was breathing heavily, on the verge of tears. "A Jewish lawyer named Siegel, Michael Siegel. He was out on the street with a sign around his neck that said, 'I'm an insolent Jew.' And he was barefoot!"

Hani suddenly felt a hot pressure in her head. "I don't understand."

"They were leading him around by a rope."

"Who?"

"The Brownshirts, the SA, the Nazis. They were laughing at him. He looked awful. Someone said they were punishing him for defending a client who was beaten by the police. That's all I know." At that, Herlinda leaned back in her chair and closed her eyes.

Hani felt a pressure in her head and chest. She could barely get the words out: "Were there people around?"

"Of course."

"And what did they do?" Hani tried to modulate her voice so that it wouldn't jump to a higher, shriller tone, which she knew happened when she was upset.

"They looked. They were just looking."

In the following days, Herlinda and other seamstresses shared more troubling news heard from relatives or gleaned from newspapers. In Munich, as across all of Germany, the offices of leftist papers had been ransacked and leaders of socialist or Social Democratic groups attacked, even killed, or "disappeared"—all this in the aftermath of a fire that badly damaged the Reichstag in Berlin. The Nazis accused communists of the arson, but more than a few people, including those in the shop, were of the opinion that it was the Nazis themselves who set the fire. Word was also filtering out about a new prison camp on the sight of the old munitions depot at Dachau where Hani's father, Benno, had been stationed during the war. People were being arrested and sent there.

Benno was quiet when Hani shared these stories at dinner. But he counseled Hani that they should not be overtaken by fear. "The Nazis are out to dampen down political opposition and consolidate their hold on power. If you are not a leader of a political opposition party, they won't have a lot of interest in you."

"Let's not fool ourselves." Anna was uncharacteristically terse. "Hitler has made his followers crazy with hatred. Who knows what they'll do?" The image of the men she and Hani saw the day after Hitler's appointment by Hindenburg to the Chancellorship was still vivid in her mind.

Benno replied with a fatherly calm voice. "For the time being we all have to be careful. But there's no point in letting fear control us, that's my point."

Hani continued to hear more disturbing stories at work. It was all people could talk about. Jewish stores were being sprayed with acid or defaced with inscriptions like "Jew, stinking Jew" and "Out with the Jews." One of the salesgirls was a frail-looking young woman in her early twenties who wore long braids with bows at the end that made her look even younger than her years. She stood behind the counter during a lull in customer visits to relate a story about a local Jewish merchant who had been practically torn apart by SA men who broke into his home. "They yelled at the poor man." As she spoke the color seemed to fade from her face. "They said, 'We've starved for fourteen years while you, Jewish pigs, have devoured everything!'"

Another worker drifted over to the conversation. "How do you know this?"

"Because my brother's best friend is in the Munich police, and he was called to the man's apartment after this happened."

"Why aren't the police doing anything about it?"

"It's been in the papers," the salesgirl answered. "The police commissioner, Dr. Stützel, who might have intervened to stop these things, was kidnapped by the SA men and beaten!"

Hani listened to such reports largely in silence. She was having trouble controlling her emotions and the agitated pitch of her voice. For the time being she decided to take her lunch breaks outside the shop to avoid more disturbing stories.

## The 1860 Club

With Hitler's ascendancy to the Chancellorship a new word entered prominently in the national vocabulary—"*Gleichschaltung.*" The word literally means "coordination." For the Nazis it meant an effort to reshape all of Germany's political, social, and cultural life to conform to a racialized view of history and society. For Jews it meant being shunned as an alien race. Newspapers in February 1933 reported on laws and measures that would set Germany on this new path. The Nazi media claimed it was about restoring "national greatness."

In March 1933, a few days after Fritz returned to Munich from an extended sales trip to northern German cities, he went to the 1860 Sports Club, the club he had belonged to for many years, looking forward to working out and seeing his friends. He'd read the news of new policies on the road, but the sign at the door of the club still staggered him. In bold letters that mimicked Hebrew script, it read, "*Juden Zutritt Verboten!*"—"Jews not allowed!"¹²

Opinion among 1860ers about the new policy was divided. Some of Fritz's friends and teammates as well as other club members were openly hostile to the change and even denounced it as "Nazi bullshit." There were threats to quit the club in protest. But nothing came of them. Meanwhile, others fell more quietly into line. Before long, even those who were genuinely outraged at the new laws and said this to their now-expelled fellow athletes, held back from expressing their opinion in front of anyone they didn't fully trust. Most of all, they kept quiet in public. As a consequence, after early opposition to the policy, a new normal began to impose itself. Former teammates swore they would continue their friendships with Fritz outside the club. But as time went on this became difficult and socially risky to do.

Jewish athletes now had no place to engage in group sports except in clubs that were exclusively Jewish. So, Fritz, along with other young sports-minded Jews, came together in Munich in their own Jewish sports club.

## BOYCOTT

In late March, Nazi Propaganda Minister Joseph Goebbels announced that a boycott of Jewish stores, cafés, and restaurants would begin throughout the country on April 1. The boycott was called, so the Nazi press claimed, in retaliation for "anti-German" protests in England, the United States, and elsewhere promoted by "Jewish hate mongers." To the ardent followers of the regime these calls for boycotting German products were proof of the power and malevolence of "international Jewry."

On the morning of Saturday, April 1, as Hani rode a Munich tram to work, she saw shops with windows and doors painted with the word "*Jude*." Most had uniformed Nazis pacing in front of them. Many Jewish shops were closed that day, either out of the fear of the boycott or because it was the Sabbath, and some

Jewish businesses were always closed that day. Hani was relieved when she arrived at work to see neither Nazis nor signs at the dress shop—apparently because the business was owned jointly by Jewish and non-Jewish owners.

The boycott day was not as terrifying as Hani had feared. In fact, she heard more talk of sympathy for Jewish store owners than antagonism. As she stood behind the cash register, she heard several men in their mid-forties, apparently in the store buying things for their wives or daughters, say to one another, "I don't care one way or another about the Jews, but I'm not going to let some brown-shirted punk tell me where I can and cannot shop!"

Another customer, while fishing around in a gawdy red purse for money to pay for a blouse, told Hani, "You should see those uniformed idiots out there in front of the Jewish stores—like they own the streets! I bought this pastry from a Jewish baker even though I really didn't want it. I think a lot of people are doing that today." She reached out to offer Hani a sweet roll. When Hani politely rejected her offer, she said, "Take it. It's defiance, honey. Hitler may control the government, but he doesn't control us!"

Hani repeated these stories that night over dinner after her mother suggested that, for the sake of the Sabbath, they should avoid talking about bad news. To that end, Anna didn't mention the call she'd gotten that afternoon from her sister Fanny describing a banner Traunstein Nazis had placed at the entrance to the town square that read, "Do not buy from Jews, they'll just kick you farmers from house and farm." Fanny told her sister, "Since we're the only Jewish family in Traunstein that does business with farmers that banner could only be referring to our family."

Fritz was home that evening, having arrived from a sales trip in the north. In deference to his parents, he talked mostly about the beauty of the Thuringian Forest near the town of Gera. He took a side trip there in the latter part of the week from Weimar where he had some important customers. The morning before he left Weimar, he saw signs of the boycott but the few customers he spoke with were opposed to it. One non-Jewish customer was outspokenly hostile to the Brownshirts whom he referred to as "turd shirts." Fritz stayed away from Jewish customers that day in order to avoid any confrontations with uniformed Nazis. "Seems to me like the boycott probably had its greatest success in keeping Jewish customers away from Jewish stores," Fritz said. He had seen unpleasant things as well—shops plastered with anti-Jewish graffiti—"Don't buy from the Jews," "Death to Judah"—and uniformed Nazis in front of Jewish shops yelling at potential customers. But he kept these to a minimum in the family conversation for the sake of his parents—and even more so, his sister.

## The "Holy Shrine"

Several weeks after the anti-Jewish boycott Hani, heading home from work, was walking along the Residenzstrasse, one of Munich's main streets in the area of the Marienplatz. She was not paying attention until she realized she was about to pass the Feldherrnhalle and the site of the street battle during Hitler's attempted Beer Hall Putsch. After 1933, Hitler declared the area a "holy shrine" and posted two armed uniformed guards on the Residenzstrasse side of the Feldherrnhalle.

Everyone walking past the soldiers was expected to give the *Heil Hitler!* (Hail Hitler) or the *Sieg Heil!* (Hail Victory) salute as a sign of loyalty to Hitler and the regime, gestures that had been adopted by the Nazis in the 1920s. After 1933 they became mandatory for all civilians. Bad things could happen if you didn't salute—especially for Jews. But, for Jews, saluting also carried the potential danger of being humiliated and physically assaulted. If you saluted and they found out you were Jewish, they might grab you and yell, "You, insolent Jew, how dare you mock us with this gesture!" In fact, in 1937, a law would make it illegal for Jews to give the Sieg Heil salute. This gave Jews the choice of risking punishment for saluting or, then again, for not—a situation only a fascist mind could find amusing.

Behind the columned Feldherrnhalle was a narrow street,

Viscardigasse. It was not uncommon for people to use that alley to bypass the shrine and the armed guards. But Hani had absentmindedly gone past the intersection. She was close enough to see the guards with their rifles, and she started to panic. To take the Viscardigasse detour, Hani would have to turn back. As she turned to look, she saw two young, uniformed Nazis behind her. What if they stopped her to ask why she was changing direction?

At that moment she dropped her handbag, and the contents spilled out on the street. She leaned down to pick up the bag and push the contents back inside. In the process she fell on the ground and one of her knees scraped the pavement. The young Nazis passed her by and said nothing. She picked up the handbag and walked shakily to the intersection. Was she going to faint? The terror only subsided when she joined others taking the turn up Viscardigasse.

When Hani arrived home, she poured out a shot of her father's schnapps, went to her room, and cried. At dinner that night, her face was drawn, and her eyes were red from crying. She sat looking at her plate but made no move to eat. "You're not hungry tonight, Hani?" her father asked.

Hani looked up. "I'm leaving Germany, Papa, Mama." Her voice broke with emotion. "I'm leaving Germany. I can't stay here anymore." Hani moved to get up, but her mother put her hand on Hani's arm, and she settled back down on her seat.

"Is there anything in particular . . ." Benno began. Anna put her hand up and Benno stopped mid-sentence.

Anna was holding back her own tears, but said to her daughter, "Sweetheart, we will support you in whatever you decide."

Later that week Hani wrote her first letter to Benno's brothers, her uncles Hugo, Markus, and Heinrich, asking for his help in her quest to emigrate to the United States.

### Sports Shoes and Racial Politics

During the early years Fritz spent on the road all over Germany—

first with Thormann and Dannhäuser and later with the Julius Levy line—he enjoyed good relationships with most of the small business owners and salespeople he interacted with. But after 1933, attitudes began to change. Even among those who had expressed progressive views and acceptance of other cultures, Nazi racial attitudes began to make inroads.[13]

Some of his contacts who'd been outspokenly anti-Nazi began to moderate their tone, if not their views. Some who identified as Social Democrats or had sympathies with communism began to backpedal and reevaluate their stated opinions of Hitler and the new regime. Some who had known Fritz for years confided that the racial discrimination was harmful and unjust, but they appreciated the improved economy and renewal of "national pride." The country was showing its defiance in the face of the "oppressive" Versailles accords. "These things have to be considered," they asserted.

After 1933, Fritz steered clear of discussions of religion and politics. Still, he sometimes became party to uncomfortable conversations. Some of these involved people who had formerly been uninterested in religion but suddenly developed a kind of passionate expertise on Jews and Judaism. "Jews," they would tell Fritz, "are the cause of a lot of Germany's problems."

One afternoon, when Fritz was in a sports shop in Berlin, he overheard a customer tell a salesman, "I want *you* to help me—I don't want to be served by that *Jew* over there."

"Very well," said the salesman. Fritz had to bite his tongue. He knew that the salesman the customer was speaking to was Jewish, whereas the other one, the one he thought was Jewish, was not!

Once, Fritz made the mistake of accepting an invitation to have a beer with a store's buyer whose views he already knew he did not share. After a few glasses of beer his drinking partner began to get agitated. "Jews," he told Fritz "I don't know if you know them well—but I do. I can tell you. For example," he leaned uncomfortably close to Fritz's face and his voice became annoyingly loud, "the Jews fucked us in the war! While our German boys were suffering in the trenches, fighting for our country, getting their arms blown off, getting their *balls* blown off, the Jews were home safe, getting rich. And the degenerate bastards were fucking our women while their husbands were dying at the front!" This was, to say the least, an unpleasant and frightening moment, as his drinking partner seemed interested in not only loudly proclaiming his profound indignation, but on having Fritz join his little hate fest.

Fritz had to hold himself back from the impulse to either get up and storm out of the beer hall or take his beer stein and smash it into the face of what he now regarded as an inebriated and ignorant fool. Rising from his chair, Fritz smiled grimly and told the buyer he had to get rest for an early appointment the next day and left the restaurant.

## Company Gatherings

Every winter, Thormann and Dannhäuser held meetings with company salesmen to discuss new products due to be introduced in the spring. The meetings aimed to build a "team spirit" among the sales staff and improve their sales techniques. Political discussion played little part in these discussions prior to 1931. Thormann was a Jewish-owned company and most of its sales staff were Jews. Company management generally downplayed the severity of the challenge the Nazis represented to the Weimar Republic and to the company itself. In the company's informal gatherings, Hitler and his party were the butt of jokes, such as, "What does the real Aryan man look like?" The answer was, "He's blond like Hitler, tall like Goebbels, and slender like Goering!"

In January 1933 the Thormann sales staff gathering took place in Leipzig the week before Hitler's selection as the German Chancellor. The tensions over the political climate reflected itself in the kinds of jokes told at that gathering. For example, "We used to say Hitler fanatics were dumb as rocks. That's still true. But now we know that rocks can kill you." And "What do you call a Nazi in a coffin? A waste of wood."

The winter meeting of 1934 was held in Dresden. The mood was decidedly more dour and there was little appetite for telling or hearing Nazi jokes. While business was holding steady, there were ugly stories of gentile businesses taking advantage of anti-Jewish government policies to undermine their Jewish competitors. And they all felt the pressures on Jewish concerns to lower their profile to appear more "German" and less "Jewish." Several of the company's salespeople had already left Germany and the subject of emigration entered their conversations.

At that same meeting the company approached Fritz and offered him an expanded territory that included lucrative accounts in Dresden, Leipzig, Dusseldorf, Breslau, and Berlin, as well as accounts on the Polish border and in Prague. Fritz, who at that moment had no thoughts of emigrating, accepted the offer.

The last night of the meeting, a sales representative from Berlin mentioned over dinner rumors that the Nazi government was moving forward with plans to force Jewish concerns to sell their businesses cheaply or even confiscate them. When silence followed his remark, the salesman apologized. "I think I may have ruined your dinners," he lamented. A colleague sitting across from him said, "It's not our dinner we're worried about being ruined. It's our lives."

## A Father-Son Conversation and a Family Dinner

Fritz returned home after the Dresden gathering. That evening he sat with his father in their living room and shared the rumors about the seizure of Jewish businesses. They had never previously talked in any depth about anti-Semitism. But on this occasion Benno offered some observations and conclusions he had come to through his life experiences and his readings of history. "Your grandfather had stories about the economic crash in 1873. It changed the way he approached business. He saw how bad economic times were dangerous for us. We saw that in 1923 with the inflation. Of course, you remember that . . . that's when Hitler's movement began to gain ground. The way I see it, Fritz, anti-Semitism is like a spasm that comes with an illness. The illness is this economic depression."

Fritz nodded quietly and took a puff from his pipe. He leaned forward on the couch and laughed. "You should hear some of the nonsense people tell me when they don't know I'm Jewish. One fellow in Thuringia—a lot of fanatics are in that area for some reason—told me, in confidence, that 'all German Jews pay a special tax to the government in *Moscow* to sustain the Soviet Union. The Soviets would have collapsed by now if it weren't for German Jews.' Where does this rubbish come from?"

"Conspiracies about Jews go back a long time, Fritz. But now the government gives these lies their full backing." Benno ran his hand over his now largely hairless scalp. "You know your sister wants to leave Germany."

"I know." Fritz took another pull from his pipe. "I can understand that. But I don't feel that way. Businesswise things are going fairly well for me in spite of everything. You know the company just gave me a bigger territory. I'm getting accounts in Berlin, Hamburg, even Prague! Father, I remember you saying there were times when things were bad, but then got better. I'm hoping that'll happen again this time."

At dinner that night, Hani, fresh from an encounter with the U.S. visa system, was anxious to talk about her efforts to emigrate. "You have to get your name on the list. Then wait for your number to come up."

"And where are you on that list?" her father asked her.

"There are hundreds ahead of me. While I'm waiting I have to work on the affidavit from the United States."

"And what if your number comes up for the visa and you don't have the affidavit?" Fritz asked her.

"I don't know what happens," Hani admitted. "I guess you go to the bottom of the list? I'm not sure. But I do know you have to have a visa and an affidavit. And since it takes so long to get them you should start the process yourself, Fritz."

"Right now I have other things on my mind." Fritz frowned. "I'm not as anxious to leave as you, Hani."

"What about the 'No Jews Allowed' signs and the sports club you can no longer belong to? What about the violence?" Hani snapped.

Fritz looked over at his father, and then at his mother. "This is my country, Hani. I'm not going to be pushed out of it so easily. This is not the first time Jews have been discriminated against in Germany."

"It's different this time," Hani answered.

"We don't know that," answered her brother.

"What?" Hani turned to Anna. "Mother, have you or Papa ever seen anything like this Nazi government?"

"No," answered Anna. "And no one can predict the future. But everyone deserves to be treated with respect. And to not have to live in fear. We've seen enough of Hitler not to expect anything good from him."

"Thank you, Mother," Hani said quietly.

Fritz said nothing to his family, but the following week he began a sales trip by driving through Stuttgart. There he stopped at the U.S. Consulate and placed his name on the visa waiting list and got information about emigrating.

## A Cousin's Defiance

Hani visited Traunstein in the spring of 1935. She, Max, and Klara, the two Holzer cousins she was closest to, went out to the town's main plaza. It was a warm afternoon, and the outdoor cafés were busy. Max, who, like his sister Klara, had a reputation as a prankster, was in a playful and defiant mood. They sat down at an outdoor table and Max went in to buy coffee and snacks for the three of them. As he came out of the café, he approached their table doing a little goose-step movement. He set the cups and food down on the table and said sarcastically, "You must drink your coffee for the Fatherland."

Hani was not amused. She looked around to see if anyone was

paying attention. She gave Max a stern look. "You need to watch what you do in public!"

"Screw the Nazis," Max said with a gesture of his hand. "Hani," he said in a loud whisper, leaning across the table toward her, "Fuck Hitler. Here in Traunstein most people ignore these Nazi pricks. The people in town know us, they've known our family for a long time. The Nazis are the biggest shits around here. They haven't been able to stop local farmers from doing business with us. We're not going to be driven out of here!" Hani took this as a reference to her efforts to leave Germany. "And we can defend ourselves."

"I don't think so." Hani leaned close to her cousin and spoke in low voice. "You don't know how nasty these people can be. I've listened to what they say in Munich. I've seen them. They have lots of people who support them, and they have people scared. No one's going to stick their neck out for us!"

Klara listened to the conversation. She sided with her brother. "They're not going to stop us from being German. And no matter what, we have the mountains, the lakes, the places to hike. They can't take that away from us. Even if they take our horses and cattle and our house—we'll still have the beauty of this land." For the moment Hani saw a different cousin from the happy-go-lucky Klara she was accustomed to.

Hani was ambivalent about the attitude of her country cousins. But their defiant confidence had, for that moment at least, a calming effect on her. On the train trip back to Munich that evening, she felt more relaxed than she had for a while. Maybe, she thought, the nightmare would go away. Maybe Jews could stand up to this.

This mood of optimism did not last long.

# PART II
# "THE JEWS ARE OUR MISFORTUNE"

## 8

# Race Riots and Racial Laws, 1935

SEVERAL WEEKS AFTER HANI RETURNED from Traunstein, in late May 1935, there were several anti-Jewish riots in downtown Munich. They took place in the middle of the day when large shopping crowds were in the streets. The windows of Jewish-owned stores were smashed, anti-Jewish graffiti was painted on walls and store windows, and Nazis, most of them members of the Schutzstaffel (protection squad), or SS, led by the staff of the rabidly anti-Semitic newspaper *Der Stürmer*, marched around the plaza threatening Munich's Jews. The event was orchestrated by Bavaria's minister of the interior, Adolf Wagner, one of the original members of the Nazi Party. Wagner's close ties with the Munich police guaranteed the rioters had a free hand.

Many people who witnessed these events or heard about them afterward expressed disgust at the public violence and thuggery. But no one from the public confronted the Nazis as the riots were going on, nor were there any significant protests or public criticism after they were over.

Several months later, Hitler declared Munich to be the "capital of the Nazi movement." For the city, this meant a proliferation of Nazi shrines, high-profile Nazi celebrations, art displays celebrating

Germany's new "Aryan culture," and events publicly highlighting the "debilitating influence of Jews." It also meant that more places where passers-by had to show obeisance to the regime by raising a stiff right-arm salute—and more impossible situations for Jews.

For Hani, Fritz, and every other Jew in Germany at the time, the proliferation of the newspaper *Der Stürmer* was a source of horror and humiliation. The paper offered a steady drumbeat of hatred, introducing grotesque caricatures of Jews and scandalous lies into the public space where they were picked up and repeated by the mean-spirited and the naïve. *Der Stürmer* relentlessly propagated the alleged "Jewish plot" to defile the German race. The paper was riddled with references to young "Aryan" girls being preyed upon by Jewish men, with cartoons of sweet German maidens being stalked by beastly figures with long noses and claw-like fingers.

The Nazi leadership publicly kept an arm's length from *Der Stürmer*. But they quietly promoted it, so that the paper became ubiquitous in factories and other workplaces, at bus stops, and on busy city street corners. *Der Stürmer* pages were posted on kiosks and on special displays on heavily traveled urban streets. Its circulation grew to a half a million. Its motto, "*Die Juden sind unser Unglück!*" or "The Jews are our misfortune!"—a phrase first coined by Heinrich von Treitschke, a prominent anti-Semite and rabid proponent of German colonialism in the 1880s—was printed in bold letters on the front of every issue.

### Racial Laws

The lawless character of Nazi street actions alienated sectors of the German public, damaged Germany's political relationships with other countries, and threatened its international commercial interests. Furthermore, Nazi authorities realized that street violence was not sufficient to achieve the goal of further isolating the Jews from the larger population. So they turned to legal means, formulating measures that would "regulate" Jewish disenfranchisement and spread it through all societal and governmental institutions.

In June 1934, the Nazis convened a conference of pro-fascist lawyers and officials to draft proposals for sweeping new anti-Jewish laws. The conference, chaired by the Third Reich's justice minister, Franz Gürtner, concentrated on two areas of social and legal policy: citizenship rights and sexual relations.

The intent of the Nazi legalists was to create strict legal separation between "racial Germans" and other groups, especially Jews, thereby demoting Jews from "citizens of the Reich" to "subjects." Only "racial Germans" would be eligible for the rights granted to citizens. Others—Jews, Blacks, Roma people, and Asians, for example—who lacked citizenship protections could be persecuted, isolated, and eventually driven out of the country under the cover of law.

Laws regarding "blood" or sexual relations were more complex and controversial. To formulate them, the Nazis drew from the same ideological sources and foundations Hitler used in his book, *Mein Kampf*. These sources included the nineteenth-century racist theoretician Artur de Gobineau and the British racist Houston Steward Chamberlain, whose writings on "Aryan superiority" and "racial history" at the turn of the century had been widely promoted in German academic and political circles. At that time a close liaison developed between Chamberlain and Germany's Kaiser Wilhelm.

National Socialist legal functionaries took two distinctly different approaches to the measures they were asked to formulate. One group, the more traditional legalist school, wanted laws based on established and conventional jurisprudence which would depend on arguments of logic, proof, or precedent. As Bernard Lösener, a representative of this approach, stated, "An effective means of determining whether a given human being has an element of Jewishness on the basis of his behavior or outward appearance or blood . . . does not exist, or at least at present has not yet been found." Lösener argued that it was not sound jurisprudence to base court rulings solely on a subjective hatred of Jews.

The other group, the so-called Nazi radicals, believed they could ignore concerns about established legal doctrine or evidence. They argued that the political goal of racial separation was basic and central to the needs of Nazi society. This was sufficient justification for laws to prohibit sexual relations between the "*Volk*" and those described as "alien races." The leader of this radical faction at the conference was Roland Freisler, who would later earn a reputation as Nazism's most bloodthirsty jurist when he became president of the Nazis' "People's Court." In arguing for what he called a "primitive" approach, Freisler pointed to two examples from the United States: Jim Crow laws that enforced racial segregation—a legal measure akin to what the Nazis sought in their citizenship laws—and blood laws. These "blood laws," or anti-miscegenation laws, which prohibited sexual or marriage relations between people of different "ethnic" or "racial" groups, especially those between "Whites" and "Non-Whites," were enforced in many U.S. states. Freisler argued that U.S. courts and legislatures required no scientific evidence or legal precedent to create and enforce such laws, so the German legal system need not require them either.

After weeks of wrangling, it was the radical faction—which more closely represented the thinking of Hitler and the top Nazi leadership—that won the day.

### Nuremberg Rallies, 1935

In mid-September 1935, in Nuremberg, a Bavarian city 120 miles from Munich, six days of events were held under the heading "Rally of Freedom." The events, best known for their large and highly choreographed rallies, were meant to accomplish three interrelated objectives of the regime: breaking with the restraints on military rearmament imposed by the Versailles Treaty; codifying *in law* the inferior status of Jews; and solidifying the monopoly of Nazi rule.

During an elaborate display of militarism, armaments, and aggressive military tactics, Hitler announced, in direct defiance of Versailles, the resumption of compulsory military service.

At the same time, a special session of the Reichstag was held in Nuremberg in order to pass the key anti-Jewish laws that had just been formulated. Henceforth Jews would no longer be granted the rights due to a German citizen. Regarding blood laws, marriage or extramarital relations between Jews and non-Jews would henceforth be legally prohibited, and German women under the age of forty-five would be forbidden from working in Jewish households. Finally, a law passed in Nuremberg enshrined the Swastika flag as the sole and official flag of Germany, thus removing the last symbolic remnant of the Weimar Republic: its black, red, and yellow striped flag.

## Legality

After the Nuremberg session, Jews had to be very careful how and with whom they moved in public. Police were empowered to arrest anyone thought to be violating these new laws. Jewish cousins, even siblings of different sexes walking down the street together or in a movie theater together, could be arrested and jailed until they could prove they were not a "mixed race couple." Jewish men who had any kind of social contact with non-Jewish women, and vice versa, risked persecution and prosecution.

By codifying and legalizing Nazi racial practices, Nuremberg encouraged an outpouring of anti-Semitic scholarship and legal commentary that found its way into popular magazines, newspaper articles, documentary films, newsreels, exhibits, classroom lectures, scholarly forums, special educational programs, "scientific" symposiums, and scholarly journals. The Nuremberg laws created the most widespread and consequential changes in German society.

# 9

# Trogerstrasse

BENNO HAD LIVED IN THE Liebherrstrasse apartment since his youth. He and Anna had lived in it together since their marriage in 1907 and raised their children there. However, the apartment was less than a block from the busy office of the Nazi paper *Völkischer Beobachter*, and, as time went on, they began to feel more and more uncomfortable there. In April 1936 they moved to a new apartment on the east side of the Isar River.[14]

The new apartment at 44 Trogerstrasse was in a slightly more upscale district, but otherwise not very different from their Liebherrstrasse home. Unfortunately, it was near the corner with Prinzregentenstrasse, one of the city's main streets, and a frequently traveled route for those coming to and from 16 Prinzregentenplatz, Hitler's Munich residence.

This proved to be unnerving, especially for Hani. Shortly after their move, she was walking several blocks from the new apartment when a caravan of Mercedes vehicles pulled up to the curb within feet of where she was standing. She held her breath as she watched Hitler and other Nazi brass exit the cars in front of her. A large man in uniform coolly brushed up against her as she backed away. Unnerved, Hani abandoned the errand she was running and returned to her apartment.[15]

## The Tailor

Fritz continued to spend much of his time on the road. His sales territory had steadily expanded, extending his travels. But his side trips were greatly curtailed by a diminished sense of comfort and safety.

While on the road Fritz had often sent his dirty clothes home for cleaning and pressing. Anna had cleaned the clothes herself. But as the years went by, she began bringing them to a cleaner's. Conveniently, the new Trogerstrasse apartment had a tailor shop on the ground floor and Anna began bringing Fritz's clothes there to be washed and pressed.

Over time Fritz became acquainted with the neighbor tailor, Ludwig Eiber, and grew to like this friendly man in his mid-forties. Eiber was slightly taller than Fritz, and he had a wiry athletic build. With his thin face, thick eyebrows above sleepy gray-green eyes, a neatly trimmed mustache and light brown hair combed straight back, he looked to Fritz like someone he'd seen in an American movie.

Fritz and Eiber found they had a mutual interest in sports, especially swimming, hiking, and skiing. Eiber had done a great deal of it in his younger days and was eager to hear about Fritz's experiences. Fritz found Eiber sympathetic to the conditions that made him, as a Jew, limit his sports activities. He found that Eiber had a deep disdain for the Nazis and this made Fritz feel comfortable talking to him.

Moreover, the Olympic Games being held in Berlin in the summer of 1936 provided them with fertile ground for lively conversation.

## A Dinner Conversation and a High Jumper

In July 1936, Mina Einstein was the last of her immediate family in Laupheim. Anna and Mina's younger brother Ludwig had died in 1916, and their father Moses passed away in 1924 at the age of eighty-one. Alone in the family house, Mina had begun letting rooms for both financial help and for companionship. Sofie Braunge, a widow, became one of Mina's housemates. When Mina came to Munich to visit Anna's family in the summer of 1936, she invited Sofie along.

In honor of the occasion, Anna organized a Sabbath dinner and invited her niece Ilse and Ilse's husband, Hermann Schuster, from Wolfratshausen. Benno invited Berthold and his wife, Hilde.

It was a hot summer day in Munich—the kind of day that made eating outside at the Marienplatz or in the English Garden a pleasant alternative to the Neuburgers' warm apartment. They would likely have done so in the past, but under the circumstances, the atmosphere for Jews made such public excursions risky. So, Anna, Mina, and Hani prepared a special meal in their apartment, a dinner for nine people. At Benno's urging they made sauerbraten as a reminder of the seder in Laupheim in 1907. Because it was Friday, Anna also prepared fish for Hermann, Ilse's Catholic husband. Hermann, a tall, sturdy man with prominent features and a warm and straightforward manner said he appreciated the gesture, but he asked for a portion of meat as well. "You need to know something about me," he said. "I'm about as observant a Catholic as you are Jews!"

Anna laughed as she looked over at Mina.

"Am I right?" asked Hermann.

"Yes. But that's not why we're laughing," Anna said. It was Mina who responded with a sly smile, "We were just thinking how much our father, Moses, rest his soul, would totally agree with you!"

During dinner, Berthold and Hilde complimented Anna and Hani on their sauerbraten, saying it was every bit as good as in the old days in Laupheim. That prompted Benno to recollect his first visit to Laupheim. It was then that the name Gretel Bergmann was stirred into the conversational pot.

Gretel, who'd grown up in Laupheim, was the center of a controversy raging around the coming Berlin Olympics. Germany had been chosen as the site for the 1936 games several years before

Hitler came to power. At first Hitler opposed hosting the Games. But when he realized the propaganda potential of holding the Games in Germany, he reconsidered.

The Nazi boycott of Jewish businesses in the spring of 1933 brought world attention to Germany's anti-Jewish policies. Now, word that the Nazis intended to exclude Jewish athletes from the games provoked a broad outcry. Averill Brundage of the U.S. Olympic committee went to Berlin in 1934 to "investigate," but he dismissed concerns for the fate of Jewish athletes. After all, he said, Jews were also excluded from his own sports club in Chicago.

Nevertheless, in August 1935, after the passage of the Nuremberg racial laws, threats of a boycott of the Berlin Games continued to grow louder in the United States. The U.S. Olympic Committee sent Charles Sherrill, a retired general, to Germany. Sherrill was sympathetic to Hitler and advised the German Chancellor that he could placate his critics and end the threat of a boycott through some public gesture.

Hitler realized that a boycott by the United States and possibly other countries would be disastrous to the credibility of the Berlin games and he called on the Reich sports director Hans von Tschammer und Osten to invite heretofore excluded Jewish athletes to join the team. One of these athletes was Gretel Bergmann, a twenty-two-year-old high jumper from Laupheim. After being expelled from a German sports club in 1933, she had left Germany for England. There she competed in the British championship in women's high jump and tied the German record in that event. When German Olympic officials invited her back to Germany for the 1936 Games, she reluctantly accepted.

Gretel Bergmann's family home was just a few blocks from the Einsteins' Laupheim home. Bergmann had, quite understandably, become the topic of a lot of talk around the town, especially in Judenberg, Laupheim's Jewish district. Mina commented that she had not seen Gretel since her return from England, and she'd assumed she was busy training.

"Mina, Sophie—what do you think of Gretel's return to Germany?" Anna asked.

Before either could answer, Hani spoke up. "Gretel should have refused to return! It's not going to be safe for her here. And if she competes, people will say, 'Oh, see, the Jews are okay in Germany. They're being included. What's all the fuss about?'"

Anna agreed with her daughter but felt bad about the pressures young Gretel was having to bear. Benno offered that her participation in the games might influence public opinion toward Jews in a positive way. He still held out hope that public pressure would force the Nazis to moderate their views.

"I don't think they're going to modify their views," Hilde responded. "The public they cater to doesn't like us. And everyone else is too afraid or too complacent to speak up."

Berthold swallowed a mouthful of sauerbraten. "I don't believe England or the United States would boycott the games for us, no matter what."

Mina looked over at Hani. "I wouldn't be so hard on Gretel. We heard from neighbors who know the Bergmanns pretty well that her family was threatened. She had to join the German team to protect them." No one at the table doubted that such threats were real. "And several weeks ago, we had some young Nazis, schoolchildren, actually, marching around Judenberg singing their Hitler songs and shouting, 'Dirty Jews, get out!'"

"Was Gretel's named mentioned?" Hani asked.

"I don't know. But one of the Jewish girls down the street from us was at her window when these nasty kids passed by, and she threw water from a cup out the window at them. I don't think any of them even got wet. But they came back a few days later when the girl . . . Tony . . . was coming home from school. They grabbed her and cut off clumps of her hair. Then they led her around the streets with a sign around her neck that said, 'I'm the dirtiest Jew in this town.'"

Sophie added, "My niece was at a Bar Mitzvah party at a friend's place in Ulm recently when some people threw bricks through the windows. Some of her friends got cut with the broken glass." She shook her head. "You know, the brick throwers just stood outside the house laughing! Then," Sophie paused, "not long after that my niece's friends got a visit from the Ulm mayor's office. They were told they'd better fix their windows because the Olympic games were coming, and the government wanted nothing that would upset visiting foreigners!"

Benno got up and put a record on the gramophone—a work by Gustav Mahler. He kept the volume low. When Mina asked if he would raise the sound, Benno turned to her, "We have to watch the music we play in this apartment. As beautiful as it is, some people in this building will take offense. They'll know nothing about the composer, but if they hear a composition that someone has told them a Jew, or a half-Jew, or a friend of a Jew, or a neighbor of a Jew, composed, then, of course, of course they'll say, 'This cannot be tolerated.'"

"People in this building?" Hermann asked. Benno nodded.

"Even when Mahler converted to Catholicism, they hounded him," Anna noted.

Ilse put her arm around Hermann's neck and looked at him, "What do we say to that, honey?"

Hermann replied without hesitation, "I say we're in this together for the long haul." Ilse gave him a kiss on the side of his face as he blushed.

Berthold said quietly, as if talking to himself, "What do they say? Once a Jew, always a Jew. But"—he raised his voice and a glass of beer—"here's to better days, we had them before, and we'll have them again." And everyone drank, joining him.

### Broken Promises

After the Nazis made their token gesture to invite Gretel and another Jewish woman athlete, the fencer Helen Meyers, to join the German team, the movement to boycott the Berlin Olympics lost momentum and the United States committed itself to participate.

The Nazis then changed course. In the weeks leading up to the games, German Olympic officials restricted Gretel Bergmann's access to practice. Two weeks before the games were to begin, Bergmann received a letter from the Reich sports director stating that she would no longer be accepted on the national team due to "under performance."

### The "Best Olympics" ever

Once the Nazi government decided to move ahead with the games, they took pains to put on a good face for the crowds of foreign visitors and worked to showcase their "new Germany." Fritz, who was almost continually on the road that busy Olympic summer, found the landscape around the country disorienting. "No Jews Allowed" signs and other evidence of racial hatred had been removed. The regime was especially diligent in cleaning up Berlin. But cities and small towns throughout the country were also sanitized of anti-Jewish propaganda. *Der Stürmer*, normally posted in special display cases and newspaper boxes, was prohibited from being sold openly.

Fritz noted that chatter over racial issues receded in step with government policy, as if someone had lowered a mental thermostat implanted in people's brains. It did not disappear, however. Overt racial hatred burst out in various forms in personal commentary provoked by the games themselves, especially the dramatic success of American Black athletes.

On the opening day of competition, the first gold medal was taken by Cornelius Johnson, a Black high jumper from the United States. Another U.S. Black athlete, Jesse Owens, won the prestigious 100-meter dash, while Hitler's favorite, Erich Borchmeyer, came in fifth. Hitler commented sourly on Owens's performance that people whose "forefathers came from the jungle" are more "primitive," and this gave them an advantage. On the third day of competition, Owens beat Germany's favorite in the long jump, Ludwig Long. Owens set a new Olympic record with a jump of

8.06 meters. After Owens's record-setting jump, Long defiantly gave Owens a warm embrace in front of the huge stadium crowd. This gesture earned him a rebuke and a warning from Hitler's close associate, Rudolf Hess.

### Races and Running Shoes

Prior to the opening of the games, the German sports shoe company, Dassler Brothers, saw an opportunity to popularize their Geda brand running shoes by offering free shoes to Olympic athletes who agreed to wear them in competition. Jesse Owens was one of those athletes who agreed to wear Dassler shoes. When Owens won four gold medals and set three world records wearing the Geda brand shoes, the company was able to cash in on his notoriety. Their sales shot up but it put them in a bad light with Hitler, Goebbels, and loyal Nazis.

Fritz admired Owens and rooted for him. That Dassler benefited from their association with an athlete whose performance undermined the central tenet of Nazism was a sweet bit of irony—one that Fritz and others like him could only enjoy openly among trusted friends and family.

Even while German athletes did quite well in these games, winning more medals than any other country, the window the games opened to the qualities of athletes of many nations, ethnicities and "races" clearly had its negative side for the Nazis. This challenge to Nazi racial dogma was notable enough that Joseph Goebbels recorded in his diary in early August, "After the Olympics, we'll get ruthless, then there will be some shooting."

Fritz made it home for a few days during the Olympics. When he paid a visit to Eiber's tailor shop to get some shirts pressed, he felt confident enough in his friend to express happiness with Owens's success. Eiber shrugged and invited Fritz to go outside his shop so they could "stretch their legs."

As they walked along Prinzregentenstrasse toward the Isar River, Eiber changed the subject away from sports to reveal his thoughts about two apartment house neighbors known to Fritz as Herr Hack and Herr Kandl. Since both came occasionally to Eiber's shop, he had heard their complaints about "the new Jews in the building"—meaning Fritz's family. Eiber moved closer to Fritz as they walked. "I need to tell you something about these fellows. I've known Hack for years. He used to be a decent guy. We used to drink together. He voted for the Social Democrats before 1933. But it didn't take long for him to 'change color' and become an apparent true believer in this cult of the ignorant." Eiber paused as they waited for traffic to clear before crossing Prinzregentenstrasse. "Kandl on the other hand has always been a shit. He was too much of a coward to be running around the streets in a brown shirt with a torch or a banner, so he settled for being an armchair fascist. He never saw any action in the war, some physical thing got him out of it. And he got into a black-market hustle at that time with all the shortages, making enough to start that small printing business of his. Printing up Nazi Party posters gave his business a boost."

Eiber stopped at a grassy area at the foot of the Friedensengel monument and took out a cigarette and lit it. As he did so he looked at Fritz sheepishly. "I only smoke occasionally and out of sight of Bertha." Fritz laughed. "After the war," Eiber continued, "when things in the western front went bad for us our Herr Kandl was among that crowd that started talking about the Jews. The Jews!" Eiber shook his head.

Eiber took some satisfaction in recounting a conversation he'd had with Herr Kandl on the street outside the apartment the day during the first week of the Olympics. "Kandl was a little upset about Jesse Owens." Eiber grinned. "I tried to avoid talking to him because, to be honest, the last thing I want is to tangle with that blockhead. But Kandl blurts out, 'You must have heard what happened at the games yesterday'—that was the day after the long jump competition—'such an embarrassment for a German athlete to lose to that ape!' He actually said that! Well, why would that surprise me? Listen, Fritz, you should know something about me," Eiber took a puff from his cigarette, "I would never call someone like Herr Kandl an ape knowing what a great insult that would be to our primate cousins." Fritz got a good laugh out of that and repeated the remark to his parents and friends in the days that followed.

## Hani's Escape, 1937

SOON AFTER HANI TOLD HER parents of her ardent desire to leave Germany in the summer of 1933, she began writing to her uncles in the United States—Benno's three brothers, Markus, Heinrich, and Hugo. Of the three, Hugo, who lived in Chicago, was the most sympathetic to his niece's appeal. He wrote back to his niece saying he would do what he could to help her.

In early 1934, word came that Hugo had passed away and Hani spent weeks in despair. Then, Hugo's son Morton, who was a few years older than his Munich cousins, responded to Hani's appeal and declared he would follow through with his father's wishes. But since Morton's mother spoke no German, he'd grown up in an English-speaking household and knew practically no German at all. Meanwhile, Hani could read some English, but her grasp was shaky. Thus communication between them was difficult.

While Hani waited for her name to rise on the U.S. Consulate's waiting list, she and Morton tried to navigate the tangled process of securing an affidavit, a necessary prerequisite for emigrating to the United States.[16]

It was Nazi policy in the years 1933 to 1939 to force Jews out of the country. By 1934, Nazi functionaries such as Reinhard Heydrich wrote in internal government documents: "The life opportunities of the Jews have to be restricted. . . . To them Germany must become a country without a future." But it was also their policy to strip emigrating Jews of as much of their money and other valuables as they could.

On the U.S. side, the quota of Germans allowed to immigrate to the United States was second in size to that of England's. But immigration quotas were scaled back because of the economic depression and other pressures. To qualify for U.S. entry, an applicant needed to provide proof that he or she would not be an economic burden on society. This was especially difficult for German Jews who had to surrender *all their wealth* as a condition to leave Germany.

Morton, never wealthy, was barely getting by as a tie salesman in a Depression economy and he had an elderly mother to support. To sponsor his cousin, he would have to show a level of income he did not make and a level of savings he did not have. He had no choice but to appeal to friends, family, and the community for help. It all took time. After many months of work, of preparing and filing documents in hopeful anticipation—as Hani's name crept up the U.S. visa list—Morton sent word that the U.S. government had rejected the affidavit he had submitted on her behalf.

Hani spent the following days in a state of shock, consoled only by the fact that her cousin was not giving up. She wrote back to Morton encouraging him to find out as much as he could about what was happening in Germany. What he found heightened his anger and his determination to continue to pursue the process.

## THE DOCTOR'S PRESCRIPTION

On the eve of a trip to Stuttgart to turn in some documents at the U.S. Consulate, Hani felt an anxiety that bordered on panic. She was unsteady on her feet. Wondering how she could function in such a state of mind, she made an appointment with a psychologist. "I think I'm having a nervous breakdown!" she confessed to the doctor, her hands cupping her mouth and tears welling out of her closed eyes.

The doctor listened quietly, encouraging Hani to express her fears. What was she most afraid of? When did she feel the greatest fear? What did she do when she felt panic attacks come on? After listening to his patient, the doctor took a notepad and wrote a message on it in large letters. He waited until Hani was calm and her breathing normal. Then he handed the note to Hani. It read simply, "I am perfectly calm. I am perfectly calm."

"Read it aloud, Miss Neuburger."

"I am perfectly calm." She looked at the doctor. "That's all?"

"Read it over again."

"I am perfectly calm. I am perfectly calm."

"Again."

"I am perfectly calm."

"Again."

"I'm perfectly calm. I'm perfectly calm. Okay, I'm calm now." She laughed and stared at the doctor.

The doctor nodded. "Are you sure?"

"Yes. Well, I am now," she said.[17]

"Good." The doctor was a short man with thick glasses that made his hazel eyes look larger than they were. He kept his eyes on Hani. She almost started laughing because the doctor suddenly reminded her of a picture she'd once seen of a large-eyed lemur. "I want you to practice something." The doctor put his hands over his eyes. "I want you to close your eyes and imagine something that frightens you. Then I want you to open your eyes and look at this paper and read the message over and over. You can practice that at home. And whenever you feel anxious, take out that paper." Hani closed her eyes to avoid his stare. His voice was calming. "Then—and this is very important—turn away from what frightens you, breathe deeply, and read those words to yourself. Read them over and over again. If that doesn't help, come back."

Hani was disappointed because the therapy didn't seem very effective. But she tried it a few times when she felt a bout of panic coming on and it did provide some relief. And yet it did not diminish her obsession with finding a way out of Germany.

## Too Old to Start Over

While Anna and Benno did what they could to calm Hani and to divert her from what Benno considered to be an obsessive fear, they supported her effort to leave Germany. It was abundantly clear that the future for young people like her was being erased.

At the same time, they didn't think emigration was for them. At that point, Benno was sixty-six, and Anna was sixty. Benno felt too old to start over in a new country. And if he and Anna did make it to the United States, what could they be, other than a burden? What kind of a life would that be?

Benno took comfort in the perspective his years had given him. "We had the Kaiser," Benno told his children. "We had the military government. Then Weimar, and now this. We lived through the war when food was scarce. We lived through the Revolution and the changes of government. We lived through the violence of the Freikorps. We lived through the inflation. We'll live through this, too."

"I'm a living witness to the growth of this city," Benno would say. "I saw its buildings go up, new streets put in, tram lines laid. I was here when horses were replaced by electric trams and gas automobiles. I visited the construction sites as libraries and museums were built. I saw them build the Science Museum from the ground up. I'm a war veteran. And," he'd say with a bit of a twinkle in his eye, "if there were ever an accounting of those who over the years drank the most Munich beer, I'm sure I'd be somewhere in the running!"

"And anyway," he responded when the subject of emigration came up with his children for the umpteenth time, "we're too old to be a threat to this government!"

## Relief and Grief

When Hani came home one day from doing errands, her mother

came to the door to greet her. "And?" Hani asked, confused by the expression on her mother's face. Then, she saw an envelope on the table in the dining room. "It's from Morton," Anna said quietly. "I haven't opened it."

Anna sat with her daughter as Hani carefully slit the envelope with a letter opener. Hani's hands were shaking. She passed Anna the envelope. "I can't look at this, Mama." Anna pulled out the letter carefully without reading it and passed it to her daughter. "No, Mama, please, read it to me." "No," Anna said. "Sweetheart, this is your letter. It's for you to read." Hani unclenched her hand from the chair. She unfolded the thin yellow onion paper. She looked up at Anna, then read slowly:

> Dear cousin,
> I'm writing to inform you that the U.S. State Department has accepted our affidavit! Isn't that great! Since you told me your consulate number makes you eligible for a U.S. visa, it looks like you are free to come to us. We will be here to receive you! We are very happy! Write to me when you book your passage from Germany. We will inform you on the best way to reach us in Chicago from New York. Don't worry about the cost, we will make it happen.
> Your cousin, Morton.[18]

When Hani finished reading, she and her mother broke down in tears.-

The U.S. Consulate in Stuttgart sent Hani a note that the way was clear for a U.S. visa. All that remained was to undergo a physical exam, book passage to the United States, and pay the exorbitant taxes on the meager possessions she'd be allowed to take with her. But she was getting out! For the first time in years, Hani, now twenty-eight years old, felt hopeful. She lay in bed that night trying to imagine what her life in a new country would be like and that brought her some moments of worry. But she slept for the first time in years without bouts of paralyzing anxiety.

## A Yom Kippur in Hamburg

The sky was just beginning to lighten on the morning of September 17, 1937. It was the eve of Yom Kippur. Hani, Fritz, Anna, and Benno stood outside their Trogerstrasse apartment as Fritz loaded Hani's luggage into the trunk of his car. Hani looked up at the apartment building for one last time. She wrapped her arms around Benno and kissed him. Then, she turned to her mother. As their arms folded around each other Hani felt light-headed and deeply sad. She felt wetness on her cheek as her tears mingled with those of her mother. "We'll write each other, Mama. I'll write as soon as I arrive in New York. You think about coming. Please think about it."

"Of course, we'll stay in touch, sweetheart." Benno cupped his hand on his daughter's cheek. "Don't worry about us, we'll be okay. And, who knows, maybe we'll see you in Chicago."

"Hani." Fritz closed the trunk of his car. "We really need to go. We've got a long trip ahead. You never know what delays there might be on the way." Fritz saw his parents in the rearview mirror waving as his car made the turn down Prinzregentenstrasse toward the Luitpold Bridge. They were beginning their 500-mile ride to the port city of Hamburg. The next day, on Yom Kippur, Hani was due to board the steamship *President Roosevelt* for the United States.[19]

Fritz looked over at his sister. She seemed lost in thought. "Are you going to miss Germany?"

"No!" she practically shouted. "Why should I? Why should I miss a place that treats us so badly! If I could, I would not think about this place again. And it can *all* go to hell! I mean it, Fritz. If only our family would all leave, I would then spit on this place for how it's treated us—and *never* come back here!"

As they left Munich on the road north that would take them to Nuremberg, Hani talked about the trials of Jewish men accused of sexual crimes which were, at that time, a constant topic in the German media. She had a recent issue of a Munich paper with her that cited one such case and she read aloud the description of a Jewish businessman brought to trial as Fritz gripped the steering wheel. He didn't want to hear about these unpleasant realities for the hours that stretched ahead. But he kept quiet. He realized what his sister was doing. Though he was not ready at that moment to admit it to her face, he knew that in their long dispute over whether to stay in Germany or leave, she had been right. For years he had accused her of overreacting to the threats, of being overly sensitive, overly fearful, and of exaggerating the anti-Jewish climate which he believed was a painful but passing phase. But now reality had proven him wrong.

A major shift in his thinking had taken place six months earlier when he met with a fellow salesman from Thormann and Dannhäuser at a café in Weimar. There had long been stories of Jewish enterprises driven out of business or forced to sell out to non-Jewish buyers at cutrate prices. But on this occasion, the salesman told him of credible reports that Thormann and Dannhäuser—and all other Jewish businesses—were going to be taken over, or "Aryanized," to use the Nazi term. The rumor Fritz had first heard at a dinner in Dresden three years earlier was now shaping up as an immediate reality. It was only a matter of time before wholesale seizures would begin. "The stage is being set for something much more sweeping. Maybe there'll be some incident to justify extreme measures, since extra-legal actions by the government are not popular with a lot of Germans," the colleague surmised.

"What do you mean by 'some incident'?" Fritz asked.

"Your guess is as good as mine. Let's not underestimate the Nazis' creativity. And the pressures are building. All it would take is for one of us to do something out of frustration, something that could be seized on as a pretext for a massive expropriation." The colleague shook his head and lowered his gaze. "It's coming, Fritz. It's time for us to wash the sand from our eyes."

It was this threat to his livelihood, along with the orchestrated assaults on Jewish men and the unending string of public insults that finally washed the sand from Fritz eyes. He'd come to realize that he, too, needed to get out. But he was still hesitant to admit this to his sister.

As they drove Hani was in a talkative mood. She spoke of her appreciation for what Morton had done and went on about what she knew of him. She mused with anticipation about what she expected of the United States She talked about what she'd read about Chicago. She talked about how she was going to improve her English and about the kind of work she would eventually like to get. She talked of her interest in seeing the things in the United States she'd heard about. "Like cowboys," she insisted at several points in the discussion.

Fritz turned to her. "Hani, there may be a lot of cows in Chicago, but not a lot of cowboys, except maybe in the movies."

"Well, I'll look for them," she countered. "If I find them, I'll let you know."

When they reached Nuremberg, they had been on the road for a few hours and were hungry for breakfast. But they did not want to risk stopping in a city that neither of them was familiar with, and whose very name left a bad taste in their mouth. Fritz proposed they continue to Leipzig. From his travels to that city Fritz knew of places where it would be safe for them to eat.

Over lunch, they talked about German and American foods. Hamburgers were the only American food either of them had heard much about. Hani thought it odd that a typical American food was named after a German city.

"I'm sure they have the same things there as we have here," assured Fritz.

"Wurst?"

"Of course. Only they don't call it that. They call it 'hot dogs.'"

"Hot dogs?" Hani got that slightly cross-eyed look of hers, which made her brother smile. "That is so strange. And it doesn't sound at all appetizing."

Fritz laughed. "Don't worry. No one starves in America. You'll just have to learn to eat fast! Everything in America is done fast."

Hani had a habit of using the expression "if it kills me!" to describe her intentions. If she were going to visit a friend she would say, "I'm going to see so-and-so tomorrow, even if it kills me." If she wanted to have some schnitzel, she'd say, "I'm going to cook some schnitzel tomorrow for dinner if it kills me." Fritz found the repeated use of this expression terribly annoying. Sometimes, when he heard it, he'd answer his sister's fatal threat by muttering under his breath, "Well, let's just hope it does!"

But on this occasion, when Hani, his nervous, sensitive, overwrought younger sister, said, "When I get to the United States, I'm going to get an affidavit to get you out of Germany if it kills me," he made no sarcastic reply. He simply answered quietly, "Hani, please do that. I'll be waiting."

At that moment a realization struck them both: Hani, the "little sister" of the family, was leaving and she would never be coming back. And Fritz, German to his toenails, was now resolved that he, too, would have to leave.

A sadness too heavy for words hung in the air. And they drove in silence for quite a time after that.

(l to r) Alfred Holzer, Hedi Holzer, Benno Holzer, Klara Holzer, Max Holzer, with cousins Hani Neuburger, Fritz Neuburger.

Benno, Anna, and daughter Hani with friends.

(l to r) Hedi, Benno, Hani, Anna, and Klara.

Fritz with others salesmen. Fritz is in the front row,
last person on the right.

(l to r) Fritz, Martha Holzer, Alfred Holzer, Klara Holzer and Hani.

Hani and Fritz, Munich.

Benno, Gestapo mugshot.

## Max Holzer, 1937

AFTER THE PASSAGE OF THE Nuremberg Laws of 1935 the Nazi press unleashed a campaign warning of the danger posed by Jewish sexual behavior. Julius Streicher's paper *Der Stürmer* was the most strident and bloodthirsty. Non-Jewish men were alerted to the dangers their "Aryan women" faced from Jewish men. More "mainstream" and respectable publications also spouted anti-Jewish hype. Non-Jewish women, "Aryan" women, were warned to beware of Jewish men.

Attacks on Jewish men by the legal system rose sharply. In 1936, 358 people were prosecuted for sexual crimes, a huge jump from the previous year. In 1937, this increased to 512. Two-thirds of those arrested and tried were Jewish men, even while Jews made up fewer than 1 percent of the population. The mainstream Nazi papers sensationalized trials of Jewish men accused of improper sexual behavior with German women.

The definition of illicit sexual relations was extended to cover nearly any kind of bodily contact between Jews and non-Jewish Germans. Under pressure from the Gestapo and the Reich Justice Ministry, those found guilty of sexual crimes, or "racial defilement," were sentenced to ever longer terms of imprisonment in penitentiaries—not just ordinary prisons.

Some Germans took advantage of the legal leverage this provided them. Businessmen threatened or arranged for Jews, including those involved in commercial competition with them, to be arrested on false charges of "racial defilement" in order to extort concessions and bribes from Jews.

Attacks on Jewish men were a potent weapon for the Nazis. Because many Germans had no contact whatsoever with Jewish people, it was easy to paint a bleak picture of them. The incessant warning that Jewish men were a threat to non-Jewish or "Aryan" women aroused German men's hostility to Jews while appealing to their masculinity. It reinforced both patriarchy and misogyny as it implied that German women were weak and easily seduced by oversexed and lecherous Jewish men. The Nazis emulated the mindset that prompted the lynching of Black men in Jim Crow America. As *Der Stürmer* advised its readers, "This is how racially conscious men in America act: They lynch any Negro who even attempts to defile a girl of the white race."

On November 26, 1937, Traunstein police accompanied by a Gestapo agent arrived at 6 Kernstrasse and demanded to see Max Holzer, the youngest son of Anna's sister Fanny.[20] This was not good news and Max's first impulse was to leave the house. But he came to the door, and the uniformed men, one of them a well-known member of the town's Nazi group, told him he was being arrested.

"What is this about?"

"You'll find out soon enough," the Gestapo man snapped.

At the police station, Max was told by one of the arresting officers that he was being charged with sex crimes. The officer said a number of women had denounced him, but he didn't say their names. Later, a police arrest order revealed the names of several gentile women who had worked as housekeepers in the Holzer home. They had claimed that Max had sexually molested them. Max was taken into custody and held in the Traunstein jail where he remained until his trial three months later.[21]

The shock of Max's arrest hit his family very hard and sent

them scrambling to find a lawyer. They were able to locate one in Nuremberg who was one of the few Jewish lawyers still allowed to practice, apparently because he was a war veteran.

## Trial in Traunstein

Fritz was in Prague on business in January 1938 when an article in a local paper caught his eye. He saw the name of his cousin Max Holzer in a headline. He saw the word *Traunstein* as he skimmed the article. He knew of the trial but was still stunned to read that Max had been convicted and sentenced to five years in a German penitentiary—five years for this feisty cousin he'd known since childhood. He got an extra copy of the article and sent it to his sister Hani in the United States. He hoped Hani could use the article to impress upon Jews in the United States, many of whom were not taking the situation in Germany that seriously, just how dangerous Germany was becoming.

When Fritz returned to Munich a few days later, he found his cousins Klara and Alfred—Max's siblings—and Alfred's wife, Martha, at the Trogerstrasse apartment. "We felt we had to tell your parents about Max, and we didn't want to talk about it on the phone," said Klara. "Papa is very distraught and we're all going crazy trying to figure out what to do." They had brought with them a copy of the local paper, the *Traunsteiner*, with a front-page article on the trial. Alfred and Martha sat at the dining room table with Fritz while Klara stood nervously next to her cousin. She read aloud a section in the article where the writer stated he was including details of the trial "in order to inform the public which has not always kept the necessary distance from the accused."

"This is what this is all about," Alfred exclaimed, responding to the words of the article. "We really already knew that, but here it is in print. This is what they've been trying to do for four years—isolate us from our neighbors, especially the farmers we do business with."

"The Nazis in Traunstein weren't able to turn people against us," Klara threw the paper on the dining room table. "Now, this is having more effect. Since Max was arrested, we've had farmers turn away from us. We're having trouble getting some of them to pay what they owe us. One farmer, who has always been friendly and supportive, said to me the other day, 'Maybe I have been wrong about you people'!"

"It's right here." Alfred pointed to the article. "'Every German-thinking businessman should take note when considering trade with the Holzers.'"

Fritz took the paper from his cousin. He shook his head as he read the first paragraphs of the article: "'In Central America, in Martinique, there is a dance among the Blacks there, the Biguine, a strange obscene midnight ritual performed in secrecy.' Odd, no?" he said.

"In the first place the writer knows nothing about geography." Martha, normally easygoing, was now bitterly sarcastic. "For starters, Martinique isn't in Central America—it's several thousand kilometers away in the Caribbean!"

Fritz looked from Martha to Alfred, "Martinique?"

Alfred struck the table with the palm of his hand. "Here's the way I understand this. The writer is saying to the Traunstein readership, 'You think you know Max Holzer as that happy-go-lucky fellow who grew up in your town and always had a joke or funny comment. No. No. The real Max, the *Jewish* Max, is like one of those *dark* people on this *strange* jungle island who engage in obscene sexual practices.' Since people in Traunstein have no contact with Black people—or have prejudices about them already—the paper can print whatever trash and assume people will believe it. Listen to this part." Alfred picked up the paper to read it. "'The accused, slumped in his fur coat sitting on the bench of the Grand Criminal Court of Traunstein,' and then this, 'The results of the trial, merit comparison with obscenities of a foreign race.' The obscenities of a foreign race!" Alfred repeated that phrase several times.

"And you'll see that the writer throws jazz into the article," Martha added. "Here, 'unpleasant memories of past years with Negro culture and jazz.'"

"Jazz, that's a Nazi obsession," Fritz added.

"Assuming everyone regards jazz as what?" asked Martha.

"Racial danger, of course!" Klara asserted. "Why, when German girls hear jazz music they just jump in bed with whoever is nearby."

"Whichever Jewish man is nearby, oversexed as they are," Martha said, tapping Alfred on the arm.

"Not funny." Alfred gave his wife a furtive look.

Martha turned to Fritz. "The French are also mentioned in the article. Your father said it refers to a time when the French occupied the Rhineland and stationed African soldiers there."

"Another Nazi obsession." Fritz grimaced. "Some Rhineland German girls got pregnant with African soldiers in the 1920s. You know, 'racial pollution.' And after 1933 those mixed race children were forcibly sterilized. They called them the 'Rhineland Bastards.'"

"The point of the article is quite clear. There are dangerous races and we're one of them," Klara stated.

"Oh, you don't read *Stürmer*, Klara!" Martha slapped the table with her hand. "We're the *worst* of them! We're the *most evil*, the *most dangerous, the most depraved, the most—*"

"Inferior!" Alfred interjected.

"Yes, *inferior* race there is!" Martha exclaimed.

Fritz looked over at his cousins. "Have you heard anything from Max?"

"They're keeping him in jail in Traunstein until they send him to Amberg, the penitentiary." Alfred looked up from the newspaper. Fritz noticed his cousin's hands were shaking. "Dad visited him a few days ago. He's scared."

"Who wouldn't be?" Klara was pacing. "That fucking trial—such a damn lie! There was a girl who spoke against Max who worked for us seven years ago. Why did it take so long for her to say something? One of the girls only worked for us a few days. Mentally unstable. You should have seen her as a witness."

Alfred turned to Fritz. "One of Max's friends spoke up against him. That was tough on him. Max wasn't always careful about what he said. The Nazis in town had their eye on him, especially Aichner."

Fritz looked pensive. "What does the lawyer say?"

"He thinks it's a setup. Max wasn't an angel. But this had nothing to do with what happened in our house. These girls were pressured to testify. Probably Aichner was behind it. The atmosphere in court was ugly."

"Who's Aichner?" asked Fritz.

"Albert Aichner, the vice mayor, a big fathead Nazi," said Klara. "He came around at times with a few of his smirking friends when we had business at the house. They stood around and stared at the farmers who continued to do business with us even after they were warned not to."

Alfred put his hand on his sister's shoulder. "Klara here is not one of Aichner's favorites, either. We came to Munich to see if we could find some other legal help for Max. Our lawyer said we need to find a gentile lawyer because a Jewish lawyer's not going to get anywhere trying to appeal his case. I don't have much faith that even if we found a gentile lawyer willing to take this case he'd get anywhere."

Klara took a deep breath. "Our lawyer told us something—just between us—there's word around that Jewish men imprisoned for sexual crimes . . . will be sent to concentration camps when their prison sentences are completed." Fritz glanced at his cousin, who looked like she might break into tears.

On March 8, 1938, just several months later, the Nazi justice minister, Franz Gürtner, announced just such an anti-Jewish measure.

## The Fight, 1938

IT WAS JUST PAST SEVEN in the evening when Fritz arrived at his family's Trogerstrasse apartment building. A summer solstice sun was still bright, and the air was pleasantly warm. As Fritz shut the door to the street behind him, his neighbor, Ludwig Eiber the tailor, peered out from the door of his ground-floor apartment. He smiled as he beckoned Fritz to come in. "Good to see you, Fritz," Eiber said, as he closed the door behind them. "Your father told me that you are getting out of here. Congratulations. When are you leaving?"

"In about a month, I'm making my arrangements."

"Difficult?" Eiber had a concerned look.

"Only if you think giving up everything you own, everything you've accomplished in life, then paying a tax on it all, is difficult."

"Bastards." Eiber put a hand on Fritz's shoulder. "I was so glad your poor sister got away. How is she?"

"Fine. She's been in the United States"—Fritz paused to calculate—"nearly eight months now. Having a hard time with her English but managing."

"I guess you'll be seeing her?"

Fritz sighed. "Yah, if all goes well. I have to prepare myself, learn to dry dishes."

"I don't understand," said Eiber.

"Nor I." Fritz laughed. "My sister writes me, 'You need to learn to dry the dishes, men dry the dishes in America.'"

"Hah. I guess there are worse things." Eiber led Fritz to the back wall of the living room, to a dining table between a door that led to the kitchen and a table where a pile of jackets, pants, and other clothing items were neatly stacked. An ironing board next to the table held an upright iron, poised next to a pair of wrinkled slacks. The scent of steam hung in the air.

On the opposite wall was a built-in shelf below a mirror; the sound of a Wagner piece wafted into the room from a shiny brown Volksempfanger radio. Eiber went over and turned down the volume. "Love the music," said Eiber. "Not so fond of the man."

"Music to iron by," Fritz laughed.

"You've got that right. You should see me when I get in rhythm!" He mimed the movement of an iron with a flourishing sweep of his hand. Fritz clapped in appreciation. Eiber motioned for Fritz to sit. "Can I get you a beer?"

"Yah, of course. Ludwig, you act as if you have something important to tell me?"

"I do. But only over a beer!" Eiber opened the door to the kitchen. Eiber lived with his wife, Berta, in an apartment near the front of the building that housed eight units and a storefront where the Eibers had their small tailor shop. A door from the Eibers' living room led to the shop. During business hours Eiber, his wife, and several employees worked sizing, sewing, and pressing clothes. Sometimes the work spilled over into the living room area, as it had this evening.

When Eiber returned he had two bottles of Gunzenhausen. "My favorite, as you know." He placed one in front of Fritz and then sat down with the other.

Eiber was wearing a crisp white long-sleeve shirt and neatly pressed light slacks. All that was missing from his normal work attire was a silk bow tie and a gray frock coat. Eiber had a habit of dressing up, even in his shop, a habit he carefully cultivated. As he would say to anyone who commented on his formal appearance at work, "No one wants to patronize a shabby-looking tailor!"

"I asked you in, well, to see you, of course, but also . . ." Eiber took a sip from his beer. "It's been a while since we've talked, and I want to know what's been going on with you. And, I have something rather immediate. I want to remind you, about the match."

"Oh, yah, yah." Fritz looked at Eiber. "The boxing match—Louis and Schmeling. I've been thinking about it, too."

"Well, it's very early tomorrow morning. You're welcome to come here and listen to it."

Fritz nodded. "Yes, thanks, that would be good."

"Fritz, you know where my sympathies lie. And I think that we might be in for a pleasant surprise. If you know what I mean."

"I hope you're right." Fritz took a drink from his beer. "I have learned some things about Louis. He lost last time, but I think this fight might be different. He's prepared himself better."[22]

Eiber looked intently at Fritz. "Well, the *swine* certainly hate Louis, and they are all huffed up about their boy Schmeling. Goebbels and his crowd don't like Schmeling personally, but he represents the, you know, 'Aryan.'"

Fritz nodded thoughtfully. "They're broadcasting the match here at three in the morning just as the fight is going on at the stadium in New York. That's amazing," Fritz said with some measure of awe.

"I think the whole world will be listening," said Eiber. "But it's better you listen to the fight here and not in your apartment. You can never tell with these idiots around here." Fritz knew who he meant. Everyone had to be cautious about what they said, and what they listened to. This was true ten times over for Jews. And then there were neighbors in their apartment building that Eiber had warned Fritz about, and who Fritz and his family knew to be cautious around, Herr Hack and Herr Kandl.

Eiber walked Fritz to the door. "Come a few minutes before the match. I'm probably going to sleep for a while, but I'll be up for the broadcast."

"I'll be here." Fritz started to open the door.

Eiber came close to him. "And invite your father too. And Fritz, I'll leave the door open, so you don't have to knock. No reason to give the snitches any cud to chew on."

Fritz arrived at Eiber's door at quarter to three in the morning. He went in the apartment without knocking as Eiber had requested. He came with a pot of hot tea and a small dish of hamantaschen cookies Anna made for the occasion. Eiber smiled. "Excellent. Your mother is such a sweetheart—and such a cook! And your father?"

"Asleep. I didn't want to wake him."

The radio was on, and Fritz heard the voice of a familiar German broadcast commentator, Arno Hellmis. It was nearly 9 p.m. in New York and the announcer was describing the scene at Yankee Stadium where 70,000 people had come to watch perhaps the most anticipated fight in the history of the sport.

Hellmis was a loyal Nazi and a regular writer for the Nazi Party's paper *Der Völkischer Beobachter*. As the crowd filtered into the stadium and preparations for the fight proceeded, Hellmis recounted the first fight between the two boxers that had taken place two years earlier in 1936. He was profuse with praise for the "mastery" the German fighter, Max Schmeling, had demonstrated in defeating the younger and favored "American negro" boxer, Joe Louis, in that previous match. Hellmis emphasized how Schmeling had sussed out Louis's weaknesses and employed his "superior intelligence" to overcome Louis's physical advantages. Schmeling outlasted Louis in their first fight because at every turn Schmeling's "Aryan instincts" prevailed. "Schmeling had a will as hard as Krupp steel," Hellmis asserted. "And he carries an autographed photo of the Führer wherever he goes."

Fritz and Ludwig looked at each other as the announcer droned on in that manner. "Just shut up," Eiber hissed at his radio as he took a bite of a cookie. "Nazi blabber is so tiresome." The cheers from the stadium crowd could be heard as the names of the fighters were called out. The fight was about to begin, and the tension increased—a tenseness shared at that moment by millions across continents. The fight not only had great "racial" significance, it had also become a proxy for the growing enmity between Germany and the United States.

Fritz felt a knot in his stomach. He put down his cup of tea and sat forward on his cushioned chair.

At the sound of the bell for the first round of the fight, Eiber rested his chin on his hands and planted his elbows on the dining table. The German announcer described the boxers approaching each other at the center of the ring. As the first punches were exchanged he sounded confident, even cocky. "Maxie"—Hellmis used the diminutive for his admired fighter—"throws a right and Louis backs away." Then, "Maxie takes a right." And then, "Maxie backs up and hits back."

But just past the first minute of the round, Hellmis's voice began to change. Louis was landing punches that Schmeling could not return. The announcer's cockiness rapidly morphed into something akin to hysteria. A minute and a half into the fight, Louis had Schmeling up against the ropes and was pounding him so hard, and so frequently, that Hellmis began screaming. Then Schmeling went down, and Hellmis implored, "Maxie, *steh auf! Steh auf!* Get up! Get up!" Then, with relief, "Maxie is back on his feet." But shortly after that, Schmeling went down again. This time Hellmis began screeching, "Get up! Get up!" After that little else was intelligible.

The two neighbors looked at each other, both stunned by the confusion in the announcer's voice, and its implication. Fritz was on the far edge of his seat.

"Sounds like Krupp steel might be melting," he said to the delight of his friend.

Barely two minutes into the fight, Hellmis's voice went silent.

From what they could make out, Schmeling was on the canvas and was not getting up.

Eiber pounded his fist on the table and looked up at the ceiling with an exuberant whisper, "*Wunderbar!!*" Suddenly the radio station cut away from the fight scene, and after an odd silence, there was a terse announcement that the broadcast had ended.

"Well, we'll never hear another word about that fight!" Eiber said, sarcastically.

Fritz whispered excitedly, "Can you imagine, the expressions on some faces around here? I would very much like to see that right now." Fritz was referring to a man whose Munich apartment was few blocks up the street at 16 Prinzregentenplatz, the man whose picture poor Max supposedly carried wherever he went. Fritz and Eiber both laughed, and, at the same time, motioned to each other to keep their voices down.

"Our Führer, are you furious?" Eiber whispered as he thrust both fists in the air.

Before Fritz left the apartment Eiber hugged his young friend. "This fight is a good going-away present to you, my dear Fritz."

Fritz had to wipe away tears. "*Danke*, to you, for your support, and for that Louis fellow."

Eiber had his hand on Fritz's shoulder as they walked to the apartment door. "If you ever see that Black fellow over there in America, thank him for me. And please tell him, and the people over there, not all of us Germans are Nazi pigs."

Halfway around the world, in Harlem, in other sections of New York, and in cities across the United States, people were dancing and shouting in the streets, unaware of the joy they shared with some Germans at that same moment.

# Fritz

FRITZ WAS PACKING WHEN THE doorbell rang. Anna, who had stood watching her son, went to the living room window. "It's the mover, Fritz." Fritz walked down to open the apartment building door. Trogerstrasse was bright with sunlight on this unusually warm day. A stocky man wearing a short-sleeved blue shirt, matching pants, and a docker's cap stood outside. The man looked vaguely familiar to Fritz, but he couldn't recall where he'd seen him. "You have something for me, no?" the man asked. Fritz nodded, and together they went up the stairs to apartment number 3. Just inside the door stood a wooden box filled with a small piece of furniture and other items that Fritz was allowed to take in addition to his suitcase. "This it?"

"Yes." Fritz grabbed the top of the crate to make sure it was secure. "You'll be taking this to the train."

"Yah, of course." The mover leaned down and shoved the box onto his hand cart. "You can come and sign the papers tomorrow."

"I'm sorry?" Fritz looked puzzled.

"You have to come to the warehouse, some papers to sign. It's just routine, when someone's leaving the country, some bureaucratic thing. Don't worry, it's all routine."

"Just routine," said Fritz, looking at his father who had just come out of his bedroom.

"You've got to sign a few papers before we can bring this to the train." The mover reached for the door. "Nothing to worry about, Mr. Neuburger." The mover pulled the crate through the doorway and closed the door behind him.

The following day, Fritz went to the warehouse with his friend Frank Mittelberger. Both men had their affidavits from relatives in the United States and their precious visas from the U.S. Consulate. They had secured passage to the United States. They were getting out. Their ships were due to depart from different ports on different dates, but they were both leaving Munich by train the next day, July 28, 1938.

"What do you think this paper signing business is all about?" Fritz, who was driving, looked over at Frank.

"I don't know." Frank combed his hand through his thick brown hair. "It surprised me too. But I think we're okay. I recognized the moving company rep. I've seen him at the synagogue. He sounded pretty reassuring."

"He said this was just routine." Fritz maneuvered his Opel through Munich traffic.

"Well, of course. Fucking with Jews from every possible angle *is just routine*." Frank reached out to Fritz and placed a large hand on his shoulder. "There's a special bureau for that, no? The Reich Bureau of Special Measures to Fuck Jews."

"For the Fatherland." Fritz thrust his clenched fist energetically toward the windshield. "Part of the great new prospects our great leader has brought to our beloved Fatherland."

"We have opened up, and we will continue to open up, for our sacred, Aryan *volk*, these great new career opportunities in our new Germany!" Frank brought his closed fists to his chest, imitating Hitler's frantic style of speech. They both rolled their eyes.

Prior to the spring of 1933 Fritz and Frank were both members of the 1860 Club.[23] Fritz was on the club's track and handball teams and Frank was a well-regarded soccer player among the 1860 crowd. They competed in their respective activities and moved in different circles. Neither associated much with other Jews in those days. Their relationships to their religion consisted of an occasional visit to a Munich synagogue, usually during the High Holidays of Rosh Hashanah and Yom Kippur, though each had gone through a Bar Mitzvah. However, after being barred from the 1860 Club in March 1933, Fritz and Frank had gotten to know each other better as they worked to help build a branch of a Munich Jewish sports club.

In the years that followed, Frank, like Fritz, had held stubbornly to the idea that the upsurge in anti-Semitism was like a virus that would burn itself out. But the steady erosion of their social lives, the growing threat of physical and psychological harm, and the realization that there would be no way to make a reasonable living in Germany finally drove him to seek a way out as well.

To get permission to leave the country they had to turn in detailed lists of all their possessions down to the last item of clothing. Each was allowed to take only one large suitcase and whatever could fit in a small wooden crate. They had to pay a punitive tax on each item.

Because they were only allowed to take a small sum of money with them, they splurged on transportation by buying first-class berths on their respective ships. They would be traveling above their class.

"I'm fortunate, Fritz," Frank rambled as they rode through Munich streets. "I have a few relatives in the United States who are putting some money away for me."

"I'm taking a little of it with me— a few gold coins, several cameras . . ."

Frank glanced over at his friend. "Declared?"

Fritz gave Frank a wary look. "No."[24]

Frank raised his eyebrows and turned his gaze to the street and pointed to a building in the distance. "I can see the tower of the technical university from here." He put his head back and laughed.

"What's so funny?" Fritz asked.

"Just remembering a conversation with the dean of the Engineering Department the day he told me I was being kicked out of the university. You wanna hear about it?"

"Yah."

"The word was getting around that Jewish students were about to be expelled. Some were getting these terse letters from the school administration saying, in so many words, 'Please get your ass out of our school.' The dean of my department asked me to come see him. I entertained the illusion that maybe they had something else in mind for me, but as soon as I stepped in his office the dean said, 'Mittelberger, I have bad news for you.' But before explaining he said, 'I need to talk to you outside.' So we walked around the campus for a while. He reminisced about his time at the school. He especially talked about Professor Willstätter, how much he admired him." Frank looked over at Fritz. "Well, you might remember that Willstätter is a Nobel Prize–winning chemist, a former colleague of Fritz Haber. It was Willstätter who helped me get admitted to the university, and he's Jewish, which is why I think the dean dropped his name. And Fritz, I don't know if you know about this, but Willstätter *quit the university* in the early 1920s because of the *anti-Semitism* there! The university tried to get him back, offered him all kinds of inducements, but he refused! Good for him!" Frank slapped his knee, and Fritz slapped the top of the steering wheel.

"So what more did the dean say?"

"The dean said, 'It *pains me* to be the one to tell you that you can no longer be a student in this school.' Then he says, 'Frank, I want you to know I don't believe in the devil, I don't believe in witchcraft, and I don't believe this racial hogwash of the National Socialists. There's no science to it at all.' So I asked him, then why am I being dismissed?"

"What did he say?"

Frank laughed and said with an officious tone of voice: "'Germany is entering a new era. It's a rebirth of our spirit, our culture. Jews can't be part of it. The Jewish disposition is harmful to the new Germany.'" Frank pounded the dashboard of the car. "Hah! It's not about our race, Fritz! It's our *disposition*! What the *fuck* does that mean?"

"Sounds like a pompous prick," Fritz said as he parked the car. The two would-be émigrés walked to the warehouse door. Inside they were met by a worker who escorted them to their packed crates and told them to wait. While they waited, they joked about things they'd heard about in New York. "I'm told in New York you have to watch out for large apes climbing buildings," Fritz deadpanned.

Frank leaned close to his friend's ear. "We'd rather take our chances with those apes than the ones in high positions here." Fritz's laugh was cut short. He saw a uniformed Nazi approaching. A pounding began in his chest and became so forceful he thought it would make a noticeable sound. The two friends looked at each other. Fritz bit his lower lip and then tried to look relaxed as the officer neared. The Nazi was tall, about Frank's height. He looked to be in his early forties. He wore a dark green uniform with an iron cross of the old Reich on his brown necktie. On his cap was the Nazi eagle with the Swastika in its talons. His tone of voice was anything but friendly. "You're here to sign papers for the possessions you're shipping with you." They nodded. He then went on with the list of restrictions they were already familiar with. "You will have to sign off on all these restrictions. And you'll need to open those boxes."

Fritz felt the blood drain from his head. He kept a calm face as best he could. A worker who'd accompanied the inspector came over with a crowbar and handed it to Frank who, with a rough jerk, pried open the lid of his wooden box. The Nazi looked at the papers he had in his hand. He pushed his uniform cap back and bent to look inside. He reached down and pulled up a bundle, wrapped in what looked like a tablecloth. He opened the cloth revealing a half-dozen framed photos. The inspector looked through the stack, lifting some. Then he went back to the box. His arm disappeared into the crevices of a neatly folded pile of linen. The inspector looked at Frank and nodded. Frank wrapped the photos securely in the cloth and put them back in the box. "You're leaving from Hamburg," the Nazi said to Frank, looking down at the paper. Frank nodded.

"And you," the inspector said, looking at Fritz. Fritz opened his box revealing a small night table with its legs wrapped in a cloth and next to it a rolled-up carpet. He didn't dare look at Frank. "Let's see that, what, table?" Fritz pulled the table from the box. It was solid walnut, with a small drawer and cabinet underneath. Its curved legs had little rounded feet. The table had been next to his bed for years, his favorite little piece of furniture. He set it on the floor. The inspector looked inside the drawer and opened the cabinet. Then he looked down in the box at the carpet and pushed it to the side. As he did so his cap dropped. The inspector caught it and pushed it back down firmly on his head. He compensated the awkwardness of the gesture with a remark in an exaggerated stern tone, "Both escaping to the United States." He looked down at the document in his hand. He looked over at Frank and Fritz. To Fritz, the Nazi's thin aquiline nose and close-set eyes made him look like a bird. His puckered mouth looked like a beak. "You Jews don't like Germany." It was hard to tell if this was a question or assertion. Fritz shrugged slightly. "You're leaving from Le Havre. With a first-class berth on an English Cunard ship, *Georgic*," the inspector noted. At least the idiot can read, Fritz thought to himself. "Why not a German ship?" The inspector glanced at Fritz who started to bite his lip again and then stopped. His heart was beating so hard now that he thought it might just push its way out of his chest. "*Juden*," the inspector put exaggerated emphasis on the first syllable, "always travel first class . . . Hmm." The inspector stared at Fritz, as though he was trying to think of something else to say—something damning. "If I had my way it would be different." He turned, took a few steps, and tossed the documents toward the open box. The papers hit the edge of the box and fell on the ground. The inspector gestured to the worker, "Get the signed documents to me." He walked away.

Fritz, then Frank, signed the papers and checked the appropriate boxes, indicating that they had obeyed all the various obligations and restrictions for travel out of Germany—obligations they had already sworn to in order to get their passports approved.

It was Frank who broke the silence back in the car. "I guess we missed our chance for an excursion to Dachau—all expenses paid."

"Lucky he didn't see what I had in that carpet. That was a foolish thing I did, I'm sorry."

"Don't worry, Fritz. I'm sure it's not the last foolish thing you or I do in our lives. Hey, at least you'll have some cameras with you. You can take some pictures and send them to the inspector as a thank-you."

Fritz felt his heart still racing. "I didn't expect the asshole to be here."

"Yah. Didn't that moving guy say this was just some routine bureaucratic thing?"

"He didn't say a goddamn thing about inspections," Fritz said bitterly. "He must have known about that. Didn't you tell me the moving guy was Jewish?"

"Yah. But it's like they say, snakes come in all colors."

## July 28, 1938

On the eve of Fritz's departure, Benno was both stoic and reassuring. He praised his son, something he was not used to doing but felt he needed to do now that his oldest child was leaving and who knew when, if ever, they would be together again. "You're intelligent, ambitious, and organized, I expect good things from you, Fritz." He put his hand on his son's shoulder. "We'll be okay here. We're old. No danger to the regime. They don't care about us. And we're not worth harming. Anyway, I need to stay here. I have the properties. They're not worth much now, but if I left there would be no one to keep an eye on them. And you know they would just grab them."

"Maybe we'll find a way out of here too," Anna said as she embraced her son. She brushed his shoulder to wipe the tears from his dark suit jacket. "But what's important is that you and Hani will be safe."

Fritz's cousin Klara Holzer watched as Fritz bid farewell to his parents. She then accompanied Fritz on the tram to the main Munich train station. They arrived early in case of any last-minute problems and to meet Kohn, a friend of Fritz. Kohn had agreed to travel with Fritz, carrying a suitcase with more clothes for Fritz to take to the United States. Since Kohn had only one parent who was Jewish, he was freer to travel than his "full-blooded" Jewish friend. The plan was for Kohn to accompany Fritz to Paris.

Klara stood with Fritz at the platform in the cavernous station and lit up a cigarette. The ground vibrated as the Paris train pulled slowly forward. "So, you're leaving, Fritz. I thought Hani might have to come back here and drag you out!"

"I've been ready for a while. I didn't tell you what I did when I got word about the visa being approved."

Klara blew out a puff of smoke. "Your mother told me you were on the road."

"I was in Breslau when my father called me about the letter from the consulate in Stuttgart. I dropped everything and drove all night to Munich—eight hours on the road. I took my physical the next day."

"I'm happy you're getting out. Why, for one thing, Fritz, you work too hard here in Germany. You need to go someplace where you can relax a little." Klara was into her trademark sarcasm.

"By the way, Klara, why are you smoking? It's not good for your health, you know that?"

"Fritz, I'm a Jewish woman living in a country run by Nazis! If only smoking were my biggest worry! I began smoking more heavily during Max's trial. Now I can't stop." Fritz nodded grimly. "When you sent Hani that article about Max from Prague you nearly scared your poor sister to death," Klara said.

"How do you know that?"

"She wrote to me about it."

"Any news about Max?"

"He's not doing well in Amberg. I didn't want to talk about it in your parents' place, especially in front of your mother. Thank God my Mama died before she had to see this. Jewish men accused of sex crimes don't do well in German prisons." Klara spoke bitterly. "They got Max. But at least you're getting out of this prison of a country. And I'll do my best to keep an eye on your parents."

"Please stay with them as long as you can, Klara. My mother really needs someone now. When I get to the United States I'll see what I, what Hani and I, can do to get them out. But what about you getting away?" Fritz looked at his cousin.

"I can't leave—not with Papa and the other family in this situation. They've been so stubborn about staying. And now there's no way Papa would leave, not with Max here in prison."

"I'll be in Paris for a few days before I go to La Havre. The ship doesn't leave until the sixth of August, that's nine days from now. I'll see our cousin Simon Vogel while I'm there. Do you have a message for him?"

"Tell him what's going on here with us and with Max. I've written him a little, but you know one can't say too much in the letters. And also tell him if I do get to Paris again, this time, he has to find me a swimming spot on the Seine." Klara laughed.

When Kohn showed up, the three walked to a door of the waiting train. Klara hugged her cousin. "Well, I hope you have a happy life in the United States. And work on that sense of humor, Fritz. Why, you need to laugh more. Don't take life so seriously."

Fritz smiled grimly as he stepped up on the train, and then turned at the door. "I guess you're right, Klara—better to die laughing than to die smoking!"

"Ach!" Klara waved her hand as though batting a fly as Fritz and Kohn slipped inside the train door. She blinked back tears as the train moved slowly out of the station.

# June to November, 1938

Anti-Jewish Measure, June 1938
The Polish government announces that it would no longer extend protection to Polish citizens living in other European countries. This has special implications for Polish Jews living in Germany.

Anti-Jewish Measure, June 1938
The Munich Aryanization committee publishes a list of 1,750 enterprises owned by Munich Jews signaling its intention to confiscate the businesses or force their sales to non-Jewish entities.

Anti-Jewish Measure, July 1938
Jewish cattle traders are denied licenses. Jews are no longer permitted to operate as traveling salesmen.

Anti-Jewish Measure, July 6, 1938
A list of businesses and services off-limits to Jews is published. Among the services are credit and real estate.

Anti-Jewish Measure, late July 1938
The German government passes a decree ordering Jews to turn

in their identification papers and apply for new ones. The new documents come with a "J" stamped on the front. This measure is meant to make it harder for Jews to evade detection inside Germany. But the J also alerts authorities in bordering countries that the passport holder might try to stay illegally or apply for asylum if allowed to enter. It effectively closes the borders to Jews trying to leave Germany without a special visa.

Hani Neuburger arrived in New York on a ship from Hamburg in late September 1937. She was nearly twenty-eight years old. She went immediately to Chicago where she lived with the relatives who had given her the crucial help she needed to immigrate to the United States—her cousin Morton and Morton's mother, her Aunt Salome, respectively the son and widow of her uncle Hugo. Not long after arriving in Chicago, a Jewish women's group helped Hani get a night shift job in a factory. But Morton insisted that while Hani lived in his home and "as long as he had food" Hani would not work.[25]

This gave Hani more time to arrange an affidavit for her brother Fritz and to attend English language school. At English night class Hani met a German Jewish student from Frankfurt named Sophie Strauss. Hani and Sophie became friends and Sophie introduced Hani to her brother, Ludwig, who was studying in the same school.

The friendship between Ludwig and Hani became serious. When Ludwig moved to New York in the summer of 1938 in search of more lucrative work, he asked Hani to join him there. This worked out well for Hani, who wanted to be in New York by the beginning of August 1938 to meet Fritz, who was due to arrive from Germany.

Hani and Ludwig were married and began living together in Astoria, Queens. Fritz, upon his arrival, took up residence with his sister and brother-in-law. He also began using an Americanized name, Fred.

That August, Benno and Anna began writing letters to their children, both now living in New York.

August 4, 1938

Dear children,

Reading your letter, I'm very happy to hear that you my dear Hani are so happy with your dear Ludwig and he with you. I wish so much to be with you and now that Fritz is with you—he'll tell you all the news.

Dear Hani, you will let us know about everything and especially about how Fritz manages with his new life. I dearly wish to be with you there.

Your father.

Dear Fritz,

I'm wishing you the best in such a faraway country. Let us know how you are doing. We are very surprised about your being together with Hani. Yesterday Ms. Krauss and Julie stopped by to send you their greetings and congratulations from all your friends.

Aunt Verona is having a hard time with you being in New York, but that's only because she would love to be with you there. I wish I could do something for you, my dear Hani, but I guess you'll stay with Fritz. I can't believe that I'm without children here but I'm happy that it worked out for you and now for Fritz as well. Even though the farewell was really hard, I will rest and take care of myself so that I'll be able to join you some day. Hopefully, my dear children, you will write to me often so that I can have some joy even though I can't be with you.

Many greetings and kisses from your Mom.

August 14, 1938

Dearest children,

We received your letter, dear Hani, which you had sent on April 11. You would like me to come right away, but that's not possible. Herr Berger is saying that his properties don't sell so fast and that he's really not in a rush at all to go abroad. I would love to be with you as soon as possible and to come to New York.

You are asking me if Tilli already left but this probably won't happen before the fall. Ilse as well will probably stay here for now.

Today Kleri Weil came by and told me that she won't be able to leave any time soon either but she's sending greetings

Greetings from your loving father

Dear Fred,[26]

You've always been industrious and hardworking and so I'm happy that you'll be taking a vacation. Your relatives will be happy to see you in Chicago.

This week I received a birthday card from Aunt Salome. I'm often longing for you and my thoughts are always with you, dear children. Klara also has sent me birthday wishes and Hansi has settled in well. I believe that Hedi will be joining you soon, but the marriage will have to wait until things look better again.

P.S. My loved ones, I'd like to add a few lines and greetings to your mom's letter. We are always so happy to hear from you. Soon your loved ones will be with you but I'm not looking forward to the farewell, even though I'll wish for you to be all together.

Loving greetings to you. Your aunt Mina.

ANTI-JEWISH MEASURE, AUGUST 17, 1938

A new law, to take effect January 1, 1939, requires all German Jews to add an additional middle name on all documents, including passports. The new names were "Israel" for men, "Sarah" for women.

Munich, September 24, 1938

Dear children,

We received your letter, and we are happy to know that you are doing well. Regarding the consulate, it should be done next week with the corrected data. I was born on 03/04/1871 and mom on 04/15/1877. Please give this information to Aunt Salome and Morton since we haven't sent anything to them yet.

They wrote us that they are looking forward to it and that they would be grateful for it.

We are wondering if you could send us linen goods. It certainly would be great if you could get it for us.

I'm overjoyed that you, Fred, have found work. It's always good to be making progress.

Please write us soon!

Greetings from your loving father.

Again, wishing you a Happy Birthday!!!

### Anti-Jewish measure, September 27, 1938

A new Reich decree bars all but 172 of 1,753 Jewish lawyers from continuing to practice law.

September 28, 1938

Dear children,

Since I haven't heard from you this week, I will update you on what's going on here. We enjoyed the holidays even though we were alone. My thoughts were with you.

I also went to synagogue. This morning Klara came by, but she will leave this evening.

How are you all doing? Fritz, are you well-adjusted with your new business? What's Hani doing? Dad and I often go for long walks since the weather is so beautiful. But I rarely make it to the movies anymore. I'm sad that you didn't write during the holidays. I would've really appreciated it. Hopefully you'll write me soon.

I don't have any news to report. Aunt Mina and uncle are writing very little as well. Hedi and Willi paid me a visit.

Please write me soon. Greetings and kisses from your Mom.

### A Munich Conference

A few days after a subdued Rosh Hashanah, Benno and Anna

were with their friends Greta and Rudy on a morning walk along a tree-lined pathway by the Isar River. A long caravan of cars tailed by police vehicles with flashing lights appeared beyond the lines of trees and bushes ahead of them. Some were open convertibles with passengers in uniforms and business suits. Swastika flags and emblems of other European countries flew from car antennas. Benno made out the red, white, and green flag of Italy and England's Union Jack. "Wonder what that's all about," Greta said.

"The Sudetenland conference," Anna reminded her friends.

"Of course. That must be it," Greta replied as she peered through the branches at the fast-moving cars.

"Headed to Hitler's apartment," observed Benno. "Chamberlain and Daladier are here to give Czechoslovakia to Hitler."

"Do you believe the Czechs are mistreating the Germans in the Sudetenland?" asked Greta.

"The Nazi papers are going berserk with accusations about massacres of Germans by Czech authorities."

"A pile of lies." Benno spoke while looking intently at the cars beyond the line of trees. "A pretext to justify Hitler's grab for the Sudetenland." Benno gave a sarcastic laugh. "Chamberlain and Daladier come to Munich to give away Czech land, but no one invited the Czechs!" As the two couples reached Prinzregentenstrasse Benno signaled for them to cross the now clear street. Once at the Trogerstrasse apartment, Anna and Greta went to the kitchen to heat up food Anna had previously prepared while Benno and Rudy sat at the dining room table talking.

"Do you think Hitler would go to war over the Sudetenland?" Rudy wondered as he and Benno sat with glasses of schnapps.

"No." Benno emptied his shot glass. "I think Hitler is playing the tough guy. That's what his supporters want. But Germany isn't ready for war. He got Austria. And as long as no one calls his bluff he'll keep grabbing more. He's promised Germany the empire they didn't get in the last war . . ."

"A war I supported," Rudy admitted.

"So did I," said Benno gravely. "I don't think England or France want a war with Germany now."

"So, he'll get the Sudetenland."

"That's already been decided, Rudy!" Benno's voice was shrill. "And this won't be the end of it. Hitler's been clear about his territorial ambitions. Chamberlain is very naïve or just acting that way."

"Can I tell you what happened yesterday?" Rudy said. "Greta and I were buying groceries on Neuhauserstrasse. As we were leaving the store, Feldman—someone I've known for years from the temple men's group—called to me. He was very excited. I've known him to be this way at times. Anyway, he said he had to talk to us, so we walked with him to Karlsplatz. He's convinced the British and French are in cahoots with Hitler. He said Hitler would never have gotten anywhere if they hadn't let him rearm. And now, they're encouraging him—first, giving him a free hand in Austria—'in violation of their own Versailles Treaty.' He had my arm in a very tight grip while he talked. 'And now the Sudetenland. The whole of Czechoslovakia is next, I'm sure of it!' Then he said, 'This is all about the Soviets, the big European powers want Hitler to go after the Soviets, crush the Soviet government. This is what the imperialists are seeking' . . . and so on."

"I'd say there's something to that. But it's not that simple." Benno pulled a cigar from his pocket but then put it away as Anna and Greta came into the room with boiled potatoes and boiled sweet and sour red cabbage and set them on the table. "Hitler knows the German military's not ready for a major war. So, this is a gamble for him."

"But he seems to be succeeding." Rudy nodded thanks to Anna for the food. "It looks as though so long as Hitler makes moves toward the Soviets, the other powers won't confront him."

"But in cahoots?" Benno shook his head. "They're in cahoots until they aren't. It's a many-sided game, Rudy. Each nation holding different cards."

"You don't necessarily see another war with Russia, then," Rudy surmised.

Anna set down a loaf of sliced rye bread and a pitcher of tea. "I have another dish," she said as she disappeared into the kitchen. A minute later she came out with a platter of cheese slices, sliced boiled eggs, and chicken.

"This is quite something, Anna." Rudy put his head back and inhaled. "The chicken smells terrific."

"My brother-in-law Willi and his daughter Hedi were here from Traunstein yesterday. They brought us the chicken and eggs," Anna said as she took a seat at the table.

"Tell them what your friend Feldman told us." Greta gestured to Rudy as she passed the plate of food around.

"I just told Benno."

"Anna's here now."

Rudy touched his forehead with his hand. "Sorry, Anna. My friend Feldman sees this Sudeten conference as evidence of a grand conspiracy against the Soviets."

"And I think there is something to be said about Chamberlain's willingness to give Hitler concessions so long as he moves east," Benno suggested. "But it's a more complex game . . ."

Rudy took a piece of bread and put a slice of cheese on it. "For Feldman it's pretty straightforward. Hitler wants to expand east. I mean he even said so in *Mein Kampf*, right? And the British and French are willing to let him. They'll even risk a new world war if it means the destruction of the Soviets."

Benno grimaced. "Wasn't it some British poet who said, 'The best laid plans of mice and men . . . ?' "

Greta shook her head. "It's all a cynical game."

"And at the moment Czechoslovakia's going to pay for it," Anna added. "No doubt the world is becoming more dangerous."

Greta turned to Anna. "On another subject, how are you doing without Hani and Fritz?"

"I miss them terribly. But we're thankful they got away."

"How long have they been gone?"

"Hani left a year ago. Fritz left two months ago. It seems longer. And he's already found himself a job in a department store in New York."

"And Hani has found herself a husband." Benno smiled and looked at Anna. "His name is Ludwig Strauss."

Greta took a bite of red cabbage. "Your children work fast!"

"Hani met him at night school in Chicago. He's from a town near Frankfurt am Main. Now they live in New York."

"Wow. At least it's nice to know there's life after Germany," remarked Greta.

"Life starts after Germany. At least for us," Anna responded.

"Sounds like you're ready to leave, Anna," Rudy chimed in.

"Very." Anna saw a worried look on her husband's face and decided to change the subject. "Hani says she likes America but complains about speaking English." She turned to Benno. "Tell Greta what Hani wrote in her last letter."

"I have it right here." Benno picked a letter out of a drawer in a cabinet by the dining table and handed it to Anna.

Anna pulled the thin paper from an envelope. "Hani went to a pharmacy to get medicine for growths on her feet. And she told the pharmacist, 'I need something for my *Hühnesaugen*.' And then, she says, 'This poor man almost choked to death laughing.'"

"And?" Greta held her fork suspended above her plate.

"It turns out that Hani had looked up the word for *huhnesaugen* and found the English translation to be 'chicken eyes,' or something like that." Anna put down the letter.

"Ay," Greta shook her head as she realized what had happened.

"In English they use another word for those growths. They call them 'corns.'" Benno looked at his wife and laughed. "The pharmacist thought Hani needed something so her chickens could see better!!"

"Ahh!" Rudy grimaced at his own slow uptake. "English! Such a peculiar language. Isn't 'corn' a vegetable? Why would you call *ein huhnesaugen* a 'corn,' as if you could eat it!?"

"Makes no sense." Benno sat back in his chair. "But if we ever get to America, we need to be careful we don't make the same mistake!"

"We should be so lucky," Greta looked at her fork as she put a piece of egg in her mouth. "I wish I were there now. Fritz and Hani must be working for you to join them, yes?"

"Yes. They want us to come," Anna sighed. "It's in every letter they write."

"Are you ready to leave, Benno?" Greta asked.

"I've been considering it lately." Benno looked at Anna. "Now that our children are gone. But I can't leave until I get paid for the land I've sold."

"The Nazis'll *never* let you take anything out," Rudy said emphatically.

"I know, Rudy, but I need the money to *get out*—to pay passage, and other expenses. I don't want to drag our children down in debt. So that's what I've got to work on."

"Certainly seems like *no one* wants us." Rudy cut a piece of cabbage with his fork. "Remember that conference in France, what, two or three months ago?"

"Evian," Benno said grimly.

"A special conference to save European Jews. Yet not one of the thirty countries—right, Greta?—said they would open their doors more widely to help us!"

"Except the Dominican Republic," Greta said with a shrug of resignation.

"And what would we do in a poor country like that? And how would we live?" Benno asked.

"America's our best option, but Roosevelt didn't even send a government representative to Evian. He sent a friend of his, for crying out loud!"

"For a French vacation!" Greta added indignantly.

"A conference 'to save Europe's Jews' where nearly everyone attending found some excuse to do nothing to save even one of us!" Anna lamented.

Greta nodded. "It made Hitler happy. 'You see?' he smirked '*No one* wants the Jews.'"

## Anti-Jewish Measure, late October 1938

Seventeen-thousand Polish Jews, including many who had lived twenty years or more in Germany, are rousted from their homes. Allowed to take only one suitcase each, leaving behind possessions acquired over decades, they are herded or driven to train stations and taken to the German-Polish border where they are ordered to cross into Poland, which refuses them entry. Twelve thousand expelled Jews are left stranded in frigid weather without money, food, or adequate shelter.

# 15

# Klara

IN THE FIRST YEARS AFTER the beginning of Nazi rule, life for the Holzer family in Traunstein did not change dramatically. In the warm spring and summer months, Klara indulged her passion for swimming by visiting the Chiemsee, a large lake an hour's drive from the town. She was friends with the owner of a small cluster of lakeshore rental cabins and she spent free days there sunning and swimming.[27]

On one occasion she sat outside her cabin, her arms wrapped around her knees, contemplating a longer than usual swim. As she readied herself to enter the water the owner of the cabins came by. "Listen, Klara. I'm very sorry to do this to you, but some big shot from the SS is here. He saw you and he knows you're from the Holzer family." This got Klara's attention. "Well, he says he doesn't want you around—he doesn't want any Jews around." He lowered his mouth to Klara's ear. "He wanted to know what you were doing here, if you know what I mean. I can't tell you how sorry I am about that, I'm really sorry, but I can't do anything about it."

"That's all right," Klara replied in her casual style. "You know, this is a big lake, I'll find another place to swim. As much of a big shot he might be, he can't take the whole lake from me, can he?"

She moved to another beach spot along the lake and waded into the water—determined to make it farther into the lake than she ever had before.

In the early summer of 1937, Klara received a letter from Simon Vogel, a cousin from Laupheim who was then living in Paris. Klara had become very close to Simon and his wife, Johanna, some years before when she lived with their family in Cologne. Now Simon invited her to visit Paris and attend the International Exposition of Modern Arts and Technology being held there that summer. Which she did.

When Klara returned to Germany, she enrolled in a school in Munich to learn sewing and clothes design. Hani had already left for the United States and Klara moved in with Anna and Benno where she helped to fill the void left by their daughter's departure.

Several weeks after Fritz left for the United States, Klara received another letter from Simon. "Please come to Paris,' " he wrote. "Maybe we can do something about the problem." She took that to mean the problem with her brother Max. The problem also referred to the relentless attacks on Jews and the growing danger of living in Germany. Earlier that summer Hitler ordered Munich's main synagogue torn down because he considered it an "eyesore."

Cousin Simon's invitation offered Klara a ray of hope. Her family was helpless to do anything for her brother Max in Germany, and she thought that with Simon's help they might appeal to authorities outside the country.

But her hope was immediately undermined by the thought of the travel restrictions imposed on Jews. In July 1938, Jews had been ordered to turn in their identity cards. When they went to pick up their new ones, they found them stamped with a big "J" across the front. People showing these at the border were being turned back since it was assumed that anyone with a "J" on their passport was coming to stay. Klara's father and brothers who had, for years, traveled to Belgium and Austria on business were now having their visa requests denied. She wrote to Simon, thanked him for the invitation, but lamented that her situation looked hopeless. Simon wrote back and insisted that she give it a try. He would be waiting for her with some ideas in mind.

Klara was nervous and depressed at the thought of going to the government office in Traunstein to renew her passport. The man in charge was a longtime Nazi. She could picture herself being mocked and then run out of the office, or worse. And even if she survived that ordeal, she would have a document that would be useless for travel.[28]

She thought about it for days and in the end decided that she had always looked at the world from the bright side and should keep doing so. She decided to give it a try.

On a cool morning in early October, Klara entered the Traunstein office where passports were issued. Her stomach was in a knot. As she entered, she saw that the Nazi she'd expected to see working at the desk was not there. In his place was a young agent who was an old friend from Klara's sports club days. "Heinrich!" called Klara, smiling broadly. Her old friend got up to greet her. "Klara, I haven't seen you in quite a while. Hope you're okay."

"I'm okay. I'm glad to see you. Are you still skiing?"

"When I can. I don't get out much like back in the Turnverein days. Maybe this coming winter." He looked at her carefully. "And you?"

"Not in a while. I've been out of the area. Anyway, I'm here. I need to get my ID renewed. I didn't expect to see you here."

"Well, the old fart head is out for a while." Heinrich gave her a playful wink. "Do you have your picture with you?"

It took a second for the words to register. A picture? "Well, I came to find out what the procedure was."

"All right. Fill out this form for me, and then come in tomorrow with your picture. I should be able to get this done for you then."

Klara thanked her friend, then stood for a moment on the street outside the office. She felt a bit wobbly but overjoyed at her good luck—she didn't have to deal with the Nazi "fart head." Heinrich's words had her laughing.

She went to a photography studio and had an passport picture taken, then picked up the photo the next morning and went to the passport office to drop it off. Later that afternoon, she returned to pick it up. Other people were in the office when she entered, so she waited in line. When her turn came, her friend handed Klara an envelope. She smiled at him, and he looked back at her with a nod.

After walking out of the office, Klara found a quiet spot on a street with a bench and sat for a while, looking to make sure that no one was around. Then she opened the envelope carefully and pulled out the new document. It all looked in order—shiny, with the right name and the right picture, and an expiration date that said it was good for five years. And, it had no "J"!

Klara was not someone easily overtaken by emotion. But, at that moment, she broke down. She cried so hard she thought she might choke on her tears.

### Paris

When Klara left her family's house on Kernstrasse for the Traunstein train station a few blocks away, her brother Benno, thirty-four years old, and her sister Hedi, thirty-two, were on either side of her, each carrying one of Klara's bags. "Why, I see you think I'm some kind of invalid now!" Klara groused.

"No, Klara, but this help of ours comes at a price—your promise that you'll come back." Benno set a bag down on the ground of the plaza in front of the station.

"Well, you should know you can't get rid of me that easily." Klara leaned down to pick up the bag. "I told Dad I'd be back the second week of November. I mean, if Simon doesn't kick me out of Paris before then."

"Papa started crying after he said goodbye to you," Hedi said. "We need you here. Papa needs you."

"I'll be back. While I'm in Paris I'll see what Simon and I can do for Max. That's the most important thing right now." Klara hugged her siblings and disappeared into the small station.

That evening, at the Vogels' apartment in Paris, Klara's cousin

Simon invited her into the dining room for a bite to eat. On her plate she found an envelope. Simon stood by the table. "Open it please, Klara." Klara pulled a legal-looking document out of the brown envelope. She looked at her cousin. "It's an affidavit, Klara." Simon sat next to her. He pointed to the name written on the front page, a name Klara had never seen before. "I got this from a business connection in Cincinnati. Now all *you* have to do is get a visa from the U.S. Consulate in Germany. I suggest you start the process as soon as you can. It's taking longer and longer to get U.S. visas."

Klara turned to her cousin, then looked across the table to his wife, Johanna. "I'm very grateful to you. You don't know how grateful I feel. But I can't leave Germany now. My father won't leave, especially now with Max in prison. He'd be alone without us kids. I can't leave them."

Johanna pushed her chair closer to the table. Klara noticed that her large brown eyes were wider than usual. "Klara, we're just realizing how dangerous life is becoming for all of you. The things we hear about Germany—maybe they're being hidden in Germany—but terrible stories are coming out about violence against people, especially Jews. The camps . . ."

"Even if you don't intend to leave now," Simon said, looking first at Johanna and then at Klara, "get your papers in order. Get that visa, make your arrangements. Once that's done, you can decide whether to leave or not. While you're here, we'll see what we can do for Max." Simon looked again at his wife. "But we need to be realistic. We don't have much leverage."

Klara stayed in Paris for nearly a month. During that time, she and her cousin visited lawyers and government offices. They wrote letters to authorities in Paris, London, and Washington, explaining the injustice done to Max Holzer. They were offered nary a glimmer of hope.

On November 7, 1938, several days before her planned return to Germany, Klara, Simon, and Johanna were in the Vogels' living room. The Vogels' children, Hans Jacob, eleven, and Walter Josef, eight, had just gone to bed when the phone rang. "*Allo,* Vogel . . . ah, *Guten tag.*" A smile on Simon's round face faded as he listened. He looked over at Johanna and Klara. "Okay, I see. And his name? And the victim, still alive? Anything more? All right. Of course, of course, I'll check the news. Thanks." Simon put the phone down and turned to his wife and cousin. "That was Meyer from the office. He's home now, but he said there's a report on the radio of a shooting at the German Consulate here in Paris. A young German shot a consular official. But so far there's no word on who exactly the shooter is or why he acted."

"That's all?" asked Johanna.

"Only that the consular official's name is vom Roth or Rath, something like that."

"And the shooter's name?" asked Johanna.

"He only heard that the shooter is a German studying here in Paris."

Klara sat back in her chair. "God, let's just hope he's not Jewish!"

# 16

# Shattered Glass

THE 17,000 POLISH-JEWISH IMMIGRANTS deported from Germany were trapped inside the Polish border. Four days after arriving, many of the deportees were cold, sick, hungry, and living on the stone floors of the Polish border station and in nearby stables, waiting for permission to enter the country. There were suicides among them.

Zindel and Rivka Grynszpan were among the deportees. They had lived in Hanover, Germany, for twenty-seven years where they ran a small tailor shop. After their sudden deportation, their daughter Berta wrote a desperate note to her seventeen-year-old brother living in Paris. "Herschel, we haven't got a penny." She implored him to send whatever he could. Tormented by his family's trauma and his inability to help them, Herschel bought a pistol and on November 7 headed to the German Consulate in Paris intending to kill the German ambassador. Informed that the ambassador was out, he was sent to the office of Ernst vom Rath, a minor consular official. There Grynszpan pulled his pistol and shot vom Rath in the stomach.

### A Hate-Filled Dinner Speech

The top Nazi leadership was gathered in Munich on November 9 for the annual commemoration of the 1923 Beer Hall Putsch. Hitler spoke at the Burgerbraukeller, and later that evening he was at a dinner in Munich's city hall when word came that the German consular official Vom Rath had died of his wounds. After consulting with Hitler about Vom Rath's death, Joseph Goebbels rose to make an impromptu speech. In remarks filled with violent vitriol against Jews he threatened violent retribution for the killing of a "loyal servant of the Reich." Goebbels noted in his diary that his speech was received with "thunderous applause. All are instantly at the phones. Now people will act."

Following Goebbels's speech, the Nazi officials gathered from around the country called their local offices to inform them of the death and instruct them to attack Jewish businesses, synagogues, and other institutions. They were told to make the assaults look as much as possible like spontaneous responses from an outraged public. Care was to be taken to make sure that non-Jewish properties were not damaged in the rampage.

### A March to 6 Kernstrasse

The Nazis in Traunstein were having their own celebration of the Putsch anniversary on the night of November 9 when the call came in from Munich. As instructed, some uniformed marchers went home and changed into civilian clothes. Then, about forty marchers, led by their leader, Franz Werr, and the town's vice mayor, Albert Aichner, marched to the Holzer family home. As they neared the Kernstrasse house, they began shouting, "Jews out of Traunstein!" "Holzers out!" Several pulled pistols and began firing into the house. Some of the men broke down the door and began trashing the house. A member of the family who was there at the time heard some of them shouting, "Where's that bitch who was in Paris?"

The oldest son, Benno, was upstairs when the Nazis broke in. He escaped the house by crawling out of an upper-story window and onto the roof. After running from the property, he found refuge with a family who owned a small bakery near their home.[29]

Willi Holzer, his son Alfred, his daughter-in-law Martha, his daughter Hedi, and a family with two young children who were visiting from the nearby town of Freilassing were taken into custody by the Traunstein police. In the brutal home invasion, Martha suffered a severe injury to her foot and later had to be hospitalized.

Louis Holzer's daughter Hansi, her husband, Paul Lowy, and their daughter Margaret were also visiting Traunstein at the time. That family had previously fled their home and business in Salzburg, Austria, after the Nazis took over the country in March 1938. Frustrated at not finding some of the family members they were looking for, the Nazis held fourteen-year-old Margaret Lowy captive for "questioning." They held her all night—a horrific night that changed her life forever.[30]

## A Fire in Judenberg

On the night of November 10, Nazis from Laupheim and other nearby towns descended on Judenberg, Laupheim's Jewish quarter. They went door to door demanding that Jewish residents leave their homes. They pounded on the door of the house at 49 Kapellenstrasse and shouted, "Out or we'll break down your fucking door!" Anna's sister Mina Einstein and her housemate Sofie Braunge thought to hide, but then realized they had no choice but to surrender. Once out of the house, the Nazis shoved the two older women into the street. Then, they marched all the Jews from the neighborhood to the synagogue and ordered them to kneel in front of the temple. The Nazis, whipped into a violent frenzy, broke into the temple, and spread gasoline in the pews and over the *aron hakodesh*, the cabinet which holds the Torah.

While Mina, Sofie, and the other Jewish residents knelt in front of the synagogue, one of the Nazis threw a match onto the gasoline-soaked floor of the building. As the synagogue burned, Judenberg's residents were ordered to shout, "We are burning the synagogue! We are burning the synagogue!" Mina and other Judenberg residents cried bitterly as they watched the building that was so central to the life of their close-knit community burn to ashes.

### Anti- Jewish Measure, November 8, 1938

The German government announces that all Jewish newspapers and magazines are to immediately cease publication. The order affects three Jewish newspapers with national circulation as well as four cultural papers, several sports papers, and several dozen community bulletins. Only one Jewish publication, the *Jüdisches Nachrichtenblatt* (Jewish Newsletter), is allowed to continue to publish so as to inform the Jewish community of the measures being imposed on them.

### Anti-Jewish Measure, November 10, 1938

Hitler meets with Reich Propaganda Minister Goebbels at the Osteria Bavaria in Munich to finalize a draft of a decree to bring the pogrom to an end. They discuss ways to deny insurance compensation for Jews while speeding up the expropriation of Jewish businesses.

### Anti-Jewish Measure, November 10, 1938

Heinrich Himmler, head of the Nazi SS, declares that any Jew found to possess a gun will serve twenty years in prison.

## A Pistol in Wolfratshausen

Early in 1938, Hermann Spatz, husband of Tilli Holzer, and his son, Wilhelm, moved from their home in Wolfratshausen to an apartment at 12 Landsbergerstrasse in Munich. On the night of November 10, Hermann heard of Himmler's threat to imprison any Jew found with a gun. Fearing that his house in Wolfratshausen would be raided and the police would find an old war pistol he kept there, he returned to his old house to retrieve the weapon and hide or dispose of it.

The next day, he was caught on a street near his house and sent to the Dachau concentration camp. At Dachau he was badly beaten and forced to agree to sell his Wolfratshausen home for well under its value to a Nazi who worked at the camp. The money from the sale was placed in a blocked bank account, and the war veteran thereafter had to ask permission to retrieve meager funds from the forced sale of his property.

### Carpets of Glass

Just before midnight on November 9, a display window at a Jewish textile shop in Munich was set on fire. Within minutes Ohel Jakob, the only large synagogue remaining in Munich, was also in flames.

In the early morning hours of November 10, groups of Nazi SA and SS members in civilian clothes took clubs and crowbars and smashed the windows and doors of Jewish businesses on Munich's Kaufingerstrasse. They entered the shops, removed the displayed products, and threw them in the street. They stole, stomped on, and urinated on merchandise. Some Munich streets were left littered with debris and carpets of glass. By the end of the night every Jewish shop in Munich was partly or completely wrecked. Munich's fashionable street looked as though it had been bombed.

On the morning of November 11, nearly every non-Jewish shop in Munich bore a sign that said: "No Jews Allowed."

### Dachau

On November 10, a memo was sent to the Dachau concentration camp to prepare to receive 10,000 new prisoners. That same evening a police van pulled up in front of 44 Trogerstrasse. Munich Police and Gestapo agents pushed their way into Benno and Anna's apartment and took Benno into custody. Benno was driven to a train station filled with heavily armed police and hundreds of other Jewish men from the Munich area.

The train carrying Munich's Jewish men arrived late at night at Dachau. En route, the passengers had to remove their normal clothes and don thin cotton uniforms and ill-fitting shoes. As they walked from the train station to the concentration camp Benno saw the rows of wooden barracks surrounded by barbed wire and watchtowers. These had replaced the munitions depot where he'd served during the war.

Benno was one of 500 Jewish men from Munich brought to Dachau that day. He was one of 30,000 Jewish men arrested and sent to concentration camps across Germany during what became known as the "Kristallnacht Pogrom" or the "Night of Broken Glass."

On November 11 Munich's mayor, Adolf Wagner, spoke to a crowd of 5,000 at the Munich circus denouncing Jews, Catholics, and the Pope, who had spoken out against the Kristallnacht violence. Following Wagner's speech, a mob attacked the Catholic cardinal's palace, smashing windows and cursing Munich's Cardinal Michael von Faulhaber. The previous day Faulhaber had responded to a plea for help from the rabbi of the Ohel Jakob synagogue by sending a truck to rescue religious objects from the temple before it was destroyed. The attack on von Faulhaber's home was retribution for this small act of kindness to the Jewish community.

### Dread in Queens, New York

Hani had just gotten back to her Astoria apartment from her job in Manhattan and was in the kitchen when Fritz came in. "How's the new job at Klein's, Fred?" Hani asked as she took a plate of leftover chicken out of the small Hotpoint icebox. Fritz's new American name, "Fred," still sounded strange to Hani, and she had to be careful not to slip back into "Fritz," his German name. She was about to comment on this but stopped when she saw her brother's anxious look.

Fred put a copy of the November 11 issue of the New York *Daily News* on the kitchen table and sat down. "Hani you have to look at this." Hani sat down next to her brother. "Oh my God!! My God!!" Her face reddened and she broke down in tears. "Ludwig is visiting his sister. I'm going to call him." Hani hurried into her bedroom. Fred heard his sister's quavering voice while she spoke on the phone with her husband. After several minutes Hani came back to the kitchen. Her eyes were bloodshot, but she was no longer crying. "Ludwig will be here soon."

When Ludwig entered the apartment he didn't take off his coat or hat. He sat down at the kitchen table and looked down at the paper Fred had spread open. Hani cleared off a few dishes so the paper could lay flat. The three of them stared at the paper with its large headline: "Nazi Mobs in Orgy of Anti-Semitism Wreck, Burn, Slay." Ludwig read aloud sections of one article, translating parts as best he could from the English for his wife and brother-in-law: "Synagogues have been burned. Stores have been destroyed and looted. Ten thousand stores in ruins. Many suicides . . ." Hani gasped at each sentence. Fred was quiet but tears filled his eyes. He tried to wipe them away without drawing notice.

Ludwig had a soft, high-pitched voice that matched his thin build. But his distress and anger expressed itself in a loud, agitated quality as he read from a long list of atrocities enumerated in the *Daily News* article. He paused. "And here"—Ludwig pointed to a section of the article—"this is some real bullshit!"

"What do you mean?" Fred looked down at the paper.

"It says here, 'The mob paid no heed to Goebbels's order to stop the destruction.'"

"Ach!" Fred got up and paced the small kitchen. "Goebbels tried to stop this!? We're to believe that the chief arsonist tried to put out the fire!" For a moment he thought about picking up a plate and smashing it against the wall. "We've got to get our parents out!"

The phone rang and Hani went into the bedroom to answer it. When she returned to the kitchen, she said, "Fritz, it's our cousin Ida from Chicago, why don't you talk to her. I mean, *Fred* . . ."

When Fred returned from the bedroom, he said, "Ida's in shock." He looked at his sister. "She hadn't taken the situation very seriously. But she sees it now. She just heard a radio report that thousands of Jewish men have been taken to the camps!"

"Who is Ida?" Ludwig asked.

"She's the daughter of our Uncle Markus—Dad's brother," said Hani. "She lives in Chicago."

Ludwig picked up the newspaper, his voice still shaking as he read and translated, "Gangs entering houses, breaking down doors of Jews and dragging them out."

Fred looked intently at his sister. "Ida says she knows a politician in Chicago, a Mr. Sabath.[31] She's going to try and see him. Getting the affidavits is not going to be the most difficult issue. It's the visas to enter this country—that's what we have to work on. So this contact of Ida's might help."

"This government could do a lot more than it has. It shouldn't be so hard for us to get visas," Ludwig fumed. "Capitalist governments *don't give a damn* about you unless they can get something out of you. This country's no different than any of them."

"I don't feel quite as negative about it, Ludwig." Fred stood up again. "We should write a letter to Munich right now, Hani. We have to be careful what we say, but we should let them know we understand the seriousness. And tell them about Ida's new resolve." Fred pulled the writing paper they used for international letters from a drawer and he and Hani began to compose a letter.

At about the same time, Anna was writing a carefully neutral letter to her children.

November 12, 1938

Dear Hani and Fred,

We have received your letter from November 4. We are happy that you children are doing so well. As to myself everything is the same. I'm alone but Dad will be getting home soon. Louis and Willi just came by.

Don't worry about me—under these circumstances, I'm just

fine. My dearest wish is just to be with you and Dad of course as well. That's all we are thinking about but when will it happen?
Your mother.

## Anti-Jewish Measures
### November 12, 1938

Head of the Nazi four-year economic plan, Herman Goering, convenes a conference at the Berlin Air Ministry. He rages at the assembled economic and domestic affairs functionaries over the losses Germany suffered in the November pogrom, such as the glass that had to be imported to replace shattered windows in Jewish businesses, the insurance claims that had to be paid to Jewish insurance holders to protect the insurance industry's credibility, the economic loss as a result of goods stolen or destroyed from wrecked Jewish stores, and the loss of tax revenue from businesses put out of action. He demands measures to mitigate these losses. The conference comes up with policies to soften the blow to the German economy. Chief among these is a plan to confiscate Jewish insurance claims and impose a collective fine on the Jewish community of a billion Reichmarks (the equivalent of about 5 billion 2023 dollars) for the damage the nation sustained during the pogrom.

November 13, 1938

My dear children,

It's a pleasure writing you again today. I'm doing pretty well so please don't worry about me.

Dad should be here any moment. My biggest wish is to be with you, my dear children. It looks like we are the only ones who stayed behind. Klara is gone and soon everyone will leave. I'm just happy that you, my dear children, got away in time. I got a letter from Aunt Mina today. She's doing all right considering what she's gone through. Well, the main thing is that we all stay healthy.

Greetings from your mom.

Dear Hani and Dear Fritz,

Thank you so much for your lovely words. You must have received our letter as well. It's a pleasure to know about your well-being. All we are wishing for is to be with you. We had to leave our home on Thursday [November 10.] That's why we are staying with your mom now. She's taking it quite well. God-willing we will be able to bear all the hardships we are experiencing now. Who knows what the next days will bring? We'll remain here until we can return home. Of course, the best thing would be to go to America right away. Maybe you could help us with a sponsorship. That would be highly appreciated.

Martha [Alfred's wife, Martha Trautman Holzer] is in the hospital. We'll be visiting her soon.

Unfortunately, we won't be able to send you the requested newspapers. They didn't come this week. Klara called us from the Vogels' home yesterday and wanted to know how we are doing. She won't come back.

Take care of yourselves and please write us soon!

Loving greetings from your cousin Hedi.

My dear ones,

It's been great looking after your mom. I just wanted to tell you that we are living with our dad [Louis Holzer] for the time being. We are hoping to emigrate soon, and we are indeed quite desperate to get to America. Unfortunately, it's taking longer than expected. I'm happy to hear that you like your new home. Your mom can't wait to see you again.

Best regards from all of us.

Yours sincerely,

Cousin Hansi.

Anti-Jewish Measure, November 14, 1938

The German Minister of Education, Bernhard Rust, issued a decree barring Jewish students enrolled in all German or Austrian universities from attending lectures. The following day,

German Jewish children were barred from attending German schools. Those enrolled are expelled.

### Anti-Jewish Measure, November 22, 1938

Munich mayor Adolf Wagner establishes the Wealth Administration Organization of Munich. The administration sets up a corporation to liquidate or "Aryanize" Jewish businesses. This enables Nazi Party officials, sycophants, opportunists, and other assorted thieves to acquire Jewish properties for a fraction of their value. They could, and often did, sell these properties to third parties for a handsome profit.

### Other Anti-Jewish Measures in November 1938

A decree calling for all Jewish retail businesses to be transferred to Aryan hands.

A decree preventing Jews from holding jobs as foremen or chief clerks in factories or stores and a prohibition from engaging in handicrafts.

A decree making it illegal for Jews to enter theaters, concerts, cinemas, music halls, dance floors, or other places of entertainment. Violations would result in punishment of the places of entertainment and more severe punishment of the Jews themselves.

A decree revoking Jews' driver's licenses and invalidating their car ownership permits.

A decree prohibiting Jews from nearly all open-air recreation sites. In some sites, special park benches were to be designated as "For Jews Only."

# After Dachau

November 25, 1938

Dear Fred and Hani,

We received your letters from November the 11th and the 15th. We just wish we could already be with you. Dad is still out doing things. Hopefully you can get your citizenship quickly. I'm sure things will get easier then. Every day we are waiting for mail from the authorities but nothing so far.

There's so much to take care of. But in the meanwhile, all we can do is wait. Yesterday Fritz's friend was here. He'll be leaving next week. Dad is trying to make things happen, but so far without luck. I'm just so happy that all of you children got away. We just have to wait to be reunited with you again. Every day I'm praying to the Almighty that we stay healthy until we get to you. How wonderful it would be if you could pick us up from the ship, you, standing at the shore, and us waving from the ship.

My thoughts are always with you and I'm sure it'll all work out in the end.

Greetings and kisses from your mom.

## The Evening of November 25

Anna had just returned from mailing a letter to her children when she heard a knock on the door. When she opened it, she gasped and cried out, "Benno!" She embraced her husband and they both broke down in sobs. His appearance spoke a great deal about his ordeal. The jacket and shirt he wore were ill-fitting and hung off a noticeably thinner frame. His face had lost its previous fullness and his eyes appeared as though they'd faded and sunk into his face. He had difficulty speaking.

On hearing Anna's cry, Willi, Hedi, and Benno Holzer came running to the entranceway and each in turn greeted Benno. He was surprised to see Willi, his brother-in-law, and Willi's two children. Willi retreated to the kitchen and came back with a bottle of beer and thrust the bottle into Benno's hand with the words "Here's the best Bavarian medicine!"

Then Hedi, her cheeks damp with tears, explained that she, Benno, and their father were his new roommates, since the family had left Traunstein and were now living in Munich. "We'll tell you all about it later," Anna said. "Now just rest. I'll make some soup."

Hedi and Anna went to the kitchen and made a sweet and sour cabbage soup, one of Benno's favorites, while Benno and Willi Holzer sat with Benno at the dining room table. Anna brought her husband the letters that had arrived from Fritz and Hani while he was in Dachau. "I didn't tell them where you were," explained Anna. "I just said you were 'out.'"

Benno spoke softly. "Well, by now they know, of course." Then his voice rose. "I would hope the whole world would know—should know—the shameful horror this country has become!"

Willi spoke indignantly. "They came and broke into our home. They took Hansi's little Margaret and held her all night. God knows what they did to her!"

"We still don't know what they did to Margaret," Willi's son

Benno told Benno Neuburger. "But she's hardly been able to talk since the night of the ninth. The good news is that it looks like Hansi and Paul will be able to get Margaret away from here."

"To where?" asked Benno.

"Colombia. Paul Lowy has some kind of contact there."

"What about Alfred and Martha?" asked Benno Neuburger warily.

"They've found their own place in Munich. Martha's recovering from a broken foot, and can't walk, so Fredi takes care of her."

Benno looked at Willi. "And your house?"

"What they haven't wrecked they'll steal. It's not our house anymore. It belongs to the Reich and the thieves who broke in that night. Our horses are no longer our horses, the same for our cows. They've taken everything. A lawyer—or now they call them 'legal assistants' since Jews can't be lawyers anymore—is looking into it for us, but they've got laws now that allow them to do this. We're trying to get something back, but it seems they've auctioned a lot off, or just outright stolen it. Our neighbors told us that some of them started to wreck the house, but Aichner stopped them. Of course, so he could have the spoils for himself!"

"Papa and Alfred were arrested but not beaten," said the younger Benno. "I was able to get out of the house when the bastards showed up. Some neighbors took me in. There are people in Traunstein angry about what happened that night. I've spoken to some of them."

"But will they do anything?" asked Benno.

"A few people are trying to get some of our things back. But anyone who stands up for us publicly risks, well, you know . . ."

"I've been contacted by a few farmers," Willi added. "One of them got a few of our horses at an auction. He got them cheap and told me, quietly, that he'd send me some money because he knows we can use it. Another asked how we were and offered to bring us food if we needed it. There are those who don't like what they did to us."

"What the *swine* did to us, Papa," interjected Hedi. "They don't like what the *filthy swine* did. And don't think they aren't proud of themselves." Hedi placed a plate of soup in front of Benno. "They're proud that Traunstein will soon be *Judenfrei*. It's in that dirty *schmatte* of a newspaper, *Traunstein wird judenfrei!*" [Traunstein will be Jew-free] Hedi began shaking.

They were silent for a time. Benno drank his beer and then ate the cabbage soup. "You have no idea how good this food tastes."

"Well, Dachau's given Benno an appreciation for home cooking," Willi joked as Hedi embraced her Uncle Benno from behind him, resting her head on his shoulder.

"I'm alive." Benno grasped Hedi's hand with his. "I'm lucky. I'm out." At that, Benno choked up. After several minutes he added, "A lot of people are still in that . . . place . . . Of course, I had to promise to give them everything we have as a condition for leaving. Someday I may tell you about it. But not tonight."

Benno looked at his relatives. "There's only one thing that matters now." Benno's voice was wavering. "That is, we have to get out of Germany. This is *not* our home anymore!!"

Nov. 25, 1938

Dear Aunt Emma,

We Holzer sisters and your cousin as well as Aunt Anna noticed with delight over the years that you and my mom had a lively correspondence going on between the two of you. Now we'd like to ask you for a big favor. We are in big trouble here and we would like to emigrate to America. In order to do that though we need sponsors and we thought that you, your sons, our cousin Julius or maybe your brother Leo (from whom we heard a lot of good things) might be willing to do that for us. We would be forever thankful to you.

We are strongly hoping to get your help in this matter since it would mean life or death for us in our situation here. Carl Laemmle might be able to pull some strings as well. We are willing to do whatever work there is to do once we are in America. Our mom taught us not to be picky when it comes to earning a living.

Here are the dates for when we were born:

Father Willi Holzer 07/03/1874
Benno Holzer 01/10/1904
Hedwick Holzer 02/17/1906
Maximilian Holzer 12/28/1909
Alfred Holzer 06/11/1907
Marta Holzer 05/26/1907

Benno, Hedwick, Maximilian and Alfred were born in Traunstein whereas Marta was born in Bergzabern.

At this time, we are all in Munich with our aunt Anna Neuburger and we are longing to hear from you as soon as possible.

Dear Aunt,

Anna's children Hani and Fritz have been in America now for a while and now they are trying to get sponsors for their parents. As soon as they have the documents they'd like to leave right away.

Our Aunt Mina gave us your address and since we don't have any other relatives in the U.S.A. we are very much hoping to get your support in this life-threatening situation.

Once again, we are very much hoping that you can help us, for which we would be indebted to you for the rest of our lives.

Thank you very much and many greetings from our family Holzer.

Loving greetings from Alfred and wife, Martha, and Willi (Holzer).

Greetings from Benno Holzer. Please help us in these difficult times.

P.S. Dear Aunt, Please have it in your heart to help your relatives. They'll be very thankful to you. Loving greetings to everyone and I hope to see you again someday.

Your cousin, Anna

### A Letter to Laemmle

In December the Holzers wrote a letter to the U.S. filmmaker Carl Laemmle in which they explained their circumstances and appealed for his help. Laemmle was born in Laupheim in 1867 and emigrated to the United States when he was seventeen. While living in Chicago in 1906, he opened one of the city's first movie theaters. Within a few years he began distributing films. His audacity in successfully standing up to a syndicate that sought to monopolize film distribution won him acclaim. He moved from film distribution to film production and eventually founded his own production company, Universal Studios, in Southern California. He was a pioneer of the Hollywood film industry.

After the Nazis rose to power, Laemmle devoted himself to helping Jews leave Germany by guaranteeing their livelihoods in the United States, thereby satisfying a requirement of the State Department that immigrants entering the country provide proof that they would not be a burden on U.S. society. In this way Laemmle was able to assist hundreds of refugees, including many from his hometown of Laupheim, who would have otherwise been unable to emigrate.

Beginning in 1937, the U.S. State Department began throwing obstacles in Laemmle's path. As the Holzers reached out to Laemmle for his help, they had no way of knowing that his ability to help them had been undermined by policies meant to prevent Jews from emigrating to the United States.

ANTI-JEWISH MEASURE, DECEMBER 3, 1938
Jews are heretofore banned from using public libraries.

ANTI-JEWISH MEASURE, DECEMBER 6, 1938
Jews are banned from using sports or playing fields, public baths, or outdoor swimming pools.

Anti-Jewish Measure, December 1938
A decree on the Utilization of Jewish Assets mandates the compulsory sale of Jewish-owned businesses with the funds generated directed to a special account controlled by authorities. It also obligates Jews to move their securities into special accounts

where their own access to the funds would be limited—effectively cutting them off from the source of their own wealth.

Munich, December 11, 1938

Dear children,

We received your letter. Hopefully we'll be able to come to you soon. It's both our dearest wish to join you as soon as possible. It would be so wonderful to live with all of you. I'm looking forward to helping you with your household. What I'm able to do I'll do. I can't wait to cook for you, Hani.

You must be very busy since you started working. I'm just so happy that you found some work—just like Ludwig and Fred. It makes for a happy life.

Today Benno and Hedi stopped by to say "Hi." They've been looking for their own apartment since our place is just not big enough with so many people living here.

As you know Dad doesn't like to have so many people around. The good news is that Hansi, Paul, and Margit are leaving the country tomorrow. They are so happy to get away.

Life just runs its course. When I receive something, I will certainly let you know. Since you left, everything has changed. We are getting by—don't worry about us.

Your mom.


My loved ones,

We received your letter from November 30, 1938, and we are very happy with its contents. We'll be so happy once we can leave. As you know we sold half of our properties in September, but we still haven't received the money for them.

Nothing has been paid for.

You really have no idea how things are. Just be happy that you got away. In the middle of October, I wrote to Stuttgart [the U.S. Consulate office].

Please write us soon! We are sending all of you our regards.

Your loving father.

## Beer Talk, December 22, 1938

Benno was in the kitchen of his old friend Berthold's apartment. Both were wearing overcoats. It was cold outside and the heater in the apartment was not working well. Berthold was afraid to make demands on the landlord who was acting less and less friendly these days.

Berthold was boiling potatoes for food and heat. They would have cabbage and cheese with their potatoes, and beer. With all the restrictions pressing in on their lives, their get-togethers over beer were a fragile lifeline. Their conversation up to this moment revolved around the problem of finding food. Now, weeks after the November 10 pogrom, the "No Jews Admitted" signs had begun disappearing from a few food stores, restaurants, and pharmacies. But places to shop were still limited and so were funds. Banking restrictions on top of dwindling assets threatened to make them destitute. Benno was selling land cheaply for cash but was having problems getting buyers to pay. Berthold's Munich store was wrecked the night of November 10 and the insurance payments for the damage were confiscated by the government.

Berthold sat at his kitchen table with a bowl of steaming potatoes. He looked up at Benno. For just an instant Berthold flashed on a moment thirty years before when he sat across from Benno in a restaurant near the Hofbrauhaus trying to convince his friend to come to a seder in Laupheim to meet the woman who was now Benno's wife. Berthold was about to mention this when another, more immediate question occurred to him. "Something I haven't asked you, Benno. If you don't want to answer, I'll understand. But what happened to you in Dachau?"

Benno had said very little about Dachau to anyone since being released. He took a deep breath. "Well, what I can tell you it's the one time in my life I thanked God I'm short."

"Could be the first time you've thanked God for anything!" Berthold let out a grim laugh.

"They had us marching for hours. Just marching. We marched

from one part of the camp to another. The word went around: Try to keep from being conspicuous. This was harder for the taller guys. The guards loved to pick on them. They were free with their beatings . . ."

Benno paused to eat and then continued. "In the mornings they'd have us standing in the cold while they took roll call. The colder it was, the longer they'd have us there in our thin clothes. They yelled if you moved when not instructed to move. They beat people for just being noticeable." Benno paused with a grim expression. "A few times they had us repeating phrases from *Mein Kampf.* They got very aggressive if you didn't shout with the proper enthusiasm. I was hit hard in the back at one of these sessions. We were yelling, '*It is the Aryan and the Aryan alone that can be regarded as what we call a man.*' That was a popular one with them.

"They had strict rules about what they called 'hygiene.' How you made your bed up and all that. How you hung your food bowl. Any imperfection was an excuse for a beating. Guys were beaten and mistreated. Some were killed. I saw guards spray water on a group of naked men, outside in the cold. Do you think they survived?"

They both sat silently for a moment.

"But I want you to know, Berthold, they knew we were coming."

"What do you mean?"

"I mean, they were prepared for us. The inmates who were there before we got there told us they had prepared for a big influx of prisoners. After Hitler took over Austria last March, they brought people to Dachau from Vienna and other cities. They had already built up the camp before the Austrians arrived. Since then, they expanded the camp even more. They were waiting for another large group. Then came the shooting in Paris and they had their pretext. But Bert, before this gets too grim, I have a joke for you." Benno was now standing by the stove to light the stubby remnant of an old cigar he'd saved.

"A joke?"

"One from Dachau."

"I can't imagine . . ." Berthold gave Benno a puzzled look.

"First the joke. Then I'll explain."

Berthold sat back in his chair. "Okay, Benno, you have the floor."

Benno sat down and leaned forward, the stub of his cigar between his fingers.

"A Jew is sitting in a restaurant reading a Nazi paper."

"This must be before November, before restaurants closed their doors to us."

"Bert, please, you're going to ruin the joke. This Jew is reading a Nazi paper when a friend of his passes by and stops and says, 'What the hell are you doing reading that paper?' The reader looks up at his friend. 'In the Jewish papers we're always being beaten, persecuted, arrested, and run out of the country. In these Nazi papers we own all the banks, we control the media, we practically rule the world. This is much better news!'"

"Hah. So that's what you were doing in Dachau when not marching, learning jokes?"

"One horribly bad day, one among many, we got back to the barracks after eating this watery soupy slop they fed us. We were hungry, tired, depressed. We're sitting in the barracks. And this guy, Karl, I think his name was, he'd worked in a club in Schwabing. He said, 'I'm not a doctor but I know that when you're being fed poison you need an antidote. Does anyone have a joke to tell?' And we're all silent. How could we even think of a joke at such a time? And this guy who was always quiet—a thin fellow with glasses, and a funny sharp nose, he perks right up—like maybe he's always dreamed of being a comedian and now he has an audience. Anyway, he has this joke. And we say, okay, let's hear it. So that's how it started."

"There were more jokes then?" Berthold prodded.

"Yes. It went on for a while, but I've forgotten most all of them. Mostly sexual stuff. And circumcision jokes. I have a bad memory for jokes . . . Wait, okay, I remember one. Two Jews are standing at a urinal. One asks the other, 'Who did your circumcision? Was it Rabbi Steinberg?' And the other guy says, 'Yah, you're right. But how'd you know that?' And the first guy says, "Cause the Rabbi's cross-eyed and that must be why you're pissing on my shoe.'"

Berthold shakes his head. "Oh God!"

Benno smiled in a way he hadn't for months. "See what you missed, Bert?"

"Benno, if you'd stayed longer, you might have learned more jokes."

"I did my two weeks in hell. At that I was lucky. I got out sooner than many."

"Because?"

"Maybe because I'm a veteran." Benno knocked ash from his stubby cigar.

"That's what they told you?"

"No, they don't tell you a damn thing. That's just my guess. But you know what they say about Germany and war veterans."

Berthold said cautiously, "No, what do they say?"

Benno took a short puff. "Germany loves its veterans so much it lets its gentile veterans go first everywhere: first into the theater, first into the opera, first into sports events, first into the cinema, and so on."

"Yes."

"And it lets its Jewish veterans go last."

"Last?"

"Yah. To the firing squad."

Berthold nodded appreciatively. "Another Dachau joke?"

"Probably."

"So, it took Dachau to make you into a comedian!"

"Who knows, maybe this begins a new career. God knows the humor in the cabarets has gone completely to shit since the Nazis took over."

"Quite likely, Benno, but how would we know? If we ever showed up at a cabaret we'd be the punch line."

"Hah! That's good, you're getting into the spirit, Bert. 'Course it doesn't apply to my nephew." Benno suddenly turned sullen.

"What doesn't apply?" asked Berthold as he pulled a bottle of beer from a kitchen cabinet, opened it, and poured the dark liquid into his gray ceramic stein.

"The remark about veterans." Benno was suddenly speaking more quietly.

"What do you mean?"

"Hermann Spatz, married to Tilli, Anna's niece. A frontline soldier for three years in the war, in an elite unit, Iron Cross and all that. Didn't mean a thing. They beat the crap out of him in Dachau. They only let him go after he signed over his property in Wolfratshausen . . ."

"To the Reich."

"To some thug who works at the camp."

They both sat quietly. Benno seemed lost in thought.

Berthold broke the silence. "I'll have to control my drinking. Beer's getting harder to come by. So, I'll start being careful—tomorrow."

"Beer-wise we're okay right now." Benno threw the remainder of his cigar in the sink. "Before Fritz left, he bought a closetful of beer for us! He said, 'I expect you and Mom to be out of here before the beer runs out.' He meant out of Germany. But I've been stupid and stubborn. So, I haven't tried as hard . . . Well, until recently . . ."

Berthold stood up and put his chair closer to Benno who was rubbing his hands together to fight the cold.

"I didn't tell you this before, Benno, and I only tell you in confidence now."

"All right." Benno drank the last of his beer.

"The evening of the pogrom, before all the destruction began, someone came to my shop and said they'd heard that there was going to be a roundup of Jewish men. He told me to come with him. He took me to his home and hid me there."

"Who?"

"I swore secrecy, Benno, and I'm going to honor that. When people came to the apartment looking for me Hilde said she didn't know where I was, that I was probably at work or buying food. She thinks they were SA types, not Gestapo, ah young, you know, nasty, but not well organized. They said they'd be back, but they didn't return. I stayed hidden for several days before going home. Thank God they never came back."

"Lucky."

Berthold nodded. "Lucky and grateful. There are still some decent people out there." Bert rubbed his eyes. Then he looked over at Benno. "And he actually told me a joke I just remembered. Let's see." Berthold paused. "Hitler goes to an asylum. And as he enters everyone jumps up and screams and salutes, 'Heil Hitler!' And as he passes from one room to another the same thing. They all stand, and scream, and salute, 'Heil Hitler!' Hitler is very pleased. Then he goes to another room and passes a person seated there, but this person remains seated and says nothing. Hitler goes up to him and says angrily, 'You're the only person in this whole place who won't stand and salute me. Why is that?' The man says, 'I'm the doctor here, so I'm the only one who isn't a lunatic.'"

Benno slapped his knee. "Good one, Bert! Once this nightmare passes, we should hit the road as a comedy duo!"

"I'll drink to that!"

### Anti-Jewish Measure, December 23, 1938

Strict orders are issued by Gestapo headquarters to all stations on the western borders of the Reich to prevent illegal crossings of Jews into neighboring countries.

### Anti-Jewish Measure, December 1938

Herman Goering orders the cessation of all Jewish business activity as of January 1, 1939.

January 8, 1939

Dear Fred,

You are writing us that you're enjoying Hani's cooking. That's wonderful! I can't wait to cook for you as well.

Hedi is, as always, industrious and I like having her around. That way I'm not always alone. Ilse is coming by less and less and

Hansi hasn't contacted us yet. I'm just wondering how things are for her, but I just have to wait so that I can tell you about it. Please write us soon.

Greetings and kisses from your mom.

Dear Fred,

It's nice to hear that you are satisfied with your life and that it seems to be going so well for you. Dad and I are keeping the living room heated. The younger people are living in the smaller rooms. They still haven't found an apartment for themselves which is surprising to us. Dad is stubborn about how things are to be run about our emigration. He just has to have his way—I'm just hoping that it will work out. Hopefully we can be with you soon.

Loving greetings again from your mom.

January 22, 1939

My dear children,

We happily received your letter from January 8th, 1939. It's good to know that you're doing so well.

It's so depressing that we haven't heard back from Stuttgart, but chances are very slim anyway.

We certainly have written them plenty of times but without an invitation it's almost impossible to get an answer. Hopefully something else materializes, otherwise it doesn't look too good.

Family Levi is trying to emigrate to Canada. So far, it's been taking a very long time as well, but their son is sponsoring them.

Dear Fred,

We are hoping that your business is doing well. Now that you're still young and ambitious—this is the time to make it happen. As you know I have to be very stingy with my money. There's just no way to earn any. Sure, I could sell something, but you can never be sure if you get paid or not.

A lot of people unfortunately are trying to take advantage of you. So many people are leaving but we, as Jews, have to wait. It's a mess and it's hard to know how to proceed next. Hopefully something is going to work out. It's just too bad that I basically have no income anymore. I'm trying to get them to pay but I don't have a lot of leverage. Levi is one of them who hasn't paid yet, and Baumann hasn't paid back the 149 Marks either. I've almost given up hope that anyone will pay me back but if it does happen, I will certainly let you know.

Your father.

January 26, 1939

Dear children,

I'm writing you again this week. So far we haven't heard anything from Stuttgart. Of course we can't wait to receive some good news.

You have no idea how Dad can get irritated about something, but dear Hani and Fred, I think you know exactly what I'm talking about. You know how he can be. I just wish you were here to calm him down a little when he's like that. It's sometimes unbearable. I just wish we could come right away. My longing to see you is all I can think about sometimes. My dear children, I can't wait to receive mail from you. If we could just emigrate to New York right away.

Your mom.

Hitler, speaking before the Reichstag on January 30, 1939, said, "I have very often in my lifetime been a prophet and have been mostly derided . . . I want today to be a prophet again: If international finance Jewry inside and outside Europe should succeed in plunging the nations once more into a world war, the result will be not the Bolshevization of the earth and thereby the victory of Jewry, but the annihilation of the Jewish race in Europe."

On February 9, 1939, authorities in Traunstein officially declared their town "free of Jews."

>   ANTI-JEWISH MEASURE, BEGINNING FEBRUARY 21, 1939
>   Jews are required to surrender all jewelry and precious metals to state pawnshops for a nominal compensation.

On March 15, Germans troops marched into Bohemia and Moravia, territories of Czechoslovakia, in violation of the Munich agreement of September 30, 1938.

March 31, 1939

Dearest children,

We received your letter from March 13th and are very happy to get mail from you so often.

My thoughts are always with you. Hopefully we'll be together soon. Aunt Mina likes being here. She finds it easier here to take her mind off things for a little while. Since you've been gone, my children, I've had a lot of visitors who stay for a few days every so often. Your room, my dear Fred, has been occupied since you've left. Aunt Mina also likes to hang out with Hedi. Ilse and Fredi are enjoying our company quite often as well. Yesterday, Mrs. Neumeier came by. She became a grandma quite recently.

Dear Fred,

You seem to be getting together with people all the time. With the situation as miserable as it is here people are leaving daily. Of course, we are wondering when it is our turn. The process of our leaving seems to have come to a stop. Herta will be spending the holidays at her parents' house.

P.S. My dear ones, to spend the holidays with your loved ones is wonderful. We are wishing to hear only good news from you. I don't have much to say about family Langheim. My circle of friends is getting smaller and smaller. Yesterday Ilse [Schuster] and her boy came by. He's a good child.

I wish I could see Tilli more often but it's hard for me to go out. But I'm very lucky to be here with your loved ones. This makes me happy! I'm wishing you the best of luck.
Yours, Aunt Mina.

### ANTI-JEWISH MEASURE, APRIL 1939

A law on renting to Jews strips them of any protection against eviction. It allows city officials to order Jewish homeowners to rent space to other Jews or Jewish families. This paves the way for concentrating Jews in residences called *Judenhausen*, Jew houses.

### BEER TALK, MAY 8, 1939

Benno and Berthold met at the Konigsplatz and walked to Berthold's apartment. Conversation meandered along with the walk as they grappled with the increasingly impossible situation.

Benno wanted to talk out of earshot of Anna. And he was relieved when, arriving at Berthold's, Hilde was out. "I've become very irritable at home, Bert. I can't control my mood. I'm sure I'm hard to be around."

"What does Anna say?"

"She's an angel, Berthold, and I'm not the only one who says it. She endures. She puts up with my moods, my anger, my foolishness."

"You don't deserve her, Benno." Berthold stared absentmindedly out the window of his third-story apartment with a view of the English Garden in the distance.

"That may be true. But I'm the one who should be saying that, not you. You're my friend, you should be defending me."

"Don't take it seriously, Benno," Berthold laughed. "I could say the same about Hilde and me. Of most couples I know. Isn't it the women who have the wisdom? What do they say? 'An old man in the house is a burden, but an old woman is a treasure.'"

"Who's they?"

"I don't know. I didn't make it up. Someone said it. And with good reason, seems to me. It applies to us, don't you think? You and I, Benno, we're good for business, but useless in the house."

"And now we have no business," Benno lamented. "Unless you count trying to collect the debts no one is willing to pay. We have no standing in the courts. Even if I could afford a lawyer."

"Or even find one, a Jewish one. And no *goyim* lawyer is going to defend one of us," Berthold added. "We no longer have rights. Someone could come into this house right now and take anything they wanted, and we could do nothing."

Benno nodded. "That's what happened to Feuchtwanger's brother on Prinzregentenstrasse. They drove right up to their apartment, a beautiful place, with a moving truck—came in, removed their furniture, their art pieces, and such things. When they finished taking what they wanted the intruder threw some Reichmarks on the table and walked out. Didn't even wait for them to be counted. He knew the family had to accept whatever he gave them."

Berthold sat down across from Benno. "Isn't that the apartment across from Hitler's place?"

"Yah. For all we know Hitler was at his window, watching and laughing."

"Such a sense of humor." Berthold swirled the beer in his large stein. "I can remember when we thought that psychopath wouldn't last."

"Yeah, so much for that," Benno sighed. "I've been wrong about a lot of things. Maybe most things. Remember when the war started, we thought we were about to be fully accepted as Germans? Such false confidence!"

"Remember Arnulf, Benno? He and his socialist friends had fewer illusions about the war."

Benno sat back in his chair. "Well, the Social Democrats may have seen some things coming, but they didn't stop a damn thing—neither the war then, nor Hitler."

"I wonder where Arnulf is now. Do you suppose he's still in Munich?"

Berthold shook his head. "If he's still here he's probably laying very low. I know his old business is closed down. I think he may have left the country. A lot of Social Democrats left Germany after 1933."

"Lucky them," said Benno.

### Anti-Jewish Action, May 1939

The passenger ship *MS St. Louis* sets sail from Hamburg to Cuba with 939 Jewish emigrants on board. After being refused landing rights in Cuba, it sails to the U.S. East Coast and then the coast of Canada. It is denied permission to pull into any port and is forced to return to Europe.

By June 1939, more than 300,000 German Jews were on a waiting list for visas to enter the United States.

### Beer Talk, Late August 1939

Benno and Berthold met at the edge of the English Garden near the Luitpold Bridge and took a path that led along the Schwabinger Bach, the narrow stream that runs through the park. Both were relieved and happy to be out of their apartments, walking in the open air. Benno spoke of the summer days he, Anna, and the children had spent relaxing along the stream. Berthold recalled similar moments. He then turned to Benno, "We're in a contemplative mood today, aren't we, my friend?"

A small smile crept across Benno's deeply lined face. "Wouldn't it be nice to be in such a mood all the time."

"To be someplace where we were free to do so." Berthold grabbed his friend's arm. "Benno, let's sit for a moment." They sat on the grass in the shade of a large chestnut tree. Berthold unfolded a newspaper he was carrying and spread the front page of the paper on the ground in front of them. He opened a bottle of beer he'd been carrying in his coat pocket, and Benno opened one of his own. "I want to hear your view of this." Bert pointed to the headline: "Germany and the Soviet Union Conclude Pact of Peace."

"Pact of peace," Benno murmured. "When Hitler talks peace it means war. What else?"

"Do you think there's some chance that Germany and the Soviets will work together?"

Benno shook his head. "No, Bert. That's not what this is about."

"You're sure of that?"

"Bert, remember last year Chamberlain and the French president, hmm—Daladier—were in Munich, basically to give Hitler the Sudetenland? The best explanation I heard for this acquiescence to Hitler was their interest in encouraging him to move east, to confront the Soviets—let the Germans and the Soviets fight it out. What could make the British happier than to see their two rivals smash each other?"

Berthold nodded. "The Soviets don't want to confront Germany alone. So they make a deal with Hitler. Okay. But I'm not clear on Hitler's angle here."

"Last year the Czechs had to be stopped from supposedly abusing the Sudeten Germans—remember all the Czech 'atrocity stories' in the newspapers? This year, it's the Poles who've been 'oppressing' the Germans and holding on to Danzig when it rightfully belongs to Germany. So says Hitler."

Berthold stretched his legs out and leaned back on the grass. "You're saying that means Poland's next."

"That's what it seems to me," said Benno. "And I think the generals are nervous that Hitler's going to get Germany into a two-front war. This could happen if Germany invades Poland, and this provokes war with Stalin and then the British and French come to the aid of Poland."

"So, to avoid that, Hitler makes a deal with Stalin. Now he can invade Poland without having to worry about a two-front war. I'd say there's something to that, Benno."

"It's a many-sided chess game," Benno said as he lay back and looked up at the branches full of young chestnuts.

"Well, let's hope the Poles can put up a fight," said Berthold.

"And let's hope we can get out of here before any of this happens." Benno sat up and watched young boys and girls play at the water's edge. The two men both enjoyed the August sun and didn't worry about grass stains on their suits.

### World War II

On August 22, 1939, Hitler summoned his top military commanders to inform them of the impending pact between Germany and the Soviet Union, which had "completed the political groundwork" for war with Poland. A week later, on September 1, the German invasion of Poland began. On September 3, the Allied powers declared war on Germany but made no concerted effort to open a war front against Germany in the west. The German Wehrmacht, with the massive use of tanks and air support, quickly overran the western region of Poland, lands that held 22 million people, of whom about 2 million were Jews. Poland's capital, Warsaw, was taken on September 27. Fighting stopped a few days after that.

The Soviet Union sent its forces into Poland on September 17. In accord with the agreement reached with Germany in August, the Soviets seized roughly the eastern half of Poland with a population of 13 million, 1.5 million of them Jewish. Thus the Soviet seizure of eastern Poland kept roughly 40 percent of Poland's Jewish population out of Nazi hands, for the time being.

Munich, September 14, 1939

Dear Hani,

Don't worry we won't lose our patience. Someday it'll happen. Since you are asking, Hedi is not coming by that often anymore. She's changed a lot the last past weeks and hasn't really been visiting her relatives all that often either. Of course, we'd love for her to come by more often. Right now Hedi's husband is here, and he talks a lot about going away. It's just not as easy as you think it is. Dad is not going to talk to L.W.—there's nothing I can do about it. You know how stubborn he can be. Each week Dad gets together with his godfather for a glass of beer.

Loving greetings, your mom.

In late September 1939, Hedi Holzer received a letter from her sister Klara, sent from Manchester, England. Klara, with help from her cousin Simon Vogel, had managed to emigrate to England. In the letter Klara told her sister that she had secured a visa for her to come to England and that a job as a domestic awaited her there. Hedi wrote back to Klara that all of their family members still in Germany were trying to secure affidavits and visas to emigrate. "I'm sorry, Klara, but I can't go to England now and leave Papa and the others behind."[32]

# Slave Labor

### Anti-Jewish Measure, Fall 1939

Having left Jews dispossessed, Nazi authorities worry that the Jewish population will become dependent on the state for survival. To avoid that expense, the Nazi state initiates a slave labor program. They demand lists of working-age adults from Jewish community organizations and assign these adults to jobs in infrastructure construction, armed forces projects, and the armaments industry. Both public builders and private enterprises profit from this Jewish slave labor.

THREE OF THE HOLZER CHILDREN—Alfred, Benno, and Hedi—along with Alfred's wife, Martha, were assigned to labor crews in Munich, initially for gardening and city cleanup, including snow clearing after a storm in December 1939. They were paid a special "Jewish wage" that corresponded to less than 10 percent of what a German industrial worker made at that time. Out of that wage they paid an additional tax of 15 percent. Older adults such as the brothers Willi and Louis Holzer, and Benno and Anna, who were all in their sixties at the time, were excluded from these slave labor jobs due to their ages.

## A Bomb in a Munich Beer Hall

On November 8, 1939, a bomb exploded at the Munich Burgerbraukeller only moments after Hitler left the beer hall, where he'd given a speech for the annual celebration of the 1923 Putsch. The explosion killed eight and injured 62 others. The Nazi press claimed that the attack was masterminded by British intelligence. Others speculated that the Nazis themselves had set off the explosion to win sympathy and build anger against England. A carpenter named George Elser was caught and eventually confessed to having placed the bomb. Elser was not Jewish. Nevertheless, in the aftermath of the bombing there were random attacks against Jews in Munich.

> ### Anti-Jewish Measure, November 10, 1939
> The Nazis complete a population census that includes a detailed accounting of "racial Jews" in the expanded Reich, Germany, Austria, and the Sudetenland. Germany's IBM affiliate's punch card system is key in conducting this census, which finds that there are 330,539 "racial Jews" in the expanded Reich—138,819 men and 191,720 women. Emigration and persecution—death during incarceration and executions—has reduced Germany's Jewish population to nearly half its 1933 level. The census gathered detailed information on the ancestry, religious faith, and material possessions of German residents. Census information on Jews is specially marked for scrutiny.

December 26, 1939

Dear children,
It's been a while since I've heard from you. Hope you are doing well. We are doing fine too. Dad is quite excited about becoming a grandpa. You have to let him know as soon as the child is born.

Dear Hani,
We are wishing you an easy birth and a healthy child. This

Christmas we'll be spending at our place.
Loving greetings, your mother.

### Anti-Jewish Measure, November 23, 1939

The Nazis rename the central region of Poland under their rule, the Government-General. All Jews over ten years of age within this region are ordered to wear the Star of David visible on their clothing when in public at all times.

December 31, 1939

Dear children,

I'm happy to report that we are all well. Thanks for your letter from October 25th. We are glad to hear that you are doing fine. We are hoping that you enjoy your life as best as you can. Don't miss out on opportunities life has to offer you. Please ask around regarding sponsorships and the necessary rules one has to follow. You might also need to contact Chicago to renew our sponsorships. I'm hoping to hear from you now more often since there are so many ships from America arriving in Genova these days. Please write us as much as possible. You are our only hope.

Greetings from your loving father.

P.S. On October 15 I received a postcard from Aunt Salome from Chicago. I'll hurry to answer her.

March 30, 1940

I sent you twice a copy of a certificate of employment, once on the 20th and again on the 22nd of September as I stated in those letters. I had all those copies made and I'm just hoping that they'll be good for something. Hopefully Washington will recognize them as valid. It's been said that people under 60 are currently not allowed to leave anymore. So maybe our chances are better because of that even though there are plenty of old folks who are still here. We are not giving up hope but of course we are asking ourselves if we'll be able to leave.

We certainly don't want you to suffer any kind of damages.

This is not in our interest, and it should be avoided whenever possible. Please make sure you'll get the best advice possible so that you'll know exactly what you are dealing with. Hopefully the Jewish organization is of some help in that matter.

Luckily Mom and I are enjoying good health. We'll be writing again soon. With best regards from your loving father.
P.S. We are happy that Karoline is doing so well. It's just too bad that we didn't receive the picture.

On April 27, 1940, Benno's niece Ida—daughter of Benno's brother Markus in Chicago—wrote a letter to Illinois representative A. J. Sabath asking him to use his authority to help her uncle and aunt—Benno and Anna Neuburger—to emigrate to the United States. She wrote in part: "Their children, who reside in New York, are capable of taking care of them and I am writing to you at this time to ask if you will be good enough to again write to Mr. Honaker, the American Consul General, Stuttgart, Germany in the hopes that he may be able in [sic] getting them out of Germany in the very new future."[33]

### War in the West

Some historians have called the eight months that followed the September 3, 1939, British and French declaration of war against Germany, the "phony war." During that time the French and British made a halfhearted land attack on Germany, but quickly withdrew their invading forces.

The most significant fighting took place on the high seas. German submarines sank many British merchant ships and some large British navy craft.

Hitler was hoping for the British and French to acquiesce to the Nazi occupation of Poland. To this end Hitler asked for a ceasefire in October 1939. But the British and French refused.

In early April 1940, Hitler responded to British moves to cut off German imports of coal through the North Sea by invading and occupying parts of Norway. On April 9, Hitler sent troops to occupy Denmark. Land and sea conflicts were still ongoing in Norway when, on May 10, Germany launched a major invasion of the Netherlands, Belgium, Luxembourg, and Northern France. The French sent their largest forces to confront the Nazi invasion in the north, anticipating that the main German forces would follow a similar invasion strategy as Germany had under the Schlieffen Plan in the First World War. The Germans, however, sent their most powerful forces into France through the Ardennes, where they were not expected because of the region's extensive forests and rough terrain.

The French military was overwhelmed and unable to counter the German attack. By late May, the British army in France was also in retreat to the north and surrounded by German divisions. The British evacuated their army to England from Dunkirk.

By June 12, 1940, the German army was rolling into Paris.

### Beer Talk, July 1940

On one of his visits to Benno's apartment, Berthold was let into the apartment building from the street by a neighbor who was on his way out the door. Just as Berthold got to Benno's apartment door a neighbor appeared in the hallway. On entering the apartment Berthold found beer and pretzels awaiting him in Benno's kitchen.

Berthold sat across from Benno and spread a thin line of mustard on his pretzel. "That neighbor of yours, I forget his name, the one that reminds me of Goering, he came into the hall as I came to your door and was staring at me."

"You mean Kandl. He likes to scowl at people who come to our door."

"He wasn't scowling. He was smiling."

"Then maybe he's hungry and imagining how much bratwurst he could take from you."

The remark caught Berthold in mid-sip and with his laugh beer squirted out of his nose. As he coughed Benno patted him on the back. "Take it easy, we can't afford to waste good beer."

"I can see I don't need to worry about the Nazis killing me, you'll beat them to it!"

"Sorry, Berthold. But it is worrisome to have that hyena smiling. I'd rather he be his normal snarling self. Most likely he's pleased with Hitler strutting around Paris."

"I would have thought the French would have put up a better fight. Did you ever imagine France collapsing in five weeks?"

"No. The Nazis are the new kings of the world, it seems." Benno pulled a cigarette from his loose suit jacket.

"No more cigars?" asked Berthold.

"Can't find them. And I can't afford them."

"They still have England to contend with, but Goering says his air force will smash England in no time," Berthold said.

"We'll see. I don't think the game's been played out. How long do you think the arrangement with the Soviets is going to last?" Benno's question was as much a statement.

Berthold shrugged. "Do you think Germany might actually win this war?"

"Maybe we should hope they do. When they lost the last one it didn't go well for us." There was resignation in Benno's voice.

"Screwed no matter what, then." Berthold picked up a pretzel. "If they win, we'll be slaves forever. If they lose, they'll toss us on a bonfire before the country goes up in flames."

"Here's to our future," said Benno, sarcastically.

In September 1940, the German Luftwaffe began an intense bombing campaign against England.

September 26, 1940

Dear children,

    Thank you very much. I received the letter with the transcriptions of the sponsorships and I'm wondering if you still have a copy of those because there are several mistakes in it. Mom's date of birth is not *1873*, but April 15, 1877, and in Bernstein's letter from Chicago, it referred to Neuberger instead of *Neuburger*. But I'm sure this can be corrected with an explanation. I'm happy to hear that you all seem to be doing just fine. That's wonderful. Our life has been pretty good as well. Thanks again for the pictures of Karoline. They have brought us a lot of joy . . .

Anyway, we are hoping to hear from you soon.

Many greetings from your loving father.

# PART III
# DESPAIR BECOMES DEFIANCE

# Trapped in Munich

### Anti-Jewish Measure, June 1940
In an intra-department memo in June 1940, U.S. Assistant Secretary of State Breckinridge Long spells out how the U.S. State Department officials are to keep European refugees out of the United States:

"We can delay and effectively stop for a temporary period of indefinite length the number of immigrants into the United States. We could do this by simply advising our consuls to put every obstacle in the way and to require additional evidence and to resort to various administrative devices which would postpone and postpone and postpone the granting of the visas."

### Anti-Jewish Action, September 1940
The anti-Semitic film *Jud Süss* opens at the Venice Film Festival where it receives the "Golden Lion" award and rave reviews. It opens in German theaters in October.

October 3, 1940

Dear children,

We would like to write you once a week. It's been going well so far and hoping that you're doing just fine as well. Hopefully we'll be with you soon. Next week Ms. Bahn will be leaving the country (to the U.S.) via Cuba while her son will be waiting for her in New York. We must keep our hope alive that it'll happen for us someday as well.

Please find out about how much a passage would cost with that shipping company "United States Lines" and we are wondering if they take care of everything. As soon as we get your letter we'll see. I'm very sorry that you are spending so much money for us without knowing if it really does any good. We are doing fine and hoping that the same holds true for you. We are always happy to hear how Karoline is doing. I guess we'll soon hear from you in regard to Cuba. We are ready to make the journey there.

November 15, 1940

Dear children,

You are probably wondering why I am writing you again since you must have just received a letter from me. Well, I'm writing you again because I don't want you to waste your money. Please don't buy the passages since it's not sure that we'll be able to leave at that time. I was wondering if you could send me some kind of confirmation which states that you pay for the passages as soon as it's certain that we can leave. It's just that if once the passages have been purchased and we can't go at least 15 percent of the money would be gone for sure. Please make all necessary inquiries so that you don't waste your hard-earned money. Maybe it's also possible to get insurance in case we can't make the journey. Besides that, I'm still hoping to find an organization or benefactor who pays for our fares.

Did you write to Ida in Chicago? Just wondering if she's able to pursue our case. I'm hoping that she is trying to work something out with the consulate.

We received your last letter on October 20, and we are hoping to hear from you soon.

Greetings to all of you and especially to Karoline.
Your loving father.

### Early December 1940, Beer talk

"What's going on with you today, Benno?" Berthold asked when he opened his door and saw the irate expression on Benno's face.

"I was about to tear down one of those filthy movie posters!"

"Of?"

"*Der Ewige Jude!*" [*The Eternal Jew*]. Benno clenched his teeth. "You see them all over, now!"

"That dreck. I don't blame you. But Benno, that would be dangerous."

"What is this Goebbels's obsession with this phrase, 'eternal Jew'?" Benno sat down heavily in Berthold's kitchen chair. "What is an 'eternal Jew'?"

"Satan, of course. The source of all evil—Jews, that is, you and I." Berthold pointed to himself.

Benno shook his head. "Now Goebbels gloats that people flock to that twisted farce of a movie..."

"Another lie!" Berthold poured a glass of beer and handed it to Benno. "There were very few people in the theater where it's being shown."

"What do you mean, *in the theater*?"

"I went to see it."

"What?"

Berthold sat down across from Benno. "I was curious."

"Berthold, you're talking *to me* about danger?"

"It wasn't so much. I went in after the movie started. It was dark. And I left before it was over. And there were very few people in the theater anyway." Berthold put up his hand. "Don't go at me about this. Hilde's already had her run at me. She said, 'Here we are trying to get out of this country, and you put it all at risk, for what?'"

"I could hear Anna saying that, too. And I'd have to agree."

"Okay, Benno, but I thought of something while watching it,"

Berthold looked intently at his friend. "Do you remember those postcards of Africans years ago?"

"No, I don't think so."

"Thirty years ago—more than that now—when Germany had a colony in the south part of Africa—South West Africa. You don't remember? They sold these picture postcards of emaciated, crazed-looking people from Africa—here in Munich at some of the kiosks and other places." Berthold stood up and started pacing, his hands in his pockets.

"I recall something like that. And your point?" asked Benno.

"The people on those cards had been starved and horribly treated by German colonists. But the cards didn't say that. The point was to show the public how wretched Africans were. To make people feel, not sympathy, but *revulsion*—so people wouldn't care what happened to them. But it was us Germans who caused the misery you saw in those people. I remember reading articles in *Vorwärts*, or one of the other Social Democratic papers, about it." Berthold started to speak more quickly. "Well, the scenes in this Goebbels movie were shot in Warsaw. Scenes of Polish Jews. People who are, many of them, in very wretched condition. The film is saying, 'Here we show you the Jews as they really are!' Well, read between the lines. This is what is happening to Jews in Poland. Terrible things are being done to them! But the movie says nothing about that."

"So what happened to Africans is happening to us? Is *that* your point?"

Berthold, still standing, turned toward Benno. "Yes. Something like *that*."

"Only, it's worse for us, the 'eternal' Jews." Benno looked up at his friend. "You're quite excited all of a sudden, I see."

Berthold ignored his remark and kept pacing. "You remember when the Freikorps came in 1918 or '19?"

Benno raised his hands in a questioning gesture. "Yes, of course."

"Well, I remember how talk really got going then about 'racial pollution.' Some of those Freikorps were veterans of the wars in Africa and became hardened haters of what they called the 'inferior races.' And here in Munich, they were making the point that Jews are the racial polluters of Germany."

"That's *Mein Kampf*, Berthold."

"I know. I am just making this connection. Where do you think Hitler picked up his shit? It came from the racist ideas about Africans. Brought here by people like von Epps, who was a veteran of the war in the German colony. And von Epps was one of the main Freikorps leaders."

"This racial stuff started before that, Berthold. There was the Kaiser's friend. I don't recall his name right now. A British writer . . . Chamberlain, I think. He was pushing that Aryan crap before the Germans stumbled into Africa!"

"I didn't say *all* of it started in the colonies." Berthold sat down suddenly. "I'm just saying that some of it came from there."

"Okay, I get your point," Benno said.

Both went quiet for a time and Berthold spoke up. "Maybe we should change the subject to something less depressing. I have something . . . Hilde made some apple strudel and there's a little left. Share it?"

"Of course. What a treat." Benno clapped his hands.

JANUARY 30, 1941

At Berlin's Sportspalast, Adolf Hitler repeats the threat he'd made two years before, in January 1939, that if another world war were to come it would mean "the annihilation of the Jewish race in Europe."

February 24, 1941

Dear Children,

We just received a notice from Stuttgart. I'll attach a copy of it. Tomorrow I'll send out a telegram concerning the passage since I was just able to get it confirmed by the local authorities. They were so swamped with applications that it took longer than we've expected.

Hopefully we'll be able to leave as soon as possible. I very much regret that you have to use your hard-earned wages to pay for our passage. We'll be happy to help you with anything you might need and hope to pay you back soon. We are looking forward to receiving a telegram from you in regard to the passage and hopefully this will settle the matter.

I'll keep you updated since the sponsorships have to be renewed by June in order to stay valid.

According to the officials in Stuttgart it's advised to name the ship, the cabin number and to have a receipt for the payment of the passage. If those requirements are not fulfilled the visa will not be issued. Many applications are denied because people are not able to give the necessary information to the officials. So, it's better to do it right the first time.

Please research this matter closely for it's very important not to make a mistake.

March 6, 1941

Dear Fred,

Your engagement is a beautiful present for my birthday. We are wishing you and your fiancée a most wonderful time. May your life be blessed with fortune, good health, love, and lots of children . . .

I'm sure you received the telegram regarding the passage. We are waiting for your answer. Once this is settled, we'll be eager to come to you as soon as possible.

P.S. Dear Fred, Please make sure that the sponsorships are still valid. I know they have to be renewed soon. Since we don't know when we'll be able to leave—it's better to renew them sooner rather than later. I'll keep you updated and please write us often. I've heard that the ships are going more frequently now . . .

Many greetings and kisses from your loving father.

March 12, 1941

Dear children,

According to your letters from January 29 and February 7 the marriage will be held this Saturday [March 15]. We'd like to congratulate you from the bottom of our hearts and wishing you much happiness in your future life. Today we received a notification from the Jewish financial aid organization about a payment of $500. If our emigration is to succeed it will depend on a variety of things. Most of all how we can get the necessary money to pay for the passage. I still have between 7,000 and 8,000 Marks (potentially) at my disposal from the sale of our property and I hope that I'll be able to come up with most of it.

I'll have to see how this is done in the most efficient way and I'll let you know as soon as possible. I'm ordered to pay a capital tax and with that the sale of the properties from 1938 will be taken care of.

March 15, 1941

Dear Fred,

Once again, many thanks for the $500. Unfortunately, it's been getting far more expensive. I might just have to ask the financial aid organization to help with some of the costs but maybe you might be able to research that from there.

Hopefully they can help with some of the paperwork so that we can finally take the passage. With the telegram I wanted to include congratulations to your marriage, but they didn't allow it as well as the congratulations to Morton's marriage . . .

Your loving father.

### Anti-Jewish Measure, March 1941

The Munich government begins construction of a barracks complex to house Munich's remaining Jews in an area called Milbertshofen. It is being built on land seized from a Jewish business on Knorrstrasse.

April 9, 1941

Dear children,

Finally, we received your letter from March 10. We are happy to know that we are all doing well. It doesn't look too good regarding our departure. There aren't enough ships leaving [Germany] and there are too many who would like to get away.

The sponsorships probably need to be renewed since it's taken us so long to get a passage.

Benno and Hedi would like to emigrate to South America, but they need money to do it. I'm wondering if you could give them some or if you could maybe ask at the Nonprofit Financial Aid agency for some money. Maybe it's possible that the family Baumeister could provide some financial aid instead of sponsorships. This would really be the best in this situation.

Loving greetings from your father

On May 10, 1941, Rudolf Hess, Hitler's deputy führer, flew a German Messerschmitt aircraft from Augsburg to Britain and bailed out over Scotland. When captured, he claimed to be on a mission to arrange peace between Germany and England. Hess knew that war with the Soviet Union was looming, and he thought he could become a hero by keeping Germany from a two-front war.

### War in the East

On June 22, 1941, Germany tore up its peace accord with the Soviet Union and launched the largest invasion ever seen in war. Nearly four million German and other Axis soldiers and personnel, hundreds of thousands of motorized vehicles, thousands of artillery pieces, and three to four thousand warplanes moved across a front of nearly 2,000 kilometers into the western Soviet Union. The invasion was code-named Operation Barbarossa. Coming off German victories over Czechoslovakia, Poland, and especially France, Hitler was supremely confident of a quick victory over the Soviet Union.

August 24, 1941

Dear children,

Aunt Mina is sending many regards especially to you dear Fred and she wanted to write herself but it's too strenuous for her to do so. Martha and Fredi are immigrating to the U.S. very soon. They have their sponsorships as well as their passage. I'm happy for anyone who can leave.

Hedi and Benno haven't received their sponsorships yet even though they are working hard to get it. They think that if Klara would've been in the U.S. already everything would be easier. Please write us soon in all detail. We are very excited to hear from you.

Loving greetings and kisses from your mom.

## Searching for a Hole in the Net: Astoria, Queens, September 1941

Fred arrived at his apartment in Queens somewhat rattled by the evening's traffic. As he entered the kitchen his young wife, Kate, opened a window above the stove, hoping to catch a little evening breeze, a little relief from the heat and humidity. Fred hugged his wife of five months and watched as she cooked.

"How was your day?" she asked in her heavily accented English.

"Tiring. We drove to Connecticut and back," Fred answered in German. They had recently made an agreement to speak English as much as possible in the house, but when Fred was tired he sometimes slipped back into German. Kate joined him.

"Why so far?"

Fred shrugged. "We had some customers who asked to see us. Ludwig wanted to visit some tailor shops in a town called New Haven. You should have seen the traffic coming back."

"Dinner will be ready soon." Kate poured boiling hot water from a pot into a colander in the sink to drain noodles.

Fred looked into the sink. "You made spätzle! You know there were times in Germany I'd drive a long distance to find a place for good spätzle."

Kate smiled. "Looks like you've done that today."

Fred laughed. "I smell something else."

"Roast beef, Fred." Kate leaned down and opened the oven door. "Were you able to get more customers for your signs?"

"A few new ones. Nothing that special. I'm not sure it was worth the long drive."

"It gives you time to talk with your brother-in-law." Kate pulled the roast from the oven and cut into it to see if it was done.

"Ludwig? Try getting a conversation out of him!" But you know, Kate, I told him some of your stories. He agreed with me—neither of us realized how tough things were for Jews in rural German towns like yours."

"It wasn't like in the big city where you could walk the streets and people would have no idea that you were Jewish. In our little Breitenbach, everyone knew everyone. It took just a few Nazi bullies to make life miserable." Kate put the roast on a cutting board and began slicing it.

"Yah. But at least it made you realize you needed to leave."

Kate nodded. "Even though none of our neighbors were ever mean to us. But did I tell you the story about my cousin Lothar?" She placed a platter with slices of roast beef and a bowl of spätzle on the table.

Fred put a piece of roast beef on his plate. "No, I don't remember that."

Kate sat down across from Fred. "My uncle Auguste had a butcher shop in town. In 1935 he died of a heart attack. His son Lothar was coming home from the funeral when a Nazi from town saw him and started taunting him, you know—'Another Jew dead, I'm so happy for my Germany'—something like that. They got into an argument and Lothar beat the fellow up. The mayor, Karl Vetter, heard about the fight. And he heard that the Nazis in a nearby town planned to go after Lothar. Well, Vetter and my uncle

Auguste were friends—they'd served together in the war. So the mayor sent Lothar a note: 'You'd better leave town, tonight. It's not safe for you here.' And he did. Lothar left that same night with a friend. They went to a nearby town. They eventually made it to the Swiss border and to Basel."[34]

"Where is Lothar now?" asked Fred.

"I don't know. Probably still in Switzerland. His father had a friend who ran a butcher shop in some town there. So he may still be there."

Fred sat for a moment at the kitchen table looking at his wife's sweet, youthful face and her long light-brown hair. He felt lucky. Lucky first of all to have gotten out of Germany! Lucky to have a job as a traveling salesman, to be able to use the skills he'd learned in Germany. And lucky to have met Kate . . . to have a home and a future. If only he could have some luck getting his parents and other relatives out of Germany.

Kate left the kitchen. When she returned, she had papers in her hand. Kate handed her husband a copy of the German Jewish monthly the *Aufbau* and a letter from Fred's parents in Munich. Then Kate sat down to eat. Fred glanced at the headlines in the paper and then opened the letter. As he started to read he shook his head in disgust—"*Ach nein!*"

"What is it Fred? Is everything okay?"

Fred waved the letter in the air. "Once again my parents write about the problems with getting passage! And that the U.S. consulates in Germany are shut down!"

"Why?"

"They don't say. As hard as we've tried to get everything arranged, one thing or another gets in the way. We're saving to get my parents visas for Cuba. But will there be a way out of Germany?" Fred threw the letter on the table.

"Fred, didn't you get a letter that your cousins had gotten their sponsorship *and passage*?"

"Yah. One of the letters said Alfred and Martha got sponsorship and a place on a ship. But, in any case, Kate, sponsorship and passage by itself means nothing. You can't go anywhere without a visa!"

"What about your cousins going to Cuba?" Kate asked.

Fred shook his head. "How? The Cuban visas for my parents will cost us five or six months of our income. Who has enough money to buy Cuban visas for all these relatives? And it's next to impossible to get a visa for the United States now."

Kate shook her head. "Even though America's not even filling the quota they have for Germany."

"Where did you hear that?"

"I think Ludwig or maybe Hani told me that. Ludwig keeps a close watch on these things."

Fred picked up a piece of spätzle and held it in his fork, "One thing is certain, the American consulates work very slowly. Especially the one in Stuttgart. I don't know what's wrong with them! The waiting list for U.S. visas is six years long! That's according to the American Jewish Committee."

"Why do they think that is?"

Fred shook his head. "I guess it's obvious. We're not a priority. Of course, Ludwig has his ideas about this. He says, 'Roosevelt and his capitalist friends don't care about us.' He's told me—I don't know how many times—he wouldn't put Roosevelt's picture above his toilet. I don't care about Roosevelt's picture. But I know Roosevelt says nice things about Jews in public and then does *nothing*. But he also has to contend with people in the government that don't want more immigrants."

"Especially *Jewish* immigrants," Kate added. "Let's not fool ourselves."

Fred shook his head. "Here's our one glimmer of hope, Kate, a tourist visa for Cuba. Even though my father says he doesn't want to go to Cuba—doesn't know how they would survive there. I tell him, it's a step away from the fire. It'll give us time."

Kate reached across the table and squeezed her husband's hand. Fred set the letter aside and returned to the spätzle. He looked up at Kate and smiled. His eyes were a little glassy. "Yah, Kate, I would drive a long way for this."

## Berg am Laim

AFTER THE HOLZERS WERE EVICTED from their home in Traunstein in November 9, 1938, they fled to Munich. Alfred Holzer and his wife, Martha, quickly found an apartment in Munich while Willi Holzer, his son Benno, and his daughter Hedi lived for a time with Benno and Anna. Some months later, they too got their own apartment.

Benno Neuburger had just returned to the Trogerstrasse apartment when Willi and Benno Holzer came to visit. They were both clearly distraught.

"We've been moved out of our apartment," said Willi.

"As of when?" asked Anna.

"Last week. We got no notice. Some men from this Aryanization department came by. It was very ugly. What should I say? One of them carried a riding whip!"

Benno Holzer came and sat on the sofa next to his father. "We need these apartments for 'the *Volk*,' they told us. They say it this way, so we understand that we aren't '*Volk*'—we aren't people." The younger Benno's voice was husky from a chest cold. "They said, 'You can take a suitcase with you.' That's it. We had to leave everything. There wasn't that much, but we had to leave almost everything we had behind. So now we're in a Catholic monastery, on Clemens-August-Strasse."

"I know that place. It's in the Berg am Laim district," Benno Neuburger said.

Willi nodded. "The monastery is pretty, and the Catholic Sisters, the Sisters of Mercy, are friendly to us. We're told to have no contact with the nuns, but when the Gestapo men aren't around, the Sisters greet us. They wave to us nicely when they pass us on the stairs."

"Some of the more Orthodox people aren't happy about being forced to live in a Christian place. But I don't mind that. What I mind is . . . everything else about it! That we're so many crammed together. There's no privacy. It's very uncomfortable." Benno Holzer looked at his father. "Papa's been doing some work around the convent with the Jewish committee people, while Hedi, Alfred, Martha, and I are at work. They now have us working at a battery factory."

The younger Benno started coughing then. When he stopped, the older Benno asked, "How many are you?"

"You mean how many Jews are there at the monastery? More than three hundred from around Munich. Just like us, the others had to leave everything behind."

Anna handed her nephew a cup of hot water for his congested chest. "You'll stay with us for dinner tonight."

"We need to eat soon, though," Willi said. "We have to be back before the curfew at eight."

When Anna served her brother-in-law a bowl of soup, Willi had to eat it with his left hand. He explained that he had injured his right shoulder digging trenches for the foundation of a barracks in a new camp being built to house Jews in Munich. "It's called Milbertshofen and it's on Knorrstrasse," Willi said as he ate. "It's pathetic to say this, but we're lucky to be at the monastery. A lot of people are being taken out of their homes and put in that wretched Knorrstrasse camp." He was especially distraught about the news he'd picked up from a Jewish committee member at the convent, that the Nazis had deported hundreds of Jews from the Stettin area of east Prussia to Poland to live with poor Jewish families there. Some of the Stettin Jews had died from cold and disease not long after arriving. "Things are desperate there," said Willi as he massaged his right shoulder. "Collections are being taken up among Munich Jews and Quakers to send them clothes and other items."

Benno Holzer paused to cough. "It looks like they're not going to send us away because they need us working, especially now with the war in Russia. The work is horrible. The pay is ridiculous. And some of our foremen—not all, but enough—treat us like dirt. But at least it'll keep us here. They need us to make batteries for the war."

Munich, September 11, 1941

Received your letter from August 27. Very much enjoyed it, especially the photos of all of you. You look so nice in one of them. It would have been so wonderful to be part of that tour you took. This area must be so beautiful. Too bad you haven't heard from Washington. I'm just wondering if it would make sense if acquaintances of yours would give it a try as well. Who knows, maybe you'll receive something, nevertheless?

Please, whatever you do—don't spend any money on this. I'm so regretting the money I spent on HAPAG. It was totally for nothing. If something could have been done, then they probably would have been able to get the visa in Stuttgart.

Going to Cuba would cost too much and we don't really have the connections to Spain.

I guess we'll just have to wait. All we're doing is waiting for the process to continue but so far nothing.

But little Karoline is making steady progress which makes us happy.

Loving greetings to all of you.

Your loving father.

ANTI-JEWISH MEASURE, SEPTEMBER 1941

A police ordinance issued on September 1, 1941, declare that beginning September 19, 1941, all Jews above the age of six are "forbidden to show themselves in public" without "a black-edged, six-pointed star of yellow cloth, as large as the palm of the hand, with the word 'JUDE' in black, clearly visible, firmly sewn to the left breast of the piece of clothing." Furthermore, Jews are forbidden from leaving the boundaries of the communities in which they are resident without written permission from the local police. Those who contravene the ban deliberately or through negligence will be fined up to 150 RM or imprisoned up to 6 weeks, and perhaps longer.

### Sunday, September 14, 1941

Before leaving for Berthold's apartment, Benno grabbed several bottles of beer from his diminishing supply and some chocolates that had arrived several days before from his children. "These will cheer us up," Benno thought. But when he got to his friend's apartment, he found that the beer and chocolates did little to lighten their grim mood. The news of the new requirement to wear the star horrified them. Thus far the endless stream of anti-Jewish measures had restricted their activities to little more than walks around the city. And now even the thought of walking on the street was frightening.

Berthold read from a copy of the Nazi paper *Völkischer Beobachter*, commenting on the new decree. "'The German soldier on the eastern front has met the Jew in his most disgusting, most gruesome form. . . . This experience forces the German people to deprive the Jews of every means of camouflage at home—'gruesome form,' that's Goebbels-talk."

"The war is not going so well, and they don't want us talking to other people," Benno speculated. "They don't want people hearing anything other than their steady outpouring of lies. Or they don't want us to know that the 'steel-like German people' are getting wary of the war and the lies. How many unhappy letters are coming from soldiers?"

"Or notices to parents about the deaths of their sons in the glorious war," added Berthold.

Their conversation turned to the camp on Knorrstrasse, which was now completed. People were being taken from their homes and relocated there. Both men mulled over their frustrated efforts to emigrate. Every hopeful prospect had so far dissolved like a mirage.

Benno had never seen his friend so morose. He worried about Berthold, knowing that an epidemic of suicides was spreading among Jews. They commented on the deaths by suicide of the Neumeyers—Karl, a professor, and Anna, a writer—both well-known members of the Munich Jewish community.

"Benno, they're taking everything from us—our possessions, our livelihood, our homes, our dignity, our humanity."

Benno looked intently at his friend. "No, they don't have the power to do that."

"What are we, then? We have to scrounge for a shitty crumb to eat. We have to hide in the shadows. We have to cringe in our homes—those of us who still have them! We shudder at any sound that might be a knock on the door. We turn our heads when we walk down the street. We want to walk away from every bit of news because it's all hurtful. I think, 'This can't be happening to us,' but it *is* happening to us! I don't want to live like this. And I don't want to die—like they want us to die!"

Benno was about to ask what he meant by that, but he knew exactly what Berthold meant, because those same thoughts were tormenting him. But he would not say them and give them the power of recognition.

"It's their inhumanity, not ours. They're the beasts, Berthold. They are the ones who make themselves feel big by bullying those who can't defend themselves. That, Berthold, is truly pitiful! Nazis are wretched worms that feed off the bodies of those they torment!"

These were words that Benno had never imagined himself saying. He was a practical man, not a religious or spiritual person. He was not someone to express great emotions. He thought of himself as good at analyzing situations but not at expressing broad concepts or grand themes. And yet he felt, at this moment, like he was fighting for Berthold's life and his own! He was determined not to let the Nazis destroy him psychologically. He was determined to do so for Anna, and for his children, however dim his hope of ever seeing them again. And the only way he could do that was to resist in some way.

At that moment he decided to do something he had been thinking about for a while. He didn't tell Berthold, Anna, or anyone else. He didn't want to implicate anyone, and he didn't want anyone to try and talk him out of it. And he didn't want to have to face them if, at the end of the day, he backed down. But in that moment, he knew he would do it. "I agree with a lot of what you say, Berthold. But they have not, and cannot, take our dignity."

Berthold looked up and placed his hand on Benno's. "Thank you, my friend."

Anti-Jewish Measure, September 18, 1941

Heinrich Himmler, head of the Nazi Schutzstaffel (SS) notifies SS General Arthur Greiser, Gauleiter and Reich governor of the Warthegau, that "the Führer wanted the Old Reich and the Protectorate [Germany and the territory of Czechoslovakia annexed by the Nazis] emptied and disencumbered of Jews" and that "this should be done by moving them from west to east as soon as possible."

### The Mail Supervisor

On Saturday evening, September 20, 1941, a Munich postal clerk, while sorting mail delivered that day from an area east of the Isar River, found a postcard with no address—but with a message that referred to Hitler as a "mass murderer." He showed it to his supervisor, who looked it over and placed it in an envelope marked with the number of the post office in which it was found, the name of the worker who found it, the general area it came from, and the date. He then went to the phone in his office and called the Gestapo and asked to speak to whoever was in charge. The Gestapo investigator who took the call sounded interested. "What did it say?"

"In the space where one would normally write a message and address it says 'The eternal mass murderer,' Hitler. And an expression of disgust."

"Is there any indication of who it came from?"

There was a pause while the supervisor flipped the card over several more times. "No, none," he answered.

"Where did the card come from?"

"We know the general area. I've already written that down. But there's no way to know which box it was deposited in."

"Do you know which carrier brought it in?" asked the Gestapo man.

"Well, there are several possibilities; we're not totally certain which carrier."

"But you have some carriers in mind?"

"Yes."

"Are they at your post station?"

"I believe they're home by now."

"But these carriers, you didn't ask them if they noticed anything unusual when they emptied the boxes?"

"I think they would have said something when they brought the mail in if they had noticed anything. Usually, they just empty the boxes in a bag and bring that bag into the sorting room."

"But you didn't ask them?" There was a bullying tone in the Gestapo man's question.

The supervisor blinked hard and tried to control an urge to give a sarcastic reply. "No, we didn't ask them."

"Well, don't say anything now. Someone will be by soon to pick up the card and the location information. Please make sure the carriers you have in mind are told that we'd like to talk to them. And in the meantime, don't show the card to anyone else."

"Of course, not," said the supervisor. "Heil Hitler!"

### Babi Yar, Ukraine

On September 20, 1941, German newspapers announced with great fanfare the fall of the Ukrainian capital of Kyiv to the German army. The news articles did not say this, but it had taken the German army three months to capture the city. This was far longer and at a higher cost than the Nazi military command had expected or planned for. The top military commanders understood that this delay was potentially disastrous. The German war machine would have to deal with long supply lines, fall rains, and the bitterly cold Russian winter rapidly approaching.

Four days after the German army completed its delayed and difficult capture of Kyiv, a chain of explosions rocked the center of the city, destroying entire blocks of buildings that housed the offices of the newly installed German military command and security forces. Hundreds of German soldiers, including many officers, were killed in the fires that followed. In retaliation for this setback, on September 29 and 30, the leaders of the Einsatzkommando 4a rounded up thousands of Jewish residents of Kyiv and took them to a ravine called Babi Yar on the outskirts of the city, where they were gunned down. A total of 33,771 Jews were killed in the largest mass execution of Jews in the war up to that point.

Einsatzkommando 4a was a specially trained unit of the Einsatzgruppen, sent by the German military into occupied territories in the wake of the massive Nazi invasion of the Soviet Union, which had begun on June 22, 1941. Einsatzgruppen Kommando units had a special assignment in the war zones. They were tasked with crushing resistance from the occupied population. They were death squads, terror squads. Their effectiveness was measured by the fear they sowed in the territories through which they passed. They especially targeted two sections of people in the conquered territories: Bolsheviks and Jews.

### September 30 to October 27, 1941

Tuesday, September 30, 1941, was Yom Kippur. With Munich's

synagogues long destroyed, and Jewish religious and community life shut down, Benno and Anna had few options for acknowledging the holiday. They decided, despite their own chronic lack of food, to observe the fast for the day, as a way of clinging on to something of their battered culture.

During the months since Willi Holzer and his family had been moved into the monastery of Berg am Laim, rumors had been surfacing of potential deportations. At the same time, the pathway to emigration for Benno, Anna, and other Jews still in Germany was narrowing, if not closed entirely.

In the afternoon, Benno told Anna he was going out to mail the letters they had written that morning to their children. He dropped the letters in a mailbox on the east side of the Isar. He then crossed over the river and wandered in the area around his old apartment at Liebherrstrasse, until he realized his wandering might draw attention to himself. He quickly dropped the second of his unaddressed postcards in the first letter box he came to and returned home.

Like the first card mailed ten days earlier, on the day Jews were required to wear the yellow star, this card had a very simple message. It read: "*Hanover Mannheim, Pfui! Hitler Pfui!*" The first sentence referred to the British bombing of the heavily industrialized areas of Hanover and Mannheim. This card was Benno's way of responding to what he believed were exaggerations and lies regarding Germany's progress in the war, and what Benno sensed was a growing aversion among some people for such triumphalism.[35]

When Benno arrived home after mailing the letter and card, Anna greeted him with a worried look. "What took you so long? You said you were just mailing a letter?"

"I decided to see if I could find something for breaking our fast."

"And what did you get?" she asked.

"I didn't get anything."

Anna spoke impatiently to her husband of thirty-four years: "You didn't take the ration cards with you."

"I . . . I guess I forgot. Well, anyway I'm back, dear. I'm sorry I worried you."

Two days later, on Wednesday, October 1, Benno placed a third postcard in a mailbox on Princeregentenstrasse. In the place for the address it read, *The son of a bitch, Hitler.* And in the place for messages, *Murderer!*

Munich, October 10, 1941

Dear children,

We received your letters from September 15th and the 21st and we are happy to know that you are all doing so well. Just as you, we are appreciating our well-being.

According to your letter there has not been any progress regarding our emigration. This is unfortunate. I've already sent copies of the certificate of employment twice because I didn't know if I wrote 34 or 32 in the first letter. People say that it might be possible to get a visa from Washington if you present them with such a document, but if you don't know anything about it then it might not be true.

We are wondering why Klara is not writing us more often. Please give her our regards. Your relatives were all happy to receive word from you and I'm happy to tell you that they are all well. Benno, Hedi and Alfred are all working. Max is working at the Autobahn in Zweibrucken where he was transferred from Amberg [Penitentiary] and he seems to be doing well.

The money from the sale of the properties in 1938 is supposed to be coming soon. We still have the Levinger properties, and we don't know what to do with them. We'd love to be with you, but we don't know when it will be possible.

Please write us soon!

With best regards from your loving father.

My loving greetings to Karoline.

Anti-Jewish Measure, October 16, 1941

In response to Hitler's order that the "old Reich and the Protectorate be emptied and disencumbered of Jews," the first of twenty trains filled with Jewish deportees were sent east. Jews from Luxembourg and Vienna were part of that deportation.

## A Desperate Hope
## October 27, 1941

Fred arrived nervous and exhausted at his brick apartment building on 30th Street in Astoria. He had spent the weekend visiting friends and contacts in an urgent effort to get the funds for a tourist visa that would allow his parents to enter Cuba.

As Fred entered his apartment, his sister Hani was on the living room sofa, her baby daughter Karoline nearby on the floor surrounded by pieces from a Tinkertoy set. "Hello, Hani. Glad to see you. There's some things I need to tell you. And how is our little Karoline doing?" Fred leaned down just as Karoline tossed a wooden connector at the couch with a slight giggle. She glanced up at her uncle but immediately returned to her toys.

"I can tell you she's a good eater!" Hani smiled.

Kate came into the room from the kitchen. "You look really tired, Fred," she said.

"After work, I went to the travel office in Manhattan—to get the Cuban visas."

"How much were they?" asked Hani.

"$860 for the visas. I had to give them $1,000 altogether to cover other expenses, whatever they were."

"Why so much, Fritz?" Hani's voice quivered with anger.

"Good question." Fred sat in an armchair across the small room from his sister. "Desperation makes for good business opportunities. And, of course, we're not the only Germans with a sudden interest in Cuban tourism." He loosened his tie. "It took everything we had. And I had to borrow some money. Fortunately, Ida and Morton agreed to help."

"What an angel that man is," Hani said.

"Without Morton we wouldn't be here." Fred stood up, took off his jacket and hung it over the chair. He looked at Kate. "We kept just enough for rent and food."

Hani looked up from the sofa. "I wish Ludwig and I could've helped more."

"We'll manage," Kate said.

"I understand, Hani . . . a new baby and all." Fred rolled up the sleeves of his dress shirt.

"We'll eat soon," Kate announced. "Fred, I made something special. Hani, are you and Karoline staying for dinner?"

"I have to get home. Ludwig will be there by now." Hani laughed. "Another hungry baby!"

"I smell something, Kate." Fred rubbed his hands together in appreciation and looked over at his wife. "It smells like sauerbraten."

"Yah. First time I've cooked it in this country. We'll see if it turns out okay."

Hani leaned down and pushed the scattered wooden pegs and connectors into the round Tinkertoy container and stood up from the couch. "How do we know this is going to work, Fred?"

"We don't. Even if all goes well with the visa there's no guarantee they'll get passage. Our parents have so little money and the money they have in the bank they can't withdraw without permission."

"Should we send them—"

"I sent them something recently."

"Fred, I've been seeing in the papers the things going on in Poland . . ." Fred was familiar with the fearful strain in his sister's voice.

"I know what you're going to say, Hani. What's happening there is beyond description."

"Warsaw . . ."

"Everywhere!" Fred shook his head. "I tell you it's hard for me to read the papers right now. I'll send a telegram to Munich in the next few days. I was told that the Cuban consulate in Berlin will send our parents notice when the visa is ready."

"Father's going to be upset that you spent so much money . . ."

"Hani, how could I live with myself if I didn't?"[36]

October 30, 1941

Dear Fred,

I just received your letter from October 9 in which you confirmed that you received the letter from September 22. Obviously, you are not receiving all of our letters because I sent you the photo for the certificate of employment on October 20. Please be careful when it comes to spending money for the passage to Cuba. If it's uncertain I advise you not to do it, but if you decide to do it anyway, please make sure you get advice from the Jewish Agency beforehand. And if you read my letters, you should know that you have to be very careful when it comes to spending money. There are rumors that the Jewish Agency pays the fare for some people, and it certainly should be considered as a way to save some money. Please don't waste any money until you know for sure that it's going to work. If you are going to lose your money, please don't do it. Emmy Springer had her passage paid by the Jewish Agency but now she can't get a visa since the consulates are closed.

Your father.

## WORRISOME RUMORS

On November 3, Anna's cousin Ilse came by to visit. Because she was married to Hermann Schuster, a Catholic, she had some protection from the harshest measures against Jews. She told Anna that she'd heard credible rumors from a friend of hers who worked for the *Israelitische Kultusgemeinde* (Israelite Municipal Association, IKG), the organization charged with informing the community of government demands. The rumors said that a deportation to the east of Munich's Jewish residents was imminent. No exact date or destination were mentioned.

November 5, 1941

Dear children,

Just two days ago I wrote you that you should notify us by

telegram before you make any payments to Cuba or any other destination regarding our emigration. I don't want you to waste your money in such a risky undertaking. To be honest I didn't even consider Cuba a possibility anymore and we hadn't talked about it lately but then I got a notice today that you made a payment to Cuba. So, I made an inquiry regarding this matter and what I found out is that there are problems to reach the port by train and also to get on a ship for Cuba.

Loving greetings from your father.

Dear children,

How much would I love to be with you right now. Who knows, maybe someday it'll work out? My thoughts are always with you. We are doing fine, and I hope you are too, my dear children. How's Karoline doing? She's probably talking more and more by now. This week I baby-sat Ilse's little boy for a bit.

Aunt Mina is doing well but Uncle Willi's health is not so good. He's going through a lot. The main thing is that we all stay healthy.

We're so sorry that you are going through so much trouble for us and that you worry so much about us. Hopefully we'll be seeing you soon, my dear children. Stay healthy!

Greetings and kisses to all of you and to Karoline from your mom.

## A Beer Talk on November 6

Benno met Berthold at the apartment of a mutual friend who said he had information that might be useful in their pursuit of a way out of the country. The "information" turned out to be less than what had been suggested. It involved a rumor of legislation under consideration in the United States that would open the door wider to Jews seeking to immigrate. "Legislation under consideration" was vague enough in its own right. Under closer examination, the rumor was even less substantial. It was the report of a remark made by a Jewish ally of Roosevelt speculating on such legislation. This was not the first time that such talk made the rounds of the Jewish community in Munich and Benno had become increasingly skeptical of these reports and doubtful of any change for the better.

After leaving the friend's apartment, Benno and Berthold headed for the Trogerstrasse apartment where they planned to take advantage of Benno's dwindling supply of beer. A chill wind blew rain toward the men from various directions and, at times, nearly blew their hats into the street. But both preferred the discomfort of wind and rain; it kept the streets nearly empty, which diminished the psychological trauma of being around people while wearing the "damnable brand," as Benno now called it. The nasty remarks and uncomfortable looks were unpleasant. But even a kind word spoken out of pity was something they wished to avoid. They wanted only to be invisible. Only in invisibility did they feel safe.

Their route took them past the Haus der Deutschen Kunst, the fortress-like art museum on Prinzregentenstrasse at the edge of the English Garden. The museum was designed by Hitler's favorite architect, Paul Troost, and it was erected on a spot chosen by Hitler.

"You remember when Hitler opened this place up?" Berthold commented as a gust of wind momentarily impeded their forward progress.

"Yes, of course. With the 'Great German Art Show' in 1937. It was to show off their 'heroic Aryan art' of the new Germany, the new utopia. All their cackling was very unpleasant. It was in June or July that year and Anna and I left town when the show opened. We visited Anna's family in Traunstein and then took a drive to Salzburg to visit her niece's family. I'm glad we did; it was the last time we got away like that ..."

"Well, you remember," Berthold added, "that they had another show at the same time at the Archaeology Institute to show the 'inferior art' of Weimar, of Jews, subversives and so on."

"I remember that too, Bert."

"Well, I went to the 'Degenerate Art Show' in 1937—to see

what Nazis think of as 'Jewish art.' The venue at the Institute of Archaeology was run-down. The displays were sloppy and amateurish. They worked hard to create a bad impression. And being selected to be in that art show was an 'honor' that could cost an artist their life," said Berthold. "Some of them had to leave the country after their stuff appeared there. I don't remember all their names but Beckmann, Max Beckmann, was one of them."

"You went to that show? That took some courage," Benno said.

"Not at all. And at that point, I still had an ID with my real middle name if anyone had asked. The place was packed, Benno! I think half of Munich was there. And they had all the different styles there—Expressionists, Cubists, and so on. There were some by Klee, Picasso. The lines of people waiting to get in were huge. I'd say a lot more people went to see that 'degenerate art' than the Nazi shit they had here at the Deutschen Kunst."

"And that must have made our new god very unhappy." Another strong gust of wind hit them, and Benno pushed his hat more firmly on his head to keep it from being blown off. "Bert, I've been giving some thought to our current situation. There are two things we should not forget from history: a two-front war and Russian winters."

Berthold pulled his coat lapels close around his neck. "It's only a one-front war now, Benno."

"No. The British aren't done. Their bombing raids on German cities are increasing. Hitler has to knock out Russia so he can turn on England. And behind England is—"

"The United States," said Berthold.

"Yes. And Germany doesn't have the resources for a long war against such adversaries. That's what happened the last time."

"You forget"—Berthold turned his back to a gust of wind—"the Nazis have just taken Kyiv, Benno, and captured or wiped out a good part of the Soviet Army."

"We only know what they tell us." Benno tucked his hands deeper in his coat pockets. "Just a few months ago the papers were full of reports that Leningrad and Moscow were about to fall. The

Soviets were about to be crushed, overrun like the French. Now they're curiously quiet about those cities."

"Benno, I want to believe what you're suggesting is true. Even then I don't see how we're going to get out of this . . ."

Benno said nothing for a long moment as they crossed Trogerstrasse and turned toward Benno's apartment. "Neither do I," said Benno as they reached his apartment house door.

Neither said a word as they entered the building until they were inside Benno's place. To their relief, neither of Benno's unfriendly neighbors appeared.

Inside, Berthold took off his wet coat and greeted Anna with a wave and told her that his wife, Hilde, was fine. "She's worried about me being out. But I don't want to cheat the Nazis by dying of boredom at home," he joked.

Benno and Berthold hung their wet coats and hats in a closet near the entrance and went into the kitchen to warm up. Anna had boiled potatoes and mixed in some vinegar that her neighbor Bertha Eiber had brought over that morning. Benno and Berthold settled over plates of warm potato salad and glasses of beer.

"Hitler needed to take Leningrad and Moscow by now, or sooner. I've been checking the papers. The weather's cold there, it's been very cold this fall in Russia. If the German armies get bogged down in a Russian winter, it'll be tough going," Benno asserted.

"How do you know this?"

"Speculation. Educated speculation."

"I like your speculation. But I don't trust it." Berthold waited until he had swallowed his food. "Hitler has the upper hand. He has most of Europe under his control—most of Europe!"

"They've eaten a big meal, now they have to digest it," Benno repeated a phrase he'd heard or read somewhere, he couldn't recall. "When you take ground, you also have to hold it. Think of the Kaiser's army in 1917—occupying parts of Russia may have cost them the war."

"Different time, different circumstances," Berthold observed.

"There are already shortages here. Shortages of meat. Shortages of gas. Shortages of clothes. Rumors, okay just rumors, of large German casualties. Remember the last war and how people began to grumble. They've put out a call for people to turn in warm clothes. What does that mean for their army, Bert? They don't have the winter clothes they need!"

"Benno, please," Berthold spoke between bites of potato salad. "If it comes to that, the German people will go down with the ship. And without a peep. Don't expect a thing from them. Don't expect any sympathy for us. We're an insignificant minority—now also a penniless one." Berthold hungrily poked at another bite of food. "What are your chances of getting out of here?"

Benno leaned toward Berthold. "Slim prospects. I don't say this to Anna, but I don't think we're going to get out of Germany. Not that I wouldn't go in a minute. But I'm afraid it's too late for us. I made mistakes. I miscalculated. I hesitated. We're trying Cuba, but it's not working. Fritz spent a lot on a visa. Nothing."

"Don't beat yourself up. We all made mistakes. But no one, I mean no country, has gone out of its way to help us, either. One obstacle after another gets thrown at any path out of here. They took in some young people, like our children. But they don't want us. 'Let the old ones die.' To them we're more trouble than we're worth!"

"At least my kids got away. And yours. Someone to remember us." Benno spoke softly.

"Well, we still have beer." Berthold raised his eyebrows and smiled.

"Not for long, Bert. I'm running low, with little chance of getting any more."

"Here's to another miracle. May our supply of beer last eight times longer—like the oil in the old synagogue. Is that too much to ask for a chosen people?"

"Chosen?" Benno looked up at the kitchen ceiling and said in a loud whisper, "Choose someone else next time."

"You have to speak to Him in Hebrew, Benno. He doesn't understand German, at least not with that Bavarian accent of yours!"

"It's good to see you feeling better, Berthold." Benno patted his friend's arm.

Berthold laughed quietly. "It comes and goes with the phases of the moon. Right now, I just hold on to what little things I can. Tomorrow, who knows, maybe I'll be ready to call it quits."

Benno looked at Berthold. "I don't want to go down without . . . without a swipe at them."

"How do you expect to do that, Benno?"

Benno shrugged. "I'm still thinking about it."

# Resettlement

ON NOVEMBER 8, ANNA'S NIECE Hedi Holzer arrived at Benno and Anna's apartment in the early evening. She let herself into the building with a key that Anna had given her, and then quietly opened the apartment door. Anna stood up when she heard her niece come in. She greeted Hedi with a hug. Hedi tried to smile, but she very quickly began sobbing. She had her hands to her face, and Anna could see the ragged scar left by the accident that had torn flesh off the back of several of her fingers at the battery factory some weeks back.

Anna guided her into the kitchen and began heating up a stew of potatoes, turnips, and greens. It was not unusual for Hedi to come by after work because her route from the factory to the monastery at Berg am Laim took her past Trogerstrasse. She was still living in the monastery with her father, Willi, her brothers Alfred and Benno, and Alfred's wife, Martha, along with many of Munich's Jews. At the factory where she worked, Hedi's hours were long and her pay extremely low, so Anna tried to keep food ready in case she or any of her family visited.

When Benno heard Hedi, he came into the kitchen. He saw Anna, her arm around Hedi's shoulder, massaging Hedi's scarred hand with ointment. Hedi looked up at Benno. "Papa, Benno,

Alfred, and Martha are being sent away." Her face was drawn and pale. Her hands were shaking. Anna got up and placed a plate before her. "Sweetheart, please eat some food." Anna was fighting back her own tears. Benno left the kitchen rather than have his niece see him cry as well.

"Where are they going?" asked Anna.

"East! To Riga, in Latvia. I know I'll never see them again!"

Anna was breathing deeply, fighting to stay calm. A surge of love and sympathy and grief for Hedi, for all her family, swept over her. She recalled how Hedi's sister Klara had implored her to come join her in England back in 1939. Klara had even sent Hedi the papers she needed to resettle there. But Hedi wrote back to Klara that she could not leave her family behind. Now her family was being snatched away.

Benno came back into the room. He looked at Hedi, her eyes rimmed in red and her cheek quivering. Her once full face was drawn. She still wore her gray work jacket with the yellow star and had a tan scarf tied tightly over her hair, a precaution she took when working around machines. Of her once mischievous smile, not a trace was left. "When are they leaving?" Benno asked quietly.

"I don't know for sure. They were told they can't leave the monastery, even temporarily, after November 11."

"How many people from the monastery are being sent away?" asked Benno.

"I don't know. Many." Hedi's voice was muted but calmer. "Everyone has to turn in a detailed list of everything they have. You can imagine our extensive list." She added a brief, bitter laugh. "And they were given a list of things to take with them and advised to bring warm clothes."

"I'll look to see what we have," said Anna.

"No, Tante, you keep your things. Elsbeth, a camp administrator, said she'd help with the clothes. They'll put out a call or get funds to buy us some things. Riga is up on the North Sea and winters there are bitterly cold. None of us have what we need for that kind of weather."

While Benno and Hedi talked, Anna placed some of the stew in a bowl for Hedi to bring back to Berg am Laim.

"Hedi, you can stay with us for the night—save you the walk home?" Benno suggested.

"I can't, Onkel. We have to be in before curfew. I have to leave soon. It takes me more than an hour to walk from here."

"And you work again tomorrow?" Benno asked.

Hedi nodded. "No urban public transit for Jews, and no exceptions." There was acrimony in her voice. In some German cities, the rules prohibiting Jews from using urban public transit were relaxed for forced laborers in essential industries like armaments. This was a measure in place not for humanitarian reasons, but to ensure greater labor efficiency. But no such exceptions were allowed in Munich. In the "capital of the movement," anyone with a yellow star caught on a Munich tram was subject to severe punishment—and there were local Nazis notorious for roaming the trams looking for Jewish violators who, if caught, faced fines, seizure of property, and prison.

Munich, November 13, 1941

Dear children,

I sent you a letter on November 5 and I haven't heard from you since. Your last letter was dated October 9. Since then, many things have happened. Benno, Willi, Alfred, and his wife have been evacuated and seem to be doing well. We haven't heard back from Cuba yet, but we are expecting a decision about our application soon. As soon as we hear back from them, I'll do everything necessary to get this off the ground. I assume that you are doing well which would be the same for us. I'm sure Karoline is learning new things every day.

Just make sure to do your homework in regard to our emigration. We can't leave anything to chance. If we get any news regarding this, we'll let you know by telegram. Please make sure you'll do the same and make sure that you check back with us before you send any money to Cuba. I'd hate to see your hard-earned money wasted without seeing results. Are there a lot of risks involved regarding this payment?

Dear Fred,
   Please update us as much as you can. We are longing to receive mail from you so please write us soon.
   With best regards from your loving father.

### Leaving Berg am Laim

Early in the morning on November 14, at the entrance to the stately Sisters of Mercy monastery building at Sankt-Michael-Strasse, there were many tearful goodbyes. More than eighty of the Jewish residents were leaving for the camp at Milbertshofen, from where they were to be transported east. Alfred, Martha, Benno, and Willi Holzer were among them.

Among those saying goodbye were the Jewish director of the camp, Curt Mezger, the camp doctor, Julius Spanier, and a coordinator, Elsbeth Rosenfeld—the first two Jewish by birth, the last by marriage. Each of them gave a personal goodbye to each of the deportees. The heartbreak was intense. Elsbeth handed each person a small card with a goodbye message. "These are from the Sisters," she said quietly. "They didn't put their names on them because—you know why." She lowered her voice reflexively, her own voice trembling. "They want you to know they care about you."

Hedi, her eyes puffy from crying and lack of sleep, grabbed her brother Benno, then Alfred, then Martha, and then her father, Willi. She held him tightly, her head on his shoulder. Karl, her fiancé, gently pulled her away as Gestapo agents and functionaries of the Aryanization commission began beckoning the travelers outside, where two buses were waiting. Leaders of the Munich Aryanization office had originally wanted to transport the deportees by cattle truck to Milbertshofen, but the Gestapo asked for buses to avoid attracting undue attention to the deportations.

After a short ride, the buses parked in an open space surrounded by barracks. As Martha Holzer got off the bus, she spotted her husband Alfred's cousin Tilli and her sixteen-year-old son, Wilhelm. Tilli had become a widow. In May 1940, her husband, Hermann Spatz, died of a heart attack while working as a slave laborer in Munich. The Holzers had heard the story of how Hermann's complaints of chest pain had been ignored. They also knew that Tilli and Wilhelm had been forced out of the Spatz home in Wolfratshausen and into a tiny apartment they shared with others in Munich. "The police picked us up at our apartment on Beethovenstrasse this morning," Tilli explained to Martha. "They took all eight of us from that tiny place. Beethovenstrasse—sounds so lovely, doesn't it?" Tilli tried to mask the fear and fatigue she felt, to put on a brave front for her son.

All that morning, police buses and vans from locations in and around Munich continued to arrive at the Milbertshofen camp. As Tilli and Wilhelm moved toward a barracks they'd been assigned to, Tilli saw her sister-in-law Flora Spatz and Flora's daughter Hertha. Tilli, Wilhelm, Flora, and Hertha greeted each other tearfully and recounted some of the events since they'd last seen each other. Flora and Hertha had spent the previous months as slave laborers in the notorious Lohhof flax camp outside Munich. Tilli felt heartbroken to see her relatives so thin and ravaged by their months of exhausting labor.

### Milbertshofen

November 17 was the date originally set for the deportation by train to Riga, Latvia. The date was postponed to November 20. In the meantime, the hundreds of deportees who arrived on November 14 were placed in the already crowded Milbertshofen camp.

The Milbertshofen camp had been under construction since March 1941. The work was overseen by the Munich Aryanization Committee, the organization responsible for seizing the properties of Munich's Jews. It was a lucrative enterprise. Jews evicted from their homes and forced to live at Milbertshofen had to leave behind almost all of their possessions. These fell into the hands of the Aryanization authorities.

In addition, it was the Jewish community that bore the cost of constructing and maintaining the camp. Internees were forced to turn over to camp managers the money they would have paid in rent for their former apartments. The Jewish community organization had to come up with the money for those too destitute to pay.

The barracks at Milbertshofen were built from older structures that had been disassembled and trucked in from another area. Five hundred Jewish laborers were forced into the task of preparing the foundations and assembling the buildings. Since the younger Jewish population was already employed in other forced labor jobs—mainly in war-related industries—the backbreaking work was done largely by older Jewish men. They were paid nothing, and there were many injuries. During construction, many of these laborers were held in the camp and isolated from the non-Jewish population. Many of them were then put on the list of those chosen to be deported.

When it was completed, Milbertshofen consisted of twelve large and six small barracks designed to hold up to 650 people. It was nearly full before the people from Berg am Laim and other areas around Munich were brought in to await deportation. New arrivals had to double up on the wooden shelves that served as beds, making for stifling conditions during the week as the deportees waited for the train to Riga.

### November 20, 1941

At 4 a.m. on Thursday, November 20, at the "Jewish settlement" of Milbertshofen, members of the local Munich Jewish Committee, Israelitische Kultusgemeinde (IKG), went from barracks to barracks rousing people and exhorting them to assemble in the quadrangle area at the center of the Milbertshofen camp.

Hundreds of weary and frightened deportees streamed out of the barracks to the camp's roll call site, clutching their luggage, their children, or both.

It was a cold and rainy morning. Alfred, Martha, and Benno huddled together. Benno went to Willi's barracks to help his father with his suitcase and a bag he had packed with a small propane heater for the winter months in Riga.

The gathering travelers were greeted by armed police and Gestapo agents, and members of the Munich Aryanization committee. The assembled deportees were instructed to carry their own bags, march silently, and to talk to no one on their way to the Milbertshofen train station. Parents with young children were told to carry bags for their children as well. The police and Gestapo men were there to enforce strict order. The Holzers—Willi, Alfred, Marta, and Benno—were able stay together, but Tilli, her son Wilhelm, and their in-laws, Flora and Herta, were told to march with another group.

Just as they were about to start marching a uniformed agent yelled out, "Willi Israel Holzer! Willi Israel Holzer! Make yourself known!"

Willi hesitated. Then he raised his hand. "Here."

The policeman approached him, along with a member of the IKG. "Are you Willi Wolf Holzer?" The IKG member used Willi's given name, not the name imposed by the Nazis.

"Yes."

The IKG member, who wore a white armband, wrote something down in his notebook. "There's a change of plans," the uniformed agent next to him said. "You're not going today. We'll be taking you back to Berg am Laim."

Willi suddenly felt the world around him spinning. His fear of deportation was now replaced by an even sharper, stabbing fear of separation from his children. He staggered and almost fell. His son Alfred steadied him. "It'll be okay, Papa. You can join us later. We'll write to you as soon as we get there. And this way, Papa, Hedi will have someone here with her."

"Bye, Papa." Benno embraced his father tightly. "We love you. Stay healthy, please, for us." Martha hugged her father-in-law. "Willi, we'll be together again someday, I know we will." But she, like her father-in-law, was fighting back tears.

Shouts of "Move now!" came from uniformed men in trench coats and knee-high jackboots. The crowd at Milbertshofen began marching toward the train station. Alfred, Martha, and Benno waved to Willi as he was led away to a van parked outside the fence that surrounded the barracks complex. The Jewish committeeman walked hurriedly to the van and shoved a suitcase with Willi's name on it inside. "Your bag, Herr Holzer," he said just before the door closed.

As Else Rosenfeld of the Munich Jewish Committee and witness to a deportation from Milbertshofen stated years later, "The Nazi officials were all there, and hoped to see a sort of entertainment—wailing and whining, begging for help, asking not to be deported, not to be separated from members of their families, and so on and so on. Nothing of this sort happened. Our people had a dignity and calmness which made my heart overflow with love and respect."

Most of the adult deportees who marched to the Milbertshofen train station that day were women. The average age of the deportees was forty-five years. With the adults there were 130 children and young people under the age of eighteen. The youngest children were Judis Cahn and Rachel Kiesler, both under two. There were many other toddlers.

The deportees were allowed to take 50 kilograms (110 pounds) of luggage. They had little to guide them in their packing, however. They assumed that their most urgent need would be warm clothing. Some were able to obtain small propane heaters. Others used their precious space to pack books in the hope of maintaining some rudimentary intellectual life. Most brought writing materials, to provide communication with loved ones. Many brought whatever medicines and medical supplies they could get and had room for. And those who could sewed some valuables into their clothing—money, jewelry, or anything that might prove invaluable at some point along the way. Most also brought photos, small prints, postcards, and menorahs or other items to remind themselves of their former lives, and the loved ones left behind.

Those on the deportation list were expected to pay for "travel expenses" incurred for their deportation. For those too poor to pay, the IKG would have to compensate the Nazi authorities.

The deportee only had limited time or energy to dwell on this injustice. They were now entrapped in a poisonous cloud of uncertainty. Everyone had heard stories of previous deportations and the hardships those "sent east" before them had encountered. Add to this the dire threats from Hitler and his minions, and the frightening rumors of violence in the east, which all magnified their concerns. Many had already succumbed to the cumulative effect of these terrible fears. On the eve of the deportations, the number of Munich Jews who died by suicide climbed precipitously.

The one-mile march to the train station took over an hour. It was still dark, and the rain and wind lashed their faces as the deportees lined up at the station and waited to enter the train carriages. A Jewish steward wearing a white armband was appointed to each wagon to ensure "order" during the trip. The first car of the train carried the Jewish transport management group, a doctor, some medical staff, and teachers to care for the children. A special car in the middle of the train carried thirteen police officers and a Gestapo agent. The last car on the train carried the luggage. According to one report, before the train departed from the Milbertshofen freight station, this car was secretly uncoupled and left behind.

After the loading of the passengers was completed, windows were closed, and the doors were locked to prevent escape.

### The Wait

Three days after the train left the Milbertshofen station, heading to Riga, Willi and Hedi came by Benno and Anna's apartment on Trogerstrasse. "Willi, we thought you left on the train to Poland last week!" said Anna.

"At the last minute they told me I couldn't go. I don't know why. But the train didn't go to Poland, it went to Riga, in Latvia."

"Have you told Louis?"

"Hedi told him, Anna. She also told him that we saw Tilli and Wilhelm at Milbertshofen before they left for the train. I'm back at Berg am Laim with Hedi."

Anna brought a plate of rye bread and jam and sat down. She pulled out a paper from an envelope. "I got a short note from Ilse Schuster more than a week ago. Here it says, 'My sister Tilli sent me a message from the Jewish camp; she and Wilhelm are about to leave for Poland with other Holzers.'"

Willi ate a piece of soggy bread he'd dipped into his tea. "It's confusing. The Nazis like to keep it that way. But we were told, before being sent to Milbertshofen, that we'd be going to Riga."

Anna and Benno were distressed to see Hedi so thin and tired, so worn out physically and psychologically. Willi, too, was a bit of a shock for them. He looked visibly older and frailer than even a few weeks before.

While Willi explained how he was suddenly removed from the transport east, Benno got a beer and brought it to his brother-in-law. "I have a few of these left, just a few. But like you said when I got back from Dachau, it's the Bavarian medicine. Not many medicines left for us."

"Thank you," said Willi, gratefully. He offered Benno a thin smile.

"Have you heard anything from your children?" Anna asked.

"No. Well, they only left three days ago."

"Three days? I thought they left ten days ago."

"No." Willi paused to think. "We left Berg am Laim on the 14th. But we were at Milbertshofen until three days ago. I'm not sure what date that was."

"The 20th," Hedi put in.

"They expect the train to take at least two days, so maybe they arrived yesterday? I don't expect to hear from them for another ten days, at least. Have you heard anything from Hani or Fritz in America?"

Benno looked at Anna. "The last letter we got from them was . . . ten days ago, I think. They are trying to arrange for us to go to Cuba. They don't want us to give up hope. As you know I've been hesitant to go to Cuba."

Anna sighed. "At this point we're ready to go wherever we can."

"I couldn't leave now." Willi's wavering voice was barely audible. "Leave my kids behind, no." He looked at Hedi. "If they had left and left me here, okay, I could live with that. But how could I leave my children here? How?" Hedi leaned over and kissed her father on the side of his head and Willi draped his arm on her shoulder.

Benno stood at the head of the table. "Well, my children are married now. There's a new generation out of reach of these monsters . . . And the Germans may have to contend with Soviets on one end and the English on the other." Benno raised his voice. "When I hear the air raid sirens, I just hope the English planes keep coming. Let them smash this place to pieces—to pieces!" Benno tightly gripped the chair he was standing behind.

"That's all we have left to hope for now, isn't it?" Willi looked at his brother-in-law. "We tried to do the best for this country, didn't we, Benno? We served in the war. We raised horses for their army. We bought the war bonds. And when we had a bit more on the farm, we tried to help our neighbors. The people of Traunstein were our friends and . . ." Willi sighed, and everyone was quiet for a moment. "Then they took my boy, my Max . . ." Willi began sobbing, his hands covering his face. Hedi embraced her father. "Papa, we are still here. Max is still alive. Klara is safe in England. We'll be together again."

"Why don't you lie down, Willi," Anna said. "Get some rest. We'll get you up in an hour or so."

## The Train Ride

The trip east took three days. The first town the train passed after leaving Munich was Dachau, just as dawn was breaking. Then it traveled through long stretches of German countryside, passing villages and farms, crossing over the Danube at Ingolstadt, and then through the cities of Nuremberg and Bamberg, with some delays along the way. The train came into Berlin as the sun was beginning to set that first day.

Several times en route, the train pulled into a station only to remain there for hours while German troop and munition trains rumbled by on their way to the battle lines in the Soviet Union. The lengths of some of these trains were staggering. Hundreds of flatbed cars carrying trucks, artillery pieces, tanks, and jeeps. There were long passenger trains presumably loaded with tens of thousands of soldiers.

As the train proceeded northeast, the weather grew colder.

Alfred, Martha, and Benno were quiet for much of the early part of the trip, each contemplating what they imagined lay ahead. Then they began to speculate, among themselves and with others in the car.

Alfred pulled out a writing tablet he'd brought along and began to make notes of the day's events. Then he began composing a letter to his father. In it, he tried to write reassuringly that they had begun to talk about their goals in what would be their new lives. They would work together to survive and prepare the way for the eventual reunion of the family. He wrote gratefully about their past, about the skills they'd learned growing up, caring for cattle and horses and breeding and judging livestock. They hoped to use these skills to rebuild their lives.

The small country villages and grazing animals they passed were reminiscent of Traunstein. Benno began making sketches of horses and cattle in the fields along the way, and some children in the car who were running restlessly up and down the aisles stopped to look at Benno's art. He and Alfred talked to the children about different breeds of animals. They also explained the differences between cows in southern Germany and the ones in colder Polish areas, as well as what they might expect in Riga. Several of the children mentioned that they were traveling with their mother. "Our mother is scared," one said. "She didn't want to leave Munich."

Alfred tried to assure them that what they faced was new, and new things are often scary but might offer interesting new possibilities. "Have you ever seen the ocean?" None of the children had. "Well," admitted Alfred, "I've only seen the ocean a few times. Once near Hamburg, the North Sea. It's beautiful." He told the children how he and his father had made trips to Belgium and how several times they'd gone to a town called Ostend on the water across from England. "In Riga, we will be by the ocean. You'll be able to stick your feet in ocean water! And you will have a chance to learn a new language. In Riga people speak Latvian."

Benno jumped in. "In German the word for cow is *kuh*, but in Polish it's *krowa*. But do you know what it is in Latvian?"

"No," said one boy.

"Well, neither do I!" Benno laughed. "See, something to learn."

Someone with a German-Latvian dictionary found the word for cow in Latvian and shouted it out. "It's *govs*." When the children heard this, they started laughing.

"I bet you kids don't know that cows in different countries have a different way of, well, speaking. Or should I say, accents."

"How do you know?" A girl of around six or seven swayed energetically as she spoke.

Benno looked over at this young skeptic. "I grew up around German cows. That's why I know about cows. And I can kind of understand German cows, you know they say 'Moo.' But Latvian cows, now they have a different accent, and I don't expect to understand them."

"How does a Latvian cow talk?" asked the girl's younger brother.

"Well, I think it's something like 'mooaah.'" Benno extended his rounded lips and repeated the strange sound. The young boy laughed.

His sister was not having any of it. "I don't think so."

"Well, have you ever heard a Latvian cow?" asked Benno.

"No, but I don't think they sound any different."

"Well, how would you know?"

She shook her head. "I just don't think so."

Benno smiled broadly. "Well, you may be right. But the only way you'll really know is if you listen to a Latvian cow. So, I hope you take the time to do that when we're in Latvia. Then you can come and visit and let us know what you find out."

The boy told Benno, "I want to have a horse when I get to Riga."

"Well, you'll have to learn how to care for a horse. Do you know anything about horses?"

"No," the boy answered shyly.

Benno leaned toward the child. "Well, the first thing you need to know is that you never act mean to a horse. You know why?" The boy shook his head. "Because horses don't forget. If you're mean and hit a horse, it will always remember such a mean act. And then they'll always be afraid of you or angry at you. Animals aren't mean to each other. Animals do kill each other, but only for food or sometimes for mating."

"What is mating?" asked the sister.

"When they want to produce babies. Sometimes the males fight over the females. But they don't hate each other or hurt each other because they don't like their color or the way they run, or something like that. Only people do that."

"Like when they were mean to my Papa?" the girl spoke softly.

"Who were mean?"

"The men who took him. They hurt him and now he can't be with us." The girl's face clouded and she bit her lip.

"I'm sorry." Benno shook his head. "You see how people can be worse than animals. Much worse. That's why we need to teach each other not to be that way." Benno gave each of the children a pencil and paper and showed them the horse and cow he had drawn. "Now you make your own picture," he told them. "You can use mine as an example."

After the children left, Alfred and Benno explained to Martha how their grandfather Moses made their parents promise to keep a kosher home in exchange for his blessing upon their marriage. "That's why they learned to prepare animals the kosher way," Alfred said. "I think it's more humane and healthy. It's okay to kill animals because it's part of survival. But it's not right to do so in a cruel way. I think the kosher rules were adopted, in part, from that morality. At least I believe so."

In this way the hours passed for the Holzers.

## Kaunas, Lithuania

Martha woke up first as the train pulled into a station. She was about to go back to sleep after seeing a sign that read "Kaunas." But then a steward appeared and announced, "We're leaving the train here."

"Here, in Kaunas? Not Riga?" many voices were heard to ask.

"Change of plans. We'll be getting off here," the steward repeated.

"And our luggage?" asked one of the passengers.

"They'll be bringing it later. We'll be walking to our destination from here. Be ready to leave the train in twenty minutes."

Word was passing, from one to another. "This is Kaunas, Lithuania. We're hundreds of miles from Riga."

"Why here?" many questioned.

"Friendly or unfriendly?" asked someone.

"Friendly to us?! What do you think?" came the reply.

The scene outside the train was not inviting. It was gray and wet, like Munich had been, but colder. Some of the travelers gulped down pieces of bread or other food they had on hand as they made their way down the aisles of the train and toward the exits.

Mothers were feeding their children and stuffing whatever food was left over in their pockets.

Gruff voices outside the train yelled, "Everyone off!" Alfred Holzer returned the paper, envelopes, and stamps to the small case he'd carried on board while Martha packed some food in a small bag and stuffed it underneath her jacket. Benno did the same.

As the deportees descended from the cars, they saw men wearing army uniforms and combat helmets, carrying long rifles. They were spread along the length of the train.

Martha looked for Tilli and Wilhelm but did not see them, but she saw Flora and her daughter Hertha several train cars behind them. She waved to them but couldn't tell if they saw her.

There was a light snow on the ground. The Jewish stewards were pleading with the deportees to get in lines of two. Then, several of the armed men approached the stewards and yelled, "Straighten up or there will be trouble." Mothers and fathers grabbed their children's hands. Women and men with infants in their arms tried to carry small bags of food and other items at the same time. One child wearing a padded blue coat that was far too big for his little frame cried loudly as he tried unsuccessfully to pull away from his mother to fetch a toy he'd dropped.

At the outset the marchers were told they were being taken to a "work camp" where they would be housed and fed. Their luggage would be cared for and taken to that camp. After that, they were ordered to start marching away from the train station.

Many of those from Munich's Berg am Laim quietly expressed their gratitude that the monastery staff had urged them to wear multiple layers of clothes. At least they would not freeze.

The environs of Kaunas had a feel quite different than those in Munich. For one thing, the cold had a greater sting to it. The sunlight was weaker for the same time of day. The houses they passed on the way through town were clearly poorer than those in Munich. The streets were not as well kept. There were half-finished houses and other unfinished buildings. Some buildings had balconies that sagged and siding that was crumbling.

People in the houses and apartments looked out at the marchers as they approached. Residents who were outside went inside. One woman looking out from her home hurriedly pulled shut a wooden storm window as the march reached the corner of her small front yard. No one, it seemed, wanted to be seen as the Germans passed by—at least, seen by these armed Germans.

The soldiers with their knee-high leather boots who marched alongside the deportees were members of the Einsatzkommando 3, which belonged to the Einsatzgruppen A. This Einsatzkommando 3 in Kaunas was under the direction of Karl Jäger. By November

1941, Jäger was already a veteran of large-scale mass murders in the Baltic area.

The men, women, and children from Munich did not know who was guiding them on their long walk, nor did they know where they were going. They did not know, as they passed by an area that looked especially poor, that it was the Jewish ghetto of Kaunas.

### The Ninth Fort

The deportees from Munich arrived tired and hungry at a fortress called the Ninth Fort, one of a string of fortresses built at Kaunas in the years before the First World War. The forts were captured in the early days of the German invasion of the Baltic Soviet Republics, in late June 1941. The Ninth Fort was a massive steel and concrete bunker surrounded by deep earthworks and honeycombed with subterranean passageways and chambers. In the warmest days of summer, it was bone-chillingly cold inside. In winter, it was an icebox.

When the marchers arrived, they were ushered brusquely into the belly of the fortress and toward a series of large iron-gated cells with concrete walls and floors. The cells had no heating whatsoever. Here, without heat or blankets, without any covering, they were ordered to sit and wait. They were only told that "arrangements are being made."

Alfred and Martha, Benno, their cousin Tilli and her son Wilhelm, along with Tilli's sister-in-law Flora and Flora's nineteen-year-old daughter Hertha, all found themselves in the same large cell. They huddled together in a corner. There were some cots in the cells, most of them with bare springs, but not nearly enough to accommodate everyone crammed into those spaces. Most people had to sit on the bare cement floor, using whatever clothing they could spare as cushioning.

In the hours that followed the arrival of the Bavarian deportees, two more trains arrived in Kaunas: one from Frankfurt the first evening, the other from Berlin the following day. Each transport brought another thousand deportees into the ever more crowded fort. By November 25, three thousand people were jammed into the freezing cells of the Ninth Fort. One hundred and seventy-five of the prisoners were small children. Among them were infants and toddlers.

By now the stewards of the Jewish committee with their white armbands were captives like everyone else. The Einsatzgruppen soldiers, augmented by local Lithuanian collaborators, guarded the fort and cells, ignoring pleas for food and water, and ignoring such questions as, "How long are we going to be here?" and "Where do we go from here?"

Late in the morning on November 25, the commander of the Einsatzkommando 3, Karl Jäger, assembled his officers in a room in the fort and gave them orders to convey to his 140 troops.

The orders the Einsatzkommando were given that day were met with some unusual discord. The word had passed to the troops that Jews under their guard had come from Munich, Frankfurt, and Berlin. "These are Reich Jews," some members of the Einsatzkommando murmured among themselves as they lined up outside the Ninth Fort. Up until that day the Einsatzkommando had dealt with Lithuanian, Polish, Belarussian, Ukrainian, and Russian Jews. These soldiers had been intensely trained in racial matters in the lead-up to the invasion of the Soviet Union, and their lessons emphasized the sub-humanity of Slavic peoples and others in the regions east of Germany, especially the Jews. These racial myths were reinforced by the impoverished state of many of the Jews they encountered, Jews who spoke different languages, dressed in different clothing, and were foreign to the Einsatzgruppen soldiers. But for some soldiers, German Jews were a different matter. One soldier even found the nerve to raise the issue. "These are Reich Jews," he reminded his superior.

"We have orders," was the reply.

Later that morning an officer and several of the Einsatzkommando troopers appeared at the door of the cell holding many of the group from Munich, including the Holzer family. "Everyone, get ready to leave the fort. Up now!" they shouted. As the deportees rose, groups of a few hundred at a time were ushered out of the cells. As these groups left, they were exhorted to move along. "Hurry now! That way, toward the doors!"

As they approached the outer door to the fort they passed through a large, bare room. There they encountered Lithuanian guards carrying clubs, pointing to corners of the room where clothing was piled. The guards shouted at them, "*Zieh Dich aus!*" ("Remove your clothes!")

Martha turned and grabbed Alfred's arm. Gasps went up among the group. There was some pushing and grabbing, shouts and threats. Blows were struck by the Lithuanian guards. Cries were heard. Shrieks of anger, pain, and fear echoed down the fort's cement hallway. The sound of gunfire from outside the fort pierced the room as the outer doors opened and as successive groups were herded through them by armed Einsatzkommando troops and uniformed Lithuanian police. Mothers and fathers held desperately to each other and their children. Alfred and Martha embraced, sobbing, then reached out to Benno, Tilli, and Wilhelm, then Flora and Hertha—"I love you," they cried to one another. "I love you."

A shrill cry of grief and rage cut through the air, amplified by the cold, hard walls of the room: "*Nicht meine Kinder!*" "*Nicht meine Kinder!*" "Not my children! Not my children! Not my children! Not my . . ." The thud of a rifle butt echoed, then the terrible wail of a daughter for her bleeding mother sprawled on the floor, being bludgeoned by a beast in a uniform.

A Lithuanian guard grabbed nineteen-year-old Hertha, who still wore underclothing. "Off with that, bitch," he grunted. But he was shoved out of the way by an Einsatzkommando trooper who yelled at him, "Keep your filthy Slavic hands to yourself." The guard glared at him but moved aside.

Amid the chaos and horror, Benno caught a glimpse of the bright little girl he'd seen on the train.

Naked men, women, and children were herded through the door of the fort and out into the freezing air, out onto an expansive grassy area into which a long pit, four or five feet deep, had been dug. For the next several hours, 3,000 people were herded in groups and forced to line up along the edge of the pit.

Some never heard the shots. Some felt a sharp sting in their legs or arms as they collapsed into the pit. Some wrapped their bodies around their children before falling face forward into the mass of warm corpses, and the half-dead writhing in pain—many, still writhing in pain—amid the blood . . . the warm blood . . . Special troops at the edge of the pit aimed their rifles at any movement or sound.

Until all went quiet.

Until these human beings, once filled with life, with all its joys, sorrows, and expectations, were now only a silent, lifeless, mass.

### The Spoils

The precise death count recorded by the Nazis that day—and eagerly forwarded by Karl Jäger to his superiors to burnish his credentials as an effective commander—was the following: 1,159 Jewish men, 1,600 Jewish women, and 175 Jewish children.

In the days that followed, workers from the Kaunas ghetto were sent to sort the belongings taken from arriving trains. One of these workers noted that the trains carried "the finest possessions that the eye can see . . . the nicest foods, all prepared with a generous hand to last a long time, the best clothing, the rarest of medicines, and various professional instruments. An endless number of books—scientific, professional, Jewish books, prayer books, prayer shawls—they were so shockingly deceived. Their first step toward a new life was their last—the pits of the Ninth Fort."

#### Anti-Jewish Measure, November 25, 1941

The same day as the Kaunas mass murder, a special Reich Citizenship law is enacted. It declares that all Jews who cross the Reich border—whether voluntarily or by force—lose all German citizenship rights, allowing the Reich authorities to "legally" seize all their properties and possessions.

From the time the Einsatzgruppen Kommando 3 under Karl Jäger began its actions in early July 1941 until the Ninth Fort massacre on November 25, the tally of Jews murdered in Lithuania alone was 137,346. Most of them were Lithuanian, Belorussian, or Russian Jews. Among the ranks of the Einsatzgruppen soldiers, these Jews were being denounced as racial and political enemies— targeted for elimination in the same way as the Bolsheviks—and accused of masterminding the growing partisan sabotage behind German lines. This self-deceiving lie fed the savage violence directed at Jews.

But "Reich Jews" were a different matter to many of these soldiers. They were, after all, Germans, and some were even veterans of the First World War. In the bizarre dystopia of Nazi racial dogma, they stood a peg higher than the Slavic "*Untermensch*"—"sub-humans."

Among the Einsatzgruppen or SS soldiers there would be no thought about disobeying their orders. But such ideological doubts and the demoralizing effect of the mass killings began cumulatively to poison the morale of even these specially selected and trained killers. This was one of the factors that led Heinrich Himmler, the leader of the elite Nazi SS, and other Nazi leaders to conclude that new methods of mass murder needed to be found.

# 22

# The Letters of November 18 and 20

FRED CAME HOME IN THE late afternoon on a Thursday with bags of deli food from a restaurant in Queens. The rye bread, sliced meats, chopped liver, and potato salad were for a Sabbath dinner he and Kate were planning for the following evening to celebrate Kate's twenty-eighth birthday, her first since their marriage. They'd invited their closest relatives. In addition to Fred's sister Hani and her husband, Ludwig, they were expecting Kate's two sisters, Ilse and Gerta, their husbands, Solly and Jack, and Kate's mother, Johanna. They had just begun discussing how they might fit everyone into their small apartment when Hani showed up. After greeting her brother and sister-in-law, Hani handed Fred two letters that had arrived in the mail that morning. He sat next to his sister and began to read. Kate sat down at the table across from them and said, "Fred, read the letters aloud. I'd like to hear what your parents have written." He began reading:

November 18, 1941

Dear children,

We are a little worried. Your last letter we have received on October 9. Hopefully you are all healthy. At least I can tell you that we are doing well.

As you probably know Tilli and her son Wilhelm as well as Willi, Benno and Alfred with Martha succeeded in getting to Poland. I don't know much more to report but I'm sure we'll hear from them . . .

"Poland," Fred repeated. The word rolled like something heavy off his tongue. Hani closed her eyes.

"I couldn't think of a worse place to be right now," Kate said.

"Nor I," Fred agreed and continued reading:

We received a telegram from Cuba, and we hope to get there from here. You probably know from other relatives that it's really hard to get away from here now.

"The rest is, 'From your loving parents,' and so on." Fred picked up the other letter. "This one was written two days later, on November 20."

Dear children,
    We haven't heard from you in a while, but we are hoping that you're well. The same holds true for us. Your telegram from Havana we received. Unfortunately, it's absolutely necessary to get the visa first from Berlin as you probably know.

Fred paused and looked at Hani, then Kate. "What does this mean?"

Dear Fred,
    Regarding our departure there's nothing to do right now. We'll just have to wait. We just didn't get the right number and so we missed it.

Fred reread the letter to himself, then slammed his fist on it and stood up. "They didn't get a visa from the Cuban consulate in Berlin! That means this visa business is a fraud!!"

Hani stared down at the letter. "Maybe it just takes longer, Fred."

"Longer? Hani, I paid for the visa on October 27. This letter was written on November 20. All Cuba had to do was wire their consulate in Berlin that the visa was paid for. Why would it take this long!"

Hani looked wide-eyed at her brother. "What are we going to do?"

Fred shook his head. "I'll go back to the travel office tomorrow. Ask them to contact Havana."

"Maybe you should contact the American Jewish Committee," Kate suggested.

"Maybe. But I think the truth is, Kate, those who want to help have no power. And those who have power don't want to help."

Fred sat back down and put his head in his hands. Every avenue for escape from Germany now seemed to be closed. Still, he told himself, he would continue to search out possibilities. He did not know that the letter of November 20, 1941, was the last he would receive from his parents.

# 23

# Late November 1941 to Mid-March 1942

AS THE WINTER OF 1941 set in, life for the Jews who remained in Germany turned ever more isolated and restricted. Food became more difficult to obtain, hopelessness more difficult to fend off.

Anna's sister Mina had been evicted from the family's Laupheim home on Kappelenstrasse in October 1939 and placed in an old Rabbinate retirement home, Laupheim's "Judenhaus," with forty other residents. This cut her off from the income she got from renting rooms in her home. Then travel restrictions imposed in 1941 made visiting Munich impossible.

Berthold and Benno still found ways to get together, finding their conversations to be an ever more urgently needed source of companionship and solace. Ironically, the suffering around them, including that which they themselves were enduring, was, at the same time, their only source of hope. German difficulties on the battlefields of the Soviet Union, the rising toll of death and destruction on the German soldiers, and the nation's diminishing military capacity fueled a rising genocidal rage in the regime. Yet it was only in such defeats that Benno and Berthold could envision salvation.

"We're old people and veterans, without any significant wealth,"

Benno reasoned when trying to account for why he and Berthold, among a dwindling number of Jews in Munich, were still allowed to stay in their own homes. But they had no confidence that this would last indefinitely.

## DECLARATION OF WAR

The December 7 Japanese attack on the U.S. naval fleet in Pearl Harbor, Hawaii, brought a flurry of screaming headlines to German papers. Japan's attack was hailed as something akin to a mortal blow to the U.S. military. On December 8, the United States declared war on Japan. Germany, allied with Japan, in turn declared war on the United States, and on December 11, the United States declared war on Germany.

Hitler had previously attacked President Franklin Roosevelt and the Nazi press had frequently criticized him. Now, in the wake of the declaration of war between the two countries, Hitler ratcheted up his assault on Roosevelt. Speaking before the Reichstag, Hitler denounced Roosevelt as a man manipulated by "Jews, in all of their satanic baseness," to use "the United States as the instrument . . . to prepare a second Purim against the nations of Europe."

Berthold commented caustically, "To believe the *Völkischer Beobachter*, Jewish influence in America is so mighty they alone forced Roosevelt to declare war on Germany. But those same almighty Jews can't get him to allow even a few more of us into the country!" These ironic words found an echo in Benno's own thoughts. His own disappointing experience navigating the contradictory pathway to a U.S. visa now, in retrospect, seemed much more like a purposeful effort to keep people like him out of the country. He had argued with U.S. consular officials that his children and other relatives would be able to guarantee his and Anna's livelihood without them becoming a burden to the country. But even when U.S. representative Adolph Sabath from Illinois, responding to the pleas of Benno's niece Ida, made this same argument to the U.S. consul in Stuttgart on their behalf, nothing changed.

Nevertheless, Benno and Berthold welcomed the U.S. declaration of war on Germany of December 11, and they toasted each other with a beer they shared, compliments of the Eibers. Benno's neighbor had put several precious bottles of *Gunzenhausen* in the food bag Bertha Eiber brought them. On one of the bottles, Eiber had written on its yellow label, "Congratulations, 12/11."

"Here's to a two-front war." Benno felt, for the moment, something approximating optimism. "And a speedy demise to the *invincible* Nazi military."

As the weeks of December passed, they observed, and they conjectured. They listened to comments on the street when they could, considered observations of friends or relatives, and scanned news articles; they looked and listened for any bit of favorable information they could ferret from the barrage of mind-numbing war hyperbole. These details, along with a kind word from a stranger on the street, a pro-war poster defaced on a kiosk, a sarcastic message written in haste by some disgruntled person on a wall, or the shattered glass cover of a *Der Stürmer* display Berthold saw one day, were the fragments they mulled over and threw on the modest fires of their conversations, trying to warm themselves with little sparks of hope.

### A Letter and a Demand

At the end of the second week of December, a letter arrived at 44 Trogerstrasse from the Munich Aryanization Committee. In a tersely worded message, it demanded that Benno and Anna compile a detailed list of all their apartment's furniture and other possessions. It asked for bank account balances as well as securities held, and investment and insurance information. The letter gave a deadline for when the information would have to be submitted. It also cited the legal authority under which the order was written. Benno reluctantly compiled the list and sent it off.

Near the end of December, Benno was struck with a bad case of the flu. Because he had a fever, Anna feared he would get pneumonia and was adamant that he should not go out. Being homebound turned his mood more sour than usual. Anna, as she had throughout their years together, worked hard to care for her husband. With help from Bertha Eiber, she was able to get some tea and honey for him. She also worked to lift Benno's mood by reminding him about their children in the United States She tried to channel whatever positive news she could glean about relatives and neighbors into positive conversation. At the same time, she withheld bad news when she could.

Anna worked hard to find something special to eat. She asked Frau Eiber to look for certain things that she knew Benno would appreciate. Bertha Eiber was able to find a pouch of pipe tobacco. Benno had given up pipe smoking years before, but now cigars and cigarettes had become a nearly impossible luxury. Anna hid the tobacco until Benno recovered. Once he was well, this precious cache of loose tobacco allowed him the pleasure of smoking by using one of the pipes Fritz had left behind.

### Four More Cards

Benno's recovery came by the beginning of the second week in January. When Anna was out visiting a friend, he wrote another postcard. Carefully, he wrote the word *Hail* above the Hitler stamp and, over Hitler's picture, he wrote *Murderer*. Under the stamp he wrote *God is in Heaven. Hitler is a hideous man. God decides for all people and doesn't tolerate other gods. He hails himself a god, indeed!* He dropped the card in a letter box on January 11. The next day, Monday, January 12, he wrote another card. It had the word *Robespierre* above the stamp and *Pfui* on the stamp itself, as well as a cross to the left of the stamp and one underneath it. Benno deposited this card in a box on Prinzregentenstrasse. He told Anna he had to get exercise after his long stay at home. On January 14, he wrote a card with the word *them* on the top half of the stamp, then a long line and a phrase across the stamp *Hail the New God of 1933–1943*, expressing the sentiment, or hope, that with the war going badly, the regime would not last. And then there was the phrase in capital letters *WHAT IS JUSTICE?* On January 17, he wrote a card with the word *Tyrant* across the Führer's picture. Underneath, he wrote *Pile of rubbish*.

### The Deadliest Anti-Jewish Measure at a Conference by a Tranquil Lake

By the winter of 1941–42, the momentum the Nazi military had enjoyed during the first years of the war was over, destroyed on the approaches to Moscow and Leningrad by unexpectedly stubborn Soviet defenses and the onset of the furiously difficult Russian winter. This failure produced a cascade of difficulties for the Nazi regime. Chief among them were limits to manpower and matériel. Hitler had counted on looting the conquered lands to the east to ease the strain on the homeland. This was clearly not going to be possible.

In early January 1942, in a major shift in policy, new economic measures imposed drastic cuts in the production of consumer goods to facilitate a huge increase in the production of war matériel.

The ferocious resistance by Soviet soldiers on the major war fronts and by partisan fighters in territory overrun by the German army, including along the German military's extended supply lines, presented an increasingly difficult barrier to German success in the war. It also constituted a grave challenge to Nazi morale—especially to the myth of racial superiority, in whose belief the most ardent supporters of Nazism sustained their confidence. The Nazi armies were now being outmatched by an enemy the Nazis had arrogantly labeled "sub-human."

The Nazi leadership realized that any sign of vulnerability would only magnify the problems they faced controlling the territories they had so far conquered. They decided to demonstrate their "invincibility" and "racial superiority" by destroying the "inferior" populations they had rendered defenseless.

On January 20, 1942, Reinhard Heydrich, the head of the Nazis' main security agency, convened a secret conference at a villa on the edge of a picturesque lake, the Wannsee, in a quiet western suburb of Berlin. The conference was called to work out plans for the mass removal and extermination of the Jewish populations in the areas under Nazi control, including those Jews remaining in Germany.

### "The Murderer of 5,000,000!"

Benno had no way of knowing the particulars of the Wannsee Conference. But he knew enough to understand the ominous trajectory of events. Two days after the conference, on January 22, 1942, he wrote and mailed his eighth postcard. On the stamp bearing Hitler's face, he wrote the phrase, *There has never been such an idiot.* And under the stamp he wrote *Ever in this world.* On another part of the card, he wrote the word *Meanness.*

On January 23, Benno wrote and mailed a postcard that had the word *Heil* written across the picture of the Führer and, under the stamp, the words *Government of Terror.* And under the stamp, *The New God.* On the reverse side of the card it read, *Murderer of 5,000,000!*

### Hitler's Speech on January 30, 1942

At a January 30 speech at Berlin's Sportspalast, Hitler restated the threat he had made in January 1939, that "if the Jews start another war, it is the Jews who will be annihilated." Benno pondered the immensity of the lie, and how this staggering untruth caused so little outcry, let alone the universal mockery it deserved! But he had come to understand that truth or falsehood were not important for the Nazi faithful. A lie that served to reinforce their belief in German, or really Aryan, greatness was far preferable to any truth that undermined it. Those who had thrown in their lot with Hitler were only interested in what they perceived as their own interests. This protected the populace loyal to Nazism from its grotesque contradictions.

Benno realized that Hitler's threat to annihilate the Jewish population was being carried out. It was the only explanation that fit the situation. He, Anna, and everyone within reach would eventually be killed, or they would kill themselves to prevent the monsters from having the satisfaction of doing it. This understanding both crushed him with a terrible anxiety and gave him the freedom to act. As a result, Benno's moods moved between paralyzing fear and righteous rage. Neither won out, and the swings were hard to predict.

Benno mailed another card on February 10. Above the Hitler stamp he wrote the word *Hitler* and across the stamp the words, *Son of a Bitch Murderer!* Below them, he wrote *Bandit, Scoundrel, Criminal.* To the left and below the stamp there was a cross, a sign of a death wish.

Numerous accounts of evictions of longtime Munich Jewish families were making the rounds. Benno wanted to visit Berthold and discuss these reports with him, but Hilde sent word that his friend was ill.

On February 21, 1942, Benno sat at the desk in Fritz's former bedroom. He had hardly slept for several nights. He was caught in a vortex of dread produced by the broadening wave of evictions. The room seemed to swirl around him. At times, he felt as though he were in a dream state. He recalled how, as a youth, he would sometimes awaken from a nightmare, relieved to realize it was the product of his own mind. Now, for brief moments, he had the sensation that this too was a horrible illusion. They were in a dreadful trap. There was no hint of a way out. How could this be? Yes, he had thought about the possibility of eviction, expected it, even. But now, as it was bearing down on them, it staggered him no less. Benno felt heartbreak for Anna. He could do nothing to protect her.

Benno tried to refocus his thoughts, to think things through, to act. He took a blank card with a Hitler stamp from his desk. It was as though all the emotions roiling in him were moving to the tip of the pen in his unsteady hand. "Feeble," he muttered to himself. But he had no other means to manifest his rage. He crossed thick lines through the green stamp with its profile of the Führer's head. Above Hitler's profile, he wrote *This,* and below the profile, *Criminal.* He failed to notice that this old card had his address stamped on it.

Benno left the apartment while Anna was napping. He walked the neighborhood in a kind of haze. The logical part of his mind instructed him to act in ways that allayed suspicion. He stopped to buy a newspaper. As he was reaching in his jacket pocket for the money, he remembered that buying a newspaper was prohibited to Jews. He hesitated, then bought the paper anyway. He circled the block. He walked self-consciously erect, suddenly feeling a kind of reckless abandon. Far from hiding the star on his chest, he brandished it. He wished someone would stop, make a nasty comment, give him an excuse to act out the rage that was coursing through him. A few people did pass him, and he looked directly at them. But they did their best to glance away, pretending not to see his branding. For once, passersby were more uncomfortable with the yellow star than he! Benno approached the letter box near his apartment and dropped the card in. He returned to his apartment and entered quietly. Anna was still asleep.

On February 23, Benno pulled two blank cards from his desk. He put a Hitler stamp on each. On the first, he drew thick lines through the head of the Führer. Above the stamp he wrote *Die a Wretched Death,* and to the left of the stamp he wrote *Beast,* and below it, *Murderer, scoundrel.* Across the stamp of the second card, he wrote the words, *Here is the Bloody Dog.*

On February 28, Benno wrote one more card. In thick letters above and below an ink-crossed Hitler stamp, he inscribed the words *The Dog* and *Murderer.*

### Eviction

During the first week of March, another letter arrived at 44 Trogerstrasse from the Munich Aryanization Department. It stated in part: "Given the needs of the Patriotic German people in this time of defense of the fatherland . . . the occupants of this residence are hereby ordered to surrender their apartment." The letter warned tersely that "no item from this residence be removed, other than those permitted by this department, under threat of punishment." And further: "The inhabitants of said apartment should make all arrangements to leave by March 16, 1942." The letter specified that each occupant would be allowed to bring a suitcase with no more than 50 kilograms (110 pounds) of possessions. Benno and Anna knew that these bags would be searched and if any real valuables were found, they would be confiscated.

For Anna and Benno, the days that followed were the worst since Kristallnacht. No—these were indeed worse. The future itself was an open wound, painful to the touch. How could they even talk about the days to come without conjuring some version of horror? So they avoided the topic. Instead they talked about what belongings to pack and how they might get some personal valuables to others for safekeeping—their photographs, some of the letters from their children, and other papers. The only relative they could count on was Anna's niece Ilse Schuster, in Wolfratshausen. Ilse was, for the time being, safe from deportation because her Catholic husband Hermann continued to stand by her. But Hermann was being threatened for his refusal to denounce their marriage and his freedom of movement was limited. Anna was fearful of sending a package to Wolfratshausen through the mail because that might be interpreted as a violation of the order they'd been given.

A week after receiving the eviction letter, Benno shoved a thin bundle of papers wrapped in a newspaper and secured with string through the mail slot of the Eiber tailor shop. In the envelope, Ludwig Eiber found several photos of Benno's father and mother and a note informing the Eibers that he and Anna had been ordered to move on March 16.[37] In the note, Benno thanked Ludwig and Bertha for their kindness and help and expressed the wish that, somehow, they would be able to stay in touch. Benno included Fritz's address and asked Eiber to reach out to his son and daughter should communication with the United States once again be possible. Anna also wrote a note expressing her gratitude for their kindness. Her letter only speculated that their new residence would be Berg am Lain or more likely, the Milbertshofen camp.

On Monday, March 16, a police van pulled up in front of 44 Trogerstrasse. Ludwig and Bertha Eiber went to the window of their tailor shop and watched as several men came to the outer door of the apartment building. Benno opened the door to several police and a person dressed in civilian clothes who showed a badge and identified himself as a member of the Aryanization Committee. The group entered the building without the niceties of asking permission to do so.

The men accompanied Benno to his apartment. Two suitcases sat in the hallway next to the door. The man from the Aryanization Committee, Franz Mugler, had become a familiar and feared face among Munich's Jewish residents. He instructed Benno and Anna to hand over their apartment keys, leave their apartment, and go to the van that was waiting for them in the street. Mugler then entered the apartment, carrying the list that Benno and Anna had written of the apartment's contents. He did little more than give each room a cursory look. He stopped at the icebox and opened it. He did the same with the kitchen cabinets. Finding nothing interesting, he closed them and left the apartment.

As Mugler walked out, Herr Kandl, wearing only socks on his feet, was in the hallway. Kandl nodded with a broad grin to Mugler. "Wonderful you got these traitors out of our apartment."

Mugler stared at the man. "Your apartment?"

"Our building," Kandl responded to Mugler's sarcasm.

"Very good. Just remember this apartment here is now property of the Reich and anyone who removes anything from it without authorization will be prosecuted."

"Of course," Kandl nodded.

The Eibers watched from the window of their tailor shop as Benno and Anna were placed in the police van. Bertha put her hands on her heart and said quietly, "Goodbye my dear neighbors, may God protect you." Then she withdrew to her apartment where she sat and cried. Ludwig stood watching at the window.

Outside the apartment building, Mugler handed the apartment key to a Gestapo agent who was sitting on the passenger side of a brown Mercedes.

### Milbertshofen

As they had suspected, Benno and Anna were taken to the Jewish transit camp called Milbertshofen. The place was not totally new for Benno. Like Willi Holzer, he had spent a week in the early stage of construction digging ditches for the foundation. And later Willi, who had lived at Milbertshofen in the days leading up to the November 20 deportations before he was left behind, had described the finished layout of the camp to him. But the realization that this crude camp with its bunk-style bed arrangement—more like shelves than beds—would be their new home, crowded together with many other dispossessed like themselves, was nevertheless shocking.

The barracks where Benno and Anna were placed was a bare wooden structure. Inside was a round wood stove ventilated through the ceiling. A false ceiling allowed for some insulation and the stove was adequate for maintaining a reasonably warm temperature. The barracks were kept spotless by the residents, which was a constant struggle, especially in rainy weather when it was nearly impossible to keep people coming in and out from bringing dirt and mud with them. The lack of adequate storage space meant that the barracks room, though clean, was always in a state of apparent disorder.

The Milbertshofen that Benno and Anna entered in the winter of 1941–42 was different from what it had been in the previous

November. Nearly all the young people, except for those used as low-wage laborers, had been moved out or deported. In a few lucky cases, some had emigrated. Now those in the "Judensiedlung I" or Jew colony, as it was called in Nazi reports, were overwhelmingly older people like themselves. And their numbers swelled, reaching 1,200 as the spring of 1942 approached and as further mass deportations loomed.

Several people were assigned by the Jewish Committee to greet new arrivals and give them an "orientation." Benno and Anna were shown the wooden racks with the straw bags that served as mattresses where they would sleep. They were brought to a separate barracks that served as a dining hall, and then another building where there were sinks for washing clothes and places to hang them to dry. These accommodations were very inadequate for the number of people living in the barracks, but they were there. Soap, among other needed cleaning products, was in short supply. Anna had brought some cleaning products with her and these were not confiscated when their bags were searched upon arriving at the camp.

On Benno and Anna's third day at the camp, Berthold's wife, Hilde, arrived. Benno saw her as she came into the camp and helped her with her bag. He asked about Berthold and then had to help Hilde sit down on a bench outside the barracks as she nearly fainted. "My Berthold is no longer with us," she said. Benno felt his heart begin to race. Unsteady on his own feet, he sat beside Hilde. "My Berty died of a heart attack, the day after we were told to leave our home."

Benno couldn't speak. He bit hard into his upper lip. A paralyzing sense of despair which he had up to this moment been able to stave off now overcame him. Hilde put her hand in his. He tightened his grip on hers. They sat silently for a time. Hilde looked over at Benno, who sat staring straight ahead. Tears were welling from corners of his closed eyes.

"I'm so sorry," were the words that escaped from Benno's lips. As Hilde leaned her head on Benno's shoulder, he wrapped his arm around her.

Sometime later, Hilde put her things in the barracks assigned to her and found Anna. She asked Anna to walk with her around the camp. As they walked arm-in-arm, Hilde said, "There's something I want to tell you, Anna, that I don't want Benno to know."

"What is it, Hilde?" Anna wrapped her arm more tightly around Hilde's.

"Bert did not die of a heart attack, Anna. He . . . he took his own life."

Anna embraced her friend. Only then did Hilde's agony pour from her. "My dear, dear Bert!" she sobbed, her body convulsing. "He said the pain was just too much for him. He said to me, 'We have only one thing left to us now—to decide how we die.'" Anna sat with Hilde on a bench outside a barrack. The two lifelong friends cradled each other in their arms and cried.

### A Tenuous Hold on Life

The brothers Willi and Louis Holzer arrived at Milbertshofen in the weeks that followed. Louis was downcast having heard nothing from his daughter Tilli and grandson Wilhelm since their deportation on November 20. But his daughter Hansi had made it out of the country and his third daughter, Ilse, was still living freely in Wolfratshausen thanks to her marriage to her Catholic husband, Hermann Schuster.

Willi Holzer was looking fragile. His separation from Hedi was very painful for both of them. When he was told that he was going to leave Berg am Laim while she would remain, he tried to console his daughter by saying that he would visit her regularly. But they both knew that his transfer to Milbertshofen meant he would soon be deported. "She is an essential worker, so she's safe for now," Willi told Anna. "What she is being paid is not enough to stay alive. But the Catholic Sisters make sure she gets things to eat. The Quakers also sometimes bring food to those remaining. Thank goodness for all of them."

Benno was not depressed as much as he was numb. When he was able to get some reading material like a newspaper, he was barely able to focus on it. He also was becoming more forgetful. If Anna saw him read something and asked him about it, he couldn't answer. He was still living, he thought, even while his life was over. There was only this breathing body and a mind capable of the most immediate and essential functions. Life without hope? Benno was cut off from all that had once been his life. Only Anna, his dear Anna, remained to sustain him.

Anna too, was largely cut off from her friends and relatives. She was still able to write to her cousin Ilse Schuster in Wolfratshausen, but their letters to each other were, by design, brief and contained little information. Hermann was fine, her children were fine, she was fine. She'd heard nothing from other relatives, including her sister Tilli and nephew Wilhelm. Ilse did not write to Anna about what she suspected nor about the rumors she heard from a relative on her husband's side, that everyone on the November 20 train to Riga had been murdered somewhere in the east.

Anna tried to keep herself busy helping to cook and clean. She joined a committee that was formed in her barracks. They tried to deal with the inadequate food supply. A woman from the Jewish Committee, Else Rosenfeld, came and counseled them on developing a system of organization for preparing food, for cleaning, and offering rudimentary medical care. Anna appreciated this kind and compassionate woman, who, while not Jewish, did all she could do to help these Munich Jews now in distress.

At first the camp dwellers were strangers and did not feel free to speak their minds to anyone but the closest friends and family, if they had them. Gradually some confidences between people developed, and they began to exchange information. But their isolation was such that little reliable information was available.

Despite everything, Benno was still alert to news about how the war was proceeding. He considered the German papers worse than useless, but one thought worked through his mind like an obsession—from every angle he could think of, with every scrap of information he could gather, he contemplated winter in Russia and what it must have wrought upon Germany's military.

## March 24

Benno and Anna had just sat down in the dining barracks when a member of the Jewish Committee called Benno's name. "Herr Neuburger, you are asked to visit the administration office," the man said.

When Benno got to the office, a camp manager was in conversation with several men in civilian clothes. "Are you Benno Neuburger?" one of them asked.

"Yes."

"You need to come with us."

"Who are you?"

"Special police."

The taller of the two men grasped Benno's upper arm tightly and escorted him out of the barracks.

"Can I inform my wife?"

"No!"

Benno was placed in a car and driven out of Milbertshofen.

## September 18 and 19, 1942

BENNO SPENT THE NIGHT IN Munich's Gestapo jail, a drab, concrete structure built in 1939 on the grounds of what was once the Wittelsbach Palace on Briennerstrasse.[38] No one spoke to him after placing him in a small windowless cell early that afternoon, nor throughout the night and most of the following day. He was given food late on the second day after his internment—a watery soup and a hard piece of bread. The soup reminded him of his weeks at Dachau following his arrest in November 1938.

In the afternoon, or at least what Benno thought was afternoon, of his second day in prison, he was taken from his cell and brought to a windowless room, bare except for several desks and chairs. The walls were painted gray. In one area there were smudges that looked like dried blood. The only light came from a single light fixture in the ceiling.

An expressionless Gestapo agent wearing a dark coat and pants seated him in a chair facing the larger of the two desks. Benno's arms were bound behind the chair's back. His legs were cuffed. He was left seated in this position for hours, unable to move. His breathing was labored because a rope placed around his torso was cinched tight.

Benno lost his sense of time. He thought it might be nighttime when the door opened, and a burly young man dressed in gray suit pants and a white shirt entered. The man was a thirty-three-year-old Gestapo agent by the name of Hermann Eckfellner. Eckfellner sat down at the desk across from Benno, opened a folder, and shuffled through a few papers in it. Before looking at Benno, he pulled out a handful of postcards and examined them, like a teacher might go through a student's homework. The interrogator then looked at Benno for several minutes without saying a word.

When he spoke, it was in a stern voice. "You are Israel Neuburger, are you not?"

Benno remained expressionless but he said "Yes" in a barely audible tone—one that reflected resentment at the insulting use of an imposed middle name and the way it was now being spoken.

The interrogator's closed hand came down hard on the desk. "I asked you a simple question!"

"Yes," said Benno.

"Tell me your date of birth," Eckfellner asked brusquely.

"March 4, 1871."

"Your marital status?"

"Married."

"What's your wife's name?"

"Anna."

"What's her maiden name?"

"Einstein."

The interrogator continued for some time to ask questions about Benno's family, his children, their whereabouts, his occupation, his income and assets, his associations. As the interrogator did so he made notes on a pad of paper on his desk. As Benno answered the questions the interrogator's became more matter of fact, almost cordial. The tension in the room lessened. Benno's intense anxiety also subsided somewhat.

"What's your address in Munich?" Eckfellner asked after a pause in the questions.

"Until March 16 of this year it was Trogerstrasse 44, apartment 3."

"Until March 16?" Eckfellner looked intently at the man sitting tied to the chair in front of him.

"On March 16 my wife and I were removed from our apartment and sent to a camp on Knorrstrasse."

"Until March 16 of this year, then, you lived at Trogerstrasse 44?"

"Yes."

"Are there letter boxes in your Trogerstrasse neighborhood?" Eckfellner asked as he gazed at Benno.

Benno hesitated before answering. "I believe so."

"You *believe* so?"

"My wife and I write letters to our children. We usually mail them in the letter boxes in our neighborhood."

"So you *know* so. You're familiar with the letter boxes in your neighborhood?"

Benno nodded.

"I can't hear you."

"Yes."

The interrogator paused. He then, once again, picked up the stack of cards on his desk and began shuffling through them. He laid down the stack and picked up several cards and waved them, one in each hand. "And you, Israel Neuburger, did you write these postcards and place them in mailboxes near your former apartment? Let me acquaint you with the contents. This one, found in a letter box in your neighborhood on September 20, 1941, refers to our country's leader, Adolf Hitler, as a 'mass murderer' and includes an expression of contempt. Do you recognize that?" The interrogator held the card in his hands so Benno could see the side with the printed words.

Benno's heart was thumping. He was feeling something between terrified and defiant. He said nothing.

Eckfellner got up from his desk and walked toward Benno with a card in his hand. "This one was found deposited in a box on Prinzregentenstrasse, in your neighborhood also, on October 1st.

After that first card, the letter carriers were put on alert for such mail, so they were the only ones to see them. All those who came across cards like these found them disgusting. This one says, 'The son of a bitch, Hitler. Murderer.' Did you write that?"

Still Benno remained silent.

"You had better say something, Israel Neuburger. What do you say? Did you write this trash?"

Benno hesitated, then shook his head no. The interrogator's open hand struck Benno forcefully across his cheek, stunning him. Before he could fully register what had happened, another blow struck him, so powerfully he almost toppled over in his chair.

"I can keep doing this, Herr Israel Neuburger. And I can have others in here who would be happy to have a go at you until your teeth are on the floor and your eyes are scattered like marbles around the room."

"Yes."

"What is that? I can't hear you, speak up."

"Yes." Benno spoke more loudly.

"Yes, what?" said the interrogator, practically screaming.

"Yes, I wrote them."

The interrogator smacked Benno again. This time so hard that the chair toppled over, and Benno's shoulder and head hit hard on the floor. The Gestapo agent stood over Benno and kicked him in the leg. Then he walked out of the room, leaving Benno tied to the chair in an extremely painful position. Benno passed out for a time. When the interrogator returned, he came in with several Gestapo officers. They righted the chair and blotted the blood from Benno's face and neck. Meanwhile, a note taker came and sat down at the smaller desk off to the side of the room.

Eckfellner, his hands folded in front of him, sat and looked at Benno. "Do you want water, Israel?" Benno nodded. A Gestapo officer who had remained in the room came over and put a glass of water up to Benno's mouth. He drank all the water in the glass. "You can tell us now how you came to write this scandalous crap, and who helped you write or distribute them. You can tell us the help you got from . . ." Eckfellner paused and stared intensely at Benno. "Anna, is that right? I should say, Anna Sara Neuburger."

"She did not help me at all," Benno spoke barely louder than a whisper.

"Speak up!" the interrogator shouted.

"She had no idea I was writing the cards," Benno said loudly.

Eckfellner, slammed his hand once again on the desk and yelled, "I want truthful answers, you Jewish worm!"

"That is the truth." Benno felt a sharp pain in his jaw as he spoke. At that moment his terrible fear was turning into anger and hatred. His life now hung by a bare thread. If he died at the hands of these soulless beasts, he would at least die as someone who, in some small way, stood up to their depravity. If he died, then so be it. This resolve helped him. He would not plead nor apologize. He would admit exactly what he did and why he did it. But he would not be forced to implicate anyone. He pleaded with himself not to capitulate.

As he proceeded, Eckfellner sensed this resolve. It made him want to continue the interrogation, wear down this old Jew until he was broken. But when, after a long session of threats and blows to Benno's face and body, he succeeded in getting Benno to say he had written all the cards and had been wrong to do so, the Gestapo man backed off.

As the principal investigator on the case of the subversive postcards, Eckfellner was tasked with finding the guilty party and providing the evidence for further action. There was interest in pursuing judicial action against Benno and he was now gathering the evidence needed to accomplish that. In this sense, he was satisfied with the way things were going.

Gestapo men were trained in the art of interrogation. This meant not just the use of brute force, which any lug could do, but the application of psychological methods as well. Extracting information and breaking the will of the accused at the same time, these were the skills valued in a Gestapo interrogator. Eckfellner had become skilled in his trade. He had risen in the Gestapo ranks because of that.

"You may want to know how we connected you to these postcards," Eckfellner offered during a lull in the questioning. "Well, it seems that the mark of your real estate company, or former company, was on the card we found posted on, let's see, February 21st, I believe." The interrogator showed Benno the card with the mark from his company. "And here," Eckfellner held out a small square block of wood in his hand, "is the stamp that perfectly matches the mark on the card. We found this in your apartment. I'd say it was not such a smart move." Eckfellner smirked.

Benno said nothing.

"You face serious charges, Israel Neuburger. The people in a time of war can't take lightly efforts to undermine morale by ugly slanders against our leader! You're a treasonous piece of shit, Herr Israel Neuburger. But what would we expect from a Jew, no? What could we expect? Still, we do have the capacity to forgive transgressions if the transgressor comes to express remorse for the damage they have inflicted. You understand me? Yes?"

Benno nodded.

### Admissions

Benno had admitted to the acts for which he had been detained and was willing to discuss the reasons for his actions. In the days that followed, Eckfellner pursued interrogations with the goal of ferreting out Benno's motives, to provide the court evidence of willful acts.

"You placed fourteen postcards in the mail anonymously, with words meant to defame our leader," Eckfellner restated at the beginning of another interrogation session.

"I don't remember how many cards, nor exactly what they said," Benno replied.

"But you did mail the cards I have here." Eckfellner showed the cards in his hand.

"Yes."

"And what led you to carry out these treasonable actions?"

Benno closed his eyes and remained quiet.

"Speak up!"

Benno breathed deeply. "I don't regard my actions as treasonable. That was not my intention."

Eckfellner sat back in his chair behind the desk. "Then what was your intention?"

"To oppose the injustice being done to me—to my family, to my community."

There was a sneer on Eckfellner's face. "Your community?"

"To my family. To the Jewish people of Germany. And Europe."

"An ambitious undertaking." The interrogator raised his voice. "Your goal was to protect 'your community' by insulting the leader of our nation?"

Benno did not try to hide the bitterness in his voice. "To respond to what has been done—is being done to us."

"Which is?"

"This government has taken our businesses from us, evicted us from our homes and forced my children to emigrate in order to earn a living. We've seen our synagogues destroyed, our community organizations disbanded..."

"Quiet!" Eckfellner came around his desk and stood over Benno. His tone was threatening. "In these ugly messages you call Hitler 'a murderer' and wish for his death. You write treacherous slanders against the leader of our nation!"

"I wrote that because Hitler has repeatedly..." Benno hesitated. "Repeatedly threatened to eradicate our entire people."

Eckfellner looked over at the stenographer. "If Jews continue to align themselves with those waging war against us, they risk... grave consequences. I believe that is a more accurate interpretation of our leader's words."

Benno looked down at his cuffed hands in front of him. "I know of people in Munich who while gravely ill and in need of medical care were deported, sent east. In other words, they were sent to their deaths."

"That's your supposition."

"My nieces and nephews were sent away months ago." Benno

looked directly at the interrogator. "We have received not one word from them. No doubt they too are dead—murdered most likely."

"You have no evidence of that," Eckfellner said sharply. "People are being sent east to be resettled, to start new lives."

Benno shook his head. "If they were alive, they would have contacted their parents, at the very least."

"But you don't know that. You are only making assumptions. You don't know where they went or their circumstances."

Benno did not reply.

Eckfellner glared at his captive. "On this card mailed on January 23, you wrote, 'Hail the New God of 1933 to 1943.' What did you mean by that?" When Benno remained quiet Eckfellner leaned forward. "I'll tell you. Your intent here is to see this government undermined and then violently defeated. Isn't that so!"

Benno shook his head. "No."

"By your hateful words you meant to arouse the people to violence against our leader and our government."

"I meant that the torment and injustice against us, against Jews, must end."

The interrogator stood up and shouted. "Through force and violence. This is clearly what you intended to provoke." He then took a drink from a glass of water on his desk and walked out of the room.

When Eckfellner returned an hour later, he questioned Benno about how and where he wrote his cards. Benno continued to insist that he wrote them and mailed them alone, without anyone else's knowledge. After several hours, he was returned to his cell.

When interrogations continued several days later, Eckfellner read through the postcards in order and asked for explanations of each word used to describe Hitler while a stenographer once again took down notes. Benno said he called Hitler an "idiot" because he thinks Jews have no minds of their own, a "thief" because of the money and properties stolen from Jews, and a "criminal" because of his vicious bullying of Jews. He called Hitler a "bastard" because he treats Jews worse than one would treat an animal.

During this interrogation period another Gestapo agent burst into the room. "Inspector Eckfellner," he said. "There is news I think you would appreciate hearing about."

"Now? It can't wait? What is it?" Eckfellner sounded annoyed.

"We have just received news of a significant breakthrough," the agent said. "Moscow has fallen into our hands! As we speak German tanks are making their way to the Kremlin, clearing out pockets of resistance. The combat is fierce, but our troops are fighting tenaciously and progressing toward their goal." The agent lowered his voice and spoke to Eckfellner, as though in private, but loud enough for Benno to hear. "There are indications that Stalin's people are seeking a means of surrender."

Eckfellner nodded pensively, then smiled. "Wonderful news. Thank you." The interrogator glanced at Benno, who did his best to hide the distress the news had caused him.

Eckfellner paused and acted as though he were reading some documents. He then looked up at Benno. "You know that all you have done is not only based on faulty assumptions—I call them delusions—and your actions have had no effect whatever on the situation you say you want to alter. You realize that, don't you?" Eckfellner continued, speaking slowly and deliberately: "You've accomplished nothing, Herr Israel Neuburger. Nothing. Except to create problems for yourself and great distress for your wife." Eckfellner picked up a paper and read or pretended to read from it. "Here is a document that discusses plans for a place, a sanctuary for elderly Jews like yourself—well, at least for those elderly Jews who represent no threat to the Reich—a special community. Let me read: 'A place, a community, where Jews can govern themselves, create their own cultural environment, and live in safety from persecution and war.' This comes directly from the authority in charge of the deportations you've been talking about. I happen to know that this community is being set up in a secure place outside Germany. This could have been your future, with your wife and other relatives—where you could have lived out your years."

Benno stared down at his cuffed hands.

Eckfellner put down the paper, stood up, and picked up a folder from his desk and walked around the desk to where Benno was seated. "I have here records from your military service in the last war." He looked at one of the papers closely. "There are favorable comments here. This is not an element in your history that we should overlook. In other words, your service to the country at one time, so contradictory to your recent actions, is nevertheless recognized. I want you to know we do take such history into account in these matters."

At that moment Benno remembered the joke he'd told to Berthold about Nazi respect for Jewish veterans—"last to the firing squad." Benno looked up at Eckfellner. "Cynical bastard," he thought, but he only nodded.

Eckfellner stood looking down at Benno. "Would you like to say anything?"

"No."

"You do regret what you've done. Isn't that so? Admissions of regret can have a favorable effect in whatever court proceedings you may face. Admit what you did was wrong."

Benno shook his head. "I did what I believe was the only option open to me. The only form of resistance possible for people like me."

Eckfellner changed to a more aggressive tone. "No. You've committed treason to our nation. And you've jeopardized your own life and caused pain to those you claim to care about. That is *all* you've done!"

A few days later, Benno was brought into the interrogation room for one last time. Here he was presented with a paper summarizing the actions he had admitted to. The confession concluded with a final paragraph that read: "In conclusion I'd like to remark that I haven't produced any other defamatory writings besides the above mentioned. I admit that I've been stupid to have written them since my hate for Hitler drove me to it. Hereby I'm stating that the above is true and correct and has been confessed by me without any force or pressure."[39]

"Herr Neuburger, is this confession accurate? Yes or no?"

Benno stared at the wall behind the interrogator and did not answer.

"Sign the confession." Benno again did not respond. "Why make this hard on yourself? You are only confessing to what you have already admitted here." To Benno's surprise, Eckfellner sat back in his chair. "Have it your way, Herr Neuburger. We have the evidence we need." The Gestapo man looked over at the stenographer. Then he got up and walked out of the room.

On April 4, 1942, after 11 days in Gestapo custody, Benno was told he would be transferred to another prison and then brought before a Munich court for formal charges to be entered. Before being transferred, he was taken to a room to be photographed for police records. As the photographer was preparing his camera, an inspector who had witnessed part of the interrogation told the photographer to wait. "Our Israel Neuburger is a formal dresser. We need to make sure he is dressed properly for his portrait photo."

The inspector left the room. When he returned, he had a bow tie in his hand. He stood in front of Benno whose hands were cuffed behind his back and placed the tie on the collar of Benno's white shirt. He left the tie angled below his neck. A colleague sitting at a desk in the room looked over at Benno's thin face, drawn and covered in bruises, his bowtie practically dangling from his shirt collar. "Hey, why don't we make a postcard from this photo and put it in the mail? Now that would provoke some terror." The agent grinned, delighted with his cleverness.

## Munich Prison

After being booked into the Munich-Neudeck prison, Benno was brought before the Munich District Court. He repeated in court what he had previously stated—that he had produced and mailed fourteen postcards denouncing Hitler and that he did so to express his outrage over the genocidal violence against Jews.[40]

District Court Judge Dr. Zeller issued an indictment on two

charges: treason against the Reich and treacherous attacks on Hitler. In denying bail, Dr. Zeller cited three reasons: one, because Benno was a Jew; two, because of the seriousness of the charges; and three, to protect him from a public that allegedly would be outraged by his actions.[41]

A week later, the main prosecutor of the special court in Munich informed the Reich main prosecutor at the People's Court in Berlin of the charges. This set in motion arrangements to send Benno to Berlin, where he would be put on trial.

Benno was not considered dangerous. From what the Gestapo men concluded, he was not part of some organization or movement and therefore, as an actor, not that important. The danger was the disquieting idea that Benno reflected something broader in society that could, under certain circumstances, become quite threatening. While the postcards did have very limited circulation, it was not true that the sentiments expressed in them could find no sympathy among the public. This was especially so because the war in the east, despite the Gestapo men's theatrics to demoralize their captive, was not going well. However much the regime's guardians avoided talking about it, this also weighed on them. It was this unease that likely brought about the decision to have Benno face a trial in Berlin's People's Court. The outcome could then be publicized in an effort to demonstrate how the Nazi government dealt "legally" with this kind of behavior.

## The "People's Court"

The Nazi People's Court was set up in 1934, utilizing special dictatorial powers granted Hitler by the Enabling Act which was invoked after the Reichstag fire of February 27, 1933. Passage of the Enabling Act, which was in the Weimar Constitution, required a vote of two-thirds of the Reichstag to become law. In order to fulfill this requirement, the Nazis took actions that were akin to an internal coup. They arrested and incarcerated the Reichstag's communist representatives. Then they used intimidation, including threats of violence, to generate the further votes they needed. Once the power was in their hands, the Nazis set about to establish an alternative court system suitable for enforcing the kind of social order that their extreme nationalist project required.

In the People's Court and other "Special Courts" set up after 1934, defendants enjoyed no presumption of innocence. There was no system of trial by a jury of peers. Defendants brought before the court were denied the right to choose their own defense attorneys. The defense was denied the right to cross-examine witnesses brought before the court. There was no genuine right to review or appeal court decisions. There was nothing but a procedure controlled totally by the Nazi Party, by which the regime could carry out its repression in an orderly fashion with the *trappings* of legality.

The court's vice president and one of its chief ideologues, Karl Engert, argued that the role of People's Court judges was to be politicians first and judges second. The meaning of that was best elucidated by one of the court's lead prosecutors, who stated that the court did not exist to dispense justice "but to annihilate enemies of National Socialism." Engert explained, "Just as the Wehrmacht has to safeguard the external existence of the state, the People's Court has a similar obligation for inner security in collaboration with the Gestapo."

To that end, between 1933 and 1945, the People's Court and other Special Courts sentenced around 16,500 people to prison or death inside Germany. The majority of these were foreign nationals, partisans of anti-Nazi groups in Europe, political dissidents, and slave workers brought to Germany during the war.

The unleashing of war in 1939 brought a leap in the repressive machinery of the Nazi legal system. When Germany invaded Poland there were three offenses punishable by death on the books. Five years later there were at least forty-six capital offenses. The number of accused brought before the People's Court for "serious political crimes" such as treason increased as the war progressed. The most dramatic increase in death sentences handed down by the court took place from 1941 to 1942 as Germany's difficulties in the war escalated. Georg Thierack, onetime president of the People's Court and later the most radical of all the Nazi Ministers of justice, defended the court's record of death sentences as necessary during wartime to maintain the home front against "defeatists and other such creatures."

### Anna's Search

When Benno didn't return from the Milbertshofen administration office, Anna felt a desperate fear. She began asking about what had happened to her husband, where he had been taken, and by whom, and why, but she got no answers. In truth, no one in the camp knew. Even those managing the camp had only been informed that he was "wanted for questioning."

Eventually word came to Anna that Benno had been taken in by the Gestapo, but no one could say why he had been arrested and what he was being held for. It took several months for Anna to find legal help. After bringing her concerns to others at Milbertshofen, including several former lawyers, she was able to arrange a meeting with a member of the Jewish Committee who agreed to help her. They reached out to Felix Koenigsberger, a former lawyer, who agreed to provide Anna with informal legal counsel. Like most Jewish lawyers in Nazi Germany, Koenigsberger had had his law degree rescinded after 1938. Unable to practice, he was reduced to the status of a "legal advisor," a position that carried no authority in a court of law. In pre-Nazi days, legal advisors were people without law degrees who advised low-income people on basic legal matters. If they wanted to practice at all, Jewish lawyers had to accept this position of simple advisors.

### Benno's Letter to Anna

On May 19, Benno was given permission to write a letter to Anna. He wrote:

Dearest Anna

I hope you are doing well. The same [I] can report about myself. I am terribly sorry that I cause you so much distress. I hope that this will change for you.

During the last few years, I suffered a great deal. I couldn't get the money from sold properties to support you.

I regret everything I did, especially since everything I have done has had no effect. And that nearly all our relatives and friends have been taken away. And as I heard yesterday, 14 days after we moved out, Erna Lohmann Wertheimer took her own life.

Such things have upset me a lot, and before.... I did get angry hearing about the exterminating and annihilation of the Jews. But it can't be tit for tat, hence, I did something which I should not have done, etc.

Now you know what I did, indeed. In fact, I never involved myself in politics—everybody is aware of this who knows me. I hope that this will clear up and I will be allowed to return home to you. For sure I will restrain myself and will never deal anymore, neither with politics nor with things which do not concern me.

I have a hard time thinking clearly now and I forget everything.

Please, dear Anna, be reassured and wait to see how everything will turn out for me.

Don't worry so much. Hopefully, something of the damage can be undone and the court deals with me in a humane manner....

Be greeted and kissed dearly from the one devoted to you.
Benno.
P.S. Please write, let me know how you are doing and be calm. I'm thinking of you and holding you tight.[42]

Two days after writing his letter, Benno ended up in the hospital ward of Munich's infamous Stadelheim prison. Anna never received the letter. The People's Court in Berlin ordered its confiscation after the prison directorate in Munich found that the letter contained a reference to the anticipated trial in Berlin.

### Awaiting Trial

On May 27, the president of the Second Senate of the People's Court set in motion preparations for Benno's trial in the Nazi People's Court. The court sent its accusations to Benno and appointed a Berlin lawyer, Dr. Heinz Bergmann, as Benno's public defense counsel. Bergmann declared he would respond to the charges from the People's Court.

On July 4, Benno was transferred from Munich's Stadelheim prison to Berlin and placed in the Berlin-Moabit prison to await trial. A date in front of the Berlin People's Court was set for July 20. [43]

Before the trial was to begin, Benno's lawyer, Dr. Bergmann, said he could not continue with Benno's case because of other matters. The People's Court appointed another lawyer, Dr. Ernst Decke-Cornill, in his place.[44]

### A Lawyer's Letter

It wasn't until June 30 that Anna's legal advisor sent a letter on Anna's behalf to the judge in Munich who had been presiding over Benno's case. In the letter he wrote:

> The wife of Benno Neuburger asked me to take on this case to clarify the circumstances of the arrest and the resulting prosecution of the defendant.
>
> Her 72-year-old [sic] husband is in custody in Stadelheim. The reason of the arrest is so far unknown. There are cases in which the crime has been determined as not too grave so that the authorities arranged that the accused before or after the sentence be transported to the East instead of going to prison. In the present case it concerns an elderly married couple where it is

likely that the wife will be, in the near future, transported to the East so that she most likely wouldn't see her husband again if he were to stay in prison in Germany.

I do not know if the crime of the accused is of such gravity that it is necessary to follow the law all the way through. But I hope that there be given concern to the advanced age and crime-free life of the defendant that it may be possible to grant him a transport instead of prison time.

I request to submit my concerns to the court.

Legal advisor Koenigsberger.[45]

Koenigsberger didn't know that the main prosecutor at the Berlin People's Court had already taken Benno's case and, on May 6, had issued an indictment. In that indictment they dropped the charge of "slandering the Führer" and focused on the more serious charge of "conspiring to commit treason." Koenigsberger received no reply to his letter.

## The "Trial": July 20, 1942

On the morning of Monday, July 20, 1942, Benno was taken by police vehicle from the Moabit prison to the Berlin People's Court (*Volksgerichtshof*) located in the former Wilhelms- Gymnasium in the city's Potsdamer Platz.

The main judge that day was Karl Engert, vice president of the People's Court. Engert sat alongside another People's Court judge, Hermann Granzow, who, like Engert, wore the official red robe. Three other Nazi officials, wearing the uniforms of their respective agencies, also functioned as judges. These were Gauamtsleiter (district party head) Fischer, Gaurichter (regional party leader) Kurt Kapeller, and Kreisleiter (district party leader) Anton Plankensteiner.

The judges sat in a row behind a long table at the front of the courtroom, with the bespectacled Engert in the middle. Directly behind Engert, carved in dark stone, sat a bust of Adolf Hitler.

Covering much of the wall behind the bust were bright red banners with large black swastikas surrounded by white circles. The dark wood-paneled walls and marble columns framing the banners lent the room an air of regal authority.

At 9:00 a.m., Engert called the court to order. Benno was asked to stand before the tribunal. Engert stated: "You, Benno Israel Neuburger have been charged with the crime of high treason."

High treason, defined as "acts that internally undermine the power and integrity of the state," was the most serious crime a person could be charged with in this court.

Neither Benno nor his defense attorney were asked how they pled to the charge.

After Benno was asked to be seated, the prosecutor, Dr. Meier, called the Munich Gestapo officer who had interrogated Benno, Hermann Eckfellner, to testify.[46] Eckfellner was the first and only witness. He presented the court with a rubber stamp that had Benno's name and address on it. "One of our agents found the stamp at the defendant's former residence," Eckfellner explained. "As you'll see, the markings on the stamp fit the markings found on a postcard mailed on February 21, 1942." The postcard and rubber stamp were handed to the judges for examination.

Then, Benno was asked to stand before the judges in order to answer questions about his personal life. Benno stood and tapped his fingers nervously on the table in front of him. His jacket hung loosely from his thin frame. The bruises from his interrogation had faded, but his face was pale and gaunt, and his eyes were deep-set. He answered the questions put to him by the senior judge about his age, marital status, the address of his former residence, and other personal information.

Then the Gestapo agent, Eckfellner, was again called to testify. The five judges had before them Eckfellner's interrogation report, a short Gestapo summation of their investigation, Benno's confession, and a report that contained a list of the fourteen postcards, the words written on them, and the dates they were mailed. Engert read several paragraphs from Benno's confession.

One of the other judges asked Eckfellner if the confession was given voluntarily.

"You'll see, in the last paragraph it is so stated," said Eckfellner.

At 9:55 a.m., the judges released the Gestapo interrogator.

Benno was once again asked to stand before the judges. Judge Engert held a paper with a list of the postcards. "Do you admit to having placed these postcards in the mail?"

"Yes." Benno's fingers once again tapped on the table in front of him.

"Were all of these slanderous remarks about the Führer written by you and put in the mail with the intention that others should see them?" Engert looked at Benno from behind his wire-rimmed glasses. "Please answer."

"Yes."

Engert looked to the judges on either side of him. "Treacherous slanders made against the leadership of our country at a time when our nation has been forced into a war that literally means life and death! Why did you write these remarks?"

Benno felt his heart racing. "To let the world know of the torment and injustices we are facing as Jews in this country."

"Injustices? Such as?"

"Such as my children being forced to leave the country of their birth to be able to survive. Such as my wife and I being evicted from our home. Such as members of my family being sent away, including some who were ill. Such as threats made to our community—"

Judge Granzow spoke up. "On one of these inflammatory cards you wrote, 'The Murderer of 5,000,000.' Where did you dredge up that slander?"

"There are ten million Jews in Europe. Half of them are in danger of eradication," Benno said, his voice wavering.

"Unjustified speculation!" said Engert sharply. "So rather than seek a legal remedy for these perceived 'injustices' you sought to instigate violence against our country. You sought to undermine our political authority—through your acts of treason."

"There is no legal remedy. All avenues of such action have been closed off. My intention was to bring public awareness . . . to the terrible conditions we are forced to live under. To the deadly injustices we are—"

"So." The judge picked up a paper and waved it. "This is how you seek a redress of grievances! Let me read from a postcard you apparently deposited in the mail on January 14, this year. 'Hail the God of 1933 to 1943.' What should we assume was going to happen after 1943? What 'God' were you proposing in place of our nation's leadership? What would our enemies think to read such a thing? Clearly this was meant to give comfort to our enemies and sap the will of our people." Engert picked up a paper from the table. "I will read from the report from our investigating agency." Engert glanced up at Eckfellner. "'The accused wanted to arouse indignation against the Führer in the population and prepare the ground for a cessation of these measures. It was, of course, also clear to the accused that a change in the Jewish policy of the Reich would only be possible after the removal of the Führer and the National Socialist government. He also undoubtedly recognized that the only way to get rid of the National Socialist government was by using force. That this means of attaining his ends was also right for him is obvious given the abysmal hatred that the accused harbors for the Führer and also follows from the content of the pamphlets.'" Engert pounded his fist on the table. "Isn't this exactly what our leader has warned us about? This Jew would see our nation destroyed by our enemies!"

"That was not my intention. I was trying to bring to attention—"

"How could anyone believe this attack on our nation was anything but an act of treason!!" The veins in Engert's neck stood out as he shouted his words. "What effect did our Israel Neuburger expect these messages to have when he brought them to public attention?" Engert looked to the judges on either side of him.

Benno closed his eyes and breathed deeply. "That there be demands for an end to our persecution . . ." Benno paused. "What I did, I did out of desperation. I've been under extreme stress with all the terrible things I, my family, and my community have been forced to endure. I was not thinking well."

"So, you were not in your own mind. Is that it?" Engert asked.

"Yes."

"You seem to be of sound mind now," Judge Granzow said skeptically.

"We have seen no evidence of any mental disfunction." Engert directed his attention at Gestapo Agent Eckfellner. "Did you find any evidence of mental deficiency, Inspector?"

Eckfellner stood up. "No, I did not."

"Did anyone else in your agency who encountered Herr Israel Neuburger notice any signs of insanity or mental instability in him?"

"No."

Engert looked at Benno. "Since there is no evidence of insanity, you can't resort to such a defense. The German penal code Article 51 allows for such considerations in a criminal case, but it is not applicable to this case. If none of the other judges have any more questions to ask"—Engert looked to either side once again—"we will move to close this session. We will listen to arguments about punishment." Engert turned to the prosecutor.

The prosecutor, Dr. Meier, stood up and addressed the judges. "The charge against the defendant has been proven without refutation. There can be no question but that acts such as those committed by the defendant in a time of national emergency require the most determined punishment. Anything less than the death penalty would be tantamount to undermining our nation's authority and integrity." At that, Prosecutor Dr. Meier sat down.

"And you?" Engert directed himself to Friedrich Wübken, Benno's defense attorney in court that day.

Wübken, who up until that point had said nothing in court, rose and walked to the defendant's table. "The defendant is an old man. He has never been prosecuted for a single crime in his life. He's a veteran of the patriotic war. And, in his own words, he was under great pressure which degraded his ability to think and act rationally. Given all these circumstances, while some punishment is due for this shameful attack on our nation and our leader, the court should consider that our cause can be served with a lenient sentence."

"Do you have a specific sentence in mind?" asked Granzow.

"The defendant is an old man. I suggest ten years. It's doubtful he would outlive his sentence."

"We will adjourn to consider these recommendations," said Engert. "Everyone, including our witness, should remain in the courtroom." The judges retired to another chamber. They returned in less than half an hour. Judge Engert stood behind the judges' bench and read the verdict in a flat but stern voice.

> In the name of the German people the People's Court hereby finds the defendant Benno Israel Neuburger guilty of the crime of conspiring to commit high treason. It sentences the defendant to be put to death. The convicted is hereby directed to pay for the costs of the trial and the execution.[47]

"The court is hereby adjourned."

Benno was led out of the courtroom. It was 10:55 a.m.[48]

The state asked for an execution fee of 300 Reichmarks and the full trial costs. These fees plus receipts for the defense lawyers, the costs for 167 days of imprisonment (1.5 Reichmarks for each day), and his last wish (2.15 Reichmarks) as well as the price for the printing and the distribution of the posters that would publicly announce the execution of his death penalty amounted to 1,065.55 Reichmarks.[49] This amount was to be drawn from Benno's account at the Munich Branch of the Dresdner Bank, an account that had been frozen to him.[50]

### Anna's Letter: July 23, 1942

In mid-July 1942, Anna was in the dining barracks at Milbertshofen with her brother-in-law Willi Holzer when Willi's brother Louis came in. Anna moved to make space for him. He sat and cupped his hands around his food bowl.

"You look worried today, what is it, Louie?" his brother asked. Without looking up Louis said, "They're sending me away tomorrow."

"What do you mean?"

"I got a note. I'm to take the transport at Milbertshofen station in the morning."

"Where are you going?" asked Anna.

"No destination was given. Though someone in my barracks said he thought it likely we'd be sent to Theresienstadt, in Czechoslovakia."

A week later, on the morning of July 22—two days after Benno's trial—Anna and Willi both received notices that they were to board a transport the next day. Anna, who still hoped that Benno would be released and allowed to rejoin her in Milbertshofen, was horrified at the news. She was further stricken by a short note she received from Benno on that same day. Before leaving on the transport on July 23, Anna Neuburger wrote a message to her cousin Ilse Schuster:

> Dear Ilse and Hermann,
> The time has come that I and Uncle Willi also are going to be moved away. I had a terrible day today and it looks as though I'll have to leave alone. I received a letter today from your Uncle [Benno]. Don't ask what he wrote. I shall talk to your father, dear Ilse. Stay healthy together you and your dear children.
> Sent you something today, hope you get it.
> The best of greetings,
> Your Aunt Anna.[51]

The next day Anna, Willi, and forty-eight other people were put on a truck and driven to the Milbertshofen train station, the same station from where, eight months earlier, Willi's family had departed, supposedly en route to Riga.

The deportees on the July 23 transport ranged in age from 45 to 83. Most, like Anna, were in their sixties. In their working lives they had been merchants, teachers, photographers, clerks, booksellers, salespeople, and homemakers. All had been forced out of their jobs and homes, stripped of their possessions, and often separated from their families by emigration, deportation, or death.

Those ordered to leave were allowed to carry only a suitcase or rucksack. In addition, they were instructed to carry their bedding, tableware and a spoon, food for eight days, and 50 Reichmarks of transport money. They and their luggage were searched before leaving Milbertshofen. Valuables that were found in their luggage were taken to be auctioned for the Reich, if not stolen by the inspectors or their bosses. The 50 Reichmarks in transport money had to be handed over to the Gestapo. If deportees had any extra money with them, it was to be held by a Jewish steward and given to the Gestapo to be placed in a special account of the Reich Association of Jews in Germany. Out of that any costs, in addition to transportation, were taken.

As ordered by the Reich Security Office, each deportation transport consisted of a single third-class car attached to a regular passenger train, such as the express train to Marktredwitz. This was done to shield these special transports as much as possible from public scrutiny.

At Marktredwitz, 200 miles north of Munich, near the old German-Czech border, the special car was detached from the express train and pushed onto a siding where it sat until it could be hitched to another train of cars filled with Jewish deportees from other parts of Germany.

### Bauschowitz Station

On the second day of travel, Anna, Willi, and the other passengers in the crowded cars saw signs indicating that the train had passed into Czechoslovakia. For many it was a great relief to know they were not going to Poland. Because of numerous stories of the brutal treatment Jews suffered in Poland, the very mention of that country caused nearly paralyzing anxiety.

On the afternoon of July 25, they arrived in the small Czech town of Bauschowitz. Armed soldiers stood along the tracks at the station as the train pulled in, and the officers among them began yelling to people to get off the train. Several men and women with white armbands, who were members of a Jewish Council of Elders, boarded the train and told the passengers that they were near their destination, Theresienstadt, which they described as "a Jewish ghetto community."

"Leave your belongings on the train, but carry your food, toiletries, and other items you might immediately need." Luggage, they were assured, would be brought to them later.

The Bauschowitz station was about 2.3 kilometers from the walled ghetto of Theresienstadt. This large concentration camp, referred to as the "special ghetto," was put into operation in November 1941. It lay a hundred miles northwest of Prague in the area that Germany seized in 1939, violating Hitler's agreement with Chamberlain and Daladier.

July 25 was a hot day, and for many passengers, already in a weakened state both emotionally and physically, it was an exhausting trek. Several passengers, unable to walk, were pushed to the ghetto in a wheelbarrow-like cart. The soldiers guarding them were grim and unfriendly.

As they neared the camp, the deportees walked between the raised embankment of the Ohre River and the massive brick walls of the fortress. Above the walls, they saw a white church steeple and the red slate tile rooftops of the barracks of what had formerly served as a military stronghold.

The new arrivals passed through the rounded gate of a short tunnel-like entrance and emerged into the fortress town of Theresienstadt. From there they were ushered into a processing barracks. Those who had brought bags or other belongings had them inspected. Each arrival had to fill out a form with personal information that included their work skills. From there, they were directed to the buildings where they were to be housed. Anna was sent to the second floor of the women's barracks with other elderly residents.

Anna had almost nothing but the clothes on her back and a bag with food, a towel, some toiletries, and her eating utensils. The luggage she and the other travelers had been promised was never delivered.

The beds in the women's barracks consisted of plain wooden stalls stacked three high. Those who were fortunate had thin straw mats to lie on. Others had to make do with a thin blanket or even little more than rags. Conditions were extremely overcrowded. The walled town had been built to hold 7,000 people, but when Anna and Willi arrived in late July 1942, it held more than 40,000. In some housing areas, there was one bathroom for as many as 50 people. In some cases, there was no indoor plumbing.

The prisoners worked hard to keep up decent sanitary conditions, but with few cleaning supplies, no way to wash clothes, and almost no shower facilities, this was impossible. The water from the faucets was discolored and smelled bad, but the deportees were forced to wash with it and even drink it. This led to widespread stomach problems and diarrhea. However healthy the newcomers may have been when they arrived, their health deteriorated rapidly.

In the coming weeks they saw familiar-looking clothes—items they had brought with them in their luggage—being sold to other deportees fortunate enough to have money or something of value with which to purchase them in the ghetto store. These were the items of lesser value. Better clothes and jewelry from the luggage never made it to the Theresienstadt store. They were shipped off to Germany.

### Theresienstadt "Spa"

It was Reinhard Heydrich, the SS general, head of the Reich Security Office, and lead organizer of the genocide of Europe's Jews, who was most responsible for the creation of the Theresienstadt complex. The idea for this "special ghetto" emerged in conversations between Heydrich, Adolf Eichmann, and Heinrich Himmler. They saw a need for a camp for elderly Jews, Jewish war veterans, prominent artists and musicians, and personages known to the public—one that would serve the goal of eliminating them without appearing to do so. Theresienstadt would be introduced to the world as a "model community," "a gift to the Jews," and "a spa." Heinrich Himmler, head of the SS, which ran the concentration and death camps, described Theresienstadt as "not a camp in the ordinary sense of the word, but a town inhabited and governed by Jews, in which every manner of work . . . is done. This type of camp was conceived by me and my friend Heydrich, and this is what we had intended all camps to be."

He was truthful in one sense. Theresienstadt was like every camp set up by the Nazis, since it had the same intended, if unspoken, purpose: genocide. For above all else, Theresienstadt was a conduit—or, in Nazi terminology, a "flood gate," a "transit hub," or "feeder camp"—for the extermination camps in Poland, Belarus, and elsewhere.

A short distance from the walled town there stood a part of the fortress complex called the Small Fort. In the summer of 1940, the Germans began using the Small Fort as a prison where Czechs considered dangerous to the occupying regime were tortured and murdered. Later, when the Theresienstadt ghetto was opened to incarcerated Jews, the Small Fort become a death camp for Theresienstadt prisoners accused of violating ghetto rules.

The first trains to arrive at Theresienstadt in the winter of 1941 carried Czech Jews, who were pressed into service as slave laborers. They prepared the old walled fortress town for the tens of thousands of Jews from around Europe who would be sent there. Theresienstadt opened for operation in November 1941. Beginning in early 1942, the Nazis interned the Jews of the Czech provinces of Bohemia and Moravia there. Soon after, Jews from other areas of Czechoslovakia, Germany, and elsewhere began arriving.

Shortly after Theresienstadt opened, Nazi authorities approached wealthy Jews from Austria and Germany, describing a community where their futures would be secured. If they turned their property and possessions over to the Nazis, they would be guaranteed a comfortable apartment in this new "Jewish settlement." They were promised domestic help, adequate food, and medical care. They were told they would be permitted to maintain correspondence with their families, that their billets would be adequate and warm, that they would be given paid work, and that their families would not be deported to Poland. They were even told that more money would guarantee them a "room with a view." The wealthier families who agreed to this arrangement were brought to the camp in first-class railcars.

When they arrived, they were left at the train stop for hours as part of a strategy of psychological torment. While this was happening, observers took notes documenting the effects this technique had on the detainees. This was a part of a larger effort by the Nazis to "improve" their methods of torment. After several hours, these wealthy deportees were stripped of all they had brought and marched into underground tunnels with dirt floors. There, they were locked into dark cages and left to slowly starve.

Between November 1941 through the fall of 1942, 16,000 Theresienstadt internees died of illness and starvation. Another 43,879 were put on transports and sent away, mainly to Poland.

Many of those who remained were sick. At the height of the ghetto's population in the summer of 1942, 30 percent suffered from illnesses, especially chronic diarrhea from the rotten, nearly inedible food and polluted water. The elderly deportees were hit especially hard. Since most were stripped of their possessions when they arrived, they had nothing with which to barter for food. While young people put to work at slave jobs in and around the camp were given enough food to continue working, the elderly ghetto inhabitants had no access to the food stores and were given very little to sustain themselves.

When Anna arrived at the ghetto, she was relatively healthy. She set to work helping with sanitation, cooking, and serving. Though she felt a deep sense of despair, she tried to push those thoughts away and concentrate on dealing with the onerous conditions. She derived her strength from her capacity to be of use to others.

Mutual solidarity was the only pillar that she had to cling to. Within a matter of several weeks, Anna's health began to deteriorate. Willi Holzer, already weak when he arrived at Theresienstadt, was also in serious decline.

Death surrounded them. In mid-July 1942, on average, 32 people died every day. By September, that number reached 131 per day. Among the busiest workers were those who pushed the carts that carried the dead to a gate from which they were taken to the burial ground outside the camp. Funeral processions, which, at one time, were organized to accompany the dead to the outer gate, essentially ceased as the sheer volume of death overwhelmed and numbed the living.

During her first weeks in Theresienstadt, Anna sought the help of the Council of Elders, the Jewish leadership in the camp, in reaching Benno. She asked to send messages to Munich to her cousin Ilse, to her legal advisor Koenigsberger, and to Jewish authorities in Berlin to let Benno know where she was. She was told that the SS camp commander had prohibited all communication by inmates with the outside world, as retaliation for a rule infraction that had occurred earlier in the year.

### The Council of Elders

In June 1942, after the last of the non-Jewish residents of Theresienstadt were removed from the walled town, the Nazis appointed a Jewish Council of Elders and gave them authority to manage the ghetto. The Council made efforts to improve sanitation and health care and to organize cultural and academic events. Because Theresienstadt had among its prisoners some of Europe's most talented singers, writers, actors, and directors, a schedule of musical performances, plays, and operas emerged. In exchange for this additional authority, the Council was tasked with drawing up lists of people for the transports leaving Theresienstadt for other camps. The SS demanded that emphasis be put on sending away, first and foremost, the elderly and the sick.

The cultural presentations allowed prisoners some momentary relief from depression and grief. They offered the deportees opportunities to laugh, to consider ideas beyond the grinding struggle for survival, and to feel a vicarious sense of justice watching a play that used disguised language to condemn or ridicule their oppressors. These were welcome, if fleeting, moments of release from the immediate reality of the camp and from the paralyzing fear and anxiety caused by the ever more frequent announcements of transports heading for unannounced destinations.

To allay these fears, the Council of Elders assured everyone that the destinations of those being sent away from the overcrowded ghetto would be no worse than what they presently suffered.

The leaders of the Council, however, eventually knew better.

### Hilde and Mina

In August, Anna saw several familiar faces arrive at the women's barracks. First Hilde, thin and tired, arrived on a transport from Munich. Anna hugged her old friend and grasped her trembling hand as they looked for an empty sleeping space near Anna's bunk. Then, on August 20, Anna's sister Mina arrived on a train with deportees from Laupheim. Upon seeing each other the sisters embraced, each feeling in their thinning bones and bodies the toll time and anguish had taken on them. Seeing both Hilde and Mina boosted Anna's will to persist. Anna explained to Mina their eviction from their home at Trogerstrasse, their internment at Milbertshofen, and Benno's arrest.

"Ilse Schuster sent me word about your deportation, Anna," Mina explained to her sister. "She wrote to me about the note you sent her before you left Munich, and something about Benno. But it wasn't clear what. Do you know where he is?"

"I think he's in Berlin, in prison . . . I'm trying to find out, trying to get word to him."

Mina grimaced. "And what about Fritz and Hani? Have you heard anything from them?"

Anna shook her head. "Nothing since November. Now with the war, it's impossible to communicate. What about Laupheim?"

Mina's faced turned ashen. She looked at Anna and Hilda with dark eyes moistened by tears. "Our beautiful Jewish Laupheim . . .is no more."

### Benno in the Plötzensee

On July 2, Benno was sent directly from the People's Court to the Plötzensee prison in the Charlottenburg-Nord district of Berlin. The Plötzensee, built in the 1870s, was originally a prison for people convicted of civil crimes. When the Nazis took control of the Plötzensee in 1933, they turned it into a prison for people convicted of acts of resistance against the Nazi state, and converted a prison workshop into an execution room.

In 1936, Hitler gave approval for a guillotine to be used for Plötzensee executions. The guillotine was deemed to be faster and more efficient than hanging.

After 1939, the pace of the executions at the Plötzensee accelerated. This reflected the increased anger of the populations under German control—including among Germans themselves—and the growing paranoia of the regime. Between 1933 and 1945, 2,891 people were put to death in the Plötzensee death house. Fifty percent of those killed were Germans; the others were Poles, French, Norwegians, Dutch, Belgians, and other Europeans, mainly members of resistance organizations or people deported to Germany for forced labor. Among the executed were three hundred women.

### The "Appeal"

Benno's death sentence provided for an automatic appeal process. The appellate judge in this case was the same Hermann Granzow who presided over the original trial, verdict, and sentencing.

In a ruling to uphold the conviction and sentence, Granzow wrote:

Between September 1941 and February 1942, Benno Neuburger mailed fourteen postcards containing disgraceful and slanderous remarks against the Führer. The contents of these cards have been documented earlier. But I would like to add the contents of postcard number nine in which it is declared that there are about 10,000,000 Jews living in Europe from which half are in danger of eradication.

He went on reiterate, almost word for word, what the court had previously declared when it found Benno guilty and sentenced him to death. Then he added a terse statement that summarized the Nazi view of Jews in general:

The only just punishment therefore is death to ensure the safety of the Reich. The idea that the defendant has been deprived of his rights as a citizen is out of the question since Neuburger enjoys no rights due to a citizen because of his heritage. Furthermore, the participation of Jews in public life is already restricted or not lawful.

Finally, the "appeals" judge affirmed, "The costs of the trial are to be fully paid by the defendant."[52]

### The "Plea for Clemency"

Responding to an appeal for clemency submitted by a "defense lawyer" who admitted he'd had no time to read the verdict in the case, the director of the Alt-Moabit prison in Berlin sent a letter on July 29 to the Prosecutor of the People's Court of Berlin stating:

Neuburger was kept here for only a short period of time from July 8 to July 21, 1942. During this time, he behaved according to the house rules and also worked satisfactorily but without any extra effort. Neuburger is a stubborn Jew who has no regrets whatsoever for his crimes. In a bold and brazen way, he said, "The state has harassed me in a most offensive way for nearly ten years. I therefore had no other expectation than a death sentence."⁵³

The director concluded there was nothing to justify any measure of clemency.

On September 3, the Reich Minister of Justice, Otto George Thierack, wrote in response to the plea for clemency:

> I conclude with the approval of the Führer not to grant a pardon but to give free rein to the course of justice. In the criminal proceedings against Neuburger, sentenced to death by the People's Court in Berlin on July 20, 1942, I deliver a final copy the enactment from September 3, 1942, with a request to urgently execute the judgment.⁵⁴

Dr. Wilhelm Crohn, Head of the Criminal Law Department in the Reich Minitry of Justice, added a comment directing that "the corpse is to be sent to the Anatomical Institute of the University in Berlin according to Article 39 of the Reich Constitution of February 19, 1939."

## The Waiting

Benno was held in a cell by himself in the Plötzensee following the trial. The other prisoners called his cell block the "house of death."

The court had issued no execution date, and Benno was given no further word about his case once he was placed in his cell. Not knowing when the sentence would be carried out meant living in fear of early mornings, when executions were conducted, or evenings, when, he eventually realized, prisoners were notified of their coming doom. It meant living with the terror of the approaching bootsteps in the corridor and the clank of keys in cell locks. It meant relief when his cell remained closed, and the sounds of footsteps receded. It meant the dismay of realizing that the price of his own relief was someone else's unjust death.

Benno had no face-to-face contact with his death house neighbors. He knew none of their names. He had no idea if any of them were Jewish, or what religion or belief they professed. He occasionally saw one or another when he was taken from his cell for exercise or a shower, once or twice a week. But communication from cell to cell was nearly impossible because each cell was sealed with a metal door that had only one small opening near the floor where food was shoved in and empty plates pushed out. Even so, he felt a quiet kinship with his cellblock mates that grew with the weeks. They were there because they hated fascism enough to have resisted. That fact alone made him feel a brotherly connection with them.

In the solace of his cell, he listened carefully to every sound for a clue to his surroundings. He tried to decipher every word a sentry spoke within earshot, every word that could be heard from any of the cells in the block. He tried to divine the rhythm of the prison from the steps in the passageway and from the creak and clatter of doors. Several times at night he heard what he thought were sobs. A few times he heard banging sounds and words in a language he didn't understand, in a tone that denoted agony.

During his third week in "the death house," he heard the cell next to his open and a new prisoner, a young man he guessed from the voice, moved in. One evening some days later, after food was brought to the cells and the sentries were gone, Benno heard what he thought was someone speaking in that adjoining cell. Through the door slot, Benno said, "*Kannst du mich hören?*" (Can you hear me?) When he heard no answer, he asked, "*Sprichst du deutsch?*" (Do you speak German?) He was greatly pleased that his words were heard, even if the answer back was "*Nein.*" After a pause, the man said, "*Ein bisschen Deutsch*" (A little German), followed by "*Parlez-vous francais?*" Benno answered with "*Je parle un petit peu francais*" (I speak a little French)— which was true, he knew very little French. They both laughed.

Benno, lifted by the meager but recognizable communication, said to his neighbor jokingly, "*Du bist jetzt in Deutschland, du solltest Deutsch sprechen*" (You're in Germany, you should speak

German). To which his neighbor replied, "*Parle français s'il te plait*" (Speak French, please!), which Benno understood. This gave him a good laugh. Realizing their conversations were going to be very limited, Benno said, "*Gute Nacht.*"

His new friend replied, "*Bonne nuit.*"

In the days and weeks that followed, they made renewed attempts to communicate. His French neighbor would tap before speaking and this became the new signal that a "conversation" would be coming. Benno did the same. Most of the time they said little more than "Good evening, how are you?" But Benno tried to push things. He was especially interested in any news about the war. By that point he had been in prisons for five months, so he thought his neighbor would have more up-to-date information. He asked, "*La guerre Russo-Aleman, finie?*" (The Russian-German war, over?)

To his delight his neighbor understood and answered, "*No finie. Les russes gagnent la guerre.*"

Benno did not understand the word "*gagnent.*" So he asked, "*Gut oder nicht gut?*" (Is that good or not good?)

His neighbor answered, "*Gut.*"

In this way Benno realized that Russia had not lost the war, had not sued for peace, and that his interrogator in Munich had put on an act. This realization made him feel better. The war was still going on and there was a chance that Germany would lose. Another freezing winter for Germany in Russia might mean defeat. Could he live long enough to see such a thing? He doubted it.

And he recalled Berthold's words, several years before: "If it looks like Germany will lose the war, they'll throw us on the bonfire."

## September 17

Benno ate his usual meal—an unsavory watery glutinous concoction, like bread soaked in water or in a thin vegetable broth—and sat on his cot. Before dinner he had paced his cell for several hours and did some exercises to stretch his muscles. He was about to lie down when he heard footsteps approaching and then the clang of a key in the lock of his cell. Four men entered, and Benno, startled, stood up.

The report of the visit was recorded by a prison clerk:

> At 8:18 p.m. they [representatives of the People's Court] went in the company of the representative and administrative assistant of the prison Herr Schmidt and the prison physician Dr. Schmidt to see the prisoner Benno Israel Neuburger in his cell. The Head of Execution after verifying the identity of the prisoner explained to him that he was there on behalf of the Senior Reich Prosecutor of the People's Court. After that he continued to read slowly and clearly to the prisoner the significant part of the judgment against him. Furthermore, he let him know that his appeal was denied by the Reich Minister of Justice in conjunction with Hitler. Finally, he disclosed to the prisoner the day and time of his execution and advised him to prepare for it and that he could voice any special last requests to the prison guards. At 8:20 p.m. the representatives left the prisoner. Lastly, I like to remark that the prisoner stayed calm during this visit.
>
> Signed: Senior State Counsel Wittmann and the Judicial Clerk Karpe.[55]

### The Last Night

Benno's last night was a sleepless one. He thought about the letter he'd written Anna expressing regret for his actions. He thought that if he'd been asked to write another one in that moment, it would be different. He often went back and forth in his own mind about this letter. When he wrote those words, Benno wanted to soften the blow he knew Anna would feel. He wanted to sustain hope in her and, yes, in himself as well. He knew he had this tendency to back away from facing reality. But he also realized that, since his arrest, whenever he'd been confronted directly about his actions, his reaction had been defiance. He felt it when facing the Gestapo interrogator, and he felt it during the farcical trial. At the Berlin-Moabit prison, when he was asked if he had regrets, his impulse was to spit in the face of the beast. He had resolved that he would rather die than bow before them, and he had managed to retain that resolve. Now he was going to die, and he would do so with a heart full of contempt for them.

During the long months he'd spent in prison, Benno had turned his thoughts over many times. He had thought about his father-in-law Moses and his plea to maintain the traditions that would keep their community anchored in the storms of oppression. But it wasn't the traditions Benno most valued. He was not attracted to an exclusive tradition that kept a community within its own boundaries. He wanted a community that drew strength from its history and connected their traditions to the broader experience of the world. He saw the uselessness of separation and exclusivity. And, in Nazism, he saw the deadliness of a worldview that elevated one group over another.

Nazism was the most extreme form of alienation and separation. It disconnected people from their common kinship. Kinship, yes! Nazism wasn't just an assault on Jews; it was an assault on the idea of human commonality. It is only in this commonality that humans are human at all, Benno thought. If he were able to go on living, what would he do with this new insight?

At one point, a thought overtook him—one that had sustained him during some very dark nights: His children were out of reach of the fascists! This had become one of Benno's preoccupations—the idea that the Nazis were not only out to murder his community, but to erase the memory of its existence. The burning of the synagogues, the closing of the newspapers, the seizing of property, the confiscation of businesses, the burning of the books, the enclosure of people in camps and prisons, the executions—what was all of that if not the attempted annihilation and erasure of a people? What did Hitler say, "for a thousand years"? The disappearance of memory was a horror even more terrifying than dispossession and deportation. But with his children, that memory would be preserved and passed on. Benno yearned for a moment to sit with his children and explain all that he had gone through and learned.

"My dear ones . . ." he said to himself as the night waned and as his body convulsed in sorrow, fed by a painful longing for his wife, his children, for his nephews and nieces, friends, the community—as he was now being pulled into the grave . . .

### Benno's Last Request

Last will and testament, Berlin-Plötzensee, on September 17, 1942:

> I, Benno Israel Neuburger, wish and decree and ask to grant me that my body will be allowed to lay to rest by the Jewish community in Berlin. Even though I'm a member of the funeral expense fund "Plonie" in Munich I direct that the expenses for this will be drawn from my account number 65331 at the Dresdner Bank in Munich. Further I request that an inexpensive gravestone or a memorial slab will be purchased for the burial place. I wish and request to be buried by the Jewish Community in Berlin in the presence of a rabbi. All those costs should also be drawn from the above-mentioned bank account. I further ask that the cultural municipality in Munich and of course my wife be notified. I decree that my last wishes be fully granted. Signed by Benno Israel Neuburger. Also, I ask that my watch and all my other possessions may be sent to the cultural municipality in Munich.[56]

### The Road from Theresienstadt

As the summer of 1942 progressed, the SS overseers of the Theresienstadt ghetto increased the tempo of deportations "to the east." They told the Council of Elders this was necessary to alleviate the deadly overcrowding. The overcrowding was purposeful and in line with goals laid out at the January 1942 Wannsee Conference—it was an important element in the Nazis' plan for total genocide. The SS Commandant Adolf Eichmann played a central role in organizing the transports.

For the prisoners at Theresienstadt, fear of the transports overwhelmed every other aspect of camp life.

The Council of Elders selected the names of deportees for each transport and posted them in the morning the day before the scheduled departure. On September 17, Anna and Hilde checked the list in the women's barracks. Much to their alarm they found their names on the register for the train set to leave on September 18. Anna saw that Willi Holzer was also on the list.

Anna told Mina about the transport and then she wrote a note to Willi and Louie, which was sent to the men's barracks through the message service the Council had set up for communication in the ghetto. Because the messages to and from people on transport lists and their immediate relatives were given priority, Willi and Louie received the message within a short time.

Willi, Louie, Anna, Mina, and Hilde met at the food line that evening. Anna was deeply distraught. At the beginning of September, she had received word from the Council that the communication ban with the outside world was being lifted. She immediately wrote several postcards in the format demanded by the SS—no more than thirty words, in German, in block letters. One card was addressed to legal advisor Koenigsberger in Munich, the other to a Jewish community organization in Berlin. She asked for help in locating Benno and requested that he be informed of her and Mina's whereabouts. She had been waiting for a reply. But now, she was about to be moved.

The dinner that evening was chaotic. Several of the residents, weak from hunger and worn down by depression and illness, vented their despair with caustic words. One older woman called out bitterly, waving her food card as she moved stiffly down the serving table, "We're leaving tomorrow. We need to eat! We need more food. We'll die on the train, weak as we are!"

The food servers were helpless, and they too began to get short-tempered. "You can only have your share, not more! If we had more, we'd give it. We're not hiding food. We're all being starved."

"I know some people get more than others around here!" the woman shouted. "Because we're old and poor, we're being shoved into the garbage bin and left to die! Don't tell me otherwise. We should be a community, but there is no community, no solidarity, no compassion! The beasts can do what they will with us because we do it to each other!"

A member of the Jewish committee tried to calm her down. Someone came up with extra potatoes and bread, and the woman took the food and sat down sullenly. Her anger was like a single crack of thunder in a lightning storm. She spoke the bitter agony that everyone felt, especially those in the elder barracks, but were too worn or too resigned to express.

Anna, Willi, Louie, Mina, and Hilde got their food and sat at a long table with a dozen others. Mina and Hilde were lucky to find tiny bits of meat in the unappetizing turnip gruel. Louie quietly pulled several potatoes from the pocket of his worn pants and placed them on the table. With a fork he cut them and gave pieces to Willi, Anna, and Hilde, with wishes for luck on their trip.

Anna told her brothers-in-law about her efforts to reach Benno.

"You're sure he's in Berlin?" asked Louie.

"This is what Koenigsberger was told by a contact of his."

"The legal advisor thinks Benno is facing a trial in Berlin," Mina added.

A man sitting nearby looked up from his food bowl. "You know someone who is being put on trial?"

Anna turned to him. "My husband. That's what a legal advisor told me."

"Your husband's a Jew?"

Anna nodded. "Yes, of course."

"They put him on trial? For what?"

"I'm not sure. I got a note from him before leaving Munich. He didn't say where he was—only that he would not be returning to Munich. He wrote"—Anna paused, suddenly overcome by the thought—"that he might not be long in this world." Anna placed a hand on her mouth. As she closed her eyes, tears spilled down her sunken cheeks.

The man's voice softened. "I'm sorry. What was the situation?"

Anna breathed deeply. "I think he put something about Hitler in the mail. He never told me, but that's what I think. One time, I saw a postcard he'd written with words about Hitler. But I never asked him about it. After the Gestapo took him away from the Munich camp, I got help from a Jewish legal advisor. He said he heard through a contact that Benno—that's my husband—was charged with a crime and sent to Berlin."

"To the People's Court, probably." The man spoke slowly and quietly. "If you say Hitler has bad breath, that's the court they send you to, if they bother to send you to court. How rare it is that they bother with such niceties with one of us."

"When Benno heard how they took sick people from the hospital in Munich and put them on a train to Riga, he said, 'This is outright murder; there has to be an outcry about this.' He was very upset when my nieces and nephews were sent away—Willi and Louie's children." Anna nodded toward her brothers-in-law. "So, when I found out he'd been arrested by the Gestapo, I thought it must be connected to that."

The man nodded. "And you think he's still alive?"

"I can't give up."

"If I were a religious man, I'd say, God bless your husband! You can be proud that he did something to resist." Anna gave a wan smile to the man. Then she took a moment to look more closely at him. She guessed he was in his early sixties. But it was hard to tell since stress and bad treatment at the camp aged people quickly. He had short, sparse, wiry gray hair. His eyes, rimmed with red, had the look of extreme fatigue, and his face was drawn and thin—not uncommon in this camp.

"Aren't you a member of the Council?" asked Mina, who recalled seeing this man explaining about rules in Theresienstadt when she arrived in August.

"Yes, was. Now, well, I'm going on the transport tomorrow. I was given a choice: a trip to Little Fort up the road or a train ride somewhere, probably to Poland. I assume, since I was given that choice, that it's no choice at all. I'll have to take my chances. But then, I guess I like to travel." He smiled grimly.

Willi struggled with his shaking hand as he took a spoonful of his dinner soup. "Aren't the Council of Elders protected from the transports?"

"They usually are. That's why I was kicked off the Council."

"Why were you removed?" asked Hilde.

"Let me explain. I agreed to join the Council in the first place because I thought that if we had some position, something to offer the SS, we could protect people from the worst abuses. We did some good, helped with sanitation and other health efforts. We were able to make use of the talent that's here—the artists from around Europe—to put on cultural programs."

Louie's face lit up. "I saw a play last week at a little theater near the men's barracks." He laughed. "I heard some funny lines, especially unflattering references to the Nazis and the SS." He leaned forward as though sharing a secret. "I looked at the SS men who were in the back of the room watching it. And they had no idea what was going on—why we were all laughing, or that we were laughing at *them*."

"We have some clever writers here," the former Council member said. "And courageous too. It doesn't take much to rouse the ire of, well, you know who. And then it's a trip to the Little Fort. And that's the end of you."

Hilde smiled. "We were at an outside concert several days ago." She looked at Mina and Anna who nodded. "So nice to have a few moments of escape from this place."

Everyone at the table was staring into what remained of their food. Hilde was the first to break a short silence. "We don't know where we're going tomorrow."

The ex-Councilman shook his head. "No."

"Riga, possibly?" Willi spoke expectantly.

"Could be Riga, could be Lodz, could be Lublin, or some other Polish ghetto or something worse." The ex-Councilman shrugged. "I don't mean to frighten you, but why lull ourselves with false hopes? People on previous transports sent cards from their destinations saying things are about the same for them or even better. But we on the Council were suspicious of those messages. So, on the last few transports, we gave people code words to use when writing their notes so that the Germans wouldn't understand them. And those messages painted a different picture—that we've been lied to."

"Some people say that it can't be worse than this here,'" Willi said.

The Councilman shook his head. "Should we forget how Hitler has threatened us, again and again?"

"It's one of the things that outraged Benno," Anna added.

"I'm glad he did something," said Mina.

"And now the Council of Elders has become something I can't be part of. The Council members use their leverage to keep people they are close to off the transports. Privileges for services rendered." The man pushed his bowl away and took a deep breath. "That's another tragedy here. We've become complicit in our own destruction. I've made compromises, but I have my limits. I told them that. I said, let's just stop all this! Word got back to Haindl, the SS thug who runs this place. So, now, I'm just a troublemaker." The man reached his hand across the table and placed it on Anna's. "Like Benno." Anna nodded. "Please forgive me for going on like this. But it's just—I've been accused of being a shit stirrer in my day." He laughed. "Old habits die hard!"

"Where did you come from?" asked Anna.

"Berlin. Before Hitler, I was in the publishing business. Before that I was a soldier in the war. I joined the rebellion that erupted afterward. I was there when the Kaiser ran away. You must remember those days?"

"Of course," said Anna. "We had our rebellion in Munich."

"Eisner, of course. We thought we could change things for the better, isn't that right?" the ex-Councilman asked.

Anna nodded, as did Hilde. "A lot of us were hoping for more peaceful times," Anna said.

"An end to this militaristic bullshit!" the ex-Councilman said, suddenly more excited. "I came out of that war very angry when we realized that people were put up to slaughtering each other, for what? So one group of bandits could prevail over another? The military didn't like us saying such things and they sent the Freikorps to shoot us down. You know what I mean by the Freikorps?"

"Of course," said Hilde. "They came to Munich, in 1918 or '19."

"They started a lot of this anti-Jewish business," said Anna.

"That too! They were Nazis before the Nazis! But then things settled down. Then there was Weimar. And I got to believing that things would evolve in a better way, little by little. Now I'm thinking like I used to. Capitalism is a bloodthirsty system and Hitler is just its latest, most vile, instrument."

Louie shook his head. "It's not really capitalism. Hitler's some twisted perversion of capitalism. Nazism is slavery, something like that. I was in business, so was my brother, Willi. So was Benno. We made our money buying and selling, working hard. But we did it honestly."

"You were small fry. I'm talking about the big fish, the industries, banks. The ones that grab up colonies for resources and find wars good for business. Who do you think these young people here in Theresienstadt work for as slave labor?" The ex-Councilman grimaced. "Sorry my friend. Forgive me, I'm an argumentative type. And what is it they say about us Jews? 'Put two of us together and we'll argue over three different opinions.'" He got up from the table. "I can't eat any more, my stomach just won't take it. I'm probably getting the enteritis that's killing so many of us here. We all have to get ready for tomorrow. You all stay together. If you can get some food or water for the trip, do it. Look out for each other. Let's hope for the best."

Mina turned to Anna. She put her hand on her sister's. "I want to go with you tomorrow. Why would I want to stay here? At least we'll be together."

"Please, Mina. Stay here in case word comes from Benno. You can join us later. As soon as I can, I'll send word where I am. Then you can volunteer to come." Neither of them had much confidence in that plan.

Early in the morning on September 18, before first light, Anna, Willi, Hilde, and nearly 2,000 others assembled with their bags at the deportation gate near the Usti barracks.

The Council of Elders oversaw preparations for the transit while the SS guards kept in the background. Councilmen were besieged by people who were about to board the train, making the case for why they should not be deported. Anna explained to one of the Councilmen that she was still awaiting word from her husband and that she needed to stay in case he contacted her. She also argued for Willi, who was trying to contact his daughter Hedi in Munich.

"If you don't go, someone else goes in your place." The Councilman patted Anna gently on the shoulder. "It's the same for everyone. The only people exempted are those who are essential to keeping the camp running." Anna thought of mentioning that there were people the Council was sheltering from the transports, but she realized it would be useless to do so.

Most prisoners walked to the Bauschowitz station. The gravely sick or dying were brought in trucks to the loading spot where they were carried onto the waiting boxcars. Each car carried at least 50 passengers. The floors were covered in a layer of hay. Although they had been given a cursory cleaning, they still reeked. The cars had no bathroom facilities. Buckets served as toilets. Almost no food and very little water was available for the trip.

Anna, Hilde, and Willi held on to each other as they climbed into the wooden boxcar and found an empty spot where they could sit together. By late morning the train began to pull out of Bauschowitz, heading northeast. The train stopped in the afternoon and one of the riders, peering through a rectangular opening on the side of the car, called out, "Dresden." The news brought a moment of hope. "Maybe we'll be staying in Germany," someone speculated. But soon after, the train pulled out, heading east to Prussia and then into Poland.

### Prison Workshop, Early Morning, September 18

At 4:30 a.m., before any hint of daylight, two guards entered Benno's cell. He was awake when they came in. Few words were exchanged. As a formality, one of the guards asked Benno his name. Then the guards removed Benno's shirt and cuffed his hands behind him. As they walked out of the cell together, Benno heard a familiar tapping. He spoke gently, "*Au revoir, mon ami.*"

At 4:45 a.m., Benno left the Plötzensee death cell block. Several minutes later Benno approached a small brick structure, the former prison workshop, now the execution room. He was flanked by two guards.

What followed was reported by the Senior Reich Prosecutor of the People's Court:

> Witnessed by Senior State Counsel Wittmann as Head of Execution, the administrative inspector Schmidt, and Judicial Clerk Karpe as representative of the court, the designated civil servants of the advocate of the People's Court went to the prison Plötzensee in Berlin in order to conduct the execution of Benno Israel Neuburger.
>
> The executioner Hehr from Hanover stated that he and his helpers, who were Herrs Albrecht, Roselieb, and Köster, were ready to proceed with the execution. In the front part of the execution room, which was brightly lit by electrical light, stood a black cloth-covered table with a crucifix and two lit candles on it. The rear part of the room contained the guillotine which was hidden by a black curtain.
>
> The representatives stood behind the table whereas the

executioner and his helpers placed themselves in front of the black curtain. The Head of Execution then ordered to have the prisoner led into the room. At 4:48 a.m. the prisoner arrived with his hands tied to his back. The door was closed. Again, the identity of the prisoner was verified by the Head of Execution. Whereupon the Head of Execution told the executioner to proceed with the execution. Immediately the curtain was pulled open, and the three assistants traded places with the prison guards. The prisoner remained silent and stayed calm. He was led without resistance to the guillotine and was laid down bare-chested. The executioner then used the guillotine and proclaimed that the judgment had been fulfilled.

From the time the prisoner was brought into the room and had been put into the hands of the executioner's assistants it had taken 18 seconds and another 9 seconds. . . .[57]

Signed by Senior State Counsel Wittmann and Judicial Clerk Karpe.

### Benno's Last Letter

Berlin-Plötzensee, Koenigsdamm 7. Sept. 17, 1942

Dear relatives,

Hope that you dear Ilse and Hermann are healthy and your father in Theresienstadt is well. Today I want to tell you that tomorrow I will not be on this earth anymore, because I will be executed on account of my mistakes—this I have never believed, but it cannot be changed. Have instructed that I shall be buried in the Jewish Cemetery in Berlin and receive a Jewish burial. Ask dear Ilse in a few days of the Jewish Community where I was buried—burial, no cremation. Also ordered that a small cheap stone or plate will cover my grave. You or some of yours will make that known to my wife, if that is possible, because it may once again be possible to hear from Jews who were evacuated into foreign countries.

I greet you All heartfully and wish that you All have a Good Future, and you keep me in your memory. I also wrote to the Community that my wife might be informed.

Many greetings to All of You.

Uncle Benno [58]

Benno's last requests were ignored. The court issued instructions on what was to become of Benno's body:

> The corpse will be used for scientific and educational means at the Anatomical and Biological Institute of the University of Berlin. The release of the body or providing any kind of information to the relatives is strictly prohibited. Enclosed find an admission card for transporting the corpse to your institute. The arrangements are to be conducted in conditions of strict secrecy.[59]

## Treblinka

The plan that emerged from January's Wannsee Conference had included a call for the construction of special camps whose singular purpose was to eliminate large numbers of human beings as quickly and covertly as possible. By the time of this meeting more than 700,000 Jews had already been murdered, but the Nazis wanted to mechanize the process and quicken the pace.

Three new extermination centers were built in Poland as part of "Operation Reinhard." Belzec became fully operational in March 1942, Sobibor started up in May, and Treblinka II began its killing operations on July 23, 1942. All of the special extermination camps were located within 300 kilometers of Warsaw.

In the 18 months these three camps were in operation, at least 1.5 million Jews (and an unknown number of Roma and Poles) were murdered in them. Their bodies were incinerated, and their remains buried to conceal the crime.

The camps were overseen by graduates of the Nazi "T-4" euthanasia program, which, beginning in 1939, had been carrying out large-scale murders of Germans deemed to have physical, psychological, or developmental disorders. Methods of mass extermination developed in T-4 were later deployed in the death camps.

Treblinka was located in a wooded area 100 kilometers east of Warsaw. The first deportation train to the camp left Warsaw late on July 22, 1942, and arrived the following morning. Thereafter, transports from Warsaw and the surrounding district arrived daily.

The first two commanders of Treblinka II had previously worked in the T-4 program. One was an Austrian psychiatrist named Irmfried Eberl. The other was a former Austrian police official, Franz Stangl. Eberl was replaced within a few weeks of taking charge of the camp because of poor organizational skills. Under his watch, people approaching the camp saw hellish scenes of mutilated bodies scattered both outside and inside of the fence that enclosed the encampment. Franz Stangl had mastered the technique of disguise during his first death camp assignment at Sobibor and he set about rectifying the situation at Treblinka when he took over. He built a fake train station with a large wooden clock and fake train schedules. He had flower beds planted and leafy branches woven into the barbed wire fence surrounding the camp.

According to a report sent to Berlin by an SS commander named Hermann Hofle at the close of 1942, in 155 days of operation, the Treblinka extermination camp ended 713,555 lives—an average of 4,600 a day or nearly 200 per hour. In the fourteen months the camp stayed open, 900,000 people were murdered.

Treblinka was the most lethal piece of ground on earth.

### Treblinka, Poland: Late Afternoon, September 19 or 20

As the train from Theresienstadt rumbled onward, many of the riders were in a daze. The heat inside the boxcar was stifling. Some riders were close to death before the train left Theresienstadt and died on the way, succumbing to despair as much as to physical torment. Some had died before they were placed on the train because the Jewish Committee had taken to sneaking bodies onboard in order to satisfy the numbers demanded by the SS, thereby sparing others.

In the Polish countryside 80 miles east of Warsaw, the train from Theresienstadt slowed as it moved past rural villages. One of the stronger passengers in the car that carried Anna, Hilde, and Willi kept a lookout from a small rectangular opening near the large main door. From there he read off the names of villages as they passed them. At one village, he saw several men in a wagon with a load of rye just harvested from a nearby field. As the train passed the lookout saw one of the men move his index finger back and forth across his throat. He decided not to mention this to the others in the car.

A short time later, a sign reading "Treblinka" appeared. Not far beyond it, the lookout said, "We're coming to a train station." From inside the boxcar, the place looked like the kind of quaint train stop found in a typical small village. The train slowed to a stop as the people inside waited tensely. Then the train moved forward again. This happened at intervals. Each time, the sound of doors sliding open and muffled voices could be heard. At each stop, the sound grew louder. When the train jerked forward for the fourth or fifth time, someone in the boxcar asked the lookout, "What's the name of the station?"

"The sign says 'Treblinka.'" No one in the car had heard of the place.

When the car came again to a stop at the station platform, they heard loud shouts from immediately outside the car. Several minutes later, the large sliding door of the cattle car rumbled open. A man in uniform wearing a blue armband and bearing a wide leather strap in his hand shouted at them, "Out, out, out! Get out now. Hurry now." The man spoke German but with an accent Anna didn't recognize. "Out, we have many more cars to unload, move out." Anna was dizzy, terribly weak, and desperately thirsty. She could hardly move. She got up slowly and almost fainted.

Guards carrying clubs and whips walked on the platform, banging on the sides of the cars. "Come out of the wagons or we'll pull you out!" Willi was propped against the back wall of the box car, listless. "Willi, we've got to get out now," Hilde said. Willi did not move. With a lot of effort, Hilde and Anna were able to get him up and out of the car and onto the platform.

Anna, Willi, and Hilde walked with difficulty along the platform next to the barbed-wire fence that was interwoven with leafy branches. Up ahead of them, beyond the platform, passengers from the train were passing through a gate. They followed the crowd. A pungent stench hung in the still air.

"Is there water?" people asked as they moved through the gate.

"Move, move, move!" one of the guards kept repeating. The man had the same accent as the other guards but spoke with a slur. He was drunk. "You bastards better move. You'll get water and food if you move along."

Most of the arrivals were directed toward several long wooden buildings—men to the one on the right, women and children to the left.

Once they were inside these long sheds, the deportees were told to remove their clothes. Uniformed men then drove the naked prisoners up a walkway called "the tube" to the "shower room." The door in front of each shower room was covered by a cloth depicting a large Star of David. "This way to the showers," guards shouted. "You need to be cleaned up after your travels! After the showers, you'll be moved to a work camp." Those who hesitated, spoke out, or even asked a question were moved along with a blow from a club or a whip.

SS men in gray uniforms and high leather boots stood aside and watched. They let the Ukrainian and Polish guards do the work of moving the arrivals along. The SS were focused on the loot that could be gathered from those who had shed their clothes and were moving to the showers. They oversaw crews of prisoners who looked through the huge piles of possessions in search of anything of value—money, precious metals, jewelry, wallets, watches, even securities, that is, certificates of stocks and bonds and so on. Their enthusiasm for the task depended upon the point of origin of those arriving in the camp. Those brought in directly from cities or towns offered prospects for hidden wealth. Those brought in from Theresienstadt were not promising. But there were always surprises.

## The Lazarett

Among the crowd leaving this train were elderly deportees so weak they had to be helped along. Some were put in wheeled carts and moved through the gate. Anna was able to walk and, together with Hilde, she helped Willi. As they moved slowly through the main camp gate a guard screamed out at them, "You three, to the lazarett, off to the right."

"Lazarett?" repeated Hilde.

"Straight off to the right!" The uniformed man pointed away from the buildings to a fenced area a few dozen yards ahead. "You are Germans, are you not? You understand 'lazarett.' A special place for you older ones." His broad face was expressionless. "Look for the red cross to find the hospital. Go."

They turned to the right and followed the path that led to the "hospital." Ahead of them, a figure in a white suit with a wide-brimmed hat seated on a horse caught Anna's eye. He held a long strap of some kind in his hand. The horseman was smiling. He seemed like a bizarre apparition.

Willi nearly fell. Anna and Hilde, walking on either side of him, held him by his arms. But they, too, walked with difficulty, with a terrible weariness. "My Max is here," Willi said as he walked. "This is where I find him. Isn't this it? Isn't this the place where my boy Max is?"

"Yes, Willi," Anna answered gently.

"Max, Freddy, Benno, Hedi—we're all getting together here." Willi smiled for the first time since they had left Theresienstadt. "We need to let Klara know. Will you let Klara know?" asked Willi.

They approached an enclosure surrounded by a wire fence, one also interlaced with leafy branches. At the opening to the enclosure, there was a large flag with a Red Cross and next to it the word "Lazarett" posted on a sign. A hazy smoke rose from beyond the fence. It carried a horrible odor.

Anna closed her eyes. She tried to conjure the image of her children.

Anna, Hilde, and Willi walked through the gate to a room with no ceiling, then beyond it to a low earthen wall behind which there rose a smoky haze. A breeze flung acrid fumes toward them, smarting their eyes, and choking them. Out of the haze a uniformed figure wavered in front of them. Was that a rifle there? Swollen eyes stared puffy and red above the uniform. Shots?

The world was suddenly quite silent.
Anna saw someone familiar walking in front of her,
moving with long, smooth strides.
It looked like her sister Mina.
But this couldn't be
Because Mina was still back in Theresienstadt.
Anna cried out.
The woman turned around.
Anna could see it was Mina!
And she wasn't alone.
Benno was with her!
"Benno!" Anna called out, suddenly feeling a rush of excitement.
"Benno, you're here, Benno!"
Anna reached out to Benno.
She touched his shoulder. And he turned and looked at her.
And Anna saw a smile on the face of her husband.
It was the shy smile she remembered
from the first time they met
at a Passover seder
in Laupheim.

BENNO NEUBURGER DIED IN BERLIN, Germany, on September 18, 1942.

Anna Einstein Neuburger died one day later, in Treblinka, Poland.

## Epilogue: Red Posters and the White Rose

Benno Israel Neuburger has been executed on Sept 18th, 1942. The convicted offender denigrated the Führer, and the National Socialist government and committed high treason against the German Reich.[60]

SO READ THE TERSE PRESS RELEASE from Berlin People's Court on September 19, 1942.

The Reich Ministry of Justice ordered fifty bright-red posters announcing the execution of Benno Neuburger to be put up at visible locations in Munich.[61]

Six months earlier, in the spring of 1942, students at Munich's Catholic University had formed an anti-Nazi resistance group. Among the original core organizers were medical students who had served in the German army as medics. Angered by the heavy-handed suppression of ideas that did not conform to the doctrine of National Socialism, the enormous loss of life in the war, the relentless assault on Jews and other so-called non-Aryans, and the growing awareness of the extremes of Nazi brutality, these students began to discuss ways to resist.

# EPILOGUE: RED POSTERS AND THE WHITE ROSE

In April 1942, copies of a sermon given by the Catholic Bishop of Munster, Clemens von Galen, appeared in the letter boxes of some of these students. Von Galen's sermon denounced a secret program organized by the Hitler government to exterminate people regarded by the regime as "unfit to live." This included children with Down's syndrome, adults suffering psychological problems, and people with physical handicaps. They were abducted from care facilities and hospitals, brought to special centers, and murdered, first by injection, and later by gassing.

The Bishop's public denunciation of this program spread outrage at the euthanasia program and planted a seed of activism among some students. Following the example of these letters, two students, Hans Scholl and Alexander Schmorell, developed a plan to write and distribute their own flyers. They chose to operate under the name "White Rose."

Inge Scholl—who after the war wrote about the actions of her brother Hans and sister Sophie Scholl, two of the core activists—described the conditions that influenced the rise of the White Rose, noting, "More and more frequently newspapers ran brief notices of death sentences meted out by the People's Court to isolated individuals who had opposed the demonic tyrants of the people, even if only in their utterances."

Beginning on June 27, 1942, and continuing at intervals for sixteen days, the White Rose sent four letters through the mail. The first letter stated in part, "Who among us has any conception of the dimensions of shame that will befall us and our children when one day the veil has fallen from our eyes and the most horrible of crimes—crimes that infinitely outdistance every human measure—reach the light of day?"

In July 1942, Hans Scholl and other members of the White Rose were sent as army medics to the Russian front. They came face-to-face with the brutal horrors of Nazi war making. They saw beatings and the sadistic mistreatment of Jews and heard stories of anti-Semitic persecution from reliable sources. They witnessed or heard accounts of war atrocities on the battlefield and against civilians. In a letter home, one of the students, Willi Graf, expressed the turmoil this caused him and his friends when he wrote, "I wish I had been spared the view of all this which I had to witness."

These experiences further galvanized their determination to act.

When they returned from the front in November 1942, they took up their work with renewed determination. Their flyers took on a sharper edge of resistance. They broadened the distribution of flyers in Munich and sent members of the group to other cities to disseminate them and link up with other like-minded resisters.

Speaking about the central message of the White Rose, Inge Scholl summed up their view this way: "It was a matter of putting up a defense against the imminent threat of a new barbarism, against the legalization of genocide, and against the piratical-elitist doctrine of the race and of the state. The defense of common humanity everywhere had to be raised above the interest of the nation. The common interest of all nations and races was greater and immeasurably more important than the differences among people."

Kurt Huber, a university philosophy professor whose lectures had been inspirational to the White Rose students, joined their group, and gave them encouragement. He said: "The isolated individuals who have stood up one by one against Hitler must be made aware that a large body of like-minded people stands with them. This knowledge will give them courage and strength to persist. Beyond this we must try to enlighten those Germans who are still unaware of the evil intentions of our government and awaken in them the will to resistance."

In August 1942, a German offensive meant to cut off foreign supplies to the Soviet Union through the Balkans and to seize Soviet oilfields in the Crimea brought the German Sixth Army to Stalingrad on the banks of the strategic Volga River. The siege of Stalingrad became the deadliest extended battle of the war. The siege continued for five months, from August 1942 to February 1943. Aroused by the enormous losses suffered by German soldiers, a mood of rebellion began to stir among some sections of the population.

# EPILOGUE: RED POSTERS AND THE WHITE ROSE

On January 13, 1943, Bavaria's Prime Minister, Paul Giesler, whose history with Nazism hailed back to his Brown Shirt days in the mid-1920s, held a meeting to mark the 470th anniversary of the founding of the city's Ludwig Maximilian University. The meeting took place in the main auditorium of the Deutsches Museum, the science and technology center built on an island in the Isar River. During his speech, Geisler directed his attention to the women students present. With contempt, he told them that instead of reading books, they should be using their "healthy bodies" to produce babies for the Reich. "And for those women students not pretty enough to catch a man," he sneered, "I'd be happy to lend them one of my young associates," promising them "a glorious experience."

As he spoke, dozens of women got up to leave in protest. Brown-shirted male students attacked the women while other male students rushed to their aid. Fights broke out among the students. The meeting broke up and a protest march of university students took to the streets of Munich.

Later that month 6,000 to 9,000 copies of the White Rose's fifth leaflet, "*Aufruf an alle Deutsche!*" ("*Appeal to all Germans!*") were produced using a hand-operated duplicating machine. Between January 27 and 29, 1943, members and supporters of the White Rose group carried flyers to Saarbrucken, Cologne, Vienna, Freiburg, Chemnitz, Hamburg, Innsbruck, and Berlin. Copies were dropped in the mail from these places.

On February 5, 1943, a few days after the collapse and surrender of the German Sixth Army at Stalingrad, Otto Dietrich, State Secretary of the Nazi Propaganda Ministry, recognizing a need to reinforce war morale among the Nazi base, issued instructions to German newspapers and magazines: "Anti-Jewish propaganda is on the same level as anti-Bolshevik propaganda. The treatment of this theme is part of an essential campaign to stimulate feelings of hate."

Meanwhile, encouraged by the changing mood among their fellow students and a new sense of urgency, on the night of February 14, members of the White Rose boldly painted slogans on walls around Munich near the university, the Marienplatz, and even on the Nazis' "holy shrine," the Feldherrnhalle. In large letters, using black tar-based paint, which proved difficult to remove, the slogans declared "Down with Hitler!" "Hitler the mass murderer!" and "Freedom!"

On February 18, 1943, Sophie and Hans Scholl decided to take the risky step of distributing flyers on the campus of the university. They left stacks outside classrooms and then, in a mood of defiance, Sophie flung extra leaflets from the mezzanine level to the floor below. They were spotted by a janitor who grabbed the students and called the Gestapo.

On February 22, Hans and Sophie Scholl and Christoph Probst were brought before the People's Court in Munich presided over by Roland Freisler. In court Sophie Scholl bravely confronted and denounced the regime. Her words recorded at the trial were: "Somebody, after all, had to make a start. What we wrote and said is also believed by many others. They just don't dare express themselves as we did."

After the brief trial, Hans and Sophie Scholl and Christoph Probst were all found guilty and sentenced to death. Their execution by guillotine took place hours later in Munich's Stadelheim prison.

## BENNO'S ROLE IN HISTORY

There is no way to precisely measure the effect that Benno's acts of resistance had on the movements of opposition to Nazism that gained momentum in the period after the winter of 1941–1942. Did anyone, aside from a few postal workers and Gestapo agents and other agents of the Nazi state, see the messages on his postcards? Did the messages on the cards have, in any way, a broader impact? Did those in and around the White Rose resistance group read the notice of Benno's execution or see one of the posters announcing his execution somewhere in Munich? Did this have any impact on their own sense of responsibility to resist? None of this is known. What can be said with confidence is that Benno realized by the fall and winter of 1941–1942 that a genocide was unfolding and that he would carry out the only act of resistance against it that he saw available to him. It was an act of desperation, but also of defiance. It's very likely that he understood that his message reflected more than his, and the Jewish community's, hatred of what was unfolding in Germany at the time and that there were others in Nazi Germany, and even in Nazism's birthplace, Munich, who despised Nazism and would have welcomed resistance.

If Benno's story has any broader importance, it is that the desire, means, and courage to resist oppression exists even in the most repressive societies. And such resistance is never futile.

## THOSE WHO PERISHED IN THE HOLOCAUST

*Postcards to Hitler* is the story of members of four interrelated German families whose lives were dramatically affected, and in some cases ended, by the Nazi Holocaust. Those families were the Einsteins, the Neuburgers, the Holzers, and the Spatzes, who during the Nazi era lived in four cities or towns: Laupheim, Munich, Traunstein, and Wolfratshausen.

Here is an accounting of what became of those family members who died in the Holocaust and whose stories were told, in part, here:

Benno Neuburger: Born in Munich, March 4, 1871. Executed in Berlin, September 18, 1942.
Anna Einstein Neuburger: Born in Laupheim, April 15, 1877. Murdered in Treblinka, Poland, September 19, 1942.
Mina Einstein: Born in Laupheim, September 6, 1872. Died in Theresienstadt, Czechoslovakia, November 8, 1942.
Louis Holzer: Born in Stein am Kocher in 1872. Died in Theresienstadt, January 1, 1943.
Willi Holzer: Born in Stein am Kocher, July 3, 1874. Murdered in Treblinka, September 19, 1942.
Benno Holzer: Born in Traunstein, January 10, 1904. Murdered in Kaunas, Lithuania, on November 25, 1941.
Alfred Holzer: Born in Traunstein, June 11, 1907. Murdered in Kaunas, Lithuania, on November 25, 1941.
Martha Trautman Holzer: Born in Bergzabern, May 26, 1907. Murdered in Kaunas, Lithuania, on November 25, 1941.
Hedwig (Hedi) Holzer: Born in Traunstein, February 17, 1906. Died in Auschwitz on March 10, 1943.*
Maximilian (Max) Holzer: Born in Traunstein in 1909. Died in Auschwitz on March 13, 1943.*
Cäcilie (Tilli) Holzer Spatz: Born in Traunstein on May 18, 1902. Murdered on November 25, 1941 in Kaunas, Lithuania.

---

*Hedi Holzer and her brother Max died in Auschwitz. Hedi was picked up in the last deportation from Munich in February 1943 and sent by boxcar to Auschwitz. Her cause of death is believed to be typhoid. Max, after serving a five-year term at Amberg Penitentiary, was sent to Auschwitz where he too died, it is believed, of typhoid.

Hermann Spatz: Born in Wolfratshausen. Died in Munich in 1940.
Wilhelm Spatz: Born in Wolfratshausen in 1925. Murdered in Kaunas, Lithuania, on November 25, 1941.
Flora Spatz: Birthdate unknown. Murdered in Kaunas, Lithuania, on November 25, 1941.
Hertha Spatz: Born in 1922. Murdered in Kaunas, Lithuania, on November 25, 1941.

## THE MEMORIAL IN MUNICH

On July 11, 2022, the Cultural Department of the City of Munich Institute for City History and Remembrance Culture, in cooperation with Munich city officials, held a commemorative event for Benno and Anna Neuburger at the Villa Stuck Museum at 60 Prinzregentenstrasse, a block from their former home at Trogerstrasse 44. Following the public gathering, a permanent memorial was placed in front of Trogerstrasse 44. For video and photos of the event go to postcardstohitler.com.

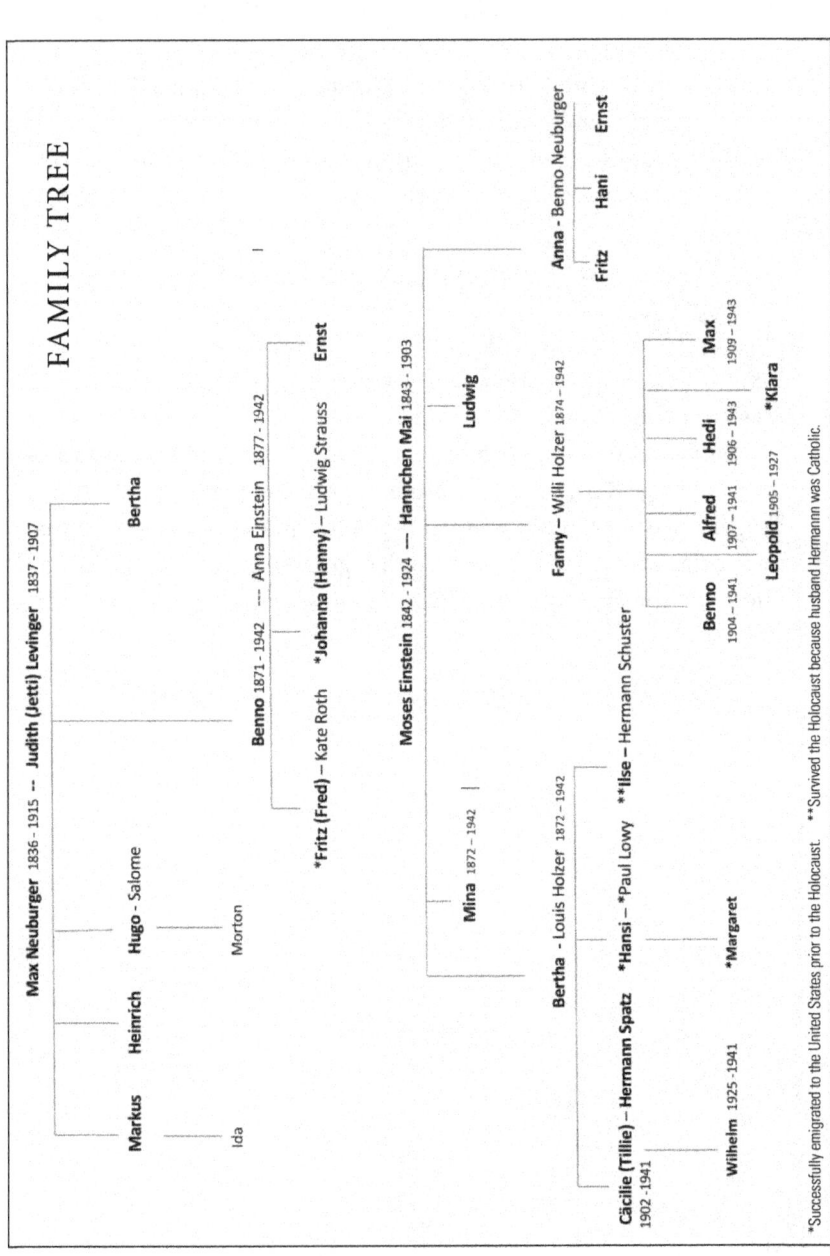

# PERSONS IN *POSTCARDS TO HITLER*

### Family

Max Neuburger: Benno's father. Born June 13, 1836, in Mönschdeggingen. Died 1915 in Munich.

Judith (Jette) Levinger Neuburger: Benno's mother. Born February 19, 1837. Died 1907.

Benno Neuburger: Born March 4, 1871. Executed in Berlin, September 18, 1942.

Anna Einstein Neuburger: Born April 15, 1877. Murdered in Treblinka, September 19, 1942.

Fritz (Fred) Neuburger: Benno's son. Born October 2, 1908. Died January 12, 1987, in Long Beach, California.

Johanna (Hani) Neuburger Strauss: Benno's daughter. Born October 24, 1909. Died 2008 in Irvine, California.

Hugo Neuburger: Born November 23, 1868. Died January 1934 in Chicago.

Morton Neuburger: Hugo's son, cousin to Hani and Fritz, obtained affidavits for their emigration to the United States.

Markus Neuburger: Born June 14, 1862. Brother of Benno who emigrated to the United States in the 1890s.

Ida: Daughter of Markus who wrote letters to U.S. Representative Sabath of Illinois, appealing for help for Benno and Anna.

Heinrich Neuburger: Brother of Benno who emigrated to the United States in the 1890s.

Moses Einstein: Anna's father. Born May 29, 1842. Died November 29, 1926.

Hannchen Mai Einstein: Anna's mother. Born November 21, 1843. Died May 13, 1903.
Mina Einstein: Anna's sister. Born September 6, 1872, in Laupheim. Died 1942 in Theresienstadt.
Ludwig Moses Einstein: Anna's younger brother. Born May 11, 1880. Died 1916.

Berta Einstein Holzer: Born March 9, 1874, in Laupheim. Died 1922.
Fanny Einstein Holzer: Born in Laupheim. Died 1936.
Willi Holzer: Born July 3, 1874, in Stein am Kocher. Murdered in Treblinka, September 19, 1942.
Louis Holzer: Born 1872 in Stein am Kocher. Died January 1, 1943, in Theresienstadt.

Ilse Holzer Schuster: Born September 13, 1904. Survived Holocaust period.
Hermann Schuster: Catholic husband of Ilse Holzer Schuster.
Tilli Holzer Spatz: Born May 18, 1902. Murdered November 25, 1941, in Kaunas, Lithuania.
Hermann Spatz: Husband of Tilli Holzer and WWI veteran. Died 1940 in Munich.
Wilhelm Spatz: Son of Tilli and Hermann. Murdered with his mother, November 25, 1941, in Kaunas, Lithuania.
Flora Spatz: Sister-in-law of Tilli and Hermann Spatz. Murdered November 25, 1941, in Kaunas, Lithuania.
Hertha Spatz: Daughter of Flora Spatz. Murdered November 25, 1941, in Kaunas, Lithuania.
Hansi Holzer Lowy: Daughter of Berta and Louie Holzer. Born June 1, 1903. Emigrated to Colombia, then the United States.
Paul Lowy: Husband of Hansi Holzer. Emigrated to Colombia, then the United States.
Margaret Lowy: Daughter of Hansi and Paul Lowy. Emigrated to Colombia, then the United States.

Alfred Holzer: Born June 11, 1907, in Traunstein. Murdered November 25, 1941, in Kaunas, Lithuania.

Martha Holzer: Wife of Alfred Holzer. Born May 26, 1907, in Bergzabern, Germany. Murdered November 25, 1941, in Kaunas, Lithuania.

Benno Holzer: Born January 10, 1904 in Traunstein,. Murdered November 25, 1941, in Kaunas, Lithuania.

Hedwig (Hedi) Holzer: Born February 17, 1906, in Traunstein. Died March 10, 1943, in Auschwitz.

Klara Holzer: Born October 4, 1908, in Traunstein. Left Germany in 1938. Emigrated to England in 1939, then to the United States in 1947. Died December 26, 1996, in Irvine, California.

Max Holzer: Born 1909 in Traunstein. Murdered March 1943 in Auschwitz.

Leopold Holzer: Son of Willi and Fanny Holzer. Died at age twenty-two before the Hitler era.

Simon Vogel: Born 1899. Cousin to Klara Holzer and her siblings from Laupheim. Lived in Cologne until moving to Paris in 1937. Helped Klara emigrate to England. Emigrated to the United States in 1941.

Johanna Vogel: Wife of Simon.

Hans Jacob Vogel: Son of Simon and Johanna.

Walter Vogel: Youngest son of Simon and Johanna.

The Götz family, Sara, Thekla, and Otto: Land investors who were partners with Benno Neuburger in a plot of land on the outskirts of Munich purchased by Maffei Locomotive manufacturer in 1936. The Nazi government confiscated the money.

Kate (Roth) Neuburger: Wife of Fred (Fritz) in the United States. Born December 5, 1913, in Breidenbach am Herzberg, Germany. Died August 1998 in Orange County, California.

Ludwig Strauss: Husband of Hani in the United States. Born February 15, 1905, in Frankfurt, Germany. Died 1972 in New York.

Karoline Strauss: Daughter of Hani and Ludwig Strauss. Born February 11, 1940.

### Friends and Neighbors

Frank Mittelberger: Friend of Fritz who left Munich for the United States on the same day as Fritz.

Kohn: Friend of Fritz who helped him bring clothes to Paris when he was en route to the United States.

Felix Koenigsberger: Legal advisor for Jews in Munich who assisted Anna in finding Benno when he was arrested at Milbertshofen.

Ludwig Eiber: Tailor, neighbor of Benno and Anna, and a friend of Fritz at 44 Trogerstrasse.

Bertha Eiber: Wife of Ludwig.

Herr Kandl: Pro-Nazi who lived in the same building at 44 Trogerstrasse.

Herr Hack: Nazi sympathizer who also lived at 44 Trogerstrasse.

Sofie Braunge: Roommate of Anna's older sister Mina in Laupheim.

### Nazis in Traunstein

Albert Aichner: Traunstein's Nazi vice mayor who led the attack on the Holzer home on November 9, 1938.

Franz Werr: A leading Traunstein Nazi and a leader of the Kristallnacht attack on the Holzer home.

### Munich Jewish Committee (IKG) members at the Monastery of the Sisters of Mercy at Berg am Laim

Curt Mezger: Camp director.

Julius Spanier: Camp doctor.

Else Rosenfeld: Economic director.

## Munich Nazi Officials
Franz Mugler: Head of Munich's Aryanization Committee.

## Those Involved in the Arrest, Interrogation, Trial, and Execution of Benno Neuburger

Hermann Eckfellner: Gestapo interrogator who testified at Benno's trial in Berlin.
Helmut Pommerening: Polzeirat: SS-Sturmbannführer, official in the Reich Security Main Office, member of the secret police.
Dr. Heinz Bergmann: Benno's original lawyer/defender in Berlin.
Dr. Ernst Decke-Cornill: Lawyer who took over for Heinz Bergmann.
Friedrich Wübken: Benno's defense attorney before the People's Court.
Karl Engert: Vice-Chairman of the Nazi People's Court and main judge who presided at Benno's trial.
Hermann Granzow: A judge who presided at Benno's trial and the Court of Appeals judge.
Kurt Kapeller: NSDAP *Gaurichter* and juror who also presided at Benno's trial.
Anton Plankensteiner: NSDAP district leader and juror who also presided at Benno's trial.
Dr. Meier: State prosecutor representing the senior Reich Prosecutor at Benno's trial.
Wöhlke: Justice Secretary as registrar of the head office.
Hehr: Surname of the executioner in charge of Benno's execution.
August Albrecht, Alfred Roselieb, August Köster: Hehr's execution assistants.
Dr. Wilhelm Crohne: Head of the Criminal Law Department in the Reich Ministry of Justice.
Dr. Georg Thierack: Reich Minister of Justice who wrote the decision denying Benno a pardon from the sentence of death.

### Other Nazi Murderers

Karl Jäger: Head of the Einstazgruppen Kommando in Kaunas, Lithuania.

Franz Stangl: SS Commandant and head of the Treblinka death camp (man on a horse dressed in white as described in chapter 24).

### Fictitious Characters

Berthold: Longtime friend of Benno's "godfather" from Laupheim; introduced Benno to Anna.

Hilde: Berthold's wife, also from Laupheim.

Gustav: Non-Jewish land investor (Benno later meets Gustav on the Luitpold Bridge in September 1941).

Julius: Small Munich clothing store owner (Jewish).

Werner: Non-Jewish civil attorney.

Rolf: Non-Jewish small business owner and friend of Berthold.

Arnulf: Non-Jewish part-owner of a ski shop, ski equipment saleman, and member of the Social Democratic Party.

Herr Katz: Old friend of Max Neuburger who shows up on the last day of shivah after Max's death in April 1915.

Cantor and other synagogue members: Conversations outside the Munich Haupt Synagogue in 1918 and 1919.

Crowd on the corner of Liebherrstrasse and Zweibrückstrasse: Commenting after the Putschist march passes by.

Rudy and Greta: Friends from Munich's Haupt Synagogue. They appear twice in the book, in 1914 on the eve of WWI and in September 1938 during the Munich Conference over Sudetenland.

Ernst and Anna Neumeier: Friends who meet at Benno and Anna's apartment the night after the failed Munich Putsch.

Herlinda: Seamstress who worked at the dress shop with Hani in 1933.

Member of the Council of Elders at Theresienstadt: Deported to Treblinka the same day as Anna and Willi.

French Resistance fighter: Occupies the cell adjoining Benno's at the Plötzensee prison.
Jewish Women's Association members: They meet at the Haupt Synagogue in 1911.
Sonia and Riva: Russian women, survivors of a Czarist pogrom, present at the Jewish Women's Association meeting.
Henny Kosman: Daughter of Ukrainian Jewish immigrants and translator at the Haupt Synagogue meeting.
Raissa: Russian Jewish immigrant and friend of Anna's.
Robert: Leader of the Zionist group meeting in Munich in 1920.

# ACKNOWLEDGMENTS

A story such as this could not have been told without the research, writing, and documentation of hundreds of historians and archivists and the testimonies of survivors and family members of those lost to the Holocaust. They provided the vital background, historical analysis, and context for the story told here.

The story of Benno's resistance came to public light when the archives of the Nazi People's Court became available to a broader community of researchers in 1989. Knowledge of German Jewish resistance to Nazism had been largely hidden until determined researchers ferreted out from police and court archives examples of such resistance, upending the false notion of Jewish passivity in the face of Nazi terror. Outstanding in this regard is historian Wolf Gruner of the Center for Advanced Genocide Research at the University of Southern California who has done extraordinary work to research, uncover, write, and speak out about acts of Jewish defiance. Bernward Dörner of the Technical University of Berlin is another such historian. Bernward took particular interest in Benno's story, drawing attention to it as important evidence to shatter two myths: the myth of Jewish passivity and the erroneous contention that no one knew, or could have known, about the unfolding Holocaust outside the narrow circle of Nazi elite. Bernward has especially focused on the postcard Benno posted on January 23, 1941, in which he warned of the coming genocide of at least five million Jews.

While on a visit to Munich in 2018, I met Maximilian Strnad,

ACKNOWLEDGMENTS

an archivist, researcher, and writer who has worked tirelessly to bring the history of Munich Jews to light. Max and his colleagues at the Cultural Department of the City of Munich Institute for City History and Remembrance, in cooperation with leaders of the Munich Jewish community, have done outstanding work to memorialize Jews of that city who were lost during the Nazi era. Max's writing on Munich's Jewish detention camp of Milbertshofen, on the deportations from Munich in 1941 and 1942, on the Nazi Aryanization committee, on the slave labor flax factory at Lohhof, and on other aspects of Munich Nazi history were of enormous value to this author in writing this book.

The historian Friedbert Mühldorfer has researched and written about the Holzer family of Traunstein. He also spearheaded the effort to put up a beautiful stone memorial to the Holzer family that today stands outside the former Holzer home at 6 Kernstrasse in Traunstein.

Aldo Bayer, Dr. Antje Köhlerschmidt, and Karl Neidlinger did outstanding work to preserve the memory of the Jewish community of Laupheim, writing personal accounts of each of those Laupheimers who perished in the cataclysm.

The writer Christian Steeb wrote a lengthy series of articles in the magazine *Merkur* on the Hermann Spatz family of Wolfratshausen.

Without the devoted work of the historians mentioned above, this story could not have been written. They have also set an important example by their determination to seek out and expose the truth of the crimes committed by their own country.

My eternal gratitude goes to Uwe Gabel and his father, Adi Gabel, from Cologne, Germany. I met Uwe in San Francisco in 2009. Uwe was making his living as a German-language teacher at that time. We met at Muddy Waters coffeehouse, where I showed him a thick file of letters from my grandparents, Anna and Benno. Would he translate them? Uwe immediately agreed to do so. But because the letters were written in an old German style, Uwe had to send the letters to his father, Adi, who copied each letter into modern German script. From there Uwe translated them into

English. Uwe also translated material from the Bundesarchiv and other documents and sections from German books and articles. Uwe's translations are available on this book's website, postcardstohitler.com.

In the writing of this book I received invaluable encouragement, support, and advice from a number of people. My friend Leonid Gornik, upon hearing the story about Benno's postcards, insisted I write about him. And Leonid persisted in this despite all my doubts and reservations. When I began to write, Leonid offered his advice, and we engaged in long conversations on the book. And while we did not always see eye to eye on how the story should be told, these conversations were *always* stimulating and provocative. Leonid read drafts, offered suggestions, pointed out errors.

Robin Larsen and I spent many, many hours in conversation about *Postcards* as it was being written, and as she was writing the story of her great-grandfather from Omaha, Nebraska. Not only were these conversations important to me, but Robin was constantly and generously making valuable suggestions about books to read on topics related to my writing.

My cousin Hugh Neuburger provided me with valuable information and sources on German history and related his experiences of visiting the birthplace of his grandfather, Hugo, brother of Benno, in Mönschdeggingen. My sister Linda Stoll and my nephew Michael Stoll spent many hours finding and scanning documents, letters, postcards, and pictures my father Fred (Fritz was his German name) left behind, thus providing essential material for this book. My nephew Steven Stoll, a prolific writer himself, frequently offered valuable insights, encouragement, and suggestions all along the path toward the completion of this book. Steven's mother-in-law, Rena Powell, helped with translations of some German documents, especially military records, also providing advice and encouragement.

I am grateful to Derrlyn Tom and David Ramos who read early drafts of the book and offered encouragement and valuable

# ACKNOWLEDGMENTS

suggestions. So did my cousin Rick Schulein who also accompanied me in travels to Prague, Theresienstadt, Warsaw, Minsk, and Kaunas, Lithuania, places pertinent to this story.

I received advice and encouragement along the way from my wife, Sharon, my daughter, Anna Moeller, and my son-in-law, Marc Moeller. They, along with my granddaughters Madeline Moeller and Eleanor Moeller, my great-nieces Batsheva Labowe-Stoll and Katya Labowe-Stoll, and my great-nephew Jaden Labowe-Stoll, made the trip to Munich in July 2022 for a memorial event for Anna and Benno at the Villa Stuck Museum. There the great-great-grandchildren of Anna and Benno read sections from the letters written from Munich from August 1938 to November 1941. After the commemoration we placed a permanent memorial stele with Benno's and Anna's likenesses in front of their former apartment at 44 Trogerstrasse.

I am greatly appreciative to Michael Yates, who brought the manuscript of this book to the attention of Monthly Review Press, and for MRP's enthusiastic support for this project.

I am grateful for several outstanding editors: Bridget Lyon, a wonderful independent editor, and Scott Borchert of MR Press—not only skillful at this work, but great writers in their own right who've offered their wise and energetic guidance. Certainly much that is positive in this book is due to their skillful work.

I am grateful to the talented graphic artist Anna Fong who put together the website postcardstohitler.com, which has received enthusiastic praise from many quarters and through which the public now has access to the interviews, letters, and archival documents from which this story is drawn. Anna also designed the book's cover. I can't express how fortunate I feel for having her talented assistance.

I hope all those many friends who asked over the months and years how this prolonged book project was going, who patiently listened to my musings on one aspect or another of the book, or who took an interest in this history and thereby helped shepherd it along, will realize how grateful I am for their interest and support.

Finally, I would like to acknowledge Enne Braun. Enne, a cousin of my mother, Kate Roth Neuburger, came to the United States at the age of eight in 1938 with the aid of the filmmaker Carl Laemmle, founder of Universal Studios. It was through Enne that I learned of Laemmle's efforts to rescue hundreds of German Jews. And I learned how the U.S. State Department obstructed and then shut down Laemmle's life-saving work. Enne, a San Francisco public school librarian and lifelong patron of the city's art and cultural scene, died in 2014.

# KEY SOURCES
(available at www.postcardstohitler.com)

Interview with Fred (Fritz) Neuburger, September 1983
Interview with Johanna (Hani) Neuburger Strauss, December 13, 1983
Interview with Clara (Klara) Holzer, April 16, 1984
Bundesarchiv documents NJ-2999 Bd. 1–4 and R3017-5257
Munich City Archive documents
Bavarian State Archive documents
Letters from Benno Neuburger and Anna (Einstein) Neuburger, 1938–1941
Letters from members of the Holzer family
Postcards from Benno Neuburger, Fritz Neuburger

# BIBLIOGRAPHY

*The 1619 Project: A New Origin Story*. Created by Nikole Hannah-Jones and *The New York Times Magazine*; edited by Caitlin Roper, Ilena Silverman, and Jake Silverstein. One World, 2021.

Bard, Michael G. *48 Hours of Kristallnacht: Night of Destruction/Dawn of the Holocaust*. Lyons Press, 2008.

Bayer, Udo. *Vignettes: The Legacy of Jewish Laupheim*. Universitats Bibliotchek Heidelberg, 2017.

Beer, Edith Hahn. *The Nazi Officer's Wife*. William Morrow and Co., 1999.

Black, Edwin. *IBM and the Holocaust*. Crown, 2001.

Bland, Luke. *Germany and the Boer War, 1899–1902*. Self-published, 2014.

Brenner, Michael. *In Hitler's Munich: Jews, Revolution and the Rise of Nazism*. Princeton University Press, 2022.

Brenner, Michael. *The Renaissance of Jewish Culture in Weimar Germany*. Yale Univeristy Press, 1996.

Browning, Christopher. *Ordinary Men*. Harper Perennial, 2017.

Buttar, Prit. *The Splintered Empires: The Eastern Front, 1917 to 1922*. Bloomsbury, 2017.

Cassell, Farris. *The Unanswered Letter: One Holocaust Family's Desperate Plea for Help*. Regnery History, 2020.

Cesarani, David. *Final Solution: The Fate of the Jews, 1933–1949*. St. Martin's Press, 2016.
Clark, Christopher. *The Sleepwalkers: How Europe Went to War in 1914*. Harper Perennial, 2013.
Clark, Christopher. *The Iron Kingdom: The Rise and Downfall of Prussia, 1600–1947*. The Belknap Press of Harvard University Press, 2006.
Davitt, Michael. *Within the Pale*. A. S. Barnes and Co., 1905.
Dekel-Chen, Jonathan. *Anti-Jewish Violence: Rethinking the Pogrom in East European History*. Indiana University Press, 2011.
Dobbs, Michael. *The Unwanted: America, Auschwitz, and a Village Caught In Between*. Deckle Edge, 2019.
Döblin, Alfred. *Berlin Alexanderplatz*. University of California Press, 2006.
Donner, Rebecca. *All the Frequent Troubles of Our Days*. Little, Brown, and Company, 2021.
Elon, Amos. *The Pity of It All*. Metropolitan Books, 2013.
Evans, Richard J. *The Third Reich in Power*. Penguin Press, 2005.
Fallada, Hans. *Alone in Berlin*. Translated by Michael Hoffman. The Penguin Press, 2010.
Feuchtwanger, Edgar. *Hitler, My Neighbor*. With Bertil Scali. Other Press, 2017.
Feuchtwanger, Lion. *Success*. Martin Secker, 1930.
———. *The Oppermanns*. McNally Editions, 2022.
Fischer, Fritz. *Germany's Aims in the First World War*. W.W. Norton, 1967.
Friedlander, Henry. *The Origins of Nazi Genocide: From Euthanasia to the Final Solution*. University of North Carolina Press, 1997.
Fritzsche, Peter. *Life and Death in the Third Reich*. Harvard University Press, 2008.
Gay, Peter. *Weimar Culture: The Outsider and Insider*. W.W. Norton, 2001.
Gellately, Robert. *Backing Hitler: Consent and Coercion in Nazi Germany*. Oxford University Press, 2001.
Gerwarth, Robert. *November 1918: The German Revolution*. Oxford University Press, 2020.
Gilbert, Martin. *Kristallnacht: Prelude to Destruction*. Harper Perennial, 2006.
———. *The First World War*. Holt McDougal, 2004.
Glenny, Misha. *The Balkans: Nationalism, War, and the Great Powers, 1804–2011*. Penguin Books, 2012.
Gobineau, Arthur. *An Essay on the Inequality of Races*. William Heinemann, 1915.
Gorodetsky, Gabriel. *Grand Delusion: Stalin and the German Invasion of Russia*. Yale University Press, 1999.
Grady, Tim. *A Deadly Legacy: German Jews and the Great War*. Yale University Press, 2017.
Gruner, Wolf. *Resisters: How Ordinary Jews Fought Persecution in Hitler's Germany*. Yale University Press, 2023.

Gruner, Wolf, and Steven Roth. *New Perspectives on Kristallnacht.* Casden Institute for the Study of the Jewish Role in American Life, 2019.

Gruner, Wolf. *Jewish Forced Labor in Nazi Germany: Economic Needs and Racial Aims.* Cambridge University Press, 2006.

Haffner, Sebastian. *Defying Hitler.* Translated by Oliver Pretzel. Farrar, Straus and Giroux, 2000.

———. *The Revolution that Failed.* Library Press, 1972.

Hansen, Randall. *Disobeying Hitler: German Resistance After Valkyrie.* Oxford University Press, 2013.

Hawes, James. *The Shortest History of Germany: From Julius Caesar to Angela Merkel.* The Experiment, 2019.

Hilberg, Raul. *The Destruction of the European Jews.* Holmes and Meier, 1985.

Hilmes, Oliver. *Berlin 1936: Sixteen Days in August.* Translated by Jefferson Chase. Other Press, 2018.

Hitler, Adolf. *Mein Kampf.* 1924.

Hoffrogge, Ralf. *Working-Class Politics in the German Revolution: Richard Muller, the Revolutionary Shop Stewards and the Origins of the Council Movement.* Haymarket Books, 2015.

Hochschild, Adam. *King Leopold's Ghost.* Mariner Books, 2020.

Holborn, Hajo. *A History of Modern Germany.* Princeton University Press, 1969.

Horne, Alistair. *The Fall of Paris: The Siege and the Commune 1870-71.* Penguin Books, 2007.

Jelavich, Peter. *Berlin Alexanderplatz: Radio, Film and the Death of Weimar.* University of California Press, 2006.

Jens, Inge. *At the Heart of the White Rose: Letters and Diaries of Hans and Sophie Scholl.* Plough Publishing House, 2017.

Jones, Mark. *Founding Weimar: Violence and the German Revolution of 1918-1919.* Cambridge University Press, 2016.

Kaplan, Marion. *The Making of the Jewish Middle Class: Women, Family and Identity in Imperial Germany.* Oxford University Press, 1991.

Karlauf, Thomas. *The Night of Broken Glass: Eyewitness Accounts of Kristallnacht.* Polity Press, 2012.

Kershaw, Ian. *Popular Opinion and Political Dissent in the Third Reich: Bavaria 1933-1945.* Clarendon Press, 1983.

King, David. *The Trial of Adolf Hitler: The Beerhall Putsch and the Rise of Adolf Hitler.* W. W. Norton, 2017.

Klemperer, Victor. *I Will Bear Witness: A Diary of the Nazi Years, 1933-1942.* Modern Library, 2001.

———. *I Will Bear Witness: A Diary of the Nazi Years, 1942-1945.* Modern Library, 2001.

———. *Munich, 1919: Diary of a Revolution.* Polity Press, 2017.

———. *The Language of the Third Reich.* Bloomsbury, 2013.

Kogon, Eugen. *The Theory and Practice of Hell*. Farrar, Straus and Giroux, 2006.
Köhlerschmidt, Antje, and Karl Neidlinger. *The Jewish Community of Laupheim and Its Annihilation*. Munich Hüttsheim, 2008.
Koonz, Claudia. *The Nazi Conscience*. Belknap Press, 2003.
———. *Mothers in the Fatherland: Women, the Family and Nazi Politics*. St. Martin's Press, 1987.
Lander, Saul. *Nazi Germany and the Jews, 1933 to 1945*. Harper Perennial, 2009.
Large, David Clay. *Where Ghosts Walked: Munich's Road to the Third Reich*. W. W. Norton, 1997.
Larson, Erik. *In the Garden of the Beast*. Crown, 2011.
Lenin, V. I. *Imperialism, the Highest Stage of Capitalism*. Foreign Language Press, 1973.
Lederer, Zdenek. *Ghetto Theresienstadt*. Translated by K. Weisskopf. Edward Goldston and Son, 1953.
Lieb, William. *The Life and Adventures of Karl Laemmle*. Putnam and Sons, 1931.
Liulevicus, Vejas Gabriel. *World War I: The "Great War."* The Great Courses, Audible.com
Longerich, Peter. *Holocaust, the Nazi Persecution and Murder of the Jews*. Oxford University Press, 2010.
Mandelbaum, Hugo. *Jewish Life in the Village Communities of Southern Germany*. Feldheim Publishers, 1985.
Mann, Heinrich. *The Loyal Subject*. Continuum, 2004.
Mann, Thomas. *The Magic Mountain*. Vintage Press, 1996.
Mayer, Arno J. *Why Did the Heavens Not Darken? The 'Final Solution' in History*. Verso, 2012.
Mendelsohn, Daniel. *The Lost: The Search for Six of Six Million*. HarperCollins, 2013.
McKeekin, Sean. *July 1914: Countdown to War*. Basic Books, 2014.
Mosse, George L., *Nazi Culture: Intellectual, Cultural and Social Life in the Third Reich*. Schocken Books, 1966.
Müller, Ingo. *Hitler's Justice: The Courts of the Third Reich*. Harvard University Press, 1991.
Neidlinger, Karln, and Antje Kohlerschmidt. *The Jewish Community of Laupheim and Its Annihilation*. Antje Kohlerschmidt and Karl Neidlinger, 2008.
Olusoga, David, and Casper Erichsen. *The Kaiser's Holocaust: Germany's Forgotten Genocide*. Faber and Faber, 2010.
Parks, James. *The Four Lives of Elsbeth Rosenfeld As Told By Her to the BBC*. Camelot Press, 1964.
Piketty, Thomas. *Capital and Ideology*. Belknap Press, 2020.
Remarque, Erich Maria. *All Quiet on the Western Front*. Random House, 2013.

Rogowski, Christian. *The Many Faces of Weimar Cinema*. Camden House, 2010.
Rosenfeld, Elsbeth. *Interview with the BBC*. Victor Gollancz, 1964.
Rothstein, Andrew. *The Munich Conspiracy, 1938*. Lawrence and Wishart, 1958.
Scholl, Inge. *The White Rose: Munich 1942–1943*. Wesleyan University Press, 1983.
———. *The Resistance of the White Rose*. Wesleyan University Press, 1970.
Schorske, Carl. *German Social Democracy, 1905–1917: The Development of the Great Schism*. Harvard University Press, 1955.
Sereny, Gita. *Into the Darkness: An Examination of Conscience*. Vintage Books, 2011.
Speer, Albert. *Inside the Third Reich*. Macmillan, 1970.
Stackelberg, Roderick, and Sally A. Winkle. *The Nazi Germany Sourcebook*. Routledge, 2002.
Stahel, David. *Retreat from Moscow: A New History of Germany's Winter Campaign, 1941–1942*. Farrar, Straus and Giroux, 2019.
Strnad, Maximilian. *Zwischenstation Judensiedlung: Studien Zur Jüdischen Geschichte Und Kultur in Bayern*. Oldenbourg Wissenschaftsverlag, 2011.
Strnad, Maximilian. *Flachs für das Reich Das jüdische Zwangsarbeitslager "Flachsr.ste Lohhof" bei München*. Volk Verlag, 2013.
Stroud, Dean G. *Preaching in Hitler's Shadow*. Eerdmans, 2013.
Talbot, David. *The Devil's Chessboard: Allen Dulles, the CIA and the Rise of America's Secret Government*. HarperCollins, 2015.
Thomas, Gordon, and Greg Lewis. *Defying Hitler: The Germans Who Resisted Nazi Rule*. Penguin Random House, 2019.
Troller, Norbert. *Theresienstadt: Hitler's Gift to the Jews*. Translated by Susan E. Cernyak-Spatz. University of North Carolina Press, 1992.
Wallenberg, Samuel. *Revolt in Treblinka*. Jewish Historical Institute, 2000.
Weitz, Eric D. *Weimar Germany: Promise and Tragedy*. Princeton University Press, 2007.
Wertheimer, Jack. *Unwelcome Strangers: East European Jews in Imperial Germany*. Oxford University Press, 1987.
Willet, John. *Art and Politics in the Weimar Period*. Pantheon Books, 1978.
Whitman, James Q. *Hitler's American Model: The United States and the Making of Nazi Race Law*. Princeton University Press, 2017.
Wyman, David S. *The Abandonment of the Jews: America and the Holocaust 1941 to 1945*. Pantheon, 2001.
Wyman, David S. *America and the Holocaust: Confirming the News of Extermination*. Vol. 1. Garland Publishing, 1990.
Zalc, Claire, and Tal Bruttmann. *Microhistories of the Holocaust*. Berghahn, 2017.
Zipperstein, Steven J. *Pogrom: Kishenev and the Tilt of History*. Liveright Publishing, 2018.

*Articles and Videos*

Berrin, Danielle. "One Man's Crusade to Prove Hollywood Mogul Carl Laemmle was a Hero." *Jewish Journal*, December 10, 2013.

Brook, Daniel. "Lithuania wants to erase its ugly history of Nazi collaboration—by accusing Jewish partisans who fought the Germans of war crimes." *Slate*, July 26, 2015.

Beattie Jr., Edward W. "Nazi Mobs in Orgy of Anti-Semitism Wreck, Burn, Slay." New York *Daily News*, November 11, 1938.

Dunmore, Helen. "Rereading Hans Fallada's *Alone in Berlin*." *The Guardian*, January 7, 2011.

Dörner, Bernward. "*Allein gegen den 'Mörder von fünf Millionen*" (Alone Against the Killer of Five Million). *Süddeutsche Zeitung*, September 18, 2022.

Eddy, Melissa. "They Resisted Hitler. They Were Executed. At Last They Lie at Rest." *New York Times*, May 13, 2019.

Gabler, Neal. "Laemmle's List: A Mogul's Heroism," *New York Times*, April 13, 2014.

Garaev, Paulina. "Hitler's Jewish Landlord." *i24 News*, April 18, 2017.

Gestapo Interrogation transcript of Alexander Schmorell. Translated by Ruth Sachs. Exclamation! Publishers, 2006.

Glaser, Zhava Litvac. "Refugees and Relief: The American Jewish Joint Distribution Committee and European Jews in Cuba and Shanghai, 1938–1943." CUNY Graduate Center thesis, 2015.

Gruner, Wolf. *Defiance and Protest: Forgotten Individual Jewish Reactions to the Persecution in Nazi Germany*. Cornell University Library, Jewish Studies Program, March 31, 2016.

Kalb, Marvin. *Refugee Crisis and the Sad Legacy of the 1938 Evian Conference*. Brookings, September 23, 2015.

Kuznick, Peter. "America's Forgotten Support of Adolf Hitler." *Truthdig.com*, June 6, 2019.

Laffer, Dennis. "The Jewish Trail of Tears: The Evian Conference of July 1938." Graduate thesis, University of South Florida, 2011.

Madley, Benjamin. "From Africa to Auschwitz: How German South West Africa Incubated Ideas and Methods Adopted and Developed by the Nazis in Eastern Europe." *European History Quarterly*, Vol. 35, Issue 3, July 2005.

Müldorfer, Friedbert. "Die Vertreibung der jüdischen Familie Holzer" [The Expulsion of the Jewish Family, the Holzers, from Traunstein during Kristallnacht 70 Years Ago]. *Traunsteiner Tagblatt*, November 8, 2008.

Paul, Pamela. "90 Years Ago This Book Tried to Warn Us." *New York Times*, October 6, 2022.

Reinharz, Jehuda. "Ideology and Structure in German Zionism, 1882–1933." *Jewish Social Studies*, Vol. 42, No. 2, Spring 1980.

Steeb, Christian. "Das Schicksal der jüdischen Familie Spatz—Teil 1" [The Fate of the Jewish Spatz Family, Part 1]. *Merkur*, August 27, 2014.

Stranex, Katherine. "How Richard Wagner Became a Soundtrack to Nazi Fascism." *The Collector*, January 3, 2022.

Tritter, Dr. Thorin. "On the Evian Conference of 1938." Holocaust Memorial and Tolerance Center of Nassau County, video available on youtube.

## NOTES

All interviews, letters, and Bundesarchiv documents cited here are available at postcardstohitler.com.

1. From the Letters of Benno and Anna.
2. Bundesarchiv NJ-2999 Bd. 1–4 017.jpg. Benno's postcards.
3. Interview with Clara Holzer.
4. Bundesarchiv BA Auftr. Nr. 864 NJ-2999 Bd. 1–4 11.
5. Interview with Johanna (Hani) Strauss. Interview with Fred Neuburger.
6. Interview with Johanna (Hani) Strauss.
7. Interview with Fred Neuburger.
8. Interview with Fred Neuburger.
9. Postcard from Fritz Neuburger to Benno Neuburger, August 9, 1930.
10. Postcard from Fritz Neuburger to Benno Neuburger, March 9, 1932.
11. Interview with Johanna (Hani) Strauss, December 13, 1983.
12. Interview with Fred Neuburger, September 1983.
13. Interview with Fred Neuburger, September 1983.
14. Interview with Johanna Strauss, December 13, 1983.
15. Interview with Johanna (Hani) Strauss, December 13, 1983.
16. Interview with Johanna (Hani) Strauss, December 13, 1983.
17. Interview with Johanna (Hani) Strauss, December 13, 1983.
18. This version of Morton's letter to Hani is the author's invention.
19. Interview with Fred Neuburger, September 1983.
20. Fanny Holzer died in 1936. The circumstances of her death are not known to the author.
21. Interview with Klara Holzer, April 16, 1984.
22. Letter from Ludwig Eiber to Fred Neuburger, January 7, 1948.
23. Interview with Fred Neuburger, September 1983.
24. Interview with Fred Neuburger, September 1983.
25. Interview with Johanna (Hani) Strauss, December 13, 1983.
26. Soon after arriving in the United States, Fritz changed his name to Fred.

27. Interview with Klara Holzer, April 16, 1984.
28. Interview with Klara Holzer, April 16, 1984.
29. Interview with Klara Holzer, April 19, 1984.
30. Interview with Johanna (Hani) Strauss, December 13, 1983.
31. Adolph J. Sabath, an Austrian-born Jew, represented Chicago in the U.S. House of Representatives from 1907 to 1952.
32. Interview with Klara Holzer, April 16, 1984.
33. Letter from Ida (daughter of Markus Neuburger) to U.S. Representative Adolph J. Sabath.
34. Letter from Lothar Roth.
35. Author's interpretation of Benno's postcard of September 30, 1941.
36. Interview with Fred Neuburger, April 2013.
37. Letter from Ludwig Eiber to Fred Neuburger, January 7, 1948.
38. Bundesarchiv BA Auftr. Nr. 864 NJ-2999 Bd. 1–4 2 & 8.
39. 13-14 Bundes Archive BA Auftr. Nr. 864 NJ-2999 Bd. 1–4 13 & 14.
40. Bundesarchiv BA Auftr. Nr. 864 NJ-2999 Bd. 1–4 26.
41. BA Berlin, NJ/2999, vol. 1, fol. 9: Munich Court, arrest warrant, April 4, 1942; NJ/2999, vol. 2, no fol.: arrest note, April 4, 1942.
42. Bundesarchive Auftr. Nr. 864 NJ-2999 Bd. 1–4 39–42.
43. Bundesarchiv Auftr. Nr. 864 NJ-2999 Bd. 1–4 50.
44. Bundesarchiv BA Auftr. Nr. 864 NJ-2999 Bd. 1–4 69.
45. Bundesarchiv BA Auftr. Nr. 864 NJ-2999 Bd. 1–4 65.
46. Bundesarchiv BA Auftr. Nr. 864 NJ-2999 Bd. 1–4 76–77.
47. Bundesarchiv BA Auftr. Nr. 864 NJ-2999 Bd. 1–4 83.
48. Bundesarchiv BA Auftr. Nr. 864 NJ-2999 Bd. 1–4 91–95.
49. Bundesarchiv BA Auftr. Nr. 864 NJ-2999 Bd. 1–4 103.
50. Bundesarchiv BA Auftr. Nr. 864 NJ-2999 Bd. 1–4 162.
51. Anna's last letter.
52. Bundesarchiv BA Auftr. Nr. 864 NJ-2999 Bd. 1–4 91–95.
53. Bundesarchiv BA Auftr. Nr. 864 NJ-2999 Bd. 1–4 182–184.
54. Bundesarchiv BA Auftr. Nr. 864 NJ-2999 Bd. 1–4 197.
55. Bundesarchiv BA Auftr. Nr. 864 NJ-2999 Bd. 1–4 212.
56. Bundesarchiv BA Auftr. Nr. 864 NJ-2999 Bd. 1–4 98–99.
57. Bundesarchiv BA Auftr. Nr. 864 NJ-2999 Bd. 1–4 213–214.
58. Benno's last letter.
59. Bundesarchiv BA Auftr. Nr. 864 NJ-2999 Bd. 1–4 203–205.
60. Bundesarchiv BA Auftr. Nr. 864 NJ-2999 Bd. 1–4 198.
61. Document # 157 in the German Bundesarchiv.